White Sand Black Beach

UNIVERSITY PRESS OF FLORIDA

Florida A&M University, Tallahassee
Florida Atlantic University, Boca Raton
Florida Gulf Coast University, Ft. Myers
Florida International University, Miami
Florida State University, Tallahassee
New College of Florida, Sarasota
University of Central Florida, Orlando
University of Florida, Gainesville
University of North Florida, Jacksonville
University of South Florida, Tampa
University of West Florida, Pensacola

WHITE SAND
BLACK BEACH

Civil Rights, Public Space, and Miami's Virginia Key

Gregory W. Bush

University Press of Florida

Gainesville · Tallahassee · Tampa · Boca Raton

Pensacola · Orlando · Miami · Jacksonville · Ft. Myers · Sarasota

21 20 19 18 17 16   6 5 4 3 2 1

Library of Congress Cataloging-in-Publication Data
Names: Bush, Gregory Wallace, author.
Title: White sand, black beach : civil rights, public space, and Miami's
    Virginia Key / Gregory W. Bush.
Description: Gainesville : University Press of Florida, [2016] | Includes
    bibliographical references and index.
Identifiers: LCCN 2016015363 | ISBN 9780813062648 (cloth)
Subjects: LCSH: African Americans—Civil
    rights—Florida—Miami—History—20th century. | Civil
    rights—Florida—Miami—History—20th century. | Virginia Key (Miami,
    Fla.)—Race relations—History—20th century. | Miami (Fla.)—Race
    relations—History—20th century.
Classification: LCC F319.M6 B87 2016 | DDC 323.1196/0730759381—dc23
LC record available at https://lccn.loc.gov/2016015363

The University Press of Florida is the scholarly publishing agency for the State
University System of Florida, comprising Florida A&M University, Florida Atlantic
University, Florida Gulf Coast University, Florida International University, Florida
State University, New College of Florida, University of Central Florida, University of
Florida, University of North Florida, University of South Florida, and University of
West Florida.

University Press of Florida
15 Northwest 15th Street
Gainesville, FL 32611-2079
http://www.upf.com

To the fighters for Miami's public waterfront
Athalie Range, Mabel Miller, Dan Paul,
Dinizulu Gene Tinnie, and Enid Pinkney

The struggle continues.

Contents

Illustrations

Acknowledgments

This book is the product of thirty years of attempting to fuse scholarship, teaching, service, and activism related to developing Miami's historical resources and preserving and enhancing the public waterfront.

I was originally hired in 1983 to teach American history and direct the Institute for Public History at the University of Miami but took my own path along the way as I bumped up against the political realities of Miami. After getting involved with others in trying to stop the Miami Heat's successful attempt to take public waterfront land for their new basketball arena in 1996, I delved into the history of the politics and perceptions involved with this incident by examining newspaper records and TV news coverage, attending numerous meetings, and completing a series of oral history interviews. Then I delivered scholarly papers on the subject at the annual meeting of the American Studies Association in 197 and the conference "Orange Empires: Miami and Los Angeles," held at the Huntington Library in 1999.[1] Along the way I also became involved with others in starting a new organization called the Urban Environment League, which focused on public planning processes and trying to save waterfront land from succumbing to various commercial schemes.

This book is thus a hybrid of historical analysis and personal memory of what now goes by the label of civic involvement. It took much longer to complete than I planned because my attention kept getting diverted. So be it.

Thanks to the National Park Service for giving me the original assignment to assess the historical resources of the Historic Virginia Key Park for possible inclusion within their system.

My "Special Resource Study: Report to Congress," assisted by many people and put into final form by Nancy Lee, was never published by the National Park Service.[2] As part of that effort, Chanelle Rose, at the time a University of Miami student and now the author of an important book on civil rights in Miami, completed a number of National Park Service oral histories. While I disagreed with the park service's decision to deny the national historical significance of the park because of the nature of their criteria, I remain hopeful that perhaps one day they'll change their minds.

I especially want to thank my editor Grey Osterud for her wise counsel, patience, and ability to rearrange and chop much repetitive material while making me rethink facets of my work. My colleague at the University of Miami, Don Spivey, provided valuable comments on several drafts, as did Ellis Berger. Sian Hunter, Stephanye Hunter, Marthe Walters, and reviewers provided valuable input, and a special thanks to Kate Babbitt for her incredibly valuable textual comments and copyediting. Kimberly Scott helped with my final draft.

My friend and fellow activist Gene Tinnie read and responded to many of my early drafts, for which I am most grateful. I have included some of his comments in the final chapters.

I learned so much from my own oral history interviews, notably those with Enid Pinkney, Athalie Range, Spencer Pompey, Bobbi Graff, Thelma Gibson, Dan Paul, Jim Murley, Lloyd Miller, Johnny Winton, Elizabeth Plater-Zyberk, Alberto Ruder, Katy Sorenson, Merritt Stierheim, Tomas Regalado, Bob and Bill Graham, and others.

Professor Raymond Mohl and Arva Parks McCabe were especially generous in sharing information and resources over the years. Thanks also to Nancy Lee and Bob Weinreb, Blanca Mesa, John DeLeon, Grace Solares, John Van Leer, Gary Milano, the late John Brennan, and others for their hard work on issues related to public waterfront space and environmental issues—and for speaking out and doing the necessary research. Other friends and colleagues have supported my work in many different ways; these include Alberto Ruder, Carmen Alvarez, Graham Andrew, Sallye Jude, Carolina Amram, and Paul George. Thanks to Irene

Secada for her advice, advocacy, and support in earlier years and to my daughter Paula for putting up with a sometimes grumpy dad.

The University of Miami allowed me time and space to do much of my scholarly analysis and writing, teach courses on the subject, and learn about Miami's politics and its incredibly complex waterfront history. Yet much of the freedom I have to say what I think is also due to the faith and support my parents placed in me over the years, for which I remain grateful.

Introduction

The Struggle for the Civil Right
to Public Space in Miami

The urban landscape of the southeast coast of Florida, like the ebb and flow of its sandy and mangrove-filled shoreline, is always changing, projecting little solidity of place or purpose. Here, the Tequesta Indians lived for thousands of years, adapting to the shifting shape of the flat landscape and shallow bays, which reflect the effects of a semitropical climate, a unique hydrological system, and periodic hurricanes. From their earliest arrival, Europeans considered the area to be a hot, mosquito-ridden, and intimidating wilderness. Starkly beautiful, this exotic area grew more attractive in the nineteenth century as transportation connections gradually linked it to the broader world.

Virginia Key is a barrier island in the northern portion of Biscayne Bay, a large shallow tropical saline lagoon at the northern end of the Florida Keys. The natural history of the bay is shaped by both daily tides and dramatic storms. Since the 1890s, machine dredging has carved a series of channels and three cuts into the ocean and has constructed numerous islands with fill. Only Belle Isle and Virginia Key are natural, though their size and shape have been transformed over the centuries. Much of the land around the bay is lined by bulkheads; precious few of the original mangrove swamps remain intact. Several creeks and rivers run from the Everglades into the bay, including Arch Creek in the north; the Little River, Miami River, and Coral Gables waterway in the middle section; and Black Creek in the south. Government Cut, created in 1905, facilitates tidal flow into the bay and divides Miami Beach from Fisher Island, one of the wealthiest zip codes in the nation. Dividing Virginia Key from Key Biscayne to the east is Bear Cut; its powerful currents hide several shipwrecks and have made it the site of numerous drownings over the years.

Virginia Key now consists of something more than 1,200 acres. As we drive from Miami's Brickell neighborhood on the mainland east on the Rickenbacker Causeway onto Virginia Key, the first thing we encounter is a landmark restaurant on the northern side of the key. The Rusty Pelican, which overlooks the city, offers spectacular views. Next, we drive or bicycle past a boatyard and boat storage area, the Miami Marine Stadium, and the causeway between Miami and Key Biscayne. We pass a building of the Miami Rowing Club; Mast Academy, a maritime high school; the headquarters of the National Oceanic and Atmospheric Administration; the University of Miami's Rosenstiel School of Marine Science; and Seaquarium, an aging theme park. North of the causeway on the extreme eastern side of the island overlooking Bear Cut is the 80½-acre Historic Virginia Key Beach Park. North of that is another public beach and cove area and a ramshackle fish house and drinking hangout named Jimbo's. Northwest of the cove and overlooking Fisher Island is a small island made of fill that contains bike trails, a large wastewater treatment plant that was completed in 1957, a 112-acre toxic landfill with god knows what in it, and a protected natural area, the Bill Sadowski Park.

What was originally called Dade County was renamed Miami-Dade County in 1997 as a promotional tool fostered by Mayor Alex Penelas. From its incorporation as a city in 1896, Miami has had a notoriously weak planning tradition, allowing broad sprawl with little attention to adequate public infrastructure or mass transportation. The public sphere has become weaker throughout the county as local and county governments have often failed to address issues related to mass transportation, park space, community centers, and maintenance or waterfront access, often deferring to the political clout of developers and promoters of tourist and sports spectacles. Pressure to sell off parks or put commercial signs up in them has continued as funding for maintenance or purchase

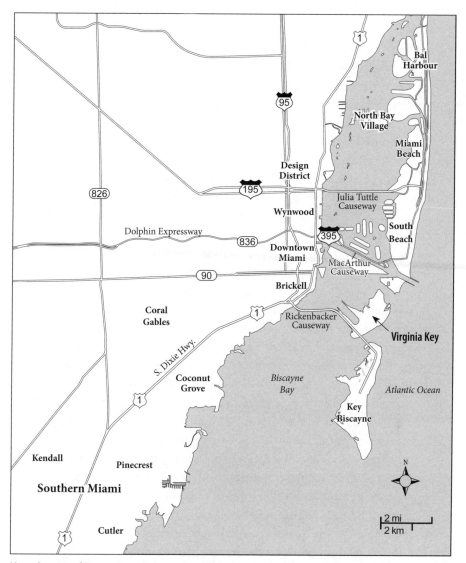

Map 1. Overview of Biscayne Bay including Miami, Miami Beach, Key Biscayne, and Virginia Key

of new parkland has often been cut back—unless it became an election issue. From a broader perspective, incumbent mayor Carlos Gimenez has written that "It used to be Miami-Dade County wanted to operate everything. . . . I don't want to operate anything."[1] The era of privatization has clearly come of age with ramifications that will be explored in this book in terms of the waterfront.

The county contains 1,946 square miles of land. It now has thirty-four separate municipalities, a large unincorporated area, and a population of 2,662,874 (2014 estimated census). It is the most populous county in Florida and the seventh most populous county in the United States.[2] It is also Florida's third largest county in terms of land area. With a population of 417,000, the city of Miami is now but a small piece of the county. But the extended metro area, up to Palm Beach County, has a population of about 5.5 million and is the fourth most populous urban area in the United States. There are few waterfront parks or even restaurants with a view of the water, all the way from Homestead to the Broward County Line. It is almost completely built up, privatized, and most residents have little consciousness of or experience with Biscayne Bay.

The bizarre mix of land uses on Virginia Key reflects the variety of groups that have had control over it and the conflicting purposes to which this supposedly vacant space has been put. It has no residents, other than a few homeless people. Its ownership is divided between Miami and Miami-Dade County, which lease out the existing facilities, and it is covered by a confusing array of zoning classifications. Previously, the key was all public land controlled by the state of Florida's Internal Improvement Fund, but it has been tossed around between jurisdictions. Virginia Key has alternated between long periods of public inattention and short bursts of political controversy. Until recently, it was not shaped by any clear or sustained plan or coherent vision.[3]

Environmental conditions in Biscayne Bay have been impacted by shoreline construction, especially the creation in the 1960s of Lummus and Dodge Islands, home to the largest cruise line port in the world. In the nineteenth century, Biscayne Bay was notable for freshwater springs, and in 1896, Henry Flagler's Florida East Coast Railway brought the railroad and tourism to Miami. Until well into the twentieth century, raw sewage was discharged directly into the bay and the Miami River.[4] Nationally prominent writer Philip Wyllie published scathing exposés about contamination. Early environmentalist Marjory Stoneman Douglas and others focused on the degradation of the bay, linking it to the fragile water system of the Everglades. By the 1940s, the bay's distinctive organisms—black coral sea fans, stone crabs, and pompano—were in decline. One sanitary engineer wrote in 1949 that "a boat trip in the bay and out near the main channel gives the visitor a chance to contrast the dark brown-gray polluted water near the city with the beautiful blue-green ocean water."[5]

Our understanding of the rich and often elusive quality of this area is deepened by closely examining its most forlorn places. Virginia Key, a relatively barren 1,000-acre island about a mile off the coast of Miami jus east of Key Biscayne, is a largely untapped landscape that is nonetheless filled with memory and hope. Its history has been shaped by a host of jurisdictional fights, competing development visions, and changing cultural values. Its delicate ecosystem is threatened by a hodgepodge of exploitative land uses. Much of it has been disturbed by the work of modern people. More recently, however, its landscape has also been rescued and restored by citizen activists.

Most important, Virginia Key provides an invaluable window into African Americans' quest for access to the coast. This is a central part of our shared struggle for civil rights to public space. The Historic Virginia Key Beach Park, located on the eastern edge of the island, commemorates the establishment in 1945 of the first legally recognized bathing beach for people of African descent. In accordance with the segregation laws of the time, it was an all-black beach. The park was created because of pressure brought by a small but important civil rights demonstration at nearby Haulover Beach led by a gifted African American lawyer, Lawson Thomas, a story that is recounted in chapter 1.

The park became an unprecedented gathering spot for African Americans in South Florida, eventually including walking trails, a carousel and miniature train, a dance floor, cabanas, and a refreshment stand as well as a popular beach. As chapter 3 reveals, it was a place of black pride and fellowship and an important link to nature. It was one of the first sites in the twentieth century to result from a campaign of civil disobedience that expanded public accommodations and created a novel leisure space within one of the region's fastest-growing cities. A response to the long, ignominious record of racial degradation and the harsh disjunctures and blatant contradictions of World War II (the focus of chapter 2), Virginia Key Beach is a uniquely revealing symbol of the complex history of race relations in Miami and the nation. Moreover, its story illustrates the recurring challenges for those who seek to claim and preserve public space. Despite the walls and boundaries of racial segregation and the types of interaction between whites and blacks in Miami from 1896 to World War II, Bahamians and African American migrants from other parts of the South created a vital community life in Miami.

Before the mid-nineteenth century, Virginia Key was connected to Miami Beach and Fisher Island but was cut off by tidal changes and dramatic hurricanes. It was doubtless the site of maroon colonies formed by people of African heritage who had escaped slavery, including black Seminoles. Oral history narratives have affirmed it as an informal gathering place for black Miamians in the early twentieth century, when the island remained largely uninhabited and was newly disconnected from the mainland. More recently, Cubans and Haitians fleeing persecution landed there as a place of refuge. Virginia Key was claimed by a mobile people searching for a place to belong amid the fragile and shifting sands of time.

Like other modern landscapes, Virginia Key Beach has multiple layers of meaning that have been asserted, forgotten, reaffirmed, and transformed over the years. Its hidden history has a unique power to disrupt modern visions of commercial development as unalloyed symbols of progress and to demonstrate the changing significance of racialized landscapes.

In the 1930s, white leaders conceptualized a "colored beach" on the island as an adjunct to the removal of blacks from downtown Miami. Their aim, in part, was to separate black people from white tourists and move them out of the way of land developers while responding to growing black demands for access to the bay. The creation of the beach was a reflection of conditions in the wider geography of the downtown area, the role of the press in publicizing the sorry state of public parks available to black Miamians, and the changing needs of white and black residents.

Miami's civil rights movement unfolded far from the gaze of the national media between the end of World War II and 1975. (I tell the story of this movement in chapter 4.) During these decades, the Overtown area, originally called Colored Town, was undermined by highway construction, suburbanization, and the depopulation of downtown Miami. Black Miamians' struggle for access to public space was part of their effort to attain a more equitable share of public services, greater economic opportunities, and a measure of political power.

Virginia Key Beach developed a starkly different set of meanings for the African American community after Supreme Court rulings and civil rights legislation mandated the integration of public accommodations. A decade or more after the 1945 demonstration that secured the black beach, oral history testimony shows, many African Americans saw the "gift" of the beach not as a victory won through militant direct action but rather as a triumph of the strategies of cooperation based on personal relationships with white leaders built up over many years by Miami's black elite. Others saw the black beach as a segregated, inferior locale compared to nearby white beaches, an embarrassing memory of second-class citizenship. Yet as a site for religious ceremonies, seasonal celebrations and entertainment, family lore, and romance, the beach became a major center of community life during the transition from segregation to what passed as integration. It attracted vacationing blacks from the North, most notably Martin Luther King, and a host of African American entertainers. Thousands of children and adults who walked the park's trails became entranced by its flora, fish, and wildlife or enjoyed the tranquility of the bay.[6]

The diverse facets of the beach were rediscovered when activists used oral history to recapture community memory and politicize the issue of preserving Virginia Key. These voices, largely silenced over the years, were first heard in the late 1990s when activists sought elders to testify to the beach's historic significance for the African American community as part of the effort to combat its neglected condition and potential loss as a public park. By 1999, the revival of that history through the memories of older black residents, many of them professional women, had become a powerful tool that activists used to block the construction of an upscale private resort on the site. The excitement of hearing these memories about the role of the beach as a community center during the days of segregation helped galvanize local activists, the press, and schoolchildren to focus on preserving, recreating, and enhancing the site.

Virginia Key Beach can claim a significant place in the national civil rights movement. In their long struggle for social justice, African Americans and their allies have sought such tangible goals as voting rights and equal access to public schools, better housing, work opportunities, and public accommodations. The public spaces of human interaction—parks, plazas, streets, and libraries—often became theaters where the human dramas of discrimination, resistance, and confrontation took place. What was all too often a sad and seemingly endless train of personal humiliations was only rarely interrupted by moments when black people's dignity was asserted and recognized. Parks and beaches, sidewalks and streets all became the site of violent clashes during the civil rights movement. Marches and demonstrations focused the nation's attention on the Lincoln Memorial, the doors to the University of Alabama, and the parks and streets of Little Rock, Montgomery, Birmingham, Selma, and countless small towns. Martin Luther King's "I Have a Dream" speech was made in the nation's foremost park to a huge crowd of participants in the March on Washington.

The overlapping questions of access to commercial spaces such as lunch counters and department stores and to public spaces such as parks and buses have been integral to the struggle for civil rights since the 1950s. Abstract concepts of rights to public space were articulated relatively recently. Nonetheless, much of the story of the past seventy years involves the legal effects of court decisions and the Civil Rights Act of 1964 on public accommodations. Desegregation expanded the constituency for public places throughout the South. But in a rather perverse turn of events, the democratization of public places has diminished their value in the minds of a new generation of public officials and entrepreneurs. As public spaces became more accessible to people of color (and the homeless), fear of crime in parks, the loss of public funding, and neglect in overseeing deed restrictions generated new pressures and provoked another wave of struggles to protect public spaces from commercial exploitation. We still live amid those conflicts today, so we need a clearer lens for understanding the history of those places as we create coalitions of concerned citizens to reinvigorate them. The case of Virginia Key provides an unusually sharp lens for that examination.

The postwar development of waterfront land policies in Miami, of which the story of Virginia Key is a vital part, is the focus of chapter 5. It illuminates the pressures on that land and changing perceptions of its value in the Miami area from 1945 to 1982 as the environmental movement intersected with expanding visions of development. In recent years, historians and geographers have delved into the complex relationships among culture, public space, localized memory, historic preservation, and the politics of economic development. Remembering the meaning of places of humiliation and resistance, terror and triumph has helped remedy pervasive public silences in African American history and the long-obscured forms of oppression experienced in daily life under the racial caste system that dominated the United States for centuries. It has also become part of a broader process of reappropriating urban spaces as Americans have begun to redefine their sense of place, revalue forms of leisure, and reassess the function of democratic power over land use.

Chapter 6 examines how the weak tradition of planning in Miami, a slavish deference to the tourist industry, and the changing shape of the environmental movement operated with many of the neoliberal policies spawned during the Reagan era and the 1990s. The shift from the primacy of civil rights issues to the more fragmented concerns of recent times has taken place as an increasing array of advocates around the nation wondered how to define the integrity of parks as public spaces. Questions and concerns often channeled narratives toward commercial or financial matters, subordinating the natural world. Why shouldn't parks include shopping malls, advertising, sports arenas, and theme parks, some wondered? Wouldn't these commercial venues attract more people and make these spaces well used in the era of television and air conditioning? What makes parks unique as open spaces for the public's enjoyment in a torrid climate? Why shouldn't parks produce greater revenue for cash-starved cities?

In recent years, other places have mattered much more than Virginia Key to most politicians in the region. Urban elites, the press, and politicians in Miami have frequently focused on funding sports venues or other monumental architecture. Former Miami commissioner Johnny Winton said that government officials spent "way too much time" trying to accommodate the Florida Marlins' quest for a new stadium in Miami. He made that comment in 2000, nine years before final decisions were made. Leaders in other cities have felt compelled to compete by offering subsidies to professional sports teams in the form of lavish stadiums instead of addressing issues of neighborhood enhancement, poverty, and residents' needs for public space. Sadly, noncommercial meanings of public space have become opaque for many urban residents. As Harvey Graff has shown for Dallas, monumental architecture and subsidies for corporate growth have defined much public spending in recent decades, masquerading as the support of public enterprise. Richard Florida and Tom Wolfe have recently promoted the idea of creating arts districts within the urban core to fuel the growth coalition behind urban revitalization. This book outlines a more nuanced understanding of growth politics as it relates to the social and natural world.[7]

Across the nation, coalitions have attempted to more clearly define community needs and offer more tangible rewards related to public space. In Los Angeles, the struggle over construction of the Staples Center garnered attention related to subsidies and scams.[8] On the other hand, a powerful coalition of advocates emerged to fight for "free beaches" and green spaces in Los Angeles, which rivals Miami in terms of its lack of park space per capita. Numerous other cities have spawned powerful park, community garden, and public space advocacy groups. Several organizations have gained national prominence, most notably New York's Central Park Conservancy, which is supported by wealthy donors who live nearby and is led by Elizabeth Barlow Rogers. More recently, writers such as Richard Louv have built a national movement out of the idea that children are afflicted by a "nature deficit disorder."[9]

Unfortunately, gentrification and the withdrawal of people to suburban enclaves have congealed alongside both the power of commercial forces and simplistic renderings of local history; these processes have led to a lack of public understanding of both the costs of long-term neglect of urban parks and the creative possibilities for public spaces. Cynicism about government competence has fueled a sense of futility about making effective use of parks. Public spaces are now in serious danger of disappearing under the weight of our fragmented consciousness and the loss of focus on the meaning of public access to the natural world. Fundamental questions remain about our civil rights to public space and our affinity with the remaining vestiges of nature around us. Chapter 7 chronicles the attempts since 1999 to use oral history and new forms of activism to revitalize Miami's Historic Virginia Key Beach Park, plan the entire island, and reassert greater public control over the public domain.

The fate of Virginia Key Beach was a reflection of other Miami waterfront parkland controversies. By the late twentieth century, it had become a major zone of local conflict as funding for parks eroded in a crime-ridden city with few downtown residents. In 1985, a large chunk of Miami's Bayfront Park was transferred to the James W. Rouse Company in order to build Bayside, a popular shopping mall and tourist destination, reminiscent of malls of other cities such as Boston, Baltimore, and Jacksonville. The company was eventually purchased by General Growth Properties. In 1996, a major city referendum provided nearby waterfront parkland for a new basketball arena for the Miami Heat, a professional basketball team, despite the opposition of the newly formed Urban Environment League. City staff had orders to develop or lease out much of the largely abandoned and underplanned waterfront parkland to private entrepreneurs. A full-scale assault on waterfront parks was in full swing by the late 1990s, seen most pointedly in the struggle to preserve the Miami Circle, an ancient Tequesta site at the mouth of the Miami River, and Bicentennial Park.[10]

Plans to redevelop waterfronts and new advocacy groups for local parks have transformed the urban landscape across the nation since the 1970s. Following the revitalization of New York's Battery Park and the Rouse Company's revival of waterfronts in Boston, Annapolis, and Baltimore, urban waterfronts became targets as "focal points" or quasi-theme parks for commercial development and public-private partnerships. Historical waterfronts were transformed from industrial areas into tourist attractions where restaurants, bars, shops, and parking structures abounded. Many argued that in a time of urban crisis and lean public revenues, it was smart to develop economic synergy within public spaces, identifying with vestiges of historical memory while expanding cultural tourism and commercial destinations. This rationale became a powerful bludgeon against urban parks, which were often set up to fail due to neglect and a lack of creative management and government funding. We now see cookie-cutter, mall-like waterfronts appearing in many cities across the nation, some of which had no natural water at all.

By the late 1990s, a complex array of political and economic developments had undermined Virginia Key Beach's value as a public park. Administrative oversight of existing deed restrictions was lacking, while maintenance was neglected. The park had been inaccessible to the public since 1982, but few seemed to care. Memories of the place seemed irrelevant. Decades after the integration of public accommodations had been established by law, the former black beach had become a forlorn, forgotten place, set up to be leased out by the city as a high-end "eco-resort" that would return badly needed revenue. Time had erased African Americans' many positive associations with the beach, and few worked to preserve it.

Chapter 7 and the afterword reflect my own perspective and experience as an advocate for public space while providing a record of local engagement and suggesting how activists in other places might approach similar issues. I became a founder of the Urban Environment League (UEL) in 1996, and over the next few years I wrote about local public space issues and conducted oral history interviews of participants in order to learn about politics and public advocacy and about the past. In late 1998, after the unexpected resignation of the UEL president, I assumed that role, which I held through three years of dramatic struggles over waterfront parks. I felt a responsibility to use my research skills to try to preserve and restore both Virginia Key Beach and the Miami Circle and Bicentennial Park. I wrote the legislation to revive the city's Parks Advisory Board, became its chair, and helped lead the effort for a Bicentennial Park/Waterfront Renewal Committee.

By examining the long struggle for Virginia Key Beach, we can better appreciate how the role of cultural memory within the African American community intersects with the challenges of funding equity and activating the bureaucratic processes to deepen consciousness of place beyond the fluid demands of capitalism. This study uses Miami, a city that Raymond Mohl described as "South of the South," to focus on African American agency and interracial negotiation over access to public space.

Yet chapter 7 and the afterword have a wider lens.[11] Recently, Charles Birnbaum deplored the national trend toward "the cluttering of reposeful park grounds with activity-oriented 'focal points'" as lamentable and perplexing, not least because park users themselves are not demanding change. The distinctive character of parks is undermined as they become privatized, even by nonprofit institutions seeking "free land" to expand or by public agencies seeking revenue. Little that is coherent and sacrosanct stands in the way of redefining parks in relation to the flavor of the day, from electronic billboards and music venues to cell phone towers.

Preserving public space for purposes beyond financial return needs clarity of definition and a committed constituency. The recent development of Virginia Key Beach Park fits clearly into the recent revival of civic engagement in designing and revitalizing public parks and with an increasing interest in black heritage tourism.[12]

In 1999, as chapter 7 recounts, the beach suddenly became the focal point of a campaign by a fragile new multicultural coalition to reclaim and redefine public space along Miami's waterfront. Beginning in the 1970s, environmentalists led by educator Mabel Miller fought to preserve the natural attributes of the island. Their appeals to public officials to enforce existing deed restrictions were ignored, though I, for one, learned much by observing Miller's persistence and civility in an endless series of public meetings. The question of the fate of Virginia Key Beach highlighted the importance of remembering segregation and African Americans' struggle for equality, which was militant in Miami at the end of World War II. The issue of the future of this historic site gained national attention in the *New York Times*, the *San Francisco Chronicle*, and other newspapers. The voices of African Americans who had valued the beach in the past became powerful tools in preserving this public space for all. Oral history was central in reviving this public beach.

"By claiming space in public, by creating public spaces," geographer Don Mitchell asserts, "social groups themselves become public."[13] African Americans had built a sense of group identity at the beach even before it had been officially designated for them. Later, as integration opened up other parks, many blacks looked with disdain on Virginia Key Beach as embarrassingly inferior to white facilities. Others simply forgot about it. Yet when Miami officials sought to take over the park in the 1990s and lease it out to favored entrepreneurs to produce more revenue, a new set of concerns fused historic preservation within the African American community with environmental preservation and the broader demand to revitalize urban public spaces. I helped identify, validate, and politicize that history. A new coalition was formed, illustrating the changing character of public space advocacy in recent years. First in 1945 and then again in the late 1990s, the struggle for public space has illustrated the power of multiracial, multicultural, and cross-class coalitions.

Boyd Shearer Jr., who created a pathbreaking website on the history of segregated parks in Lexington, Kentucky, writes that "black parks, like schools and churches for African American communities, were crucial daily geographies that empowered black identities despite the dehumanizing eclipse of racism, which initially created this segregated landscape."[14] Places for leisure activities reawakened a sense of community and renewed a weary people's sense of self. They involved a form of aesthetics that, Shearer suggests, is "not just a theory of art nor an elitist concern with appearances, but rather . . . a process of capturing identity in an act of self-possessing space." Robin Kelley comments that "even modes of leisure could undergird opposition to white supremacy. For members of a class whose long workdays were spent in backbreaking, low-paid wage work in settings pervaded by racism, the places where they played were more than relatively free places to articulate grievances and dreams. They were places that enabled African Americans to take back their bodies, to recuperate, to be together. . . . Knowing what happens in these spaces of pleasure can help us understand the solidarity black people have shown at political mass meetings, [and] illuminate the bonds of fellowship one finds in churches and voluntary associations."[15]

Enid Pinkney, an African American leader in Miami and a member of the Historic Virginia Key Beach Park Trust, personifies this link between historic preservation and community building within and beyond the black community. "If you're a preservationist, you are a preservationist without prejudice," she has declared. "There's great tradition and heritage over in Virginia Key beach, and to lose it would be to lose a part of our history." Preservation and enhancement of the beach have become important to the African American community and link the older generation with younger people of all races. When public spaces are connected to the past through recording oral histories, creating video documentaries, and other forms of direct personal involvement, the lost sense of identification with place can stimulate a more profound connection to the built and natural environment. As Wallace Stegner observed, "we don't know who we are until we know where we are."[16]

Doing and disseminating oral history has enabled people to discover the potential of public parkland on the waterfront and to comprehend, critique, and challenge the nature of power in Miami. I have found that showcasing the voices of long-ignored people can overcome silences and bring neglected questions into the public sphere. I learned from white leaders about the weakness of prevailing advocacy groups in behalf of public spaces and sought to transpose that weakness into what some have called "advocacy oral history" that became, as Lynn Abrams suggests, a "means by which participants themselves are empowered to transform their lives."[17]

The struggles to win access to the beach and to reclaim it a half-century later are partly about racial oppression, but even more significantly, they testify to black resistance, negotiation, and community-building within the prevailing racial caste system. The times, the spaces that provided meaning to their lives, and the character of their community have all changed, but older black Miamians seek to pass on a powerful and unique legacy. They are determined not only to remember the past but also to transform the future. Many have seen their neighborhoods deteriorate as professionals and middle-class families moved out and crime impacted working-poor families who had nowhere else to go. Forms of racial oppression have become more opaque to some, taking shape in increasing economic inequality and isolation from mainstream institutions. Observing the role of activists in New Orleans, Kim Lacey Rogers has commented that "a common collective consciousness, historical understanding, and vision of necessary social change distinguish activist generation[s] . . . from other temporally related groups that do not realize themselves in public action."[18]

This account, like recent interpretations from other regions, underscores the importance of local advocacy and grassroots activism in the struggle for civil rights in the years before 1964 and links it to the expanding notion of civil rights to public space that has emerged more recently. As a white and relatively privileged academic, I did not personally experience the forms of discrimination African Americans felt. Through conducting oral history interviews, doing documentary research, and strategizing with black community activists, however, I became intimately aware of the loss of public space for all, intensifying my conviction that collective memories of sacred spaces and collective struggles are powerful tools for reshaping community life in South Florida and beyond.

In sum, this book is about the power of previously lost voices to redefine and reclaim the woebegone piece of land at the center of this narrative. Silences about and neglect of Virginia Key Beach have had powerful political and economic ramifications for African Americans. So too, revitalizing the memories of black people who experienced the beach as a site of community solidarity has helped save a forgotten public place by recalling and contextualizing life under segregation. Recent developments illustrate the potential of new forms of civic engagement in public planning processes. As a place of interaction with nature, entertainment and fun, fellowship and longing, this beach became a common ground of hope for a better future. Our continuing challenge is to make it—and the rest of Miami's public waterfront—a model for community engagement and to guard it as public space for future generations.

Wade-In

Lawson Thomas and the Potent Combination
of Direct Action and Negotiation

On the afternoon of May 9, 1945, the day after war ended in Europe, two black women and four black men removed their street clothes and, clad in bathing suits, waded into the crystal-clear waters of the Atlantic Ocean at Baker's Haulover Beach State Park, located fourteen miles northeast of Miami. On the shore stood Lawson E. Thomas, an African American attorney. Hoping that his companions would be arrested and taken to jail for violating an ordinance that reserved public beaches for whites only, he carried $500 for bail money.

The group included a housewife, two grocery store owners, a union leader, and several sailors from the large military contingent training in South Florida. Most were members of the National Association for the Advancement of Colored People (NAACP), the most prominent civil rights organization in Florida. Since 1937, its work in Miami had focused on achieving desegregation through legal channels. It was not a party to this direct action, but its presence helped exert pressure on the city's white leaders. Judge Henderson, president of the Negro Citizens' Service League, was quietly placing a call from the headquarters of the Longshoreman's Association, an integrated union with which he was associated, to the sheriff's office with the message: "There are some Negroes swimming at Haulover Beach"—an implicit threat that he could mobilize more people for the demonstration.

When the deputies arrived, Thomas all but urged them to arrest his friends, knowing full well that this would create public controversy and provoke negotiations, a two-pronged strategy that became a powerful force for change within the civil rights movement. But the bathers were ordered out of the water and made to wait, while back at the police station Sheriff D. C. Coleman tried to figure out his next move, perhaps weighing the potential threat of a group of black longshoremen showing up at Haulover to heighten the confrontation. Finally Coleman told Thomas: "I can't put them in jail." By then, the sheriff had reached County Commissioner Charles Crandon. Crandon asked Thomas to meet him the next morning in his chambers to see if they could "work something out." The next day the *Miami Herald* reported that some fifty to sixty "bathers were involved in testing their right to use county-owned bathing beaches." When a deputy sheriff was advised that this demonstration would take place, he responded that "there was no law under which they would be subject to arrest." Judge Henderson summarized the situation: "We weren't arrested so as far as I know we will be going to the beach from now on. If they arrest us, we will appeal to the courts."[1]

And so it was that three months later, on August 8, 1945, six days before World War II finally ended in the Pacific, more than 100 blacks participated in the opening ceremonies at Virginia Key Beach. Located miles south of Haulover and more than a mile out in Biscayne Bay from Miami, the new beach on county land just east of Key Biscayne was created as a response to the demonstration. The excitement of winning access to the sea must have been powerful and positive, even though the beaches remained segregated. Virginia Key immediately became a popular destination for black Miamians. Marvin Dunn relates that within "two weeks, nearly four thousand blacks had used the new swimming facilities." Never mind that the place was dangerous for swimmers and could only be reached by ferry. Acquiring access to Virginia Key Beach was a stunning achievement for the African American community.[2] The wade-in was a remarkable act that has been largely lost to history. A militant and well-coordinated protest involving just seven participants had led to negotiations with the county's most influential politicians and enabled black Miamians who had been systematically excluded from the waterfront to obtain a beach of their own.[3]

Until that moment, segregation in South Florida had ravaged lives, but most African Americans thought that nothing could be done about it. Yet in subtle and sometimes visible ways, social and economic changes were undermining Jim Crow, and black people had begun to confront and challenge white supremacy in new ways. Securing a beach was at the top of the list of priorities for blacks in postwar Miami. The plan Thomas and others hatched in the lively black community known as Overtown, located northwest of the railroad tracks from downtown Miami, focused on gaining access to waterfront leisure space by making it seem politically innocuous and socially acceptable. In a city that depended upon tourism for its economic lifeblood, the white power structure needed to avoid ugly racial confrontations.

The wade-in at Baker's Haulover and subsequent dedication of Virginia Key Beach were historic events in the local and national struggle for equal rights. Nine years before Rosa Parks refused to move to the back of the bus in Montgomery, Alabama, and fourteen years before the sit-ins in Greensboro, North Carolina, the Miami wade-in received only minimal media coverage by the local press. Equally surprising, Miami's black beach received little public recognition.

Access to Public Beaches and the Civil Rights Movement in Miami

The creation of Virginia Key Beach was the result of a confluence of national, state, and local factors. Economic, cultural, and political changes related to land use converged after the U.S. victory in World War II. Strategies of confrontation came from the threats from the African American community to publicize racism at home after blacks had fought against racism in Europe. The agreement was negotiated by an emergent and established set of white and black leaders who had built a modicum of trust over the years.

Civil rights activism in Miami fits with the understanding of the "long civil rights movement" developed by historians Jacqueline Dowd Hall and Glenda Gilmore, which highlights the role played by interracial left-wing unions and Communist Party activists in promoting desegregation during the 1930s, before the Montgomery bus boycott and the *Brown* decision elevated the movement into national prominence. In 1951, the Christmas Eve bombing and subsequent deaths of Florida civil rights activist Harry T. Moore and his wife and the virulence of anticommunist attacks against other civil rights activists dealt a serious blow to the movement in Florida. Local growth politics and postwar anticommunism were serious constraints, despite the continuing process of civic engagement and black community-building in Miami. As Mary Dudziak has shown, "civil rights groups had to walk a fine line, making clear that their reform efforts were meant to fill out the contours of American democracy, and not challenge or undermine it."[4]

Public accommodation of African Americans on the waterfront reflected the growing assertion of their recreational needs at the end of the war and their calculated militance born from their wartime sacrifice. The ability of blacks to enjoy common or segregated waterfront spaces meant a new, relatively "free space" for leisure, building community solidarity, sharing stories, and experiencing the natural world. In Miami, beaches, pools, and golf courses joined schools and streets as places of hope and sociability to which blacks sought access—part of a burgeoning political dimension of African American life in the city.[5]

African Americans' assertion of demands for political rights, greater social equality, and recreational space coexisted with forms of solidarity and resistance in black churches, bars, social clubs, alleys, and parks. What Harry Boyte and Sara Evans have called "free spaces" created by movements such as abolitionism were in fact counter-spaces, or what de Certeau has seen as defensible spaces.[6] These sites of community solidarity and celebration enabled the black community to cultivate significant power based on race. Some of these spaces were later lost and forgotten because of the transformation of black consciousness, the demands of consumer culture and the impact of upward social mobility, and the illusions of half-a-loaf integration. As David Nieves writes, "In proposing a new polis, or civic realm, African Americans were in effect destroying previous understandings of the landscape and refashioning for themselves a new spatialized ordering device based on social justice." The recent revival of those spaces, such as Virginia Key Beach, raises larger questions and poses new challenges to our understanding of the challenges of obtaining access to public sites within the changing matrix of the growth coalition. All too often, these notions eviscerate and obfuscate the principle of the civil rights of all residents to access and use attractive public space.[7]

By focusing on the struggles of African Americans and other racial-ethnic minority groups for access to public land and recreational spaces in the twentieth century, we come to understand that racialized spatial dynamics and jurisdictional struggles over property and developmental rights exhibit the plasticity of public-private partnerships through the appropriated language of local forms of community consensus. Historians and sociologists have recently shown how those ever-changing "free spaces" reflect the shape and function of local urban cultures and the resulting conflicts over land use. Racial divisions and collisions are among the most powerful of those forces. Demands for voting rights, school funding, decent housing, respectful treatment by law enforcement, and access to recreational space have all been part of local drives for equality. For example, walled enclaves and publicly supported commercial arenas helped perpetuate Los Angeles's class system, as Mike Davis has shown. Harvey Graff's work on Dallas's monumental architecture, elite cultural spaces, and uneven infrastructure development has demonstrated how an urban design expanded in a way that rationalized the spatial segregation of the rich and the poor.[8]

Recreational spaces were subsumed under broader patterns of urban planning that were pervasively racialized. The value of urban expansion became the driving assumption of planners. By the 1920s, many major cities had established new planning commissions and regional planning had begun in metropolises such as Los Angeles and New York. Yet, as Robert Fogelson writes, "From their conception of congested eastern and midwestern metropolises, the planners assumed that the great city was no longer the most pleasant place for living or the most efficient location for working. They proposed as an alternative, residential dispersal and business decentralization."[9] Subdividing the land and providing adequate streets and highways became among the highest priorities of white elites.

Black access to recreational spaces, which already was severely limited, became even more problematic in the context of the new privatized spaces of suburbia and consumer culture. Cynicism and confusion developed about the uses of public space. In addition, the problem of blacks' exclusion from public spaces was invisible to many. Understanding of the history of government, development, and racial-ethnic relations has remained abysmal in the past half-century in many cities. Even with the increasing interest in including black history in school curricula, the power, complexity, and richness of blacks' collective struggle for justice and equality has often been simplified in the broader context of American urban history. David Thelen and Roy Rosenzweig have shown that white Americans have little sense of history, let alone of black history. Nonetheless, racialized contests over memory and public space, notably in the South, continually arise in new forms. "The determined refusal of blacks to surrender their claims on the South's public spaces and life sustained a tradition of contestation that began after the Civil War," W. Fitzhugh Brundage has written. And, he adds, the "revision of the South's civic landscape is no mere chimera but rather the tangible consequence of blacks' enlisting public institutions to record and honor their past."[10]

Thomas's strategy of calculated provocation followed by negotiations that he pioneered at Baker's Haulover Beach State Park was soon adopted nationally by the Congress of Racial Equality (CORE), the Southern Christian Leadership Conference (SCLC), and the NAACP. By 1945, nonviolent civil disobedience had a long history in America, yet it was only during and right after World War II that the strategy was used in the cause of desegregation. Dr. Oscar Braynon pointed out that the demonstration in Miami

> happened long before the other cities. It wasn't heard [of] at that time. This was 1945, before the war ended. The other cities came about in the fifties, after the war. So this was very new. Those folks had no idea what was going to happen to them, but they were willing to take that chance because they knew . . . that the men were coming home from the service. And they weren't just going to tolerate being treated like they had been treated before. You pay your taxes and they tell you, "Pay your taxes but you can't go in the water."[11]

Thomas's adoption of nonviolent civil disobedience, his wife explained, came primarily from his reading of the thought and action of Mohandas

Gandhi and was indirectly linked to the efforts of such civil rights legends as A. Philip Randolph, a native of Crescent City, Florida, who organized the Brotherhood of Sleeping Car Porters, and James Farmer, co-founder of CORE. Leaders focused on recreational space as the most viable zone for a struggle that they knew would involve many other demands and, they hoped, would secure many concessions.

Miami had been segregated since its founding in 1896. The demand for a waterfront beach became the first rallying cry for justice after World War II, although at that time it meant a segregated beach for blacks. After living with the cultural legacy of the *Plessy v. Ferguson* "separate but equal" decision for half a century, Miami's black leaders saw the beach as their first reachable postwar target. Thomas's actions underscored how delicate the balance was between pushing the limits of political possibility while at the same time promoting dialogue between blacks and whites. This story is more subtle than those of the dramatic events in the later history of the civil rights movement, but it is no less important.

Segregated Beaches in Modern American History

As places that change over time, beaches are unique staging grounds and metaphors for the fragility of human existence, enlarging and eroding within a large and sometimes unfathomable universe. Rachel Carson, Anne Morrow Lindbergh, and other writers have explored the fundamental instability of beaches, which are composed of rocks, grasses and trees, and grains of sand drawn together by the tides. Serving as gateways to the mainland, they have been sites of violent conflict, whether between Europeans and native peoples in Florida and the Caribbean or between the Allied and Axis armies at Normandy. They have also been places of organized and spontaneous recreation; they evoke visions of status for some and of peaceful reflection for others. In modern America, beaches near population centers became overlaid with constructions of class, gender, and race. Boundaries around beaches blocked access for some through private property laws and through formal and informal norms about propriety.[12] Scholars, public officials, and environmental organizations have long ignored the pervasive problem of unequal access to public recreational spaces for African Americans, Hispanics, and other minority racial-ethnic groups. Issues related to beachfront access illustrate how power regulates access to a resource that enables people to experience joy, engage in recreation, and live in harmony with nature.

Four types of black beaches evolved in the United States before the civil rights movement of the 1960s. In one model, blacks played in places that were invisible to whites because they were physically isolated or undesirable for other reasons. For example, blacks in Miami could swim only in dangerous water-filled rock quarries or along the industrial waterfront. In the years before 1945, Virginia Key was such a place. A second type of black beach emerged through private ownership: black entrepreneurs purchased beachfront land and developed black-associated spaces, or white property owners allowed blacks to congregate on their land for a fee. Black middle-class tourism grew after World War I. Sometimes quietly and sometimes through struggle, African Americans obtained access to beaches and other waterfront locations around the nation, but they always had to defend their rights. In southern California, for example, a small black beach resort was created when the city of Manhattan Beach was incorporated in 1912, but in 1932, as pressures to develop waterfront land rose, the resort was condemned. In the 1920s and 1930s, a number of African Americans bought waterfront land. Several of the best examples in Florida are Abraham Lewis's American Beach, Frank Butler's land on Anastasia Island near St. Augustine, and Mary McLeod Bethune's Bethune Beach near Daytona Beach. These places sometimes featured summer cottages and hosted public picnics, religious gatherings, and a few commercial establishments. The Black Pearl, part of Atlantic Beach in South Carolina, was formed initially by Gullah/Geechee people who had long lived on the Sea Islands and opened hotels, restaurants, and shops. Selective "coastal zones" were thus owned or operated by blacks and used as recreational spaces, sometimes begrudgingly tolerated by whites in parts of the Deep South, but ultimately, by the later twentieth century, as historian Andrew Kahrl has shown, absorbed into the broader matrix of "coastal capitalism."[13]

The third model developed in only a few places where protracted negotiations with local officials brought about formally segregated black summer homes and beaches, although they were often in undesirable locations for white buyers. Russ Rymer's personal account, *American Beach*, showed how a black beach that dated back to the 1930s conflicted with corporate development visions for Amelia Island near Jacksonville. His book highlighted the fervent advocacy and idiosyncratic environmental perspective of a black woman, MaVynee Betsch, who faced corporate takeover of a historically black beach in the 1990s.[14] In Miami, black real estate owner Dana Dorsey attempted to create a black bathing beach on Fisher Island just south of Miami Beach after World War I but failed to sustain it. These experiments were shaped by low real estate values and the isolation of the beachfront space blacks were allowed to use. Most black recreation in Miami took place in churches, schools, lodges, and streets and on porches. Miami blacks also had access to several small parks that were largely dominated by sports and seldom functioned as major community gathering places.

The fourth model, an all-black public beach, evolved over time in many places in the South but emerged in full force in Miami. Historians have recently identified a wide variety of places throughout the South in which local strategies that suited local conditions were not in sync with the vision of national leaders. The fate of segregated public space became more openly contentious over time as the issue was shaped by the changing nature of land use, politics, and commercial pressures or by competing visions of public purposes for land.[15]

World War II changed the situation significantly. The potential for violence in clashes over the uses of public beaches was vividly brought before the nation during the Detroit riot of the summer of 1943. The riot began at Belle Isle Park when a young black man crossed a well-understood racial line and was hit by a stone; the incident was similar to the one that sparked the race riot in Chicago in 1919. In Detroit in 1943, African Americans fought back as mobs rampaged through the city's streets.[16] As World War II ended, many blacks in the South felt bitter about returning to segregated cities when they had risked their lives to free the world of fascism. Black leaders in Miami decided to focus on access to Miami's waterfront as a test case. In *Smith v. Allwright* (1944), the Supreme Court had outlawed the white democratic primary, and blacks in cities throughout the South were developing various strategies to confront inequality and segregation. Gaining legal access to beaches seemed less directly threatening to whites than voting, yet it was a visible sign of justice.

After the war, whites who were determined to maintain their exclusive right to public space actively opposed the black community's major push to desegregate beaches. Accounts of other areas, notably Gilbert Mason's story of the struggle he led to open beaches in Biloxi in 1959 and Suzanne Scheld's study of New York's Orchard Beach, show different approaches to the shifting politics of ethnic users of waterfront parks. Access to beaches and other recreational spaces was hotly contested.[17] In 1957, for example, the Montgomery, Alabama, city commission adopted an ordinance declaring it unlawful "for white and colored persons to play together, or [be] in company with each other . . . at swimming pools, beaches, lakes or ponds."[18] Willcox Lake near Petersburg, Virginia, was off limits to African Americans. Rev. Samuel Robinson recalled, "You'd come by and see the swimming area and the picnic tables with all the food, but you could just look, and then you'd have to keep going." In 1951, Governor John Battle warned that Virginia might close its state park system rather than accept integration, and in fact, a 1953 petition to integrate the swimming pool at Willcox Lake resulted in its permanent closure.[19] In this longer-term perspective, the 1945 victory in Miami is all the more remarkable.

Lawson Thomas: From Gradualism to Confrontation

Lawson E. Thomas was born in Ocala, Florida, in 1898, two years after the *Plessy v. Ferguson* decision and the incorporation of the city of Miami. After graduating from the Florida Agricultural and Mechanical College for Negroes in 1919, he went north to the University of Michigan because blacks were not allowed to attend Florida's law schools. Thomas practiced law in Detroit for six years and then returned to Florida, living first in Jacksonville and then settling down in Miami in 1935. One of only a few black lawyers in the city at the time, he associated with prominent black doctors and preachers. In 1953, Thomas married his secretary, Eugenia Bell Brooks, who remained a committed activist for decades, although she is now deceased.

Thomas's legal challenges to racism began on his first day in court, Thanksgiving 1937, when he sat at the front of the courtroom representing several defendants. The bailiff directed Thomas to "sit down with the rest of the niggers." Thomas refused, ignoring the bailiff's threat to "toss [him] through the sixth-floor window." It was a threat that Judge James E. Dunn, upon taking the bench, quickly ended, telling the bailiff

Figure 1. Lawson Thomas, lawyer, speaker, and leader of the first post–World War II civil rights demonstration in the South, which was held in Miami. In the early 1950s he became the first black judge of a black court in the South since Reconstruction. Credit: Arva Parks Collection.

that "under Florida law . . . Thomas was entitled to sit where he pleased." Working occasionally with Thurgood Marshall, the NAACP's lawyer, Thomas won several critical cases that brought some hope of equality to African Americans in southern Florida. One of the cases he initiated, a 1947 lawsuit against the Broward School Board, challenged the closure of black schools during the winter months when agricultural labor was needed in the county. Another won the right for blacks to serve as jurors in Dade County. He also participated as *amicus curiae* (friend of the court) in a 1946 suit that "prevented Dade county from formally zoning the county along racial lines."[20] One of his most important cases helped convince the U.S. Supreme Court to require equal pay for black teachers. Representing the NAACP, he challenged the indictment of a black man for first-degree murder on the grounds that blacks were "unlawfully, arbitrarily and systematically excluded from the grand jury which indicted him solely because of his race."[21] These successes, combined with his dialogic, relationship-building approach to white leaders, opened a clear path for his appointment by Governor Fuller Warren in May 1950 as the first black judge of a municipal court, presiding over cases involving black citizens of Miami who had been arrested by black policemen.

In the aftermath of the wade-in, Thomas drafted the agreement with city officials to designate a black bathing beach at Virginia Key. In subsequent years, Thomas's powerful public speeches articulated a demand for equality and a strategy of cooperation. He built on his experiences both inside and outside the courtroom to take deliberate action in the streets. His stature and the respect his civil rights work had garnered him are evident in the 1942 publication of his article, "The Professions in Miami," in the NAACP's magazine, *The Crisis*. Commenting on his mode of operation in the face of Miami's racial conditions, Thomas said:

> The importance of the business we handle is measured chiefly by our ability, diligence, character and the confidence Negroes have in their own. The latter is modified directly and inversely by the former three. Our opportunities are gauged by a population of 40,000 Negroes whose business and property holdings are comparatively high. We have never been refused a courtesy by a white member of the bar or a clerk of court. We use the County Bar Library and none has ever resented our presence. The practice of law in the South throws a Negro among the most highly trained white people in the South. They have intelligence. They are fairly tolerant. However, they cling to many of the old southern traditions. It places the burden upon us who dare to go to the bar in the South to show such adroitness, preparation, diligence and character that their own intelligence will require them to give us the respect and consideration we desire.[22]

By the late 1940s, Thomas was recognized as a popular speaker and a guiding intellectual on race relations not only among black leaders in Miami but also throughout Florida and to some extent elsewhere in the South. His views can best be appreciated as an extended explication of his strategy of combining assertive legal tactics with pragmatic persistence in dealing with the white power structure. To an audience of teachers in 1947, Thomas declared: "One of the elements of leadership is [the] sense of tolerance. You can captivate the fancy and gain the undying loyalty of the high and low if you but be tolerant with his point of view, and approach people with understanding of their motives, their fears, and their aspirations. This requires two things, patience and thick skins. Leaders do not blow up under fire. They will not only listen but refrain from being impatient when others will not."[23]

In late 1947, speaking to the Tampa chapter of Omega Psi Phi, the first fraternity founded on a historically black campus, he said that although segregation "is a part of the democratic process, that might does not make right." Listing the unmet needs of southern blacks, he articulated the notion of a civil right to public space:

> If there is anything which on its very face may be found to be generally disgraceful in the south, it is total lack of recreational facilities for Negroes. We do not know of a single, adequate gymnasium for physical culture for Negro children in any public school in the State of Florida. . . . We do know of a few so-called parks, most of which amount to no more than a baseball field and here and there a few hundred dollars' worth of recreational facilities for small and grown up people. It has been scientifically shown that there is a direct relation between juvenile and consequently grown up delinquency and crime and recreational facilities which direct the spare time of human beings into proper wholesome channels.[24]

Pointing to the numerous positive developments in race relations, Thomas highlighted the importance of the NAACP, the American Civil Liberties Union (ACLU), and regional interracial groups such as the Southern Conference for Human Welfare, then in its ascendancy. Significantly, he did not mention the CIO or other labor organizations, perhaps fearing their association with the left. He emphasized that "no national organizations can be effective in the advancement of racial relations except by and through local persons. . . . Local social and civic organizations are by far and large the most important bodies working in this field. The accomplishments made in the field of interracial relations and inter-group understanding have been done in two ways: (1) conference and conciliation and (2) plain, straight lawsuits. You only have to remain a Negro a goodly number of years to be convinced both methods are necessary as well as proper." This approach combined dialogue with legal action and did not rely on civil disobedience.[25]

Aware of the connection between the Cold War and the image of race relations in the United States, Thomas warned about overreliance on material goods and technological achievements to sustain the American system. He found hope in whites' growing awareness that racial injustice revealed monstrous discrepancies between rhetoric and reality as the United States tried to combat communism. In 1947, he told an audience in Delray Beach: "We cannot stand a national light to the world for freedom from fear with part of our citizens parading in bed sheets, by the dark of night, and burning crosses before the humble homes of their black fellow citizens who seek expansion into new, decent and clean places to live. Racial intolerance and segregation are sapping the moral fiber and killing the soul of the American people, thus leaving us unfit to assume the leadership of a world in which most of the people are other than white."[26]

He went further the next year when he addressed a black AME congregation in Jacksonville:

There are considerations far more important than material wealth, inventive genius and industrial development which we must consider and love, as Americans, if our system is to be perpetuated. The basic principles of the Declaration of Independence and the Constitution are not material. They were not devised for the creation of a great material empire. Their concepts are purely moral, and spiritual; and our system, our way of living, our ability to maintain the moral leadership of the world does and will depend upon how well we, the American people, display at home and abroad the spiritual fiber first found in the breasts of the founding fathers of our republic.

The "white public," he said, had begun "to catch itself up short and question whether or not injustice, racial prejudice and racial discrimination are sapping the moral fiber and spiritual strength of the American people. It is, and they know it." Thomas called on educated blacks to stimulate dialogue and confront the inequities around them. "It is the responsibility of each of us to wage incessant intellectual warfare in our respective communities for better living conditions for the masses, better facilities and more equal distribution of school funds, better jobs and more avenues of employment, recreational facilities, not only for people of school age, but with consideration for how the grown-ups occupy their time and why we have some of the amusement conditions which exist in our several communities."[27]

Black Miamians' access to the waterfront at Virginia Key Beach was the direct result of the work of this groundbreaking barrister. According to his wife, he seldom had time to sit on the beach, but he understood its significance to others. His exemplary career on the bench has been little noticed by civil rights historians and later activists, largely because he served in government. Some later criticized Thomas for agreeing to oversee the black court in Miami from 1950 until it was abolished in the 1960s after major decisions by the U.S. Supreme Court, just as they later regarded the black beach as inferior to those reserved for whites. But during this crucial transitional period, Thomas was well positioned to speak to the white power structure on behalf of black citizens.

A Wilderness on a Metropolitan Waterfront

In choosing Virginia Key as the site for Miami's first "colored beach," Charles Crandon agreed to create a park on this deserted and forlorn place that was not of interest to white real estate developers and would not jeopardize white tourism and the future land development on Key Biscayne. One map of Virginia Key allegedly dating from 1918 shows the space where the park is located as containing a "negro dancing pavilion"; thus an African American presence predates its formal designation as a park.[28] Yet in fairly short order, Virginia Key became a subject of controversy as competing and incompatible land uses were proposed by groups promoting economic development. In 1947, a causeway that linked Key Biscayne and Virginia Key to mainland Miami was completed, and Virginia Key became a focus for developers. What was once useless wilderness became increasingly coveted. But an agreement about a comprehensive plan for the island proved elusive.

Virginia Key, which was carved out as a separate island from Key Biscayne after the 1835 hurricane, was charted and described first by Alexander Bache and then by biologist Louis Agassiz in the 1840s. Documentation of its early use by people of African descent remains elusive, although it is likely that Seminoles, escaped slaves, and black Seminoles (of mixed African and indigenous ancestry) sought refuge there in the nineteenth century. Jurisdiction over 20 million acres, which included Virginia Key, was shifted from the federal government to Florida's Internal Improvement Fund in 1855. The state owned most of the submerged land and islands off the coast and had sweeping power to sell or give them to investors or to local communities for public use. Communities controlled local land use under deed restrictions that were seldom enforced. Titles to land on Virginia Key were disputed from 1898 until the 1930s,[29] and because of these conflicts the island was undeveloped and largely uninhabited.

During the interwar years, as Miami grew at a rapid pace, many leaders presented grand visions of hotels, parks, port schemes, an airport, and upscale housing developments connected to the mainland by a bridge system. Although they came to naught because of the Great Depression and World War II, these proposals from those who had power to determine the future are instructive and prophetic. Ever since its incorporation, Miami has been identified as a modern American playground and has been characterized by a culture of leisure, spectacle, and health—all the fruits of modernity.[30] The wealthy entrepreneur Carl Fisher envisioned Biscayne Bay as a metropolitan region, linked by bridges and causeways, that could host lavish entertainment and recreational activities.[31] Soon after famed designer Warren Manning created and landscaped nearly sixty acres of fill in 1926 to create Bayfront Park, located just north of the mouth of the Miami River, the new park became the city's prime attraction.[32]

At first, few residents seriously questioned Miami's growth ethos or worried about the impact of urban density and economic development on the fragile ecology of Biscayne Bay. Ralph Middleton Munroe, one of the founders of Coconut Grove, a Miami neighborhood located several miles south of the downtown area, and scientists such as Charles Torrey Simpson and John Kunkle Small, questioned the encroachment of development, but their opinions were largely marginalized by those who promoted the culture of boosterism. Some elite clubwomen promoted elements of the City Beautiful movement in Miami without success. Although city planning was emerging in industrial cities by the early 1920s, Marjory Stoneman Douglas's attempt to promote beauty and planning in Miami came to naught. As she later recalled, "I could argue that land should be set aside for parks, while land was cheap, I could talk about this new thing, zoning, and the newer and hazier thing, city planning. . . . No one paid attention."[33]

Miami's broader waterfront, of which Virginia Key was an offshore element, was the subject of contention. Entrepreneurs and civic groups sought to create artificial islands in order to expand facilities for cargo and cruise ships and yachts. The inadequacy of the channel was vividly illustrated in 1926, when a large sailing vessel that was to be converted into a floating nightclub sank, blocking the channel.[34] But plans for harbor development were impeded by factionalism among civic and business leaders. John B. Orr and the Miami Planning Board submitted a plan for a deeper channel and a chain of islands that would extend from the Miami dock to Fisher's development on Peninsular Island. These were to be the sites of warehouses and piers and were to be connected with the mainland by a railroad. Part of this plan was implemented in 1927, when the channel was dredged to a depth of twenty-five feet. The low islands lying south of the channel today are a result of this plan.[35]

Opposition to the larger plan was led by E. G. Sewell, a prominent member of the Chamber of Commerce who later served as mayor. Staking out a strong position, he argued that the plan would use public funds to build bridges that would serve private interests. In his view, it was a classic bait-and-switch instigated by clever developers and would destroy the magnificent view of the water Miamians had long enjoyed. He also worried that "obstructing the free flow of the tide" that swept away "the sewage coming out of the Miami River and along our Bay front" would "cause an unsanitary condition which may bring on an epidemic of typhoid fever."[36] The wrangling over Virginia Key must have seemed endless. In May 1926, Rand Properties of Miami sought to purchase a major parcel on the key. The company planned to build docks and terminal facilities "at the north and west sides of Virginia Key, while the rest of the island [would] be developed into a high class residential property." It envisioned a causeway from Point View to the southwestern tip of Virginia Key that would include airports that served commercial and government aircraft. Local officials also contemplated constructing 3,600 acres with dredged fill to use as port facilities. Fisher's Terminal Development Company sought rights to build across Norris Cut; in this plan, "bulkheads from Virginia Key will extend northwestward to leave a ship channel between the key and Peninsula Island."[37] None of these projects were undertaken in the aftermath of the devastating hurricane of 1926, the Wall Street crash of 1929, and the Great Depression.

A year after Franklin Roosevelt became president, a citizens' committee that sought to create a system of parks connected by a scenic highway encircling metropolitan Miami proposed that a causeway across the bay be built. However, the committee warned that "work on such a causeway would not be started until the city had obtained public use of the beaches on the keys."[38] Late in 1937, the city tried to purchase 1,300 acres of nearby bay bottom from the state, but the state deferred action on the application pending funding.[39] A few months later the city tried to purchase Virginia Key and the adjacent bay bottom to provide what was touted as a "public ocean bathing beach."[40] These plans were stymied by the South Side Civic Association, which served "legal notice" against city officials to prohibit "spending or pledging city credit" on a causeway. This action sought to undermine the project by convincing the federal government not to deliver the funds it had pledged for the project.[41] The endless debate over the expansion of Miami's industrial waterfront involving Virginia Key continued through the New Deal years. Four million dollars in potential federal funding was a major inducement, but the inability of stakeholders to agree on an overall plan proved fatal. The *Miami Herald* and others who favored the plan decried the political wrangling.[42]

Amid all this feverish, yet fruitless scheming to develop Virginia Key, a *Miami Herald* reporter took a boat ride with a friend and happened on a group of men living there. One told him, "This place . . . is the one and only. There is no other place like it in Florida. It's the South Seas and the tropics combined. There are some guys living down here that have found a way to beat the depression." This man, a former ironworker from up north, described his idyllic life on the abandoned island. Friends had staked him the money to buy a small boat, and he had built a house with driftwood. "Plenty of loose planks drifted in, and inside of six months I had a fairly presentable place, what with palm fronds and the like for a roof and sides over the planks." He survived by eating "lobster, fish and sometimes bread, coffee, if a passing boat could spare any. Drinking water was a problem for a while, but I solved that by making a watershed of my roof and storing it. I also got a five gallon bottle every once in a while from a boat." When someone asked what time it was, one of the men in the camp said, "We don't need [a clock]. It's either high tide or low tide, you're hungry or you're sleepy around here."[43]

A Waterfront Park for African Americans?

In the early decades of the twentieth century, several of Miami's white political and business leaders expressed interest in addressing African Americans' demand for access to the waterfront. In the 1920s, the visionary George Merrick planned and developed the successful upscale city of Coral Gables to the south and west of Miami. The city, which featured broad boulevards, a grand city hall, the Biltmore Hotel and the mansions of its owners, Spanish-named streets, and lush Venetian-style waterways to the sea, attracted thousands of northerners with an aggressive advertising campaign. Marjory Stoneman Douglas, the prominent writer and daughter of the publisher of the *Miami Herald*, also promoted it.[44]

Merrick, who also served as head of the Greater Miami Planning Council, was interested in displacing blacks from downtown Miami in order to expand the business district. Merrick called for "slum clearance . . . effectively removing every negro family from the present city limits." He envisioned half-acre plots, presumably created further west in the Everglades, linked by a "county wide, county controlled transportation system. Whereby these negroes and other workers can be brought back and forth at a very cheap rate." These plans were never adopted because of resistance from the black community. At the same time, Merrick expressed interest in creating a waterfront park for blacks—a concession that was widely interpreted as a form of appeasement. His plans mixed exclusion with sensitivity to blacks' predicament. In 1937, he told several white organizations that "today one third of our present population is negro. . . . Today this third of our present citizenry are effectively denied water access and 'water use.' Now, collectively as well as individually, we cannot receive fairness, unless we give fairness to this deserving one third of our citizenry." Within his vision of a fifty-mile loop of highways circling Biscayne Bay, he suggested that at "a proper point . . . a great Bay beach be established and forever preserved for negro use. And that similarly, on the ocean side of the Loop that similar advantages be established and preferably at one whole little island facing on the Gulf Stream, which could ideally be made there for them an ocean and Gulf Stream park."[45]

In 1938, pressured by real estate and shipping interests, the city adopted a plan to turn Virginia Key into a huge seaport with terminals on its north side. The U.S. Navy, after lengthy delays, approved the Virginia Key Harbor Project, which would have garnered $4–5 million in federal funds for the purpose of developing a combination airbase and seaport. But conflict ensued between Coral Gables, which had taken over control of Key Biscayne, and city of Miami and Dade County officials. A causeway and road linking Miami, Virginia Key, and Key Biscayne was again proposed. In 1940, as plans were being made to build what was later called the Rickenbacker Causeway, the city of Miami bought much of the island with federal funds it received when the project was turned over to the government. According to county parks director Doug Barnes, the state conveyed 64.3 acres on Virginia Key to the county by a deed dated May 24, 1940.[46]

That same year, County Commissioner Charles Crandon led the way in persuading the wealthy Matheson family heirs to donate 808 acres of land on nearby Key Biscayne for a public park. This development led to the inclusion of Virginia Key in a larger plan that sought to link both keys to the mainland with a causeway.[47] As it turned out, however, conflicts of interest inhibited overall planning and the idea remained contentious for years.[48] Crandon, a powerful political leader and staunch park advocate, persuaded the influential head of the du Pont interests in Florida, Edward Ball, to help promote and finance the causeway to Virginia Key and Key Biscayne.[49] Crandon envisioned real estate development and large public parks. The county promoted a plan that called for a causeway from the mainland to Virginia Key and Key Biscayne and a $2 million bond issue to finance construction of a park on Key Biscayne and another park at Baker's Haulover, now called Haulover Park. Virginia Key was to be a combination deep-water seaport, beach park, and public aquarium site.[50]

While the Miami area had rebounded from the worst ravages of the Depression, the coming of World War II altered the political and the economic situation, and the status of Virginia Key changed significantly. In early May 1940, plans were published for new parks on Key Biscayne and Baker's Haulover, but shortly thereafter President Roosevelt vetoed a bill that would have funded the dredging operation, noting that the War Department's energy should be devoted to military preparedness. However, doubtless under political pressure, the Navy Department later approved Dade County's application to construct the causeway from Miami through Virginia Key to Key Biscayne. It was also announced that the park on Key Biscayne was to be named for Crandon. By March 1941, lobbyists were seeking the navy's endorsement of the idea that the Virginia Key causeway was "needed for defense."[51]

By January 1942, Miami officials, in consultation with the federal government, had devised various plans to transform Virginia Key into an airport for overseas flights. In May, the navy approved the project and recommended a budget of $5 million (which eventually rose to $17 million). The scheme included a causeway, a harbor, docks, a bridge between Virginia Key and Key Biscayne, and extensive recreational facilities. There were difficulties with negotiating the deal for the use of the other parcels on the island, however. Crandon called for a halt in construction on the Virginia Key causeway in 1943, after delays and a different set of orders came down from the War Production Board. Development languished throughout the war, although the island was often used as a training locale. In late 1944, city and county officials were still seeking federal appropriations to make the air-seaport a reality.[52]

How, amid myriad land use plans, funding schemes, and conflicting jurisdictions, did Virginia Key become the site of a black beach? The answer is found in a combination of federal actions, including the creation of a navy training base and a study that emphasized the need for recreational spaces for African Americans, and pressure from the black community. The timing was dictated by the exigencies of World War II and the clout of Charles Crandon. Yet the critical event that brought the black beach to life came from African Americans themselves.

In 1941, a study of Dade County's recreation parks was prepared by the county park department with the cooperation of the National Park Service. After noting the relatively high birth rate of African Americans, the report stated that "it is the part of wisdom to provide [parks] for the maintenance of health, morale, and interest in regular occupation." The report identified numerous "acute complications," including the fact that blacks had few opportunities for work "above the laboring and domestic classifications. It is deemed wiser therefore to confine the negro park problem to simple lines of development in order to more adequately satisfy the needs of the colored population as it exists here." The average "negro is in a very low income bracket, and relatively few possess cars or sufficient income to pay considerable amounts for transportation, particularly if they have families, Hence their travel radius is largely restricted to close-to-home movement and activity."

> Attentive study of the county map with the geologic limitations on settlement and recreational development together with analysis of the spectacular growth of the region in the past three decades from fishing village to sub-tropical Riviera must make it painfully clear that there is inadequate ocean beach frontage for the higher type development to which area lends itself. Since any negro development would be ruinous to a large neighborhood area, it would be unwise and impractical to set off a negro reservation on the beach. In fact, such an area would be used by but a limited group and would not justify the economic penalty. It would be more sound practice to set aside a bayfront area with a small pumped-in beach with the intent to enlarge it if and when colored patronage justified doing so.[53]

This limited vision illustrates the usual combination of disregard for black Miamians and an emphasis on profitable real estate development.

Federal funding for communities impacted by the war was provided through the Defense Housing and Community Facilities and Services Act of 1940, popularly known as the Lanham Act, which authorized federal grants and loans to public and private agencies for the purpose of operating public facilities. Best known for funding child care for mothers employed in war industries, the Lanham Act was a significant factor in creating more "colored" facilities during the war. Federal funds were thus slated to help build local housing and recreational facilities.

In 1941, the Interracial Committee of the YWCA offered to work with Miami's recreation department to plan playground programs for black children. The need for a swimming beach that would be available to Negroes was mentioned in a committee survey, and city and county commissioners were urged to consider it. The report also noted that there were three main parks in Miami for African Americans: Dorsey, Dixie Park, and Liberty City.[54]

The older tradition of black use of the area east of Bear Cut on Virginia Key was reinforced by the navy's decision to use the area to train black seamen near the end of the war. According to minutes of the County Commission in March 1944, "the County Engineer reported that a request had been received from Admiral W. R. Munroe for permission to drive temporary piling on county-owned bay bottom land adjacent to Virginia Key, and to establish swimming facilities for training Negro personnel of the U.S. Navy. After considering the request, it was moved by Commissioner C. H. Crandon that the permission be granted, with the understanding that the use would be temporary and that the property would be vacated on 30 days['] notice from the County. The motion was seconded by Commissioner Hugh Peters, and, upon being put to a vote, was duly carried." A notation appeared on the right-hand margin of the page: "U.S. Navy granted permission to establish swimming facilities for training Negro personnel."[55]

Dade County's Interracial Committee included high-level white participants such as Commissioner Crandon and Sheriff Coleman and major black leaders, including Lawson Thomas. It urged that a health center and another federally assisted public housing project be established in Miami, presumably in Colored Town, renamed Overtown. At the end of a meeting in August 1944, Crandon "revealed to the committee [that] the county might announce within two or three weeks its plans for the establishment of a recreational park with bathing facilities. He said a plan was underway before the war but that military needs prevented its being carried out."[56]

Yet in January 1945 the future of Virginia Key remained in limbo. Jurisdictions, financial interests, and personalities competed to define the uses of the key. In late January, Crandon announced to the press that a "half mile negro bathing beach, large enough for 100,000 bathers, will be established by the County on Virginia Key adjoining the tract to be occupied by the proposed $15,000,000 airport-seaport project. The 46 acre negro beach, a negro baseball park and the county's $1,000,000 aquarium will be constructed on the south end of Virginia Key on 140 acres owned by the County." There was to be parking for 1,330 cars and an additional 980 parking spaces for the aquarium. "This area will also be served by a bus line which will serve Virginia Beach, the County aquarium and Crandon Park," he said. The black recreational area was projected to be opened before any projected aviation facilities were to be built on the island. Altogether, Crandon estimated, the parks at Crandon Park, Virginia Key Park, and Haulover Beach Park would provide more than five miles of beaches, enough to accommodate more than 600,000 bathers.

Over the next several weeks, however, a fight broke out over the location of the new airport. Mayor John Levi of Miami Beach and a Miami city commissioner opposed its location on Virginia Key. Arguing that "we don't want airplanes flying over our heads day and night," Levi called for the airport to be developed out in the Everglades. It was strongly hinted that Crandon opposed the creation of the private airport further south because it would be two miles from his house on Red Road.[57]

The "half-mile Negro bathing beach" would cost the county $150,000. Its amenities would include landscaping "with palm trees predominating. Groins will be constructed to prevent erosion, and a pavilion will be constructed for picnics and small gatherings. Other facilities will include bathhouses and an outdoor picnic area with built-in ovens. . . . Wharves and docks will be rebuilt to accommodate small boats. A large section will be set aside for baseball diamonds and for other sports." As if to underscore the distance between Virginia Key Beach for blacks and the newly projected Crandon Park for whites, "Virginia Beach is separated from Crandon Park by an expanse of water known as Bear's Cut which is approximately [one] half-mile wide." Despite this announcement, officials were hampered by jurisdictional fights and refused to make the park a reality.

It took an act of protest by civil rights activists to turn the promise of waterfront access for the black community into a reality. On May 9, 1945, Thomas's legal knowledge and diplomatic skills, effective civil disobedience strategies, and outrage at injustice came face to face with the power of Commissioner Charles Crandon. A unique place emerged from the complex politics of waterfront development, and African Americans were brought together in the largest recreational public space in the state specifically designated for black people. The complex negotiations that brought it about involved not only development politics but also the relationship between the races and public space in South Florida. The next chapter explores how the dynamic of race and space played out in Miami before World War II.

Beyond Colored Town

The Changing Boundaries of Race Relations and African
American Community Life in Miami, 1896–1945

At the turn of the twentieth century, white supremacy was firmly in place throughout the South. In the wake of the Populist challenge to the prevailing class and racial order, New South elites had imposed tighter spatial boundaries and harsher political constraints on African Americans. Yet in southern cities, vibrant black communities emerged behind the walls that confined them. Blacks created churches and mutual aid associations, formed civic organizations, held commemoration ceremonies, and conducted a rich, informal social life, sustaining group solidarity in the face of adversity. The emergence of a black middle class was profoundly threatening to whites. In Wilmington, North Carolina, they responded with a devastating riot and political rout in 1898. Atlanta was scarred by a race riot in 1905. Almost any show of resistance was met with violence, while the scourge of lynching continued unabated. Indeed, Florida had one of the highest rates of lynching of any state in the period 1890–1930. Even in the 1980s, black residents were reluctant to recall the 1934 lynching of Claude Neal for historian James McGovern. Yet the limits imposed on black advancement varied from place to place. In some cities, particular local circumstances opened small windows of interracial negotiation and cooperation.[1]

Miami, an "instant city" in the nation's southernmost state, was largely built by the labor of African Americans. Low-paid black laborers worked in construction, on the railroads, and in agriculture, while black women served in the households of whites. Several black neighborhoods grew up, including Colored Town, located just north of downtown Miami. Soon after the city was established in 1896, black business owners and professionals established themselves. By 1905 a Colored Board of Trade had formed. The first black lawyer, R. E. Toomey, went into practice in 1913. Dana A. Dorsey, a black carpenter who came from Georgia in 1897, profited from the building boom and became one of the wealthiest men in Dade County. In 1913, Geder Walker opened the Lyric Theater on 2nd Avenue, a "major center of entertainment" that offered vaudeville acts, motion picture shows, and theatrical performances. By the 1920s, an array of nightclubs and hotels had earned Colored Town the moniker "the Harlem of the South." Although Miami's social order was shaped by racial inequality, the configuration of race relations there was unique for a southern city. It was an unusual hybrid of well-heeled northern transplants and tourists, southern whites, and southern and Bahamian blacks.[2]

In recent years, historian Raymond Mohl has characterized Miami as "south of the South," a city defined by a vastly more complex set of cultural, demographic, and economic forces than those that prevailed elsewhere in the region. Mohl and other scholars have delved into the history of New Deal housing and building projects in Miami, the complex history of labor organizing, and the conflicts between African Americans and Cubans that have shaped local politics since the 1960s. More attention needs to be focused on race relations in Miami, the ground upon which so many controversies were fought and so many compromises were forged and then forgotten.[3]

Miami was (and in many ways remains) a racially divided city. Some walls were physical; a boundary between white and black residential areas located just east of the Lyric Theater that opened in 1915. Others were symbolic or situational, such as the elaborate etiquette that required blacks to defer to whites they encountered on the street, prohibited even indirect physical contact between the races through the use of common textbooks or water fountains, and prevented blacks and whites from sharing recreational spaces. In fact, black Miamians were formally excluded from most city parks until the 1960s. The legacy of the psychological distance, demeaning gestures, and legal strictures defines some residents in Miami to this day.

In 1945, when Miami's blacks advanced the cause of civil rights by gaining access to recreational space on the oceanfront, the compromise that gave them access to Virginia Key Beach did not overtly challenge the status quo or arouse concern among whites that organized black citizens would go on from their "separate but equal" beach to demand access to all public accommodations. Whites were able to "give" blacks Virginia Key Beach because it represented little or no threat to their real estate interests and political power—or so they believed at the time. Yet the creation of waterfront park on Virginia Key had unforeseen consequences. It provided a new gathering place for the black community in a natural setting. Churches and social groups used it for entertainment, organized recreation, and everyday beachside activities. It was a distinct, defensible, and largely self-policed public space where blacks could be free of white surveillance and control. It was a place that generated solidarity and fueled later civil rights activism in South Florida.

It was a place to remember, yet in time it was largely forgotten. Only recently has it been remembered anew, as oral histories have revealed the rich community life that African Americans enjoyed there. Unusually, the effort to save the land and the memories was initiated by environmentalists who found common cause with African Americans. Until the late 1970s, the historical experience of the black community remained largely invisible to outsiders. Since then, historians have illuminated important facets of Miami's black history. However, little attention has been paid to the city's tradition of interracial dialogue as it intersected with the development of the urban environment, the creation of public parks, and changing patterns of land use on the waterfront.[4]

Recent portraits of other Florida cities have painted a picture of complex social and political conditions that shaped black-white relations. Nancy Hewitt has examined how women from differing racial, ethnic, and class backgrounds "vied with one another, with city officials, employers, and coworkers, and with men in their community to claim public space, fashion political agendas, and construct activist identities" in Tampa. The "boomtown character of life on the Florida frontier and the blurred boundaries between racial and ethnic communities ensured the expansive character of women's roles."[5] Similar conditions existed in Miami. White women played a powerful role in promoting Royal Palm Park in 1915. In 1999, a small group of black women was central to the re-creation of Virginia Key as a public beach. Yet how gender and race relations operated earlier in Miami's history remains a mystery. Paul Ortiz's *Emancipation Betrayed*, which explores forms of black resistance, commemoration, and organization building in Florida between the Civil War and 1920, concludes that "African Americans in Florida . . . created the first statewide civil rights movement in U.S. history." Irvin Winsboro's edited collection illuminates more recent forms of black resistance to segregation and challenges the notion that in the 1950s, Florida, under the leadership of Governor LeRoy Collins, was more moderate than its southern neighbors. How does Miami fit into this evolving understanding of race relations?[6]

When I interviewed Bahamian immigrant and World War I veteran James Nimmo in 1984, I first realized that memories of segregation, still fresh in the minds of a dwindling group of elderly residents of African heritage, are critical pieces of evidence that help us understand power and place in Miami's past. Capturing memories through oral history involves gathering, organizing, contextualizing, and analyzing work that has been done, and often forgotten, by others. It also involves asking new questions of elders. All too often, historical and educational institutions have promoted bland and consensus-oriented narratives or pursued a limited range of esoteric questions. At the same time, nonprofit advocacy groups and the public have lacked the research and conceptual tools to build alternative narratives that challenge the contemporary configuration of political and economic power. Multiculturalism itself has become mainstream, absorbed into corporate thinking about competition between global cities instead of enhancing neighborhood and community life. Focusing on the political culture of land use within the modern growth economy and on the constraints and possibilities of public space can shed light on black-white relations. This chapter builds on the work of others to portray the history of black Miami and the process that led to the 1945 wade-in at Baker's Haulover beach.[7]

How did segregated black neighborhoods in Miami evolve within and beyond the dominant white culture? Given the disgraceful social conditions they were forced to endure, when and how did blacks, who came to Miami from diverse places, build a powerful sense of solidarity, commemorate their own pasts, and effectively demand their rights and negotiate with whites? How did segregation limit the freedom of African Americans while shaping their aspirations and sense of possibility? Was there any real coherence in the southern racial system that was imposed or affirmed by white leaders in Miami?

Racial Segregation and Miami's White Power Structure, 1896–1914

Miami, which preacher and promoter E. V. Blackman called the "Magic City," was founded in 1896 where the Miami River meets Biscayne Bay. Most of the new residents at the time were likely unaware of the previous history of the place they called home. Near the site of a Native American burial mound, William English established a plantation that relied on the labor of enslaved Africans in the 1830s, even before Florida had become a state. The enterprise failed because of the area's isolation during the Seminole Wars, and the entire region remained largely uninhabited until the 1880s. The city of Miami was incorporated in 1896 after Rockefeller partner Henry Flagler agreed to extend his Florida East Coast Railway south from Palm Beach and build an upscale hotel.[8]

The memoirs of Miami's early developers affirm the invisibility of blacks for whites. Yet black laborers made substantial contributions to the city's growth. In addition, the rhetoric of A. C. Lightbourne, a black champion of incorporation, and the fact that black voters enabled the city to reach the population threshold incorporation required were essential. The disappearance of black Miamians from early histories of the city attests to whites' understanding of urban development as their own accomplishment within a racialized system they benefited from disproportionately. Whites' conception of themselves as pioneer entrepreneurs, aided by Flagler's money, influence, and initiative, fit into the values of the dominant American culture at the time.[9]

Soon after the railroad reached the bay, the first newspaper, the ambitiously named *Miami Metropolis*, began reporting on the city's growth. The descriptions and images it published suggest the distance whites established between themselves and blacks. Photographer J. W. Chamberlain made one of the first photographs of the new city. In the background are twelve black men with wheelbarrows, picks, and axes. In front of

Figure 2. Black laborers and white supervisors captured by photographer J. Chamberlain as they broke ground in 1895 for Henry Flagler's Royal Palm Hotel at the mouth of the Miami River—in the process destroying a Native American sacred mound. Used by permission of HistoryMiami.

them stands a smaller group of relatively young, well-dressed white men, most of them from the South, who became prominent business-men, real estate developers, and local officials. This scene underscores the normative, asymmetrical pattern of black labor overseen by whites. In the background are the remnants of the long-standing Native Ameri-can burial mound that John Sewell, Flagler's construction boss, had his black laborers destroy, in the process digging up and desecrating count-less human remains. From that day on, disrespect for the indigenous people who had been there before marked the city; history was shoved aside in the name of progress. Another photograph of an unpaved Miami street includes a half-dozen two-story buildings and a group of black construction workers that Sewell proclaimed to be his "black artillery." Sewell used them not only as a work crew but also as voters in order to count enough residents to incorporate the city, although blacks' voting rights were soon taken away by state law. In his memoir, Sewell wrote that, twenty-five years later, five out of the twenty-five black construction workers "seem to be well and are prosperous." He never mentioned the existence of segregation in Miami.[10]

Miami's white business and civic leaders exhibited what Don Doyle has called a "new paternalism." They believed in the racial inferiority of persons of African descent, the need for clear separation between whites and blacks, and measures that enforced whites' control over blacks. Many were self-identified "crackers," southerners who had moved from northern Florida, Georgia, or Alabama to find opportunity within the Flagler orbit. They followed patterns of race relations in other southern cities by limiting funds, living space, work opportunities, and political rights for blacks. Many were evangelical Protestants, although a few were Catholic or Jewish.[11] They founded an array of exclusively white institutions, including trade associations, churches, and social clubs. White residential areas reinforced racial divisions as streets along or near the river or the bay became high-status addresses.[12]

Although Miami shared the South's political culture, it attracted an unusually diverse mixture of people that included immigrants from Europe and the Caribbean. Unlike most southern cities, it was not based on a plantation economy or on the extraction and processing of raw materials. Nonetheless, northern entrepreneurs, notably Henry Flagler and his Florida East Coast Railway, his hotels, and his Model Land Company, deferred to southern customs and laws.[13]

At the same time, the presence of northern tourists during the winter season was a powerful factor in defining local life under racial segregation. It was a double-edged sword for blacks and whites. On the one hand, northern tourists tended to defer to Jim Crow so as not to offend white southerners. The humor that entertained guests at the Royal Palm Hotel reinforced racist stereotypes. The hotel hosted an annual "Cake Walk, put on in the dining room by the black waiters. The highest stepper—the one with the most pizzazz—took the prize, a huge cake. The blacks also danced buck and wing and sang spirituals." The white elite appropriated a version of black culture that reinforced subservience. On the other hand, harshness toward black people was offensive to some northern whites, and they appreciated the personal kindnesses blacks showed them, notably members of the Coconut Grove community. Some northerners sought to soften the conditions under which blacks were forced to live, but they met with little success. Blacks remained largely invisible and politically marginal.[14]

A continuing source of concern for whites was the moral disorder in the area called North Miami and, later, Hardieville. Alcohol, prostitution, venereal disease, and crime were perceived as rampant and as threats to the white community, especially since residents of Hardieville socialized across racial lines. The first issue of the *Miami Metropolis* called for a "resident deputy sherrif [*sic*] of nerve and good character in North Miami. Many very worthy people have built their homes and live at that settlement. Their sleep should not be disturbed during midnight hours by loud shouts, screams or singing. Nor should their families be subjected on Sunday to the sight of nude negro bathers." John Sewell described these illicit activities: "The night after payday there were great times, the workmen spending their money getting drunk, fighting, shooting and killing. I have known as high as three or four dead men there after one night's jamboree. They had a number of dance halls, and you would hear the dancing and music for half a mile around until the dead hours of night."[15] Whites associated crime with blackness, and white officials arrested black citizens for vice and vagrancy. The city's police chief explained that "I take especial care that no negroes are permitted in the white district of Miami after the hour of 6 o'clock, unless the police department is acquainted with their business," but he worried that some might occasionally slip into white areas. The county sheriff closed down illicit businesses in the racially mixed business area known as Hardieville in 1913.[16]

The press occasionally praised blacks for their exemplary behavior. In contrast to the way blacks in downtown Miami were regarded, a small black section of Coconut Grove that was located south of downtown and was dominated by Bahamians, was portrayed more positively. Its inhabitants were described as a "wide-awake, well-behaved class who are realizing more and more that knowledge means power and power money, and that knowledge is found in the school room. Then, too, the white people of the Grove have taken such an interest in them that they are encouraged and helped in very many ways."[17] As this example attests, local patterns of interracial interaction might allow some scope for blacks within the white supremacist order.

The Power of Violence and the Politics of Fear

Racial segregation created separate communities in the new city not only through residential and occupational restrictions but also by means of threats and violence. The system was based on increasingly stringent state laws and city ordinances and was enforced by white police and paramilitary organizations.

The 1885 state constitution mandated that "white and colored children shall not be taught in the same school," and in 1913 it became unlawful for whites to teach in black schools and for blacks to teach in white schools. State laws required separate railroad cars in 1887, the division of railway depots in 1907, and separate jails in 1909.[18] The 1901 Florida Primary Election Law excluded blacks from voting in the Democratic Party primary. Segregation laws and local fears intensified following the Populist revolt of the 1890s and the Spanish-American War. According to historian Samuel Proctor, "When Florida liberals thundered for railroad-corporation regulation, antitrust legislation, and a wider participation in government by the common people, their program did not envision racial tolerance or political equality for the Negro in the state." Napoleon Bonaparte Broward, who was elected governor in 1904, advocated the removal of blacks from the United States through a policy that would prevent "white people from living among [Negroes and] . . . Negroes from migrating back to the United States." He argued that blacks were "the wards of the white people, and that it is our duty to make whatever provision for them that would be best for their well-being."[19]

John S. Beard of Pensacola, a candidate for U.S. senator in 1907, articulated the views of many Miami-area whites of the political rights of blacks. Calling for the prohibition of the sale of alcohol, the "regulation and control of corporate power," the "preservation of the states and of their governments in all of their reserved rights and powers," and a constitutional amendment that would limit the franchise to white males over the age of twenty-one, he concluded: "It is hard enough for a respectable, home-loving white man to have his vote offset by the qualified vote of a negro; but it is time to call a halt when the vote of a white man—the taxpayer and property owner of the county—is offset by the illegal vote of the ignorant, shiftless negro of the city."[20]

White reformers repeatedly linked concerns about public health and morality with politics. The *Miami Metropolis* illuminated the connections between a desire to institute prohibition and the desire to preserve segregation and limit blacks' political rights. Commenting on a statewide election that failed to institute prohibition, the newspaper observed that

> in Miami the fight was the strongest. With the opening of the polls . . . the saloon men, supported by many negroes, practically all of them voting wet, voted early and then got to work corralling other votes. . . . The negro saved the day for the wets. He was an important factor and was so treated by the saloon advocates. The negro indulged in social equality for one time in his life. Some of the wets so far forgot themselves and their white supremacy to take the brother of black by the arm and escort him into the polls.[21]

According to the newspaper, some believed that more than 100 blacks voted against prohibition.

A decade later, as the nation was about to enter the Great War, Rev. J. L. White of the Central Baptist Church delivered a sermon entitled "The Ministry of Women." He asked the "God-fearing men and women of this community to stand with him in his demand that the segregated district be rooted out . . . to heal this cancer which is eating at the very vitals of our beautiful city." He focused on saloons, defining them as the "festering cancer in our midst" as "a place steeped in wickedness, where intoxicating liquor is drunk and sold, where murder is often committed." He conflated the sale of alcohol with the poverty and alleged crime of black districts, warning politicians to blot out saloons and the power of the liquor industry in the city. Linking women's suffrage to prohibition and prohibition to the need to address the poor living conditions in black urban neighborhoods was an increasingly powerful strategy throughout the South as the war became a reality. While a few white leaders showed some sympathy for blacks who endured degraded conditions, their primary motive seems to have been a desire to rid black neighborhoods of alcohol. In the North, immigrants and the political machines they supported were blamed for upholding the power of saloons. Prohibition was formulated as a women's issue because drunken men were understood to beat their wives and waste money, depriving their families of their wages.[22]

Fear engendered by racial violence in other parts of Florida and the South had long affected blacks and whites in Miami. A race riot in Key West in 1897, sparked by the alleged rape of a white woman by a black man, the attempted lynching of the black man, and his protection by black citizens, captured Miamians' attention. "There is no telling at what moment some fiendish act similar to that at Key West last week may occur in this city or vicinity and precipitate a race war," the *Miami Metropolis* warned. It called for "the organization of a company of naval reserves at the Port of Miami . . . [as] a big advertisement for the place and splendid medicine in the case of a race war or riot over quarantine or health regulations, contingencies which should always be kept in mind."[23]

The overt violence of white supremacy was manifested locally during the Spanish-American-Cuban War by the behavior of some of the 7,000 soldiers brought to Miami to protect the area in mid-summer 1898. Most lived in Camp Miami, a base with inadequate sanitary facilities that had been constructed at the behest of Henry Flagler. Southern soldiers frequently harassed local blacks, once going so far as to drive them out of Coconut Grove.[24]

The ideology of white supremacy that prevailed in Miami clearly linked racial dominance to gender dominance. A photograph of a KKK parade in downtown Miami in the mid-1920s affirms the respectability the group had attained. The positive reception of D. W. Griffith's film "The Birth of a Nation" helped launch the new KKK in 1915. The film presented the ideology of white supremacy with a narrative in which the Klan redeemed the honor of white women during the sordid period of Reconstruction when blacks ran amok, corrupting politics, humiliating white men, and violating white women. *Miami Herald* editor Frank Stoneman, a Quaker and municipal judge, disliked "the anti-immigrant and anti-black obsession" of the KKK, as did his daughter, journalist Marjory Stoneman Douglas. Douglas described her father's sense of justice by recounting incidents when Yankee women, having heard wild tales of the South's injustice to Negroes, came into Stoneman's court to witness the horror with their own eyes. They never failed to speak to him afterward. "Why," one woman said, "you treat negroes and white people with exactly the same justice, Judge Stoneman." He said, "Madam, that is the purpose of this court." Father and daughter perceived the racial violence the Klan practiced as a holdover of the "old South rather than a product of the New South," a debatable perspective today but at the time an effort to uphold a higher standard.[25]

Even those who eschewed membership in the Klan might endorse its vigilantism. Rev. J. L. White of the First Baptist Church spoke again in mid-March 1925, telling an audience that one of the root problems with Miami's moral order, aside from gambling, liquor, and loose women, was "black crime." "I am not a KKK but I want to say that . . . the KKK saved our Southern homes, saved the virtue of our women, saved the interests of our people and saved our country from wreck and ruin. I don't think the KKK is organized to enforce law. But I want to tell you something tonight. If somebody doesn't enforce the law in a legal way, then citizens ought to see that it is enforced in some right way."[26]

By the mid-1920s, Klan activities had become a form of entertainment in Miami. Huge holiday crowds trooped into the new Bayfront Park to see the sold-out performances of a KKK-sponsored circus in 1926. The KKK was still going strong in the late 1930s, aiming not only at blacks who tried to vote but also at black-owned gambling clubs and strip joints.[27]

The Miami police, who were intertwined with the KKK, were often criticized for protecting whites and for being unwilling to offer even a semblance of security to blacks. Their legendary cruelty was the subject of several investigations. In 1928, a grand jury report excoriated their "underworld alliances, summary executions, revival of the torture of the Middle Ages and despotism of such nature as to destroy the freedom of our citizens." Police Chief Leslie Quigg was singled out as "wholly unfit for office," even though he and three of his men had been acquitted for killing a black prisoner.[28]

Demographic Changes and Heightened Discord, 1914–1921

In the mid–1910s, tensions generated by the burgeoning numbers of black migrants to Miami and the revival of white racist paramilitary groups were intensified by the onset of World War I. A series of conflicts over residential expansion, access to recreational space, mobility, and labor rights both underlined the divergent perspectives of white and black leaders and generated new forms of dialogue between them.

The black community was split. On the one hand, many blacks armed themselves in self-defense and threatened to fight back against white oppression. This perspective proved fertile ground for the black nationalist movement, especially Marcus Garvey's Universal Negro Improvement Association (UNIA). On the other hand, many established black leaders, notably the members of the clergy, businessmen, and professionals, sought to negotiate with white leaders with the goal of preserving the community's economic gains while advancing civil rights. This division continued through the 1920s.

The composition of Miami's black community changed during the years before World War I as thousands of immigrants arrived from the Bahamas. Almost two-thirds of the foreign-born were West Indians, and by 1920 Bahamians comprised over half of the blacks in the city. The Bahamian presence distinguished Miami from other southern cities. In 1909, the *Miami Metropolis* expressed a commonly held opinion that "as a rule . . . the native colored people are more satisfactory laborers and house servants than the so-called 'Nassau niggers.' . . . The Nassau negroes are inexperienced in agricultural pursuits and make a failure of their work" at first. According to Katharine Beard, Bahamian immigrants "established an economic niche as skilled laborers . . . [and] service providers in communities of native born and immigrant blacks and because racism and economic inequality reduced their economic and social opportunities, they tended to develop industrious habits and avoided spending their earnings frivolously."[29] They were often shocked by the harsh repression in Miami and were more inclined than native-born blacks to resist white supremacy, although they often did so surreptitiously. Judge John Grambling warned against "the great number of Nassau Negroes who upon their arrival here consider themselves the social equal of white people" and was encouraged by the fact that their encounters with the Miami police had "altered their views."[30]

In Coconut Grove, Bahamians were consigned to a specific district and had no access to parks or the waterfront. The KKK paraded down Grand Avenue in their regalia every Saturday afternoon throughout the 1920s. Bobbi Graff, a Jewish civil rights advocate, recalled that even in the early 1950s, when Jews were not yet accepted as white, she saw the KKK parading in front of a house to intimidate civil rights activists.[31]

In 1910, 41 percent of Miami's residents were black. As the black population grew, its residential neighborhoods expanded across the Miami River and north of downtown's colored district. Whites remained concerned about conditions in Colored Town. Not only were prominent white men alleged to have contracted venereal disease there, but whites feared that black hired help might bring disease into whites' homes. Over the next decade, the proportion of Miami residents who were black fell to 31 percent, although the surge in Bahamian immigration helped stem the decline. By 1920, "Miami had a larger population of black immigrants than any other city in the United States except New York," which also attracted people of African descent from the Caribbean.[32]

As the city expanded, the importance of enforcing the color line preoccupied many whites. In 1914, as construction on Miami Beach was beginning, the Central Labor Union informed the Board of Trade that "the proper place for negro skilled labor is negro town; for white is white and black is black." One speaker asked rhetorically:

> Are we as citizens going to sit down and see them put a bunch of niggers over there on the beach? It seems to me that if you, as citizens, don't want them as your business and social equals, then organized labor should have your support. I think that when a color line has been established as it has here that a protest should be made against a thing of this kind. Let that go over on the beach and it will spread. It is white territory over on the beach the same as it is here, but those niggers are living in a house there. Would you like to have a nigger family living in a house next to you? The niggers go bathing with the whites. Would you want to go bathing with a nigger?

The crux of the matter was residential segregation and, as the final image suggests, intermarriage. Blacks were prohibited from living on the beach.[33]

By 1915, as blacks moved into neighborhoods north of Colored Town, whites struck back. Masked men used KKK tactics to force blacks out of the district bounded by Avenues I and J and Fourth and Sixth Streets. One family received a note saying, "No nigger can live in this house. Move out by Monday night or we will blow you up. Signed by 200 white men." Soon no blacks remained in the area.[34] White groups limited or got rid of blacks who moved into their neighborhoods. On the south side of the Miami River, the Riverside Improvement Association requested that the city commission remove about 100 black families who were renting white-owned houses. Then the city commission passed an ordinance setting explicit boundaries on the south, east, and west but allowing the black population to expand to the north. The *Miami Metropolis* remarked that "the new color line is not to be an imaginary affair, but will be a real line, with a high wall or hedge marking the boundary." Although the city attorney informed the commission that a segregation ordinance would not be legal, he added that "if the consensus of public opinion is that the ordinance is a good one there will be no question of its actual enforcement."[35]

The right of black men to drive cars was also contested. After the completion of the Dixie Highway in 1915, more northern tourists drove to Miami rather than taking the train, and some had black chauffeurs. Automobiles also became more affordable for middle-class blacks. Just as the United States entered World War I, a series of violent incidents erupted that were sparked by white anxiety about the mobility of blacks and color boundaries in the Miami area. The presence of African American drivers on city streets offended many whites, for uniformed chauffeurs functioned as status symbols and blacks who drove their own cars seemed to be asserting their social equality. But the city depended on tourist dollars; "We cannot afford to have people come here to be mistreated," the *Miami Metropolis* warned. The newspaper pointed out that Miami was "probably the only city of any size or importance in the United States where negroes have not been allowed to drive automobiles, under any circumstances." Despite several public hearings about the problems of black chauffeurs, local authorities did nothing about the issue. Dr. William B. Scott, a black physician who was driving his newly bought car in early June 1917, was attacked by a mob and struck by an iron bar. Five white chauffeurs were brought before the police court, fined $5, and threatened with ten days in jail, but the sentence was suspended. In early July 1917, several whites attacked a black chauffeur. Later that evening, the black chauffeur assaulted one white man he believed was responsible. According to the paper, "the negro was arrested, convicted and fined after several hearings." The recent race riots in East St. Louis had undoubtedly heightened fears of racial disorder in the Miami area.[36]

Later that month, a black Odd Fellows Hall on First Street was dyna-mited at 2 a.m. by unidentified whites. Many blacks were furious, and some called on people to arm themselves to protect their community against rampaging whites. The Colored Board of Trade responded that "we neither advise nor countenance violence as a means to settling ques-tions which concern the rights and interest of our people. But we rather denounce any resort to violence as both imprudent and lawless." None-theless, its members also insisted "that negroes as citizens of the com-monwealth have certain definite legal and moral rights in the exercise of which they are entitled to the protection of the courts and all law abiding citizens." Blacks threatened to leave town in large numbers if police pro-tection were not forthcoming. White minister, Rev. J. L. White, worried that "there is a powder keg here just waiting for a match to be applied. Thousands of men armed themselves Saturday. And unless there is cool judgment and well considered action the outcome may be serious." From a financial, moral, or humanitarian point of view, he said, the city could not afford race troubles. A committee of seven white and seven black men was formed to find ways to defuse the situation.[37]

Black Miamians had some leverage because the city's economy de-pended on low-paid black workers. As the demand for labor soared just before and during the war, some blacks were recruited by the armed ser-vices for stevedore regiments and the medical corps. Others were lured by manufacturing jobs in the north. Late in the summer of 1918, the Miami Chamber of Commerce communicated its concern about the re-cruitment of black labor to Governor Sidney Catts. Of "several hundred negroes who have flocked away during the past week, many are married men who have virtually deserted their wives and children." Worried that these families would have to depend on public charity, local business leaders condemned nonlocal labor agents for offering free transporta-tion, admonishing residents that "the causes for local dissatisfaction among the negro population" were already known and it was time "to correct some of the alleged abuses." The call to reform conditions in the black community was motivated, in part, by fear of losing black labor.[38]

After the end of the war, incidents perpetrated by the KKK occurred in new black residential areas such as Highland Park. Mayor Smith ap-pointed a biracial committee to examine ways of establishing new residential boundaries. Judge Branning, who led the effort, said that "both races must live and remain in Miami and each has its share of the work to do. Neither race could do without the other, and therefore it behooves both to exist with as little friction as possible." Blacks complained about white merchants doing business in their section, while whites complained that their property values had remained static because of the proximity of the "colored settlement."[39]

On the evening of June 29, 1920, two bombs were thrown from speeding cars and blew up two unoccupied houses in Colored Town. Blacks rapidly armed themselves and gathered in groups. When the mayor called on the American Legion to patrol the streets of Colored Town, 300 members did so, many armed with rifles furnished by Frank T. Budge's hardware store. No further violence was reported. The next year, Archdeacon P. S. Irwin of St. Agnes Episcopal Church on NW Fourth St. was gagged, handcuffed, and driven off by two cars of masked men. He was stripped, tarred and feathered, threatened with lynching, and dumped back in town. Archdeacon Irwin described the incident and his refusal to comply with the demands of his kidnappers: "The men told me that I had been preaching social equality to the negroes and had advocated intermarriage of the races and that this was the South where the people did not believe in that sort of thing and no person would be allowed to advocate or preach it under threat of instant death. I was then asked if I intended to heed the warning to leave within the next 48 hours and I told them no."[40]

The Limits of Cooperation

Some influential white Miamians, particularly those who had not grown up in the South, were not fanatically committed to segregation, though few chose to counter it. Prominent developers George Merrick and Carl Fisher and journalists *Miami Herald* editor-publisher Frank Stoneman and his daughter, Marjory Stoneman Douglas, all hailed from northern states yet acquiesced in segregation and restrictive covenants on real estate. Lawyers, bankers, developers, merchants, and journalists had common interests. Although race relations was seldom among their most pressing concerns, they were conscious that Miami's continued prosperity depended on retaining a black labor force and that bad publicity about the sordid conditions in Colored Town could spark riots and damage the city's image and harm its economy.[41]

Wartime incidents of racial conflict led to limited efforts to ameliorate conditions in Colored Town. Little came of these initiatives during the 1920s, given the lack of an effective police presence, the absence of code enforcement, the double standard of justice for blacks and whites, and whites' control of political and economic resources. Notably, a few prominent white women attempted to examine the issues. When the Community Study Committee of the Miami Woman's Club met in May 1920 at the height of the Red Scare, when concern about communism became briefly linked to race relations, the club president told the mixed black and white audience that new legislation would be futile because existing laws were not enforced, such as the curfew that prohibited unaccompanied children from being on streets after 9 p.m. and the ordinance that regulated the ages of girls allowed to attend public dances. Proposed corrective measures included a housing code to prevent overcrowding, supervision of jitneys so that young girls would not form close acquaintanceships with strange drivers, the creation of supervised public playgrounds, and censorship of moving picture shows and vaudeville acts.[42]

At that racially mixed meeting, Rev. J. R. Evans, the black pastor of Mt. Zion Baptist Church, provided information on conditions in Colored Town that had been gathered by six committees of local residents. Describing places "where 100 families live in one block with four and five individuals in one room," he blamed both white and black real estate speculators. He reported that there were "1,500 children in colored town; 600 are in public schools and 663 in private schools. . . . The reason the private schools are so popular is because the public school teachers are not made to pass sufficiently rigid examinations. . . . From 50 to 75 colored youths and girls leave Miami every year to attend colleges and academies to obtain higher training than is offered here." Evans asked for more police, since there were just two officers for 10,000 residents. In addition to the regular collection of garbage, residents requested "a day nursery with playground. In one block it was found that there were 63 children locked up in the houses for safe keeping all day long while the mothers are working in hotels and homes in white town. Regarding parks and playgrounds, W. S. Frost said that they are badly needed in colored town. He relates that he sent a complete baseball outfit to the colored branch of the YMCA several weeks ago, but they haven't yet been able to find a place to play."[43]

Blacks sought a voice in the deliberations of the local school board, where they were shown some ceremonial deference but wielded little power. In 1921, the school board minutes reported: "The subject of appointing a committee of colored citizens to act in the capacity of an auxiliary board for the colored schools of Dade County was brought up . . . and discussed. On recommendation of prominent and influential citizens of both races the Board appointed the following negroes; D. A. Dorsey, Dr. W. A. Chapman, and Dr. John P. Scott. This committee has no power under the law but is created by the School Board as a go-between to facilitate the proper supervision and regulation of the colored schools of the entire community."[44] But by then registered white voters in Dade County outnumbered blacks fourteen to one. Black political power was being eroded, and the wretched conditions in Colored Town deteriorated even further. According to Paul George, "the area's infant mortality rate was twice that of white Miami."[45]

A few white merchants developed limited relationships of mutual trust with black businessmen. Roddey Burdine, the Mississippi-born son of a Confederate soldier who built Burdines Department Store into the largest retail chain in the South, privately financed the businesses of black real estate developer E. W. Stirrup and funeral director Kelsey Pharr.[46] Pharr was born in 1880 to ex-slaves in Salisbury, North Carolina. After attending normal school and a local AME Zion college and earning a bachelor's degree from Trinity Methodist College, he entered Tufts Medical College in Boston "with the intention of serving his race." He came to Miami planning to "work as a waiter and bell hop in the old Royal Palm Hotel in 1914, in order to finish his medical course." Instead, he completed a course in embalming and returned to Miami. When "I needed a little money to expand my undertaking business," Pharr recalled two decades later, "I went to Mr. Roddy Burdine and . . . asked him to loan me some money. He said I had an honest face, and he loaned me nine hundred dollars without any security except my word. That's the kind of friend he was. He never said very much about what he did, but I am not the only one he has helped, both white and black. . . . Few people know anything about all the good he did and how often he gave a helping hand to those he befriended."[47]

Personal and financial connections between blacks and whites did not appreciably diminish the cultural invisibility and political powerlessness of Miami's black residents. One can notice this time and again in the historical accounts about Miami history that were written by many of the white founders of the city and began appearing by the 1920s. Writer Michel-Rolph Trouillot writes that silences are "an active and transitive process: one 'silences' a fact or . . . silences a gun."[48] Beyond the occasional voices heard in the white press, the absence of black voices from the newly solidified historical accounts indicate that they were often silenced, both by being ignored and by being repressed.

Nonetheless, black newspapers served as a voice for the black community. H. M. S. Reeves, who came from the Bahamas, founded the most enduring paper, the *Miami Times*, in 1923. The paper had the widest readership and longest-lasting local impact in the black community. His son Garth Reeves told an interviewer that his father "had a way of saying what he wanted to say without intimidating others. He was not a blood and thunder militant as you would have today or in the 1960s. He made his point without fear. He pointed out the injustices, discriminatory practices against black people; he brought them to the attention of the white people." The white press seldom published information about activities in Colored Town, the blacks in Coconut Grove, or other neighborhoods, except for sensational stories about black crime. Few photographs of blacks exist from this period because photography was a racially and class-biased medium.[49]

As the aftermath of World War I brought social tensions involving blacks into sharp relief, some whites called for greater interracial understanding. In 1919, under the headline "Avert Race Riots by Aiding in Work to Uplift Blacks," the *Miami Metropolis* reported on a sermon delivered by a prominent white preacher, Rev. R. N. Merrill. He began by asserting that he was not arguing for social or political equality but for "religious equality." He averred that science had shown that there was no essential difference between white blood and black blood. He assured whites that blacks were "not the ones to plant dynamite under public buildings"; immigrant anarchists were to blame, or so many thought during the Red Scare. Yet black Americans' respect for law and order did not mean that they acquiesced to inequality. "Hope deferred maketh the heart sick, but the colored man does not carry resentment and harbor bitterness. He pays taxes but he does not get a playground or a park. He needs water as much as any of us but he does not get access to the ocean." Merrill admonished white Christians that their churches should be ashamed that while they were condemning the local Motor Club for "taking folks away from the churches on Sunday trips," black Miamians had "made insistent demand for parks and bathing beaches for colored folks while we remain silent."[50]

The relative political impotence of blacks defined the ground on which racial segregation and economic deprivation were constructed and re-inforced. After a concerted statewide campaign to register black voters and bring them to the polls in the 1920 election, Miami whites terrorized black men, deterring them from participating in elections for years to come.[51] In 1928, James Beard, a former state senator, spoke to an audi-ence of 4,000 in Bayfront Park about how important it was for south-ern whites to maintain control of local politics. Beard declared that "the negro race must hold the balance of power in every instance where the white vote is divided in a southern state. . . . Where there is political equality of the races there must soon come a certain amount of social equality, perhaps not to an absolute degree, but in such things as holding office and in providing common schools and like accommodations."[52]

Blacks found ways to resist the rigidity and harshness of segregation. Some simply left town for less hostile places. In 1914, blacks boycotted white-owned businesses in their neighborhood because they refused to hire black clerks and managers. The boycott succeeded, and numer-ous black clerks were hired. In 1919 and 1920 there were serious racial disturbances when blacks began moving into new, formerly all-white neighborhoods.[53]

By 1928, blacks were concentrated in defined but expanding residen-tial, commercial, and entertainment districts. Colored Town, later re-named Washington Heights and then Overtown, was the most densely populated. This eighteen-block stretch featured hotels, nightclubs, and a vital social life. Fred Brown recalled: "The boundaries for blacks if you lived in the area of First Avenue west of the railroad tracks, was on Sixth Place. The boundary to the south was Fifth Terrace. And the boundary to the north was 21st Terrace. We had to stay within those boundaries. At night after about 6 p.m. or 7 p.m., you couldn't cross those areas."[54]

The Question of Black Access to Public Parks and the Waterfront

Public parks had been off limits to blacks since the late 1890s. Their recreational activities were confined to streets and alleys, businesses such as bars and barber shops, and private homes. There were no "separate but equal facilities"; black people were simply excluded from all public facilities. Even segregated parks were difficult to obtain. Calls by blacks and some whites for access to parks began before World War I, and after the war residents of Colored Town were finally allowed to make a park of their own.

White elite women in Miami, like women in northern cities during the Progressive Era, advocated reforms to address the ills of urban life. Mrs. Henry Gould Ralston, whose husband was on the city council, penned a powerful assessment of the city's needs that was published in the *Miami Herald*. Praising the diversity of the city's population, she admonished civic leaders to "provide some positive attractive substitute" for the moral evils that were endemic to urban life. She called for YMCA and YWCA buildings with recreational facilities; parks to "serve as breathing spots, so necessary in our tropical climate"; playgrounds; and "bathing beaches." Her vision took no notice of the needs, or even the existence, of blacks.[55]

A 1916 editorial in the *Miami Metropolis*, however, declared that "the city should give the negroes a park, equipped with a band stand, supervise its beautifying and provide playground facilities for both young and old. The property will always be an asset to the city, and the negroes are entitled to a public park. Nor would it be abused. There are numbers of responsible, self-respecting men and women among the negroes of Miami who would take pride in making the park as attractive as any other park in the city."[56] Several months later, after Henry Gould Ralston "called attention to the fact that there are over 5,000 negroes in Miami and that they are entitled to parks," the city council authorized the city to purchase land for two parks in Colored Town.[57]

Three years later, though, nothing had been done. The *Miami Metropolis* editorialized that "Miami has been woefully negligent of the comfort and rights of the colored people in the matter of public improvements for their sections of the city, and an opportunity to remedy this negligence is an opportunity to benefit Miami as a whole. Several years ago it was generally understood that . . . a park was to be provided. The citizens of Colored Town are quite as entitled to their share of the public tax money as are the citizens of White Town. They are entitled to a park . . . and to well-kept playgrounds."[58] In 1921, Ralston, then serving as director of public safety and public welfare, granted permission to the Colored Board of Trade to "clean up the property bought several years ago for a negro park, lying west of the gas plant. The request was made by Allen Stokes, president of the Board of Trade. He said that the negroes would clean up the park and put it in shape for recreation. It is now in the original pine and palmetto state. The negroes were also granted permission to hold a barbecue there on Labor Day, providing they clean up the debris after the big event."[59]

A few years after Miami Beach was incorporated in 1915, although white developers decided to allow black workers access to beachfront recreational space, they sought to contain their presence. They were concerned that "on Sundays especially, the negroes come over to the beach or Miami Beach car load after car load." Early resident and later Mayor Thomas Pancoast wrote to developer Carl Fisher that "some people favored putting a stop to it absolutely, while others stated that the negroes are our servants and we could not well get along without them and we must to some extent take care of them, and there was no one needed an ocean bath worse than the negro, therefore to cut them off without giving them some other place to go would be wrong." Pancoast felt that while the site should be accessible by car, it had to be out of the way of white tourists.[60] Fisher responded that "the negroes should have a place of their own to bathe . . . [and] it would be to our advantage to build it. . . . The best way to keep them off our Beach is to . . . give them a place of their own."[61] This exchange illustrates the dilemma whites who were compelled to address their "negro problem" faced.

In 1918, in one of the first attempts to develop a black beach and resort in Miami, Dana Dorsey, a black carpenter turned real estate agent from Georgia, purchased eighteen acres on what is now Fisher Island, located directly south of Miami Beach. His plan had failed by the early 1920s, however, in part because the location was accessible only by water.[62]

When the NAACP spelled out its objectives in 1919, the list included securing voting and educational rights, ensuring fair trials, defending against lynching, obtaining equal service on railroads, and attaining the "equal right to the use of public parks, libraries and other community services." During the 1920s, the status of Africans Americans was even more precarious than it had been before the war. Rosewood, a black town in central Florida, was burned down early in 1923, and lynching continued, targeting black veterans. Florida had the highest per capita lynching rate in the nation between in the period 1882–1930. Nationally, the American Federation of Labor allowed member unions to exclude black workers and refused to meet with officials of the NAACP. Historian Harvard Sitkoff recounts that "symptomatic of the age, at the dedication of the Lincoln Memorial in the mid-twenties, far from the gaze of the Emancipator, Negroes were roped off in a segregated section across the road from all whites."[63]

Resistance and Remembrance in Colored Town, 1920–1941

The continuing oppression African Americans suffered, the growth of black organizations, and the division between moderates and radicals within the black community were clearly visible by the early 1920s. Although interracial communication was largely ad hoc in the post–World War I period, it bolstered the voices of black moderates who operated through churches, fraternal societies, and the Colored Board of Trade. Recently, researchers have recovered evidence of the burgeoning influence of the more radical UNIA.[64]

Historian Paul Ortiz has uncovered the history of organized resistance to segregation in Florida. In the late nineteenth century, a broad range of groups and customary "Days of Remembrance" galvanized African Americans' interest in seeking equality. "This was the methodology of black public history: the young and untutored were introduced to history via parades, dramatic role playing, and participatory learning." Those forms of organization, passive resistance, personal expressions of anger, and public remembrance were important in providing focus and linkages to the past. They were, however, fragile and were delegitimized by official public sources.[65]

On New Year's Day in 1918, in the middle of World War I, Miami-area blacks celebrated their fifty-five years of freedom at a service at the Bethel AME Church. The *Miami Herald* reported, "Both the white and colored residents participated in the program . . . which was well filled." The celebration featured an automobile parade and the singing of old plantation songs led by Kelsey Pharr. The master of ceremonies was R. E. S. Toomey. Lincoln's Emancipation Proclamation was read, along with poems celebrating blacks' accomplishments since 1863. In a speech endorsing the ideology of Booker T. Washington, "Henry O. Jones, a former slave, who is one of the wealthiest negroes in Dade county, owning a couple of the Florida Keys, told of some of his experiences as a slave and his experience as a negro. He stated that the way for a negro to gain the respect of a community was for the negro to respect himself and to save money."[66]

James Nimmo, who had fought in France during World War I, came to Miami from the Bahamas in 1916 and enlisted in the U.S. Army. In France, he heard a black chaplain affirm that segregation would be a thing of the past when they returned to the United States. He cried while telling a student interviewer a story about what happened when he returned. At Camp Gordon, a white sergeant yelled at him and his buddies, "Make it snappy you niggers, we're not in Europe anymore, we're in Georgia." After the recorder was turned off, he said with startling conviction, "I'll never forget it." By 1920, Nimmo had joined others in Miami's branch of the UNIA. Its growth illustrates the power of black solidarity and organized resistance to heightened forms of oppression.

Nimmo described the social distance between whites and blacks in Miami.

> When I first came here I really had no contact with white people. When I worked in the pressing club [of laundry workers] I worked with a black man. When I worked in the hotel, it was a brief period, and there were three black people working there, and I would always be with them. Didn't come in contact with no whites. I came in contact with a white lady once when I knocked on the door and I was a little frightened and I kind of hurried out. I never was so afraid in my damn life. Because crackers would be like "what the hell is he doing in the room with that white woman?" They would

lynch niggers for that. I was that close to a lynching and that's why I was frightened to be in the room with the white woman. White people were uncivilized back then. Especially down in this part of the country.[67]

Black ministers were key promoters of Marcus Garvey's UNIA. Rev. John A. Davis of Ebenezer AME Church attended the 1920 UNIA National Convention in New York City, which featured colorful parades that included the African Uniformed Legion, the Black Cross Nurses, and tens of thousands of spectators. Addressing an estimated 25,000 in Madison Square Garden, Garvey told his audience that "the nations of the world were aware that the Negro of yesterday has disappeared from the scene of human activity and his place has been taken by a new Negro who stands erect, conscious of manhood rights and fully determined to preserve them at all costs." Others such as Alain Locke soon noted the rising awakening of black culture and nationalism, observing in 1923 that "the new spirit is awake in the masses."[68] Davis organized the first Miami meeting of the UNIA on September 16, 1920, in Colored Town. Several months later, Dr. Alonzo Burgess Holly gave a fiery speech that related local conditions to the reasons behind "the revolutionary activities of his native country of Haiti." Such speeches soon gained the attention of the newly created FBI.[69]

In early December 1920, the FBI reported that the Miami UNIA had 400 members and was holding weekly meetings. Agents reported that speakers preached equality and interracial marriage. The FBI was deeply concerned that "90% of the Negroes in the area are in possession of fire arms." In February 1921, Garvey visited Key West, where the UNIA was also growing. Representatives from Miami attended the Key West gathering and heard fiery speeches from leaders followed by threats against their lives by the KKK and the president of the Key West Chamber of Commerce. After they returned to Miami, several of the local representatives were subsequently run out of town.[70]

Showing little understanding of black organizations, the *Miami Herald* said that the UNIA was a clandestine branch of a radical Bahamian organization that included numerous Bahamians in the United States. Such ties were in fact minimal. By mid-decade, the FBI had noted that the Miami branch had a membership of more than 1,000. The organization took a year's lease on the old Airdrome Building in Colored Town at 19th Street and 4th Court, renaming it "Liberty Hall. In reaction, local officials obtained nineteen machine guns, riot guns, and a large cache of ammunition. James Nimmo commented that "a few blacks feared the 'crackers' and felt that organizations like the UNIA were dangerous for the fragile race relations existing in Miami. Most of these blacks worked in the homes or businesses of whites and were told that those Garveyites wearing UNIA buttons or displaying the movement's colors of red, green and black outside their houses, wagons and vehicles were out to get whites." Nimmo became the head of the African Black Legion, which had 150 to 200 uniformed men led by two officers. The legion drilled with wooden rifles and had weekly parades. Dances, speeches, and the spectacle associated with parades filled black Miamians with a sense of pride many had lacked before. In 1926, Garvey's successor, Fred A. Toote, was welcomed by huge crowds in Miami.[71]

The UNIA movement became fragmented because of the rising influence of Laura Koffey. An inspiring speaker and allegedly a princess from Africa, she came to Miami in May 1927. According to Kip Vought, "Miami's UNIA took great care in order to not alienate the [existing local] ministerial alliance, because approval from this alliance was necessary for any association to survive in the black community." Koffey upset that delicate balance by "mixing the Garvey-like nationalism with a religious overtone." After breaking with the UNIA, she was assassinated and a mob killed her alleged assailant. The leader of this group was never identified, though Nimmo was suspected. Koffey's death brought an end to the UNIA in Miami, but its growth demonstrates blacks' deep discontent with the prevailing order.[72]

Divisions also surfaced within black churches. Kelsey Pharr decried the influence of Father Divine, a charismatic African American preacher who set up interracial communes.[73] After Father Divine visited Miami, Pharr said that "many of our people are carried away with him, and there are some who follow him who are not colored." He condemned his mission as "just another scheme to get ignorant, easily impressed victims into the net" and exploit them for financial gain. Pharr also deplored the practice of voodoo, which was prevalent among Caribbean immigrants, particularly Haitians, in Colored Town. He told a journalist, "It holds the Negro because he is naturally a superstitious creature. That is one of the things which the church and the school must persistently and strenuously resist. We have to educate our children to know how foolish [these] things are. . . . We have to lift them out of their superstition and give them new ideals."[74]

By the late 1920s, there were black Baptist, Methodist, Episcopal, Seventh Day Adventist, Pentecostal, Church of God, African Methodist Episcopal, and African Orthodox churches in Miami. The most significant black business organizations were the Colored Board of Trade, the Young Men's Business Club, and the Negro Uplift Associated of Dade County. Social clubs, hotels and night clubs, and visiting conventions brought business and excitement to Colored Town, helping forge a sense of community despite the squalor. Ninth Street boasted the Masonic Hall, a three-story wooden building where fraternal orders met. The ground floor housed businesses and the law office of R. E. S. Toomey. In 1927, the all-black Booker T. Washington High School opened in Colored Town and soon became a place of pride and community identity.[75]

Garth Reeves, son of the publisher of the *Miami Times*, told an interviewer that

> growing up here in Miami, things were pretty tough but . . . we didn't know, really, about all the things that happened in the outside world. I guess that was the secret of our parents because . . . most of our parents were dirt poor but they acted like they were rich or like we were not missing anything and . . . they made us feel that we were blessed to be here and to have an opportunity, as limited as it was. So . . . we felt pretty good about ourselves. We had our own neighborhood, which was Overtown, and we all lived among ourselves. All our schools were segregated, and all the entertainment places. We sort of got along and didn't worry about a lot of things. We had unpleasantries, but we kind of grew used to the segregated pattern of life because to resist it, you always lost, you were always outnumbered, and you did not understand a lot of the things that happened nor did you go along with things that were denied you. But your parents were always there to remind you that don't rock the boat, don't get in trouble. . . . I remember [later] when I went into the Army, my mother told me, "Learn to be— just learn to stay alive, learn to come back home, and then you can

do something about these things that you complain about now." I guess we learned to be people who could exist, who could manage to stay alive, despite the disparities of the day.[76]

Reeves, like many others, remembered having a strong sense of community. In an interview with Julian Pleasants, he said:

Neighborhoods were really neighborhoods. Any mother in the neighborhood could discipline anybody's child. It is quite different today. If Mrs. Johnson next door saw me getting out of line, she would straighten me out even to the point of punishing me, spank[ing] me. Then when my parents came home, she would tell them what happened. Well, then I would get another whipping. . . . Booker T. [Washington High School] was a closely knit school. We had a lot of pride in that school. No graffiti on the walls or anything like that. Nobody was tearing up anything. Back in those days, I guess, the segregation did not bother me that much because I had not seen anything of the outside world, and I seemed to have had everything in my neighborhood that I thought I needed or wanted. I really never did get downtown much then. I might get downtown, maybe once a week or something like that, if I had to go down to the store to get something. Growing up and after I grew up, when I went to college, I would come back home, and Miami was alive. We had more black businesses then than we have now. As to nightspots, we had clubs that we really enjoyed where we would have our dances. Nobody really wanted to go out of our neighborhood to anything. We had our own movie houses. Growing up, the one thing [we didn't have] was swimming pools. That is why so many black kids would drown. I learned to swim in a rock pit.[77]

The Great Depression and the New Deal

The depression started in Miami when the real estate bubble burst in September 1926. As banks and businesses failed, the tourist and construction industries slumped. By 1932, as the Great Depression engulfed the country, local officials had a list of "15,100 unemployed and thousands not listed are in as serious a condition as those registered. . . . Nearly half our population lives below the minimum necessary to maintain health and efficiency."[78] Three-quarters of Floridians voted for Roosevelt in 1932 and 1936. Although New Deal programs helped Miami-area residents, they also exacerbated class and racial tensions. Works Progress Administration (WPA) funds were major stimulants for local business and culture, winning both white and black support. Miami's moderate black leadership became more sophisticated and better connected nationally, but at the same time it was challenged by new, more aggressive champions of civil rights on the political left.

"By 1930," according to Raymond Mohl, "most of Miami's black population of approximately 25,000 was crowded into an area about fifty small blocks covered over mostly with long narrow shotgun shacks and slum housing. Racial zoning policies kept blacks confined to Colored Town and a few other areas of the city."[79] Residential segregation was reinforced by the Federal Housing Administration, which imposed new rules and maps and dispensed grants for new, low-cost housing projects but redlined less desirable sections. Support for the federal housing program "was widespread among Miami's business and political leaders," Mohl reports. "The Miami civic elite sought to eliminate the downtown black community entirely to make way for further expansion of the business district."[80]

This plan to remove blacks was furthered by press exposure of slum conditions in Colored Town. The media was ambivalent about addressing segregation and poverty in the black community, prodding white leaders when public health seemed jeopardized or bad publicity threatened the tourist trade but seldom challenging the power structure. Under pressure from black leaders such as Bahamian-born Father John Culmer, a recent transplant from Tampa and a member of the Negro Civic League, the *Miami Herald* published a series of exposés about municipal services in Colored Town, slamming the "deplorable slum district" and "plague spot." It attracted attention with lurid headlines, graphic photographs, and damning statistics.[81]

During the Depression, Judge Gramling and six others created the Southern Housing Corporation to secure funds from the federal Reconstruction Finance Corporation. The application stated:

> This population is living in one-story negro shacks and there are from three to fifteen shacks on a city lot of 50' × 150'. The sanitary

conditions are a menace to the whole city. The living conditions are inconceivable and are a shame and a disgrace to the responsible citizens of Miami. This area is principally owned by white people who have erected these small shacks and get exorbitant rent from them so that they pay for themselves every two to three years. . . . Many houses have no toilets connected with the house, no bathrooms, nor bathing facilities.

Taking the point of view of white Miamians, it concluded, "This project will be one of the greatest blessings that Miami ever had. It will not only eliminate the possibility of fatal epidemics here, but also fix it so we can get a servant freed from disease."[82]

Federal and local housing officials conferred with an advisory "committee from the negro section" about the planned project, and black leaders, including Toomey, supported it. They "envisioned a community of houses, with a civic center, parks and playgrounds," and a health clinic. Divisions over where to locate the new housing and about how to create buffer zones between blacks and whites marred the planning process, and Pharr and Sawyer, who served on the advisory committee, said that their opinions were "blatantly disregarded." The plans originally included a swimming pool, but that amenity was cut after a white physician expressed his concern that the pool might spread venereal disease and other whites deemed the expense "frivolous," despite the fact that Dade County had twenty public pools exclusively for whites. The federally funded Liberty Square housing project, built on a 62-acre site located north of 62nd Street NW between 12th and 14th Avenues, opened in February 1937.[83]

Many white Miamians were deeply resentful of black encroachment in the Liberty Square area and were jealous of the federal assistance blacks received. Mayor E. G. Sewell complained to Harry Hopkins that "we hear a great deal of talk at this time that the bum or darkey can come nearer getting relief than the former businessman who has lost his position or his business."[84] Responding to a chorus of complaints from whites, the Dade County Commission passed a resolution in 1935 prohibiting a "colored CCC work camp" near Matheson Hammock Park (the county park closest to Miami on the south) because "they would come constantly in contact with people enjoying park facilities." The rigidity of segregation in public spaces was reinforced even as the boundaries that delimited black areas shifted.[85] The KKK continued to link its policing of the color line to maintaining moral order, taking action against what many saw as illicit nightlife. As late as 1937, in a famous incident, the KKK gained national attention when dozens of its members showed up to try to shut down the gambling and strip-tease joints in the area associated with the La Paloma Club.[86]

The New Deal provided unique opportunities to advance public culture and increase appreciation of blacks' contributions to American life. Through the Florida Federal Music Project, black ensembles such as the St. Agnes Marching Band performed at public concerts. Under the Federal Writers' Project, Stetson Kennedy, Zora Neale Hurston, and others created an invaluable record of black life. Ex-slaves in Miami were interviewed about their experiences before and after slavery. Kennedy and Hurston lugged around immense recording machines, compiling a unique record of folklife throughout Florida and recording a series of life histories that are among the earliest in the state. Kennedy told me that as a University of Florida student in the early 1930s he helped organize an Intercollegiate Peace Council that "was the first interracial student body in Florida. . . . We had to meet behind closed blinds." He became state director for folklore, oral history, and ethnic studies, a unique exercise in promoting public culture. Hurston, he recalled, "was probably the world's greatest interviewer."[87]

Yet black Miamians remained relatively invisible in travel guides and press accounts. In 1941, the WPA guide to Miami and Dade County stated that Miami had about 30,000 black residents year-round, plus a winter influx of about 1,000 chauffeurs, domestic workers, and hotel employees. "The famed amusement facilities and bathing beaches of the Miami area are not open to Negroes. Their popular diversions are church entertainments and club activities, bolita and bingo gambling, and the traditional fish fries." After these opening remarks, the book paid almost no attention to African Americans. It devoted many pages to the Seminoles' history and exotic customs, yet it disregarded blacks, despite its acknowledgment that "the Negroes in Miami have become a pronounced social and economic problem, to which the city's rapid growth has added an ecological aspect."[88]

Conditions in black residential neighborhoods were not materially improved by New Deal programs. A 1940 report found that Miami had 35,000 black residents.

> Negro slums are appalling. . . . This condition with outside toilets, outside water supply, no baths and houses so close together that proper ventilation is impossible, is the cause of most of the disease and crime, especially juvenile crime, among the Negroes. The Grand Jury in 1939 condemned the slum condition of Miami's Negro section and called it the "City's Plague Spot." . . . Reports from the Public Health and Public Safety Departments of the city, the Tuberculosis Association and other agencies show that 75 percent of the Negro houses in Miami are sub-standard, and all Negroes live in slum areas; that the greatest number of communicable diseases, 80 percent of the tuberculosis cases and deaths, and the largest percentage of crime comes from sub-standard living conditions in slum areas.[89]

The New Deal heightened racial tensions over the allocation of public space. Both the Civilian Conservation Corps (CCC) and the WPA spent considerable federal dollars in Florida and the Miami area on recreational facilities, arousing some resentment among both whites and blacks. A 1938 report observed that "recreation in Florida . . . was, and is, Big Business, from which thousands of the state's residents derive a livelihood but in which, until recently, comparatively few of them participated." The report criticized the "discrimination against the year round resident" that resulted from the "sheer shortage of publicly owned recreational facilities." It was "paradoxical" that "Florida, which has the longest coastline of any state in the union, . . . has an unusually large proportion of both adults and children unable to swim." Thus, while blacks had a special resentment regarding the lack of public recreational facilities, working-class whites had their own forms of resentment.[90]

Excluding blacks from local beaches while containing them in segregated neighborhoods and exploiting their labor in construction and in house and yard work remained an important interest of many whites in the coming decades. Black women found jobs as maids in whites' households more readily than black men found work in agriculture and construction, and black women were often paid more than black men. In 1938, the Miami Beach City Commission voted to stop "negro jitneys" from operating between Miami Beach and the mainland and set up special buses to transport them. The city manager, Claude Renshaw, recommended the action because it would "prevent their loitering on streets after working hours."[91] Fred Brown recently recalled: "You had to get a pass to work on Miami Beach if you were black. . . . You had to go to the Miami Beach Police Department. Every January they would renew your pass." Even as late as the 1950s Miami Beach required all blacks to be off the streets and out of the city by 8 p.m. unless they were engaged in domestic service or delivering merchandise.[92]

Remarkably, in 1938 the Dade County Planning Board, which was appointed by Governor David Sholtz and was led by George Merrick, evaluated over 150 WPA projects in Dade County and called for a "coloured" park in the southern part of the county and a public bathing beach designated for blacks. Yet nothing was done to allow blacks access to public parks and beaches.[93]

Despite this pattern of segregation and exclusion, a determined person could reach the beach, either surreptitiously or in a few remote locations. Enid Pinkney recalled that Miami authorities would "permit black people to go down Thirty-sixth Street and then go over the causeway, and I was baptized over in that area. We would walk from the church, all the way over there." Athalie Range recalled in 1999 that before the creation of Virginia Key Beach, "there was a place on the island, which was called Bear's Cut. This was the only place that blacks could actually go to swim, or were permitted to go to swim without interference from the law or others who saw us there. These were the days early on when fishermen who went out to make their living would take families on small picnics, church gatherings over to Bear's Cut for a picnic of a day."[94]

Garth Reeves recalls taking a boat to the beach as a kind of ritual.

I remember I first went to Virginia Beach I'd say about 1930 when I was maybe eleven years old. . . . My dad was a member of a group called the 3rd Avenue Angler's Club and all the business men around his area on 3rd Avenue used to go fishing every Monday. We went out on a boat owned by a black guy. . . . It was a short ride to a place called Bear's Cut. . . . It was not a beach; it was very deep and my dad would not let me go in the water. He would take me out on the edge, maybe. That was what is now today's Virginia Beach. . . . We used to get off the boat and swim a little bit and cook our fish and that was a big day on Monday. I looked forward to those during the summer, going on those fishing trips with them.

Blacks also swam in secluded places in Homestead and in rock pits in Coconut Grove. David White recalled that "the Hole was dangerous for us, but we had no other place to go. We had no lifeguards, no protection. The larger boys looked after the smaller boys."[95]

It was in this context that George Merrick, realizing the desirability of granting blacks access to a beach far from the gaze of white tourists, publically identified Virginia Key as a suitable site. Although his plan sounded benign, it complemented the proposal to remove blacks from downtown Miami and was part of a design to extend segregation amid the continued expansion of the city and the development of the region. The 1945 wade-in and the subsequent negotiation that led to designating Virginia Key Beach as a space "for coloreds" must be seen as part of a long-standing pattern of white racial anxiety and blacks' grudging acceptance of the boundaries that defined African American life in Miami. Forms of deference and social control differed from those in other southern urban cities because tourism had attracted a diverse population from the Caribbean, the Northeast, and the South. The spatial dimensions of areas set aside for blacks had been constrained by a variety of state and local ordinances from the time of the city's founding, but the dynamics of Miami's rapid urban growth pushed blacks to expand into other neighborhoods.[96]

The expansive and seemingly consensual vision that imagined Miami as a "Magic City"[97] required deference to white tourism and was promoted by elite white men with a limited view of public planning and local needs. Nothing, aside from the organized black community, pressured the ruling group to grant black Miamians "separate but equal" facilities. Eventually, however, the black press, new civic organizations, and black leaders such as ministers John Culmer, Edward T. Graham, and Theodore Gibson; attorneys R. E. Toomey, Lawson Thomas, and G. E. Graves;

dentist Dr. Ira Davis; funeral directors; and educators became forceful agents of change. As historian Chanelle Rose writes: "The protection of the Magic City's tourist image greatly motivated moderate white leaders' efforts toward fostering conciliatory race relations with distinguished members of Miami's black elite. The city's emergence as one of the first cities in Florida to establish an African-American advisory committee to the City Commission in 1944 presaged the ascendancy of interracial cooperation that would shape the development of Miami's civil rights struggle in years to come."[98]

Black Organizations and Community Activism during the Late 1930s

The Miami chapter of the NAACP was organized in 1937 after the police brutally murdered a black Miamian. According to Melanie Shell-Weiss, the NAACP was organized relatively late, as African Americans did not believe that this elite interracial organization would attract working-class Bahamians and other Afro-Caribbean immigrants, who were seen as more militant than native-born blacks. The founding of a local NAACP chapter was not possible until the late 1930s, when distinctions among black Miamians of differing origins had diminished.[99]

A *Miami Herald* article published in September 1934 lists the members of the Dade County Interracial Committee. The black members were drawn from the Negro Civic League. Undertaker Kelsey Pharr served as president. White women agreed to assist black women to organize a "garden club to help further the goals of the slum clearance project." While the initial goal of the Friendship Garden and the Civic Club was to "improve the appearance of the Black Community by urging residents to plant flower gardens and landscape," its projects expanded to include programs for youths, such as a Vacation Bible School.[100]

The Negro Citizens' Service League, which was previously known as the Negro Civic League and the Negro Service Council, was established in the earlier days of Colored Town. Initially this racial uplift organization promoted Victorian mores and the eradication of vice and avoided challenging the white power structure. It included businessmen, professionals, clergy, and other community leaders, including Father John Edwin Culmer of St. Agnes Episcopal Church. A Bahamian-born liberal

Christian and racial accommodationist, Culmer joined *Miami Herald* editor Frank Bryant Stoneman to convince the WPA to construct Liberty Square. He also negotiated a deal with the city to allow his parishioners to use Hollywood Beach for their annual picnic. Other members were more radical. Sam Solomon, an undertaker, founded the *Miami Whip*, a militant black newspaper, and was willing to challenge the white power structure. This "Black Moses," as he was locally known, led a black voter registration campaign in 1939. His battle against the KKK garnered national attention, and Harlem Renaissance poet Langston Hughes immortalized him in "Ballad of Sam Solomon."[101] The Negro Citizens' Service League, a group that had gone through several title changes, was effective because it united the black middle class in spite of ideological and political differences among its members.

In May 1939, just before a local election, the KKK sought to intimidate blacks from voting by driving through downtown Miami wearing white robes, passing out voting cards to black voters, and hanging effigies from lampposts with signs reading "this nigger voted." The next day, instead of the usual 200 black voters, more than 1,000 blacks turned out in a concerted demonstration of black resistance to white intimidation. Their action was featured in *Life*, the popular pictorial weekly. The election attests to the burgeoning sense of self-direction, popular participation, and community building in Miami's black neighborhoods and to the growing resistance to forced subservience and glaring inequalities. It marked a profound shift in the boundaries and mobility of Miami's black population.[102]

National events in the late 1930s galvanized blacks' resistance to the injustices they had long suffered. Boxer Joe Louis beat German Max Schmeling in 1938 in a match that pitted an African American against the symbol of Nazi racial ideology. After the famous concert singer Marian Anderson was denied permission to sing in Constitution Hall by the Daughters of the American Revolution, Eleanor Roosevelt led the effort to have her sing at the Lincoln Memorial in 1939.[103] The most transformative event, however, was international.

The Impact of World War II on Race Relations

At the beginning of the war, Mercedes H. Byron expressed the anger of many young black men in an article in the March 1942 special issue of *The Crisis* on Miami.

> I am a Miamian, young, free, intelligent, personable—but BLACK. And so for me there are two of them—("Amis": I mean)—Mi-ami and Their-ami. Their-ami is the "ami" that I and hundreds, yes, thousands of other boys and girls whose faces, too, are black may see in newsreels and colorful advertisements, or as maids, chauffeurs or other servants of men and women who represent any race except Negro Americans—Germans, Japs, Jews, Chinese, Dutchmen, Cubans, Indians, Spaniards—but definitely no American Negro. Their-ami is the "ami" that the vacationist dreams about— miles and miles of beautiful Atlantic Beach with a background of towering coconut and royal palms, majestic hotels and apartments, attractively furnished and finished. For Their-amians, there is beautiful Biscayne Bay, ideal for yachting, fishing, sailing, beautiful moonlight rides. It is the "ami" of wide thoroughfares and avenues, of the renowned Orange Bowl Stadium. Yes, Their-ami is the "ami" I can only imagine and dream of.[104]

Ironically, although African Americans were not allowed to swim in Biscayne Bay, which was part of "their-ami," they toiled as longshoremen on the waterfront in "my-ami." This portrait of a landscape starkly divided by race underlines the resentment black Miamians felt about their exclusion and their new determination to gain access to the "amis" of their dreams.

During World War II, despite harassment by the FBI, the concept of racial equality became more prominent to many African Americans as the Allies fought the Nazis, whose actions were based on racist ideology. African Americans at home spoke of the Double V campaign against racism both abroad and at home that drew attention to the stark differences between the ideals for which many African Americans fought and died and the racial realities at home. Blacks who had provided military service and worked in war production were not disposed to tolerate second-class treatment after the war. The impact of World War II on both blacks and on white leaders became an important factor in the push for a "black beach."

Miami was an important training ground for black and white servicemen, who served in separate units. Those who were not from the South were sometimes shocked by the racial segregation they encountered in the city. From 1943 on, "work or fight" orders were aimed at African Americans, and blacks who were unemployed and were not in uniform were picked up and charged with vagrancy. African Americans were angry about Governor Millard Caldwell's call for sheriffs throughout the state to "use their good offices" to "eliminate idleness;" they contended that exclusion and segregation, not dereliction of duty, were responsible for black unemployment.[105]

The arrival of so many strangers put considerable pressure on the racial boundaries that existed in Miami and Miami Beach.[106] Gary Mormino has described wartime Miami as "a combination of Casablanca and Grand Central Station," noting that "the city bustled with newcomers bearing strange accents." Servicemen and their families took over hotels and drove up the cost of housing.[107] Boundary and transportation issues were increasingly fraught. In 1944, Miami's public safety director ordered two buses, "95% of whose passengers" were black, "to stop across the railroad tracks in the Negro section, instead of on the other side in front of a large hardware store, to avoid intermingling between the races."[108] Occasionally competition between blacks and whites for space produced curious compromises that actually benefited blacks in terms of recreational space at the expense of expanded housing opportunities. In 1943, the County Commission instituted condemnation proceedings for twenty-eight acres at NW 50th Street and 29th Avenue in order to create a "negro park." The *Miami Herald* reported "the commission decided to acquire the tract after white residents had protested the sale to negroes for home-sites of lots in the area. To avoid possible conflict, the commission hit upon the plan of converting the tract into a park to form a buffer between the white and negro residential areas surrounding it."[109] Although no major racial disturbances took place in Miami during World War II, the city's segregation ordinances and its KKK-infiltrated police force remained oppressive. City ordinances and police actions legitimized periodic sweeps that targeted black vagrants. Whites grew increasingly alarmed about crime in black neighborhoods and in September 1944, after considerable pressure from blacks, the Miami City Commission established a small black police force to secure order in the Colored Town area.[110]

By 1944, the nation had become more aware of wrongs perpetrated against blacks in the past, as Lillian's Smith's novel *Strange Fruit* attested. At the end of the war, however, global issues such as international communism overshadowed civil rights, despite Gunnar Myrdal's magisterial study commissioned by the Carnegie Foundation, *An American Dilemma: The Negro Problem and Modern Democracy*. Whites' misperceptions about African American community life persisted even among those who recognized the need for progress in race relations. Wallace Stegner, whose sympathetic discussion was published in *One Nation*, commented: "Soldier or civilian, the Negro cannot sit in the parks, swim in the pools or at the beaches with whites, or go to the same bars. The best they can do is what his fellows do: wind up in the juke-box jive joints." That description did not reflect the situation in Miami. In 1944, as mentioned earlier, Dade County was planning a waterfront park for blacks, but the plan had become enmeshed in a complex wrangle over seaport and airport facilities on Virginia Key. Local activists did not wait for white leaders to give them a park. At Haulover Beach, in a brave and unprecedented action, they demanded one.[111]

"The World War II era furnished the staging ground for the black revolution," historian Steven Lawson has written. "It revitalized black solidarity, tested innovative protest tactics, and moved the federal government closer to the side of racial equality. . . . The war loosened some of the old chains of subservience imposed by the southern caste system and freed blacks in hundreds of locales throughout Dixie to join together to overthrow Jim Crow."[112] According to Lizabeth Cohen, "a cacophony of complaints about the violation of black rights as citizen consumers would greet the arrival of peace, binding citizen and consumer ever more tightly in the African-American quest for equality as Americans. . . . The struggle for access to what was deemed 'public' in America had a radical demand for equality at its root, which appealed to lowly army privates and defense workers no less than the black bourgeoisie."[113]

Tactics shifted from behind-the-scenes negotiation to open confrontation. Nonviolent civil disobedience had a long history in the United States that stretched from Henry David Thoreau's refusal to pay taxes during the Mexican War to the General Motors sit-down strike in 1936–37, but it had not been used in desegregation efforts. Previously, advocates had brought legal suits, engaged in boycotts, organized national demonstrations, and defended black communities from white mobs. Reflecting on the first demonstrations against segregation CORE led during World War II, James Farmer remarked that "the technique of nonviolent, direct action received no notoriety and we were considered a few nuts or crackpots sitting in at lunch counters."[114]

World War II brought a broad coalition of labor advocates together with blacks in the Miami area. In 1943, civil rights activist Bobbi Graff recalled, "a public meeting in Bayfront Park, Miami, broke the segregation barrier. Eight thousand people, black and white, including many of the newly organized workers from the shipyards, laundry services and the black ghettoes as far away as Ft. Lauderdale, jammed the park." After the war, the Congress of Industrial Organizations (CIO) initiated Operation Dixie, a labor organizing drive in the South, while the progressive Southern Conference for Human Welfare began to promote notions of integration throughout the South, including Miami. Those associated with the Communist Party were also leading some of the efforts.[115]

The issue of access to a waterfront park was a natural outgrowth of the racial tensions that were heightened during World War II. Blacks' acute awareness of the disjuncture between fighting racist regimes in Europe and the degraded conditions under which they were forced to live in the United States helped transform their consciousness. The war became a clear turning point in the minds of the Miamians and servicemen who demonstrated at Haulover Beach and in the minds of the thousands who would later come to Virginia Key Beach to enjoy oceanfront recreation and build community solidarity.

Black leaders associated with the NAACP, including lawyer Lawson Thomas, Rev. John Culmer, and Dr. Ira P. Davis, made the tactical decision to focus on securing the waterfront park they had been promised. Their determination was heightened after hearing that Broward County officials had written to black clergy saying that black Dade County residents were no longer welcome on Broward beaches; local officials found the number of black beachgoers overwhelming.

The beachside bravery of Thomas and his supporters in May 1945 illustrates an important model of change: confrontation, dialogue, and negotiation. The asymmetries of power among those who engaged in behind-the-scenes bargaining were revealed and challenged by the power that blacks demonstrated on the beach as they transgressed the racial boundaries that had so long delimited public space. The victory that secured a beach for Miami blacks provided hope of continued progress toward justice. But the courage of the activists who waded into the ocean also underscored a historical connection between the black community and access to Biscayne Bay. For years, African Americans had gone to what was then known as Bear Cut and was later renamed Virginia Key Beach and built up their own traditions in this recreational space—as limited as they may have been. For more than a quarter of a century, the beach had functioned as a prime, albeit unofficial location for release from the confines of a segregated city.

The heyday of Virginia Key Beach came in the years immediately following World War II. For a decade and a half, African Americans enjoyed their access to this new public space. However, when the city's parks were finally desegregated, the beach designated for blacks began a long descent into oblivion.

Island Pleasures

Memories of African American Life at Virginia Key Beach

In the mid-1950s, on any given weekend, you could see row upon row of parked cars in the grass and paved lots of Virginia Key off the southeastern shore of Miami, a symbol of the inevitability of change in a race-conscious nation. And more change was coming. Although no one could really imagine it at the time, the actions of African Americans and the decisions of the U.S. Supreme Court eventually led to the gradual abandonment of public spaces for black culture such as Virginia Key Beach. But that is a story for a later chapter. Here, captured in photographs, the occupants of these cars, families, residents of segregated neighborhoods, and religious congregations, have come to bathe in the ocean, plant their feet in the sands of new civil rights, and experience the fluid nature of their freedom.

The cars also were an answer to the belief that being black meant being poor in terms of money, politics, and culture. In post–World War II Miami, many blacks were driving cars of their own, some quite luxurious, others not. The vehicles in figure 3 tell a story of upward mobility and success in the midst of poverty and segregation. The vast number of cars testifies to the immense popularity of Virginia Key Beach, however secluded and segregated it was.

Figure 3. Parking lot of Virginia Key Beach Park, 1950s and (*inset*) 2006. Source: Historic Virginia Key Beach Park Trust.

The beach appealed to Miami's blacks precisely because it was segregated. It was, after all, the only beach in Florida's largest and most cosmopolitan city where blacks could bathe in the sea and entertain themselves safe from the oppressive judgments of white America. Robin D. G. Kelley has written movingly about the role of parks in the lives of African Americans. He writes:

> Even modes of leisure could undergird opposition. . . . For members of a class whose long workdays were spent in backbreaking, low-paid wage work in settings pervaded by racism, the places where they played were more than relatively free places to articulate grievances and dreams. They were places that enabled African Americans to take back their bodies, to recuperate, to be together. . . . Knowing what happens in these spaces of pleasure can help us understand the solidarity black people have shown at political mass meetings, [and] illuminate the bonds of fellowship one finds in churches and voluntary associations.[1]

Black-identified places such as Virginia Key Beach enabled black Americans to forge the solidarity that eventually empowered them to overcome, in many cases move beyond, segregation itself. Without overt political associations, Virginia Key Beach was a space that enlarged the sense of being a cohesive community—through fraternal organizations, church services, and musical concerts—and produced a sense of pride and accomplishment in making change happen towards a better life.

Boyd Shearer observes that parks provide a glimpse of "the daily patterns of existence where we can begin to read power from and into the density of black life."

> Whether we look at spaces of recreation or political solidarity, it is on and through individuals that a community identity rests in a fusion of language, dress, movement and expression. If we are to value how black communities forged meaning into daily life, we must understand how individuals sculpted, shaped, and represented this life. We must understand their daily aesthetic. Thus when we look at segregated parks, we should acknowledge but move beyond [the] oppressive force of racism to ask: what was expressed and established in this daily geography of recreation and leisure that strengthened a positive sense of self and place?[2]

This chapter addresses how the black community nurtured its identity and solidarity at Virginia Key Beach.

A Haven for African Americans

There is no official account of Virginia Key Beach's popularity during its heyday in the late 1940s and 1950s. Its reputation as a recreational haven for blacks rippled across the country, first in the South, then reaching up into the Northeast. Black visitors to the city headed across the causeway for a day on the sands of a substantial beach with a growing set of amenities, now entirely their own.[3] People came by car, by boat, by bike, but there was no ticket counter, no swing-arm of a toll booth ticking off how many came, no census to accurately measure who used the cabanas, mini train, snack stand, and parking lot. We simply do not know how many visitors, both ordinary and famous, came to Virginia Key Beach. This dearth of official information, however, is remedied by the wealth of

Figure 4. The pride of African Americans related to self-policing is clear in this picture of a mounted police-man. Source: Historic Virginia Key Beach Park Trust.

recollections from oral histories and photographs in image archives held in city repositories and family albums. The hundreds of cars in figure 3 show us the popularity of Virginia Key Beach.

The photographs of Virginia Key Beach tell a story in a language all their own. The photographers were the family members who came to walk under the Florida sun away from the glare of racism. They were the bathing beauties in two-piece suits leaning against the trees, their cameras dangling like handbags from their shoulders. They were the cooks who came to wade knee-deep in the surf, the seven-year-olds digging in the sand, the teenagers taking rides on the mini-train, circling childhood one last time. They were neighbors making reservations for a cabana with four months' notice, the drift of boaters and young seaside explorers, the tourists escaping the New England cold. They were the mechanics, the preachers, the corner market clerks, the lawyers, the business owners, the incipient civil rights activists, all arriving at a place delineated by the evil drama of segregation but sustained by a community of black activists. It was impossible to come to Virginia Key Beach and *not* be a civil rights activist; the place was created in the wake of protest and before the awakening of the law.

The photographers who documented the popularity of the beach were the counterparts of singular figures such as Lawson Thomas, whose intrepid demeanor and political dexterity earned him and thousands like him the simple opportunity to visit the sea. There are no extant pictures of the 1945 demonstration at Haulover Beach, and there was little reporting on the incident. The small group that waded illegally in the surf there engaged in a measured protest against the lack of opportunities for black leisure space. The bravery of those few men and women confounded local officials; this was the first demonstration about the civil

Figure 5. Woman in bathing suit, probably from the 1950s. Source: Historic Virginia Key Beach Park Trust.

right to public space. "Wade-in," a term that, though not used then, was effectively born in 1945 at Haulover Beach, gained traction in the following two decades of struggle.

Using oral history, the scant television news coverage that exists, and a nuanced reading of some of the missing elements in public documents, a different perspective on Virginia Key Beach emerges: a picture of a vital community whose self-image belies the images of blacks that prevailed in the mainstream press and in the minds of whites. In the South, as W. Fitzhugh Brundage has written, "public space serves to reproduce social relations that define some members of a society as worthy of access to public life and others as unworthy. Struggles over the control of space have been formative for both black and white southern culture. The breadth and tenacity of the historical memory that occupies public space serves as one measure of who has exerted power there."[4]

The "separate but equal" segregated facilities and spaces that developed during the Jim Crow era helped instill a collective identity. Virginia Key Beach Park, as one of those segregated spaces, helped bring about the sense of community that was necessary for the success of the civil rights movement. Indeed, the history of Virginia Key Beach confirms that marginalized communities can work under conditions of oppression to effect change. While our current images of the civil rights struggle in the United States are shaped by massive protest, tear gas, and water hoses, Virginia Key Beach represents the (limited) possibilities in the postwar climate for peaceful, negotiated solutions to racial issues, although those solutions were still racist and inadequate. Interracial pacts were stimulated by moments of carefully planned confrontation.

In retrospect, gaining a beach that was ostensibly equal but was segregated was certainly not ideal. But Virginia Key Beach nonetheless stands as a unique attempt to promote racial equality in the South. The black beach provided some of the necessary conditions for community and solidarity. Ultimately, Virginia Key Beach became one of the most significant beaches for African Americans in the nation. No other outdoor place was as popular with major entertainers such as Nat King Cole. No other place attracted Martin Luther King and his allies as a place of leisure to the same degree.[5]

The place also illustrates the power of cultural memory for a people subjected to segregation and erasure. It underscores the critical importance of the older generation, notably women, who have felt compelled to ensure that preserving an African American identity and sense of justice is integrally related to the making sure that this beach will continue to be a public space.[6]

In the summer of 1999, when the Miami City Commission agreed to a process that would establish Virginia Key Beach as a civil rights park, a *Miami Herald* editorial remarked that "nothing could be more fitting or astute than for [city of Miami] commissioners . . . to agree to turn the beach on the southern portion of Virginia Key into a park free of development, mindful of history and open to the public. . . . For decades Miami has rushed to make a buck off of some of its most valuable land. . . . But the Beach of Virginia Key, with its gorgeous view and natural, though deteriorated, beauty, could be a sparkling jewel of redevelopment." The importance of the park as a symbol of the struggle against racism was underscored by the attention the issue raised in the national press, notably in an article by *New York Times* writer Rick Bragg. The *Miami Times*, the local black newspaper, opined that "the fact that corrupt and inept bureaucrats and politicians bungled the city's finances should not mean that places that are signposts of Miami's history should be disposed of without regard to their significance. If it has come to that, then there is no need to preserve the city as an entity unto itself."[7]

Heritage, Collective Memory, and the Politics of Land Use

We live in an era when a broadening appreciation of the struggle for urban public space is often considered separately from the destruction corporate capitalism sometimes wreaks upon the landscape impacting issues such as poverty, jobs, housing, and quality education. Yet they are all intertwined with the public's sense of its own history and the possibility of reorganizing our lives and the political order under which we live. The public realm symbolizes the power of people to act collectively and to effectively define our culture and the actual physical space involved in parks, streetscapes, community centers, schools, and other public spaces and forms of collective expression. Spatial design has become a central part of the democratic process of defining the creative and sustainable city—and rural areas as well—for the twenty-first century.

The waterfront park that the city of Miami created for blacks may have separated them from whites, but it became a place where blacks could reinforce a deepened sense of community and further develop a relationship with the natural world.

Cities need what David Harvey calls "places of hope" that nurture both viable, long-term urban visions and small organizations and microcommunities. Finding such places in some proximity to the natural world is critically important for expanding the viability of our changing sense of freedom. "Place," Sharon Zukin has written, "expresses how a spatially connected group of people mediate the demands of cultural identity, state power, and capital accumulation." In the mid-twentieth century, Miami remained driven by boosters' visions of sports venues and monumental buildings, and scant attention was paid to the small-scale spaces needed for community organizations, small scale moments of leisure and refreshment, and immersion in the natural world. One looks back at Jane Jacobs's and William H. Whyte's sensitive understanding of the scale of public spaces and their relationship to neighborhoods and the complex character of human community in lower Manhattan a half-century ago and wonders whether such sensitivity might have made a significant difference in the evolution of Miami—even the somewhat lonely outpost of Virginia Key.[8]

Historically, the built landscape was a male-dominated world of business, mass media, and sports that used space in ways that purported to serve the will of the democratic market. Urban development in the Miami area rather simplistically associated the natural world with the sea to the east or the Everglades to the west and converted sites on the older, industrialized urban waterfront into spectacles of consumption or upper-class housing. In Miami, that meant erasing the physical evidence of the presence of African Americans.

For African Americans, the erasure of evidence of their interactions with Virginia Key involved multiple displacements. By the 1960s, thousands of blacks had been displaced from Overtown. Around this time, as the city's parks were desegregated, many blacks stopped visiting Virginia Key Beach in favor of other parks because of the black beach's association with segregation and their understandable desire for the freedom to choose alternative sites of leisure. Finally, a community-based relationship to the natural world was displaced in favor of a view of that world from the position of the tourist or local spectator. Although the space the black community had made on the island was unique, real, and valuable to them, it shifted with the winds and the tides of what passed as progressive, growth-oriented modernity. Virginia Key illustrates how the "creative destruction" of the natural world became subservient to a politically acquiescent corporate culture bent on constantly re-creating places in ways that responded to demands for speed, spectacle, and status. These values legitimized the creation of inauthentic places. The intangible values of community or place-based identity became obsolete for many in the context of the lure of new sports arenas, shopping experiences, and televised spectacles that were seen as boosting the local economy. Meeting places for nonprofit organizations were ignored in this milieu.[9]

The island of Virginia Key is a strange anomaly. It represents nature and a place away from the hustle and bustle of city life. It offers some of the most stunning views of the city, the bay, and subtropical flora and fauna of any place in South Florida. Yet it also contains an unregulated 112-acre dump and a wastewater treatment plant. It is relatively accessible to Miami-area residents, yet it has few amenities that beckon people to spend a day wandering around its varied places, many of which are unique and beautiful. In 2015, it has poor signage, no island-wide public transportation, and no orientation center that could make it a compelling public attraction. It remains an icon of official indifference to the possibility of connecting metropolitan life to an array of open spaces, historical structures, and usable facilities.[10]

Some cross-cultural comparisons can help us assess the fate of this island. According to David Lowenthal, "English heritage enshrines a mystique based on inequality and hierarchy," while "the marginalized are most apt to demote material legacies." Recently, the legacy of industrialization and urban neighborhoods have attracted attention alongside the estates of the gentry, but "the new salience of minority heritage exacts costs. . . . For one, it tends to smudge or vitiate local distinctiveness."[11] Since Lowenthal made this comment in 1996, a new generation in England and elsewhere has developed novel forms of local engagement with history, demanding and experimenting with democratic planning based on the gathered memories of the past in cities across the world. Historians such as Jeff Wiltse and Andrew W. Kahrl have rediscovered long-forgotten leisure and work sites of the African American experience.

For his part, Karhl underscores the importance of fully appreciating the "manner in which black coastal landownership disintegrated and how such lands became incorporated into modern coastal economies."[12] Archaeologists in Florida have uncovered long-lost sites from the former bastion of Africans, from Fort Mose in the northern part of the state to the powerful long-lost home of the Tequesta Indians at the Miami Circle located at the mouth of the Miami River. Yet how are they to become part of a broader understanding of local culture? Scholars such as Andrew Hurley, Ned Kaufman, and Peggy Bartlett have used oral history to explore a more profound sense of place. Lost sites and stilled voices are emerging to challenge older historical narratives related to the African American experience. Indeed, stories have become so enticing that businesses, advertisers, political groups, and newspapers trying to breathe life back in their operations are using the device of locals "telling their story" as a way to reinvigorate their authenticity.[13]

Oral history can help empower the relatively powerless and subvert the dominant narrative of a community or move a cynical public to embrace a more inclusive planning process. Michael Frisch notes that oral history can "promote a more democratized and widely shared historical consciousness, consequently encouraging broader participation in debates about history, debates that will be informed by a more deeply representative range of experiences, perspectives and values." It can expand notions of civil rights and the complex forms of sharing needed to democratize the landscape while keeping the natural world more central to our sense of place and our sense of ourselves as actors in time.[14]

The Black Beach Celebrated and Remembered

Before Virginia Key Beach was created, Fred Brown remembered, black Miamians would head north of Miami to swim in the sea. "We would look for the one day a year to go to Ft. Lauderdale Beach so we could get some beach because we were not allowed to go on Miami Beach. We weren't allowed to go on Ft. Lauderdale [Beach either]. But they did give us one remote area in Ft. Lauderdale to go to the beach. And we went like cattle, all a bunch of kids piled up in the back. But it was fun. You know, we were kids, we didn't know any better."[15]

Figure 6. Park activities included the mini-train (shown here) and the dance floor and carousel. Source: Historic Virginia Key Beach Park Trust.

African Americans had gone to Bear Cut for years before the formal designation of the colored beach in 1945, and they had built up their own traditions in this place that were separate from mainland forms of segregation. Garth Reeves remembers that "coming up in Miami everybody in Miami seemed to have known their places and that's why you didn't have a problem. You knew the white man didn't want you. You couldn't go to this theater. Or we couldn't go to the beach to swim. We stayed in our places and hoped for a better day."[16] Those who asserted their right to swim at Bear Cut were claiming familiar territory, but now they were doing so openly.

Virginia Key Beach provided a place of pleasure in nature and a preeminent social location. It was a site for church gatherings, sports events, music, and entertainment. It provided the attractions of water, sand, and walks through the dunes. Religious ceremonies, especially baptisms, took place in this space. In later years, it contained amenities such as a concession stand, a small railroad, a carousel, a dance floor, and cabanas and cabins for overnight accommodations. Families came for the whole day; some would stay overnight in the cabins. It was a place where people could visit with friends in a place of freedom. The beach became a space for consolidating and enjoying community, a place of pride and a demonstration of power within constrained circumstances.

Eugenia Thomas, the widow of Lawson Thomas, remembered: "You know the beauty of it all is it's the best, the prettiest beach here. You can look as far as you can see and there is nothing blocking the beautiful waters." Wilhemina Jennings conjured up a series of associations, and perhaps myths, in her mind as she recalled the beach: "There was no fighting, no cursing, no skipping, no saying this is mine or getting back of the line. Everybody was just orderly because, you know, you had your parents and you were being watched so you wanted to be on your best behavior. Like it was all we had. As a child I was happy." The beach provided a place for the black community to gather more freely and on a larger scale than people could do on the mainland. Barbeques and picnics were held on the beach. Adults joined kids on the mini-train that circled the park from the ocean side to the tree side. Churches gathered at the park and families came for Sunday dinner. People sometimes vied for space, coming early so they could find a place to lay their blankets down.[17]

Until 1947, when the Rickenbacker Causeway finally connected Key Biscayne and Virginia Key to the downtown Miami area, African Americans used a boat operated by the county. Dr. Edward Braynon recalled that it was "a beautiful boat ride over there. And we were able to catch the boat very near where we lived, Northwest 7th Street and 7th Avenue. . . . We had to pay, but the county provided it. It cruised down the Miami River, a beautiful view of Miami River. That was before it was all developed, then. It was very beautiful across the bay to the island, Virginia Key."[18] Fred Brown remembers that the boat did not operate daily; "certain days you could go over there and certain days you couldn't." Often the ferry to Virginia Key could not accommodate everyone who wanted to go. "The boat would be so crowded, a long, flat boat with maybe a hundred or 150 people on the boat. They would make two or three trips to get everybody over there."[19] Others used private forms of conveyance to reach the beach. Some launched improvised floatation devices from

Figure 7. This photograph of African Americans launching boats from Virginia Key Beach underscores the fact that some blacks in the late 1950s could afford late-model motor boats. Source: Historic Virginia Key Beach Park Trust.

the urban waterfront, breaking segregation laws in order to reach the land specifically designated for them.

After the causeway was completed, blacks began using personal cars, carpools, and buses to get to the beach in startlingly large numbers. At first, said Dr. Braynon, "very few people had automobiles. But in the black community there was a main thoroughfare, Northwest 3rd Avenue. Youngsters, especially, [those] that did not have automobiles, would get their gear and stand along the side of the road. Those fellows driving those large trucks would stop and pick them up. And everybody would get to the beach. That was the attitude of the community."[20]

Churches played a central role on the beach, holding weddings and baptisms and Sunday afternoon picnics and recreational events there. In March 1948, an Easter sunrise service was held on the island. Rev. Edward T. Graham, pastor of Mt. Zion Baptist Church and a pivotal force in the local civil rights movement, preached the sermon. Buses conveyed worshippers from NW 20th Street and Third Avenue, Liberty Square Auditorium, Douglas Road, and Grand Avenue, while provision was made for parking more than 1,000 cars. The next year, the newspaper said more than 10,000 had come for the service and many had been turned away. The event, which was sponsored by the Young Business Men's Club, included a chorus of more than 200 boys and girls from local schools. It also featured a special spotlighted cross.[21]

Leah Sands recalled:

My family [were members of] Mt. Zion church, and that was also my extended family, cousins, uncles, aunts. We lived in Richmond Heights so my parents, before coming to church on Sunday mornings, would pack the car. I can remember my mother packing the car with our changes of clothing for the beach as well as church, and . . . the traditional staples such as pigeon peas and rice, fried fish, potato salad. She would have iced tea. These are things we grew up having on Sunday. Our Sunday meals would be at Virginia Key Beach after church.[22]

"The churches . . . were the pillar of the community," Sidney Wynn affirmed.

So whenever [the beach] was available, they used it. They had the churches' baptisms out there. They utilized it. They encouraged people to go. Why, a couple of Easters ago they had the Easter sunrise service, and many persons went there. I went there because I wanted to go back to where I used to be. It's good to go back. And then you go forward much faster. It was well attended. But they closed the gates after a couple hours. . . . It should have been open the whole day so families could enjoy. You know, why go for sunrise service, and you can't enjoy the whole beach?[23]

The close connections between Virginia Key and the churches, the central institution of the black community, cemented the cultural solidarity of Miami's African American community. That sense of community lived on in older people's recollections of the place.

The creation of amenities and county services for the park sometimes became politically contentious. Fred Brown recalled that there were few facilities at first, but "they kept fighting until they got a black concession over there." In the summer of 1948, work began on twelve beach cabanas. Each was equipped with four chairs, a coffee table, and a ten-foot porch

Figure 8. For an additional fee, families could rent overnight cabins or cabanas (shown here) for more private time in the public park. Source: Historic Virginia Key Beach Park Trust.

with awning. They rented for $3.50 per day or $500 per year. Getting the county to bring over a dredge became important after a freak storm stripped sand from the beach. A larger picnic area and a softball field were planned as well.[24]

Enid Pinkney painted a broader picture of the place of the segregated beach within community life. "We never looked at a situation and said this is forever," she began. "We felt we had to do something about the prevailing inequality and lack of access to any beach."

> We knew that we had to use the system to get our rights and that we had to stand up for our rights. And so, a lot of the history of the people who helped the civil rights movement can never be told because people don't know about it. You only know about the famous people, the people who became famous in the struggle. But other people who did things that called attention to the problems of segregation—you will never read about them in the history books but they played an important part in bringing about changes in our society.

St. Agnes, the historic Episcopal Church on Third Avenue in Overtown is really an historic site because it was the place where civil rights was fought for and where people were encouraged to vote. I think if you will check the records of St. Agnes you will find that that was a place where much of the struggle began. My fondest memories of the beach would be with my father and my mother and church going to the beach for baptisms. My father, after he had had a revival and people were saved and they were brought to the church, there would be a baptism. And they would wear robes, white robes. . . . My father would walk into the water with the baptismal candidate. He would take them out and hold them and say, "In the name of the Father and the Son and of the Holy Ghost, I baptize you." That will always be with me. Even though he's gone, the memory of taking people out to Virginia Key Beach and have them baptized after they had accepted the Lord as their savior is something that I will always remember.

Of course we also had picnics out there. We went out there just for relaxation. But I think what I cherish the most is the experience of the baptisms. It was our beach. Colored Only. That was the sign out front. We were colored back then. You know, we've gone through Colored, Negro, Black, African American, whatever. But back then, we were colored. So that was us, that was our beach.[25]

Leah Sands recalled that when she was a young girl "there was always a lot of laughter. There was also singing. I can remember if someone went to a particular sermon and it was really good, they would share with the group what the message of the day was and some of the traditional hymns. Because of our Bahamian heritage there were a lot of songs that I grew up listening to before I realized what they were. And so I can just hear some of the songs my father always sang. He's a baritone. And so he always had this voice. And he still does. I can remember hearing family members just joining in. The next thing you know there's a group of people just singing, and here we are at the beach, and we're eating, and we're having a very good time."

Many saw the beach as a major accomplishment that brought a sense of ownership to the black community. Dorothy Fields noted that she "never expected to be able to be in a room with white people as an adult.

Figure 9. "Colored only" sign at the entrance to Virginia Key Beach. Source: Historic Virginia Key Beach Park Trust.

It never occurred to me. Because it was not something that was to happen. So living in segregation was just living. Could not go to Crandon Park. Could not enjoy Miami Beach. Being black and being segregated was just a part of life."[26]

Miami Times publisher Garth Reeves told an interviewer that the white power structure had given blacks just enough to placate them under the circumstances. He recalled that whites thought:

"You want a beach, you got a beach. And that was it. Are you happy now or something?" But later on they started adding amenities to the beach like the train. And then we started having parties out there. Disc jockeys would come, and we'd have dancing and things like that. But originally it was just a beach. It was a place where black people could go to keep them from going to the white beaches. That was what Virginia Beach was. It [didn't have] a lot of extras, but enough to keep us happy, I guess. It was a fun thing because . . . if anybody went to the beach you know it would be Virginia Key Beach, because that was the only place they could go. So you saw everybody, you saw your friends. In fact, if any whites came to the beach, they were shooed off. They would not let them stay. The police would run you away; they would run all the whites away. This was a black thing only.[27]

Not only did the beach bring the black community together, it also connected the community of the 1940s with earlier generations. Wilhemina Jennings recalled that her "father was a fisherman. See, there were three girls. It being, you know, the old time, he didn't believe in his girls getting out there in the water. It had to be in the twenties. Before Virginia Beach, we had Fisher Island [the island just to the north that was owned in the early 1920s by wealthy black developer Dana Dorsey and had operated briefly as a black beach]; he used to take people in his boat to Fisher Island. He took people to Virginia Beach before it was organized as Virginia Beach." The continuity with people who went there before World War II remains an important topic for research. The informal day outings Garth Reeves noted in his oral history hint at other activities in the area by boaters who were able to come to the island.[28]

Virginia Key Beach thrived throughout the 1950s, and with the popularity came more interest in the cabins and cabanas. "There would be a waiting list for blacks to live in the cottages," Dorothy Fields remembers.

They were duplexes, as I remember—one row of no more than four duplexes. At least two sets of them would be connected. I remember very clearly, having the opportunity—that was a thrill—at least while my aunt and uncle were here, for two weeks for me to be able to live with them at Virginia Key. That was really something to look forward to. While none of us could swim, we would use the cabanas. Because they were renting the cottages, we had use of the cabana. And I could use the carousel, just everything. I mean, it was wonderful. We had parties out there, and it was just a wonderful event.

Sydney Wynn recalls the popularity of these facilities: "There were some cabanas but they didn't have enough. You had to make reservations very, very early in order to get one. So most people didn't look at the cabanas as a pleasure for all. They just put a blanket on the hot sand. Since there were a very limited number of trees, you just enjoyed it."[29]

According to Athalie Range, "many, many affairs were held over here,

Figure 10. The number of excited kids at the concession stand in this photograph from the 1950s testifies to the popularity of Virginia Key Beach Park. Source: Historic Virginia Key Beach Park Trust.

[including] some weddings. There had been a place built where a family could come out and rent cabanas. This meant when you wanted to be away from the big crowd of people, if you could afford it, you rented a cabana for your family during the day. It was up on the north end of the beach. This made a difference with the service you got on the beach. There were also a few cottages, which people used for possibly a weekend."[30]

Dr. Braynon remembered courting his wife there. "We used to ride over there at night. It was a nice ride, a nice breeze, and even at night it was safe." Wilhemina Jennings recalled that when she got "married, that's where they had some apartments over there, small apartments. We went over there to Virginia Beach. . . . And we're still together. It's been over 50 years. So it must have been a lucky place." She added that "one of the very important things was, it was a place you felt comfortable. For many years they had one police officer that controlled that beach. All those midsummer holidays, the Fourth of July, every black person who could find a way went there. It was crowded. And there were no problems. One officer controlled the crowd because they respected him. I knew him well. He was one of the first black officers hired by the Dade County police department."[31]

Bernice Sawyer remarked that "it was just such a wonderful thing and it was enjoyed by everyone. You had your school picnics, your different organizations, the camp clubs. The teachers had their clubs. And churches went. It was just nice. I think this is a famous landmark and it's something that gave you hope and gave you inspiration. You know you could be so tired or disturbed and . . . you'd be able to forget about it and think about something positive. It was important for the blacks to have it because it gave them a sense of having their own. They enjoyed it. We didn't think about whether it was like the white beach or the other beaches. We were just glad to have what we had."[32]

Leah Sands also discussed the insulation the beach provided from the insults and discrimination blacks encountered on the mainland.

> Growing up we knew, we trusted our parents. So they had the fear because they had the experience of the negative interaction with people who didn't want them around or who didn't feel they were worthy of being around. But we didn't get it as much. They would just tell us, be careful. We were limited. . . . We would have to go in groups. So, for instance, if there was something that was going on in the community or even at the other side of the beach, we would see birthday parties and during Christmastime or during Easter, they would have different celebrations at the other side of the beach and we would want to go. Our parents . . . never said to us, "you cannot go because you are black and they don't want you there." My parents would always say to us, well, once we finish doing what we're doing, we'll come back. They never instilled in us that because we were not of the same color that we were deprived of that experience. So they had a way of protecting us. But also they had a way of letting us know that we were no different.

Sands recalled that the beach attracted well-known entertainers such as James Brown and Smokey Robinson. "Lou Willy Johnson who lived down the street from us, he lived two houses away. They would always give things at Virginia Key. Muhammad Ali before he became Muhammad Ali, his name was Cassius Clay. He would always give events at Virginia Key. . . . Cab Calloway. Anyone who was at the Nightbeat or anyone who was at the Lyric Theater, if they were in town on a Sunday, or a Saturday or in the afternoon, they would come out to Virginia Key Beach and visit with the locals."[33]

Black tourists quickly came to regard Virginia Key Beach as a destination for winter vacations. Along with the Hampton House on 27th Avenue in the Brownsville section of the city and the entertainment district in Overtown, the beach was written up in various black tour guides as a major Florida attraction. Dorothy Fields remembered: "My uncle and aunt, Ben and Australia Jenkins, . . . were from Miami, but they moved to Boston. They would come every February because that's when the golf tournament would take place. Later the headquarters for the golf tournament was the Hampton House. So you had blacks coming from all over the country, in February especially. Black history month, then Negro history week."[34]

Lottie Houston, a retired junior high school counselor from Richmond Heights who was born in 1921, commented to a New Times reporter that she first went to Virginia Beach in the late 1940s, when she began traveling from Quincy, Florida (northwest of Tallahassee), to spend winters in Miami. The beach, rather than the water, was the main attraction.

> To tell you the truth I never went in. I was afraid of water. . . . I sat on the edge and observed and enjoyed the breeze. . . . I used to go in the cabanas and put my bathing suit on and sit down in the sand and probably let my feet touch the edge of the water, . . . The [cabanas had] two rooms and there were faucets all over the place and showers and everything. . . . It was well taken care of. . . . You'd take your lunch and your suit and your sandals and sunglasses and stuff and your music and have a big day. You had radios. And they had barbecue pits out there.[35]

There were, however, very real—and very physical—limits to the sense of community at the beach. "We knew about Crandon Park," Dorothy Fields remarked.

> You could ride through there, I guess. Or maybe in the early days, you couldn't even ride through there. But in later years we knew there was a Crandon Park. We knew that their carousel was larger than ours. We knew that everything that they had was better and

more substantial. It was clear that it was separate and not equal. Even after times passed. There are people who, by their very nature, see the good and remember just that. And then there are those who see the bad and remember that as a part of the good. I guess maybe the older the people are the more they realize and understand and remember the experience, the pain, of getting the beach.[36]

"When we started going there it was separate and unequal," Kenneth T. Williams said. "We just felt inasmuch as we paid the same taxes for everything, we wanted to go to any one of the city of Miami's beaches. We just filled that beach. We were so glad we could get somewhere to go. But it never, was never separate and equal."[37]

Black Miamians' memories exhibit a kind of "nostalgia for the blacks-only Virginia Beach . . . mixed with lingering resentment." Houston explained: "There was nothing wrong with it, only it was segregated. [Whites] were trying to satisfy us so we wouldn't want to come to their beach. It didn't make any difference, because we felt that we had a right to go to all of them. We enjoyed [Virginia Key Beach], but we didn't like the idea that we had to go there and nowhere else. To tell you the truth I enjoyed being among my own. But you want to know . . . you can integrate if you feel like it, that you don't have to stay there. Then you have a sense of freedom."[38]

As one looks south from Virginia Key Beach, the Rickenbacker Causeway that connects mainland Miami to the shores of Virginia Key extends like a one-fence solution to the problem of race, a physical reminder of the route to equality. The beach on Virginia Key occupied that rare liminal space between land and sea, between laws and lived experience, between public and private space. The private cabanas, which were located under power lines both real and imagined, were extensions of the porches of Overtown and Coconut Grove and provided spaces for both interaction and shelter, where parents could watch their children playing in the water and the sand while they visited with friends. The cabanas of Virginia Key Beach widened the narrow boundaries of community and the cramped spaces of people's homes.

Virginia Key Beach in the National Context

The demonstration that led to the establishment of a beach for blacks on Virginia Key offered a nonviolent strategy of civil disobedience that was used in the civil rights movement to desegregate beaches and lunch counters throughout the region.

The vital importance of Virginia Key Beach to an older generation of African Americans challenges our current understanding of the civil rights movement. This book questions the culture that views sites of racial conflict as inherently more valuable than sites of political and social negotiation between blacks and whites. Although Virginia Key Beach may have been a space that was intended to appease or accommodate African Americans after World War II, it also symbolizes a space in which a black community was able to work peacefully with existing power structures to successfully secure unprecedented rights. Just as importantly, it symbolizes a space in which a community could form, strengthen, and prosper.

Today, the beach evokes a sense of lost or incipient community for African Americans and others, including those with close associations with religious and educational institutions. One advertisement from the 1950s notes that "the difficulty of finding a picnic location for large organized groups has long been recognized, but happily at Virginia Beach, the picnic facilities are sufficient to accommodate several hundred persons at a time."[39]

Nonetheless, it remained segregated and second class in the minds of many black Miamians. Through most of the 1950s, blacks were banned from other county parks. The struggle to expand their rights of equal access continued in the courts and at golf courses and nearby Crandon Park. Even though the wade-in at Baker's Haulover beach in May 1945 did not receive much local or national publicity, many local blacks learned valuable lessons about how to demand equality of access to recreational facilities. Virginia Key Beach became a haven for blacks throughout the East, a symbol of freedom, success, and shared community life and a stepping-stone to larger goals in the long struggle for civil rights.

The political, economic, and social ramifications of the fact that blacks had access to Virginia Key Beach remain largely hidden, unspoken and culturally illegible. But the role of that recreational space in constructing an African American community proved important for the incipient civil rights movement. Even today, as urban land is becoming increasingly expensive and is a growing area of contention, public space and natural areas take on new meaning as they evoke cultural memories about the complex impact of segregation. The idea of public space has become more sharply defined since the 1960s, but the concept of recreational space still has not entered national discourse as a civil right.

In Florida, the struggle for beach access after World War II became a significant testing ground for the African American community. The state's unique position as a major tourist destination required activists to implement a new strategy in order to secure civil rights; from 1945 until the passage of the Civil Rights Act of 1964 they pursued access to public accommodations via access to recreational waterfront land. Nowhere does this strategy come into such sharp relief as it does in the state's most populous city, Miami, and that city's only historically black beach on Virginia Key.[40]

Once the park was established, major black entertainers and civil rights leaders, including Nat King Cole, James Brown, Martin Luther King Jr., and Thurgood Marshall vacationed at the beach, and a historically neglected space became one of the preeminent destinations for black tourism in the South. Its position as a preeminent leisure space for blacks across the South underscores the point that seeking access to recreational space was a decisive political strategy within the civil rights movement. The constant presence of celebrities and community leaders reflected the area's importance as an entertainment and leisure center. Dr. King's spokesperson remarked on this special role, saying that "those of us who were used to the charged atmosphere of the civil rights movement found it relaxing." Such sentiments, and such celebrity, lent Virginia Key Beach an air of dignity, even if it was an island in a sea of a race-anxious culture.[41]

Civil rights activists used parks and beaches not only as places for refuge but as strategic sites for organization and support that provided momentum to the burgeoning movement in the years leading up to major Supreme Court decisions and congressional legislation. The decision of South Florida blacks to demand a beach and the negotiations over Virginia Key Beach as a dedicated space for African American recreation were initial steps in a campaign to secure access to public space generally.

4

The Shifting Sands of Civil Rights in Southeast Florida, 1945–1976

At the end of World War II, Miami-area blacks had some reason to hope that their political, economic, and social status might improve. Many had sacrificed and died for the Allied victory, and it was hoped that this demonstration of loyalty would translate into greater civil rights. The Supreme Court had recently struck down the all-white primary, and Gunnar Myrdal's compelling indictment of racial segregation was attracting the attention of whites. The opening of Virginia Key Beach provided a new, self-policed space by the sea. But the black community still faced grinding poverty, poor housing, inadequate education, restricted voting rights, and lack of access to public facilities. Many of the tens of thousands of servicemen and women who had come to South Florida during the war returned there to live in the postwar years. New suburbs emerged in response to the rapid population growth of the area, a boom in tourism, and the advent of air conditioning. The popularity of Miami Beach and other waterfront locations led to the formation of a uniquely multicultural region, most notably with the vast influx of Cubans after 1959.[1]

Rising expectations of increased civil rights occurred alongside virulent anti-communism and a racialized vision of growth politics. For many black Miami veterans, the searing experience of racism in the military during World War II continued to raise questions about the limits of social justice. When Garth Reeves, a black veteran and son of the founder of the *Miami News*, the city's chief black newspaper, was asked by an interviewer whether he was patriotic, he responded:

> Patriotic? As well as I could be. I still have something today against flying the American flag on a flag pole. I always saluted it and I respected it and I stood up at the Star Spangled Banner. But in my home, I have a twenty-five foot flagpole on my pool deck where the boat is and I never ran up the American flag on my pole. . . . One time I had Mandela's flag, and one time I had the flag of the Bahamas where I was born, but there's something that always kept me from running that American flag up the pole.

His memory of the war was shaped by the contrast between the treatment of black GIs and that of enemy prisoners of war, which he observed as a guard at a POW camp. He and other black soldiers "couldn't go into the PX. . . . We had our own post exchange and it was for the blacks. But, believe it or not, the prisoners of war from Italy were using the white post exchange. Now, I could not understand that. . . . Here are the prisoners we once were fighting against, the enemy was getting more rights to be white. I thought that was very strange and that was something that I couldn't live with. But what could you do about it? Nothing."

When he returned to Miami, Reeves faced the question of whether to stay in the area or move to a more integrated city.

> We were still locked down in Overtown. . . . I thought about all the good times I had down on Second Avenue, the clubs we went to, we had the big bands to come to town. . . . People were worried so much about integration. As long as I had a fair shot at being able to enjoy myself, I don't have to be in a white person's company. . . . [But] you didn't want to accept segregation. . . . When I was in the Army, I went to a lot of places and I came back home and I talked to my mother. I said, "I think I'm leaving town." And she said, "Why?" I said, "I've been in a lot of big places . . . I like a lot better than Miami." She said, "Name a few." So I said, "Chicago, I like New York, I like Seattle, Washington, I like New Orleans." . . . She said, "Well, I'll tell you what: I want you to stay home because your

father has a business here and I think he wants you. He would be disappointed if you left home. But let me tell you, anywhere you go today in this country, you're going to find prejudice and discrimination. You might go places . . . where you can ride in the front of the bus and go to any theater or any restaurant you want, but you will find that you will be segregated the same way once they see the color of your skin." I thought about that for a long time.

My mother said, "Why run away from what you don't like? Why don't you stay here and do something about it?" So I said, "What can I do?" She said, "You can make changes. Make changes. If you don't like it, say so. Your daddy's got a newspaper, use that." She kindled something in my mind about using the press in order to fight your battles instead of with guns and sticks. . . . I . . . started writing articles about discrimination and prejudice.

At that time, the main thing was, really, it was still lynching and discrimination and segregation, and that's what we talked about. We pointed it out to the people. You might not be able to do anything about it, but at least we want you to know . . . that what you're doing is wrong and it should be corrected. I think that our newspaper did a good job because the *Miami Herald* and the *Miami Daily News* . . . didn't publish anything much about civil rights. . . . But the *Miami Times* was always talking about the segregated patterns. . . . We kept pointing out the inequities of the system, which were many. I think that today a lot of people have benefited by our protest.[2]

Reeves's comments underscore the returning serviceman's commitment to Miami's black community and his determination to struggle for equal rights. He stayed and tried to make a difference in advancing the racial politics of the area.

A 1944 editorial in the *Miami News* gives some sense of the racial climate Reeves entered when he returned from the war. It argued that Miami's race relations set it apart from those in other southern cities. It praised the work of the Dade County Interracial Committee, which focused on "improvement of housing, health and recreational facilities for the negroes." The editor wrote that the committee "brings together a group of responsible, moderate, non-fanatical people on each side who want to see problems settled constructively and who can sit across a table from one another in complete frankness and good spirit." The editorial was full of self-congratulation: "The happy thing is that where other cities have let these irritants slide until they reached the exploding point, Miami officialdom has moved to do something about them while yet a peaceable atmosphere exists." This complacency on the part of so-called progressive whites in Miami was part of the problem Reeves had to consider as he weighed his decision about whether to stay where he was and work for change or migrate North.[3]

Thelma Anderson Gibson, a nurse who grew up in the African American section of Coconut Grove, provides information about how living conditions improved in her household after the war because of new employment opportunities. "All through my childhood . . . I could call everybody by name. . . . When I came back, here were all these strange people. . . . If you leave and come back just a year or two later it's a different town." But living conditions in West Coconut Grove remained dismal. "It's amazing when I came back in 1947, we were still living in a house . . . with no running water. We used to pump water. We used to study by lamplight. We used to have go outside to the bathroom. With my first check from Jackson Hospital, I paid a young man . . . $50 to wire our house . . . so we could get a refrigerator. Before that we were having to buy ice. . . . That was the way we lived."[4]

Despite such hardships, the black community continued to exhibit great vitality within its own separate world. Booker T. Washington High School functioned as a major community center. Enid Pinkney recalled that it "was not only an institution of learning, it as an institution of culture and heritage. It was an institution of joy." She particularly remembered Fellowship Day, when black students from across the city gathered together. She also recalled how much at home young people felt in public: "It was safe to walk in Overtown at night. We kept our doors unlocked and windows opened."[5]

Thelma Anderson Gibson's husband, Rev. Theodore Gibson, returned to Miami in 1945 as the priest of Christ Episcopal Church. Soon, Raymond Mohl recounts, Gibson teamed up with a white woman named Elizabeth Virrick to advocate slum clearance. Gibson's wife explained that Virrick "heard him speak to a woman's group one morning and he was saying to them that his people were living in filth. . . . She . . . came to his office the next day and said to him, 'Father, I want to help.' From that day on they became fast friends and went before the City Commission and intended to get an ordinance passed that every house had to have running water and inside plumbing and electricity."[6]

The Anticommunist Offensive against Civil Rights

How do these memories fit into the larger movements of the times? Miami's experience was tied to the economics of the Sunbelt and the political and cultural changes affecting the state, region, and nation. White officials considered black requests for access to public spaces in the context of rapid economic growth. Florida's supposedly moderate stance, which has often been attributed to Governor LeRoy Collins's leadership in the mid-1950s, has long been contrasted with the massive resistance to desegregation in other southern states. Recently, however, scholars such as Irvin Winsboro have contended that "Florida stubbornly perpetuated its Old South habits through an effective system of New South illusion and Down South delays." The tourist economy, which, of course, centered on public space created unusual dynamics that shaped Florida's civil rights movement. This context has largely eluded scholarly attention.[7]

After the war, a flood of tourists and new residents descended on South Florida. Tourism was becoming a year-round phenomenon. Writer Isaac Bashevis Singer observed that vacationing at "Miami Beach was a chance to be among my own people. In those days Miami Beach was a magnet for Jewish people." Even before the Cuban Revolution, Cubans and other Latinos were coming to Miami in larger and larger numbers, often as summer tourists during the season when northerners stayed away. *Newsweek* reported in 1949 that "it sounded as if as much Spanish as English was being spoken on Miami streets."[8] Yet the influx of other nonwhite ethnic groups did not translate into improved conditions for local blacks. Chanelle Rose has shown that Cubans and other Latinos, even those with dark skin, were often served in restaurants and other businesses, while native-born blacks were not.[9]

In the aftermath of the war, outspoken black activists seeking civil rights were sometimes joined by liberal and progressive whites, but this alliance was soon threatened by virulent anticommunism and a revival of violent white racism. Stetson Kennedy, a white native of North Florida, frequent visitor to Miami, and oral historian, published *Southern Exposure* in 1946. This powerful indictment of the legacy of slavery exposed the KKK and affirmed the rising power of blacks, who were demanding an end to inequality. Kennedy supported the emerging alliance between the CIO and black workers that was combating the racist system that divided and thereby weakened the working class.[10]

In 1947, Elizabeth Virrick, assisted by her friend Marjory Stoneman Douglas, joined Rev. Theodore Gibson to form the Coconut Grove Citizens Committee for Slum Clearance, which tried to address the unsanitary living conditions in the western portion of Coconut Grove. Lawson Thomas spoke throughout the state in the late 1940s on behalf of civil rights and was joined by attorney Grattan Graves in initiating a series of lawsuits related to educational inequality. The NAACP was active under the leadership of Harry Moore, whom some national officers deemed too uncompromising in pursuit of racial equality. In the decade following World War II, an array of left-leaning labor advocates, in alliance with the Communist Party, the CIO, and the Southern Conference on Human Welfare, sought to form a biracial labor alliance to challenge the white business establishment in terms of labor organization and the prevailing racial climate in Miami and across the state.[11]

Press coverage of separate visits to Miami by Communist Party member Elizabeth Gurley Flynn and former vice president Henry Wallace in February 1948 galvanized the first wave of postwar repression in Miami. On February 17, Flynn spoke to about 150 supporters at the Edwards Hotel, appealing for funds to defend alleged communists who were scheduled to be deported to the Soviet Union. Reporters from the *Miami News* photographed audience members leaving the building, portraying them as dangerous subversives. The *News* published self-congratulatory comments from local leaders and the chief counsel of the House Committee on Un-American Activities about its exposés. The chief counsel remarked that "the boys who broke this story really did . . . as fine a job as I have seen anywhere." One story reported that its staff was investigating "indications of a shifting of the national Communist party 'orbit' from Hollywood, Cal., to Miami." Front-page stories highlighted conflicts related to the CIO's attempts to expel local union officials with Communist Party associations.[12]

Henry Wallace's 1948 presidential campaign, which called for peace with the Soviet Union and a broadened social agenda at home, gained widespread attention in Miami. In a speech given at the Roney Plaza Hotel on February 19, Wallace acknowledged that he would likely get the votes of many communists and called on blacks to pressure Washington for civil rights legislation. The next day, the former Vice President spoke to an estimated crowd of 12,000 in Bayfront Park. Decrying the power of the "Wall Street military group," he anticipated President Eisenhower's 1961 warning about the development of a military industrial complex when he said that "the three way co-operation between government, industry and the military . . . will end in a military–big business dictatorship—unless we fight back." The *Herald* commented that "a negro girl led in singing of The Star Spangled Banner" and that "negroes" were present "both in the audience and on the stage." Local elites regarded this mixture of racial and leftist politics as a significant threat.[13]

Interracial efforts to create a better future were undermined by the unusual virulence of anticommunism in Miami, which was fueled by fears of a potential coalition between Jews, blacks, and the labor left. The FBI, local police, the Ku Klux Klan, judges, business leaders, and the dominant white press all attempted to link Jews, labor organizers, and civil rights activists to the Communist Party through the 1950s. By then, the revolution in Cuba and the arrival of reactionary refugees had added a special dynamic to the situation.[14] Miami journalists obsessively searched for Communist Party members and sympathizers, condemned as "fellow travelers." Spurred by sensational stories in the *Miami News*, local law enforcement officials vied with congressional investigators to ferret out subversives. A 1955 cover article in *The Nation* written by civil libertarian Frank Donner labeled the resulting repression "The Miami Formula." The special assistant attorney general for the state of Florida, Ellis Rubin, threw a wide net around African Americans, Jews, and others who could be associated with the left. Several synagogues were bombed, stimulating the formation of the Dade County Council for Human Relations. Instead of questioning Klansmen, however, Police Chief Walter Headley released a statement charging that the investigation of the bombing "pointed strongly to the conclusion that it was part of a Communist plot to incite racial hatred."[15]

In 1954, after the passage of the Florida Subversive Activities Act, a new wave of anticommunist activities took place in Miami. In June, *Miami News* reporter Damon Runyon Jr. published a series of front-page articles in which FBI informer Al Spears revealed the purported inner workings of the Communist Part in South Florida.[16] The combination of anticommunist rhetoric and intimidation perpetrated by shadowy law enforcement operatives silenced the political left. Anonymous threats were sent to civil rights activists. A subpoena was thrust into the hands of Bobbi Graff, the local head of the Civil Rights Congress, one day after she had given birth. These developments compelled many alleged subversives, including Graff, to leave the area.[17]

On September 3, 1954, Circuit Judge Vincent Giblin held a hearing on the charge of Ellis Rubin, special assistant attorney general for the state attorney's office that attorney Leo Sheiner should be disbarred for membership in the Communist Party and the Southern Conference on Human Welfare. Giblin's written opinion included comments that caricatured intellectuals as "pygmies on stilts . . . who pose as defenders of civil liberties and promoters of international good will."[18] This event appears to have galvanized those who sympathized with civil rights activism. A week later, *Miami Life* published an editorial declaring that "Judge Giblin in the Sheiner case has literally thrown the Constitution out of the window. . . . How much longer will Miami stand for this nonsense from the jurist?" Several TV debates presented the issue of the constitutional rights of defendants more objectively. Even the anticommunist WWPB radio interviewer Sam Gyson criticized the excesses of the witchhunters. The anticommunist crusade threatened to undermine the tolerance and cosmopolitanism many Miamians wanted to be known for.[19]

In a sign of the times, Rev. Joseph Barth gave a remarkable sermon on June 27, 1954. Returning from a vacation in Maine to read a story by Damon Runyon Jr. about communist activities within his church, Barth gave a sermon entitled "When Fear Strikes Our Community." Quoting from Paul Tillich and Erich Fromm, he commented that "nationally perhaps the check on spiteful scapegoating may at last be beginning. Locally, the tide still seems to be rising." After chastising the city's "yellow journalists," he concluded that his Unitarian church was a place where "(unlike the State Department) sex perverts and statesmen belong and all of them belong together."[20] On October 8, Judge Holt ordered Rev.

Barth and his secretary, Mrs. Helen F. Williams, to show cause why they should not be cited for contempt of court because they had signed an affidavit charging the judge with prejudice. The affidavit stated that the judge had signed contempt citations against fifteen Miamians linked to the Communist Party a few days before they appeared before a grand jury, proving that he had prejudged their cases. The following day, the *Miami Daily News* reported that Judge Holt's orders were signed prematurely by "clerical error." In early November, the Florida Supreme Court threw out the charges against fourteen of the accused.[21]

Writer Louis Harap commented in the December issue of *Jewish Life* about the false façade of tolerance in Miami and suggested one strategy the nation's Jewish community could use to fight back:

> Miami, advertised as "the nation's playground," has become the nation's nightmare. Fascism is getting a tryout there. Fascist terror has hit tens of families, mostly Jewish—and the end is not in sight. There can be one form of counter-attack that can be promoted to the greatest possible extent—a boycott of Florida as a resort. Such a boycott of the state's major "industry" would awaken all elements of the community, including its business men, that officers of the law in Florida cannot destroy the Constitution without protest from the thousands of Americans—and there are many Jews among them—who plan to vacation in the state.[22]

Harap's article points out that the need for social calm in a tourism-based city was an important factor undermining the anticommunist crusade in the mid-1950s. The self-proclaimed patriots had evidently gone too far.[23]

In 1992, I interviewed a former president of the local chapter of the Civil Rights Congress, Matilda "Bobbi" Graff. Originally from New York City, Graff had gravitated to the Communist Party, come to Miami with her husband for the health of their child, and become a fervent advocate of civil rights. She supported Henry Wallace and eventually headed the local office of the Civil Rights Congress after threats from the KKK forced its previous head, Victor Emmanuel, to quit. She recounted what happened one night when she went to visit him.

> I saw the Klan. . . . This friend and I had come from a Civil Rights Congress meeting where . . . Victor Emanuel had just said that he

had sent letters to the *Herald* and the *News* and the Klan stating exactly what the Klan wanted him to say, condemning the organization as a Communist front and resigning from his position. He said he had to do it in order to save his family. Well, after the meeting, this friend and I went in his pickup truck to see the attorney for the Civil Rights Congress and tell him what had happened. . . . When we drove onto that block, it seemed eerie. The first thing that we noticed was that the brother-in-law who lived next door to Vic had put a light on with an arrow so that they should not make a mistake and come to his house. The lights picked up about twelve of them marching and two by two; the lights picked up their eyes shining through the holes of the hood. It was like a procession from the grave. It was the most terrifying thing in my life. I had nightmares for weeks and weeks after that. I would be afraid to close my eyes because I would see those eyes shining. We turned the pickup around real fast and went to the nearest phone and called the police. They weren't interested in our telling them that the Klan was at a particular place. All they kept asking was, "What's your name? Where do you live?" And I said, "They don't want to know because they are right there. These are the police in the Klan uniforms." It is a tossup between whether it is going to be one uniform one time, and another uniform another time, but they were doing the same kind of work.[24]

The fact that the pervasive terror the KKK perpetrated in Miami was effective in limiting advocates of civil rights throughout the 1950s makes the activists' achievements all the more remarkable.

Contesting Leisure Spaces in Cold War America

By 1945, building on the community pride of Overtown and the influence of moderate black leaders, a dialogue between whites and blacks had developed in Miami that, combined with the calculated use of visible protest, advanced blacks' demands for equal though segregated public leisure facilities. As noted earlier, in 1944, Miami leaders, notably Otis Munday, pushed successfully to get black policemen hired to patrol the

Overtown area, which improved residents' security. Over the next decade and a half, as the Truman and Eisenhower administrations provided limited support for civil rights, blacks in the Miami area engaged in lawsuits and acts of defiance to gain access to other public spaces and to equal education.[25] After the wade-in led to racial equality in access to the beach, demanding access to other spaces for leisure activities became central to the civil rights movement in South Florida. The NAACP's strategy of demanding equal facilities as a step toward desegregation was pursued though a wide range of educational and recreational challenges throughout South Florida in a way that was more organized than has been previously assumed. Yet the struggles were also perceived to be local. The victory at Virginia Key Beach encouraged blacks to demand access to other recreational places and facilities.

In the postwar years, blacks negotiated for access to new spaces in a context in which whites and developers were also competing for public space. In 1946, a group of African Americans asked that seats be made available to them in the Orange Bowl football stadium and implied that they would take legal action if their request was denied. Father John Culmer explained that "we do not seek social contact with white people; we only want to see some football games." The *Miami Times* reported that "some had thought that a crowd should force its way into the stadium and be arrested, so as to have the matter settled, but it was finally decided to bring this matter before the city commission then, if necessary, make a test case through the courts." It took several years for the city to grant them the right.[26]

On April 12, 1949, seven black men entered the publicly owned Miami Springs Country Club. The group included Garth Reeves and two lawyers, John Johnson and Grattan Graves, who had been trained at Howard University Law School, moved to Miami at the urging of the NAACP, and set up an office in Overtown. A few days later, the manager of Miami Beach's Bayshore course said that four blacks had called him to request use of the course.[27] Commenting on these incidents, the *Miami Times* remarked that "in cases such as this kind it is not that Negroes do not know their rights; but those rights are so often taken from them. Being such a pitiful minority, they cannot demand, but must ask and patiently wait. That's a rather undemocratic way; but that is the way it is." In the ensuing months, blacks were allowed to play golf at the club on a specific day each week. In spite of threats from the KKK, Johnson and Grattan appealed a related case to the Florida Supreme Court, where they lost. They concluded that they should have sued in federal court instead. In 1955, the U.S. Supreme Court finally ruled in favor of desegregating public golf courses, although Dade County still delayed full implementation of the decision.[28]

During this time, African Americans also pushed for more equal funding for inner-city recreational and leisure facilities. "There isn't any place in Miami, except our schools and churches, where our youth can have supervised recreation," Edward T. Graham, the executive secretary of the Negro Service Council, noted in 1947. Reports cited statistics that showed a pattern of discrimination and neglect. White groups occasionally helped raise funds for black recreational centers and public facilities. The Miami Beach Young Men's Hebrew Association and a separate group of leading Miami businessmen helped the Negro Service Council raise funds for a Negro Recreation Center. Attorney Clyde Epperson said: "Members of this committee feel that the white race should not neglect the needs of our negro population in helping them finance a monument to intelligence and initiative."[29]

From the late 1940s, more subtle changes in race relations grew out of personal encounters as Miami-area blacks found their voices and spoke out against their oppressors. Miami blacks were often seen as more forceful than those in other parts of Florida. Enid Pinkney recalled standing up for her rights when she went to Bayfront Park in downtown Miami the 1940s. "There was a parade, and we wanted to get up close to see what was going on. There were a lot of people and what I remember about that was that this white person was telling me to stay back. I guess I was always pushing. I spoke up, because from my father's studying the Constitution he thought you had rights, and I thought we have a right to be here, so I tried to get up to the front." Enid concluded that her father had a "strong sense of justice, what's right and what's wrong. . . . He felt that as long as he was within the law of the United States he should stand up for his rights. I think that had a great influence on me, and I still find myself getting involved in justice issues."[30]

Pinkney then told another story about her father, a Bahamian immigrant, who sought to claim his rights under the U.S. Constitution.

I remember once when he was pastoring, coming home on State Road Nine, he was stopped by a policeman, and the policeman told him to get out of the car. . . . When he got out of the car he had a hat on his head, and the policeman told him to take the hat off, and he wanted to know where in the constitution it said he was violating a law by keeping his hat on. The policeman got so angry at him for having the audacity to question him . . . [that] he knocked the hat off his head, and my daddy stooped down and picked his hat off and put it back on his head. This incited the policeman.

We were out there on State Road Nine, and the policeman said that he was . . . gonna have to take him to jail. So my daddy said, "Fine, then, take me to jail." My mother was trying to tell my daddy to please cooperate with the policeman and do whatever he said because we were gonna be left on State Road Nine. She couldn't drive. I couldn't drive. My brother could drive, but he had no license. And she was pleading with the policeman "Please don't, don't take him." My father told her to shut up, because he was in charge of his big problem, he's the one that got up and got his hat smashed off, and he wanted this policeman to take him to jail. My mother said no. She was very afraid because what she thought was that they were trying to kill him. . . . But he was so adamant about this that he would not back down, and he told them that's what he wanted because he knew that he could make one telephone call, and he was gonna call Mr. Albert Pick, his boss.

So they took him away. . . . My mother . . . was afraid. . . . We stayed there . . . and we saw a police car coming back toward us. . . . The police car stopped across from us, on the other side, and when we looked it was the same two policemen that took my father away, and he was sitting in the back seat. They came over to my mother and said, "Do you think you could teach him how to respect a police officer?" My daddy told her to shut up again. Then the police said, "Well, if we let you go, will you learn to speak to a police officer if you're stopped again?" My daddy said, "If a police officer slaps me and knocks my hat off, I'm gonna do the same thing all over again," and my mother thought she was gonna die. She pleaded with him to please cooperate with the policeman so we could go home. He never did, and they released him.[31]

This triumph exemplifies the personal courage that some Miamians displayed before law enforcement officials who sought to violate their rights.

A performance by famed black singer Marian Anderson made headlines in late January 1952, shortly after the bombing of a black housing project at Carver Village. Her contract stipulated that she would not perform before segregated audiences. The Miami concert attracted about 2,000 people, 60 percent black and 40 percent white. The event was a triumph for Miami, signaling that the city could rise above racist hatred. That May, the Dade Council on Community Relations was formed. It sought to increase interethnic relations as Puerto Ricans and other working-class Latinos came into increasing conflict with blacks.[32]

The Role of Television in Mediating Racial Conflicts

In the spring of 1956, a series of incidents erupted over control of beaches and pools in Delray Beach, a small city about fifty miles north of Miami. This struggle had broad ramifications throughout South Florida. An ordinance "to prevent inter-racial riots" that the city commission passed in emergency session that May forbade any mingling between the races on the beach, the first of its kind in the Southeast Coast of Florida. In late May, blacks sought access to a municipal golf course in West Palm Beach. Almost simultaneously, in Tallahassee, two Florida A&M University (FAMU) students, Wilhelmina Jakes and Carrie Patterson, were arrested for refusing to give up their seats to white passengers on a city bus. FAMU students joined with local black residents to boycott the bus company. They formed the Inter-Civic Council (ICC), an organization of businessmen, clergymen, and laypeople, to coordinate the protest. In response, the Tallahassee city commission proposed that bus seating be on a "first come, first served basis" but that blacks and whites be forbidden from sitting together. The ICC, a coalition of 1,000 boycott supporters, and C. K. Steele rejected the proposal and announced that they would no longer accept segregation of any kind on buses.[33] A police crackdown on carpools led to numerous arrests. The US Supreme Court ruling on the case of Montgomery, Alabama, bus boycott ultimately helped resolve the dispute in Tallahassee, and open seating in buses became the norm.[34]

Earlier, the movement in Tallahassee had spread to Miami. On June 7,

1956, Rev. Theodore Gibson, speaking for the Miami NAACP, demanded an end to segregation on buses operated by the Miami Transit Company. Demonstrations were met with arrests for disorderly conduct. If the bus company did not concede, he threatened, "we will call a boycott or go to the courts, or both." A week later the NAACP, led by local attorney G. E. Graves and Thurgood Marshall of the national office of the NAACP, filed suit to desegregate the county's schools. Rev. Gibson and Dr. John O. Brown were two of the six plaintiffs. Headlines about lawsuits and arrests for refusing to sit in the back of the bus heightened white and black leaders' concerns about potential disorder. Miami's Negro Service League called an emergency meeting. Its president, Sam Solomon, who had led a successful voting rights effort in 1939, said that his members were "alarmed at the threat of a bus boycott. We feel that before people become frenzied and form opinions, we should meet and take a definite stand in order to avoid unnecessary trouble." Established black leaders appeared to support a legal approach rather than direct action, which they feared could be counterproductive. Finally, federal Judge Emmett Choate ruled that bus segregation laws across the entire state were unconstitutional.[35]

Debate over the desegregation of schools, buses, and beaches raged for years after the U.S. Supreme Court had ruled in *Brown v. Board of Education*.[36] Shots were fired against black and Mexican youths in West Palm Beach, and in Riviera Beach an emergency segregation order was issued "in order to prevent and suppress the occurrence of riots."[37] Local and state officials scrambled to control the situation, but instead exacerbated it by defying the implementation of federal law. A few localities responded differently. In Fort Lauderdale, an inter-racial council was formed to work out a "calm studied approach to the problems of the community."[38]

In the summer of 1956, Florida segregationists worked to associate these disparate local movements for desegregation with communism. The *Miami Herald* quoted citizens and prominent officials who emphasized that communists were stirring up the trouble. One woman noted that the Supreme Court decision was "based on Communistic ideas" and that "Communists are behind the move to reduce us to a mulatto race." A state representative from Fort Lauderdale warned that "the Colored people . . . should be extremely careful whom they deal with. When approached by anyone claiming to represent the NAACP, they should insist on credentials, to make sure the person is not affiliated with Communists." A state legislative committee spent years trying to connect civil rights activists with communism.[39]

Florida governor LeRoy Collins called a special session of the legislature in the spring of 1956 and offered to mediate the dispute in Delray Beach. Blacks represented about 40 percent of the city's 8,500 residents. Spencer Pompey, a black leader who taught American history, wrote to the governor: "We are . . . in the throes of a very serious racial conflict. . . . It now seems that all avenues of communication are fast closing." Controversy over the construction of a pool for blacks and black access to the beach on the Atlantic Ocean had held center stage for several months, with black leaders rejecting an offer of 100 feet of beach to accommodate 3,000 people. That spring, some white leaders even sought to separate the black section from the city. At this point, blacks were not insisting on integrating swimming facilities; they were demanding adequate space in separate facilities. They could swim only in rock pits unless they went "to spots like Virginia Beach in Miami, which they do at times." Denying that their battle was inspired by the NAACP, Pompey said "we are intelligent enough, without outside guidance, to realize that we and our children are entitled to go swimming, too."[40]

Miami News writer Milt Sosin underscored to readers how counterproductive it would be for Delray Beach to exclude black neighborhoods from the city. A Miami lawyer affirmed: "I don't think that will solve the racial problem on the beaches. There's nothing in the law which restricts the use of a city's beaches to the citizens of that particular municipality." Although there had been no incidents in the two weeks prior to the passage of the emergency ordinance "barring Negroes from the municipal beach and pool," commissioner Catharine Strong, who had voted against the bill, explained: "I did not vote for the exclusion plan because I think it would only hurt our race relations, and they are already at a low ebb. In addition, I don't believe the move is unconstitutional and will probably lead to more wasteful legal wrangling. I will urge Gov. Collins to veto this bill on the grounds it will only worsen an already bad situation." Significantly, the lone woman on the Delray Beach Commission was the only fervent advocate for greater black equality. Catherine Strong had come from New York City and was in the roofing business with her husband. Her outspoken advocacy and testimony in a federal suit made her the target of threats. In the spring of 1956, the city passed an ordinance allowing police to search for and seize weapons "to prevent interracial riots."[41]

Eventually, at the urging of WTVJ-TV owner and Miami business leader Mitchell Wolfson and the quiet intercession of business magnate Arthur Vining Davis, newsman Ralph Renick took a camera crew to Delray Beach to attempt peaceful negotiations. On July 2, after speaking to white and black leaders, including Pompey, Renick brought them together under the glare of TV cameras and forged an agreement that avoided further altercations. A group of five blacks and the city commissioners would form a committee to find a beach as soon as possible, a swimming pool would be rapidly built, and the exclusion act under which the "Negro section was to be ousted from the city would be dropped immediately." Aided by the series of articles in the *Herald* as well as the role played by Renick and WTVJ, the conflict was resolved.[42]

Significantly, WTVJ never mentioned allegations of communism in connection with civil rights activism in its 1956 special report, "Incident at Delray Beach." TV had become a critical negotiating tool. Whites were apparently motivated to negotiate by the need to keep the dollars flowing from northern tourists who would, it was feared, avoid an area beset by racial violence. African American leaders understood and took advantage of this dynamic. "Incident at Delray Beach," which was broadcast throughout South Florida, sent a powerful message to area residents: given the economic importance of tourism to South Florida, social conflict related to blacks' access to beaches and pools would be harmful and should be avoided. As the Delray Beach meeting was being adjourned, Mayor Yargates spoke directly to the camera: "It is more than anyone has hoped for. Ralph Renick and WTVJ have done an outstanding thing that will go down in history as a public service." Pompey spoke words of hope as well.[43] While TV and print media had been powerful agents in promoting anticommunism, they also served as effective agents in reinforcing the need for racial dialogue. The program put white Miamians on notice that excluding black residents from public spaces was no solution to the dilemma of recreational inequality.

Relying on Local Leadership

After interviewing Spencer Pompey, one of the leading African Americans involved in the 1956 negotiations at Delray Beach, I came to appreciate the careful calculations blacks and some whites made in their efforts to advance civil rights without provoking unnecessary violence. Beyond the nonviolent civil disobedience that soon became associated with the SCLC and Martin Luther King, blacks and whites were involved in numerous delicate dances that combined confrontation and negotiation—the strategy Lawson Thomas had developed in 1945. As blacks in Miami and other cities gradually gained political influence, some white journalists, lawyers, business leaders, clergy, and reformers recognized that the ugly spectacle of white violence against blacks had to be suppressed in order to create a business climate that would attract northern investors. Yet they all remained unsure about the racially integrated society they were helping to create.[44]

In an interview I conducted in the summer of 1999, Spencer Pompey provided fascinating detail about the strategies blacks developed in Delray Beach in consultation with the NAACP's Thurgood Marshall and leaders from Miami, notably Rev. Edward Graham and Rev. Theodore Gibson. Locals such as Pompey shied away from identifying with national civil rights personalities or organizational affiliations. Faculty from Florida A&M University, the black public college nearby, met at his house. "We took the position [that] we didn't have to bring outsiders in Delray." Instead of inviting Martin Luther King to town, "we got to solve this thing here ourselves, because when Martin Luther King leaves, then we got to be the ones to" defend what they had won and protect activists from reprisals. "Here in Delray, what we decided is that we need to get examples. Marshall had convinced us . . . that if we're gonna make this thing work, we were gonna have to do it and supply the material, so as a result of that, different communities tried different things." This approach was characterized by experimentation and adaptation to particular conditions. "Here locally, we had a group of citizens that brought a suit against the city for the use of the [beach]. . . . First of all, we knew that we had something that you couldn't close, the ocean. Secondly, the national rights were there. And thirdly we had, we thought, maybe two miles of the best beach south of Daytona here in Delray Beach."

Pompey credited whites as well as blacks for playing a positive role in the negotiations. He described LeRoy Collins as the "most statesman-like governor that this state has turned out." Commissioner Catharine Strong was a trusted ally, and "the Mayor, Yargates, was a New York Yan-kee." Pompey praised the press and WTVJ, especially Ralph Renick, Mir-iam and Hank Cohen, and Henry Burns. Before the TV cameras started to roll, "We had worked it out beforehand, what it is that we could accept. We had to be careful with what we said." Pompey, who served as the black spokesperson, had experience on TV: "I had a pretty good pres-ence. . . . And they knew I wasn't afraid . . . I wasn't afraid of anybody." In a powerful reversal, it was the whites who felt threatened: "One fella who was on the city commission said 'that if Blacks were to lose the pool—red blood would flow in the streets.'" Blacks' voting power also mattered. If "we went to the polls, we could determine who was gonna be elected." In 1956, they elected "Dougal Campbell, the New Yorker," with an under-standing "that we were gonna have a Black elected city commissioner next year. We were quite astute politicians."[45]

Winning Access to Crandon Park and City of Miami Pools

The conflict over Delray Beach helped shift power relations in Miami. Looking beyond buses, lunch counters, and schools, Miami blacks con-tinued to focus their attention on integrating recreational spaces such as beaches, swimming pools, and golf courses.

Shortly after the *Brown v. Board of Education* decision in May of 1954, the *Miami News* published a survey of Florida's beaches, noting which ones excluded blacks, which ones were segregated, and areas where blacks had no beach access at all. "Practically all the communities ques-tioned said there had been no demands from Negroes for admittance to beaches used by Whites." The only trouble spot appeared to be Fort Lau-derdale, where physician Von D. Mizell, chairman of the Negro Beach Le-gal Redress Committee, said that "unless a beach of their own is provided by the Fourth of July, Negroes will start using public beaches in Broward County." The county attorney reported that the owners of a beachfront tract near Port Everglades had sought permission to lease the land as a "Negro beach."[46]

Segregation continued to be enforced on Miami's beaches. Crandon

Park on Key Biscayne, Haulover Park, and Matheson Hammock Park, which had safer swimming areas and nicer amenities, remained closed to blacks, and police enforced their exclusion. Black leaders periodically tested the waters, but for the moment this issue did not galvanize the public. On November 7, 1955, the U.S. Supreme Court extended the *Brown* decision to parks, playgrounds, and golf courses. Yet it was cautious about implementation. The *Miami Times* commented that "the ruling had given the State and the community a tremendous problem to solve, and once again the challenge is to local leadership to meet that problem and all its consequent, attendant difficulties. Not only time, but also wisdom and great patience will be required of all concerned."[47] In the summer of 1956, "rumors swirled from Pensacola to Key West that the NAACP planned to invade white beaches." Several days after the agreement in Delray Beach, African Americans selected Lido Beach in Sarasota for a protest. City officials closed the beach and "passed a bill allowing the sale of public recreational facilities to private parties." The Dade County Commission created a second segregated beach for blacks in 1956 at Homestead's Bayfront Park, separating the space between blacks and whites with a canal.[48]

In late 1959, a confrontation with Dade County officials and a wade-in led to the desegregation of Crandon Park, located across Bear Cut from Virginia Key Beach. That struggle was waged amid a revival of the anticommunist campaign waged by segregationists that targeted and badly crippled organizations seeking to advance the civil rights of African Americans. By 1959 the NAACP had been joined by an energetic group of black and white, predominantly Jewish, activists who worked through CORE. The city's Interfaith Ministerial Alliance was also central to the effort. But, according to Marvin Dunn, "the black middle and upper classes in Dade County assiduously avoided the civil right movement." He quoted Dr. John Brown: "They couldn't get forty black schoolteachers to join the NAACP, and it only cost two dollars a year to join." The level of fear was simply too high.[49] The smear campaign that associated civil rights with communism and social disorder took a terrible toll in this most liberal of Florida cities. Nonetheless, the expanded civil rights coalition focused on a variety of issues related to recreation, education, and transportation; developed local political alliances; and used a variety of tactics to influence South Florida's leaders. Because of the importance of the tourist industry, this coalition was able to make progress. They benefited from the increasingly sympathetic, though sometimes condescending, coverage by local television news and the press; the support of a more racially liberal set of local politicians, including Miami mayor Robert King High; and regional communication among black leaders. Beginning in the early 1950s, black leader Charles Hadley began various registration drives, notably an "Operation Big Vote" in 1959 that drew thousands of black Miamians to the polls.[50] Spurred on by decisions in the federal courts, by 1961, the Miami-area civil rights movement had succeeded in integrating a variety of public and commercial spaces, using a combination of sit-ins and forceful demands aimed at government officials.

As white backlash intensified, Florida's attorney general, Richard Ervin, proposed a bill that could close schools and other public facilities such as beaches, parks, swimming pools, and playgrounds upon a vote of the people as a "last ditch" stand against integration. But he soon found himself on the wrong side of both history and the law.[51] As before, economic motivations affected political decision making. In early September 1956, the governor warned that racial tension could threaten the state's economic boom. "We have been tremendously successful in bringing new businesses into the state but if Florida is seething with racial tension and discord, it could entirely handicap our progress."[52]

By the late 1950s, FBI director J. Edgar Hoover was openly involved in the effort to smear the NAACP as a communist front. His book *Masters of Deceit* detailed the alleged relationship between communism and civil rights organizations. Ruth Perry of the *Miami Times*—at first reflecting the broach scale deference to the FBI Director at the time—endorsed Hoover's book, while Florida mandated a high school course called "Americanism vs. Communism" that used it as a text. In addition, the FBI was covertly monitoring civil rights leaders. In private comments, Hoover affirmed his belief that "delicate situations are aggravated by some overzealous but ill-advised leaders of the NAACP and by the Communist Party, which seeks to use incidents to further the so-called class struggle."[53]

The NAACP kept up its fight even though the Florida legislature's Johns Committee came to Miami in November 1959 seeking to investigate communist infiltration of the Dade County branch of the NAACP.

Miami Times columnist Ruth Perry became increasingly outspoken against red baiting, commenting: "Most people recognize political moves, prejudiced intimidations and legal red herrings. Because it is obvious that if the NAACP is Communistic, then so is democracy; and if the aims and purposes of our organization are fostered by 'alien agitators,' then so, too, were the aims of the Great Emancipator, Abraham Lincoln." A number of NAACP attorneys were present as Rev. Theodore Gibson walked out of the Johns Committee hearing "in a dramatic fashion." To thunderous applause, Gibson denounced the committee as a "star chamber" that had "disqualified itself to sit as an objective fact-finding body" by its harassment of Ruth Perry, who had refused to turn over local NAACP membership records.[54] Gibson also refused to hand over the list and was given a six-month jail sentence and a $1,200 fine. Protesting that "the NAACP is simply a good American organization," he fought the case all the way to the Supreme Court. In one of the concurring majority opinions in the important 1963 decision, Justice Hugo Black wrote, "In my view the constitutional right of association includes the privilege of Americans to associate with Communists or anti-communists, Socialists or anti-Socialists, or with people of all kinds of beliefs, popular or unpopular."[55] Ruth Perry remarked that "my friend, Theodore R. Gibson, by his action, wiped out the pain of the . . . indignity. It was right and fitting that this should happen, because it symbolizes what we are fighting for in the NAACP." She added, "There comes a time in each of our lives when we must make a stand for what we believe. If we don't then what we are fighting for becomes a mockery. . . . All of us have faith that our stand will be justified."[56]

Two years later, the issue of full and equal access to swimming pools emerged in Miami alongside a broader push to integrate public beaches. The black community was angered by the drowning death of a twelve-year-old boy in an alligator-infested rock pit because black children were not allowed to swim in the nearby white pool. "The cry for a swimming pool in the Liberty City–Brownsville area has been going on for many years," the *Miami Times* reported. "Now the Negro tax[-]paying homeowners are wondering if the city officials are sincere in their meager promises. Many feel that a federal suit to integrate all municipal recreational facilities is the only answer to their do-nothing attitude."[57] In late

October 1959, the *Miami News* announced that "City Manager Ira Willard today threw Miami's swimming pools, parks and all other recreational facilities open to Negroes. The unexpected decision came in a conference between Willard and the Rev. Theodore Gibson. Gibson and other representatives of the NAACP sat down with the city manager and the attorney and asked pointedly, '"Is there anything in the code or the city charter that requires that the swimming pools be segregated?' The city attorney, William Powell, replied, 'I'm not aware of any language in either the code or the charter that specifies this.' Willard wondered aloud, 'In other words I have no choice but to grant their request?'"[58] Providing more detail, Merrett Stierheim, then a newly hired assistant in the Miami city manager's office and later the Miami-Dade County manager later told me, "Willard turned back to Father Gibson, who smiled that beautiful, infectious smile that he had, and he said, 'And I presume that they are not segregated; they're integrated.' Willard kind of thought for a little bit and he said, 'Yes.' Gibson said, 'Thank you very much.' And they left." Stierheim continued: "We had nine public swimming pools at the time. Willard then turned to me and said, 'Merritt, I want you to go out to the pool managers, because the NAACP will be testing. They'll come up in a car, and they're gonna want to go in and go swimming, and we don't want any incidents. So make sure everybody knows what's happening.' I did."[59]

The desegregation of the swimming pools did not go as smoothly as this meeting did. The city commission countermanded the manager's order and barred blacks from the six city pools and other municipal recreational facilities. A reporter noted that the head of the Dade County Property Owners Association, David Hawthorne, said nothing during the commission meeting, but his presence was decisive. "What we came down here for was accomplished. There's no need to talk," he said. Although tensions were high, there were no significant violent incidents, although Mayor Robert King High said that he had "grave fears about what might result if Mr. Willard's order was put into effect."[60] A writer in the *Miami News* condemned the city commissioners: "Until this week we had been working out the race problem as if we had good sense. No other city in the South had done so well. . . . Cautious men worked on this problem with intelligence and a sincere persistence." The city commissioners, in contrast, handled this issue "as if children full of spite were managing things."[61]

The NAACP filed a petition in U.S. district court for a declaratory judgment and an injunction blocking the recall of the city's park and pool integration order. The NAACP brief acknowledged "that the immediate desegregation of the public facilities owned and operated by Dade County could possibly bring about some discontent and may create some social problems. However, to assume that such would be the case in advance is a matter of conjecture and speculation, but in any event these matters should yield to the implementation of constitutional rights which at the present time have been established without question."[62] Noting the Supreme Court's 1955 decision in *Mayor and City Council of Baltimore v. Dawson*, enjoining racial segregation in beaches, the federal district court ruled that "racial segregation in recreational activities can no longer be sustained as a proper exercise of the police power of the state; for if that power cannot be invoked to sustain racial segregation in the schools, where attendance is compulsory and racial friction may be apprehended from enforced commingling of the races, it cannot be sustained with respect to public beach and bathhouse facilities the use of which is entirely optional."[63]

In late November 1959, Dade County officials agreed to integrate county parks. County attorney Darrey Davis's opinion stated that "there are no statutes, ordinances, regulations or directives we are aware of that prohibit the use of county recreational facilities by persons of the colored race. Thus, the affirmative action demanded by the NAACP would require that established social habits, customs and practices of this community be summarily reversed and eliminated by means of a directive issued by county officials." Echoing the language of the U.S. Supreme Court, he called for moving toward desegregation "with all deliberate speed." Two days later, the *Miami News* reported that eight African Americans had "used bathing facilities at Crandon Park without incident." Rev. Gibson was quoted as saying that "another beach party was planned today." After receiving no definitive answer from the county commission, the bathers took advantage of a chilly day and sparse attendance by whites to make their protest.[64]

Miami Times publisher Garth Reeves later reflected on the black leaders' meeting with the county commission.

Here we are . . . asking for a redress of our grievance. You are telling us we cannot go to another beach in town, that we can only go to the black beach. . . . We pay our taxes, and we are law-abiding citizens. We think you're wrong. And we want to know why you feel that way. They didn't answer us. They refused to answer anything. . . . So we said, "We are leaving, then, if you are not saying anything. But we will be back at two o'clock this afternoon, and we are going swimming out here, in your white beach, Crandon Park. If you want to lock us up, or put us in jail, or beat us up, or whatever, then so be it. We think we should bring this to closure." And we left. That was ten o'clock in the morning. We went back to Father Gibson's house where we had our meeting, and we decided we would go back at two o'clock. There were a lot of officers out there at the beach. All the county police were there standing around. I think it was just intimidation, figuring they would scare us from going down to that beach and getting in that water. We expected that we would be put in jail, arrested for disorderly conduct or something, but we were more surprised than they were, I guess, when we went in the water and nothing happened. From that day on all the beaches in Dade County were automatically integrated.[65]

Shortly thereafter, Attorney General Richard Ervin said that "Dade County must integrate its tax-supported public facilities," but added that "overnight integration is not required and a slow and gradual program should be worked out so as not to 'upset the community.'" Delay remained the modus operandi for many whites in power.[66]

By 1960, blacks had also begun to swim at Miami Beach. In August, the police said their policy was to "let them be" when a black family sought to swim there. The movement soon spread to other southern states. Dr. Gilbert Mason led an Easter wade-in on a Biloxi, Mississippi, beach on April 17. When he led a larger wade-in on April 24, he was met by violent resistance. "The mob of white thugs who met us on the beach west of the lighthouse had first assembled around the law enforcement vehicles that were parked nearby. When some of these law enforcement officers pulled away, it seemed to be a signal for the white thugs to move onto the beach. When the white gang made their move, the Biloxi police had purposefully made themselves scarce. . . . The riot proceeded with the police viewing it from the sidelines." Two teenagers were killed in the next few days of widespread rioting.[67]

Recreational facilities became crucial targets and central symbols of regional power because of the vital importance of tourism to South Florida's economy. The civil rights movement in Florida was led by local residents and remained measured in its approach. Attacks on the NAACP for its supposed ties to communists made many fearful of being associated with national civil rights organizations. White violence against blacks was increasingly disparaged in the press and by the business and political establishment in Miami. Reflecting the perspective of Governor Collins, many business leaders and racially progressive whites spoke a racially neutral language of growth politics, bureaucratic planning, and urban renewal. Above all, they sought to avoid identification with social disorder while presenting an attitude of business cosmopolitanism that paid greater attention to the growing influence of black voters.

Avoiding and Then Entering the National Spotlight

After the creation of a new Miami-Dade County metropolitan government in 1958, the downtown area reflected the views and practices of professional planners and urban renewal programs. Yet planners were caught in a political maelstrom that constrained their ability to influence evolving and complex land use and social relationships as the area was becoming suburbanized. In this context, it is curious that Miami did not enter the national media spotlight of race relations after 1961, as the social impact of Cuban immigration also became widely felt in South Florida, notably in the Little Havana area near downtown. The media covered the mass migration of Cubans, the traumas they experienced, the crises surrounding the Bay of Pigs invasion and the Cuban Missile Crisis. Yet it was largely silent about how endemic black poverty in Miami was exacerbated by the increased competition for jobs and housing between African Americans and Cubans. Later, Miami attracted national attention during the August 1968 riots surrounding the Republican National Convention which took place in Miami Beach. By then, the split between black nationalists and advocates of nonviolence, the eruption of urban uprisings elsewhere, the assassination of Martin Luther King, and the growth of what Richard Nixon would call the "silent majority" had diminished the reach of the civil rights movement.[68]

In the aftermath of the election of Richard Nixon and the continuing war in Vietnam, several parallel factors affected race relations and public space in Miami. First, national leaders had been unable to forge an effective cross-class and biracial political alliance that could constitute a politically coherent center that worked to advance civil rights and address urban poverty. Instead, white fears in response to forced busing for school desegregation and the growing fears of "big government" prevailed. As Matthew Lassiter has shown, Nixon cleverly manipulated and exploited southern whites' fears of integration. A rising crescendo of conservatism focused on school busing issues and ignored the need for comprehensive solutions to urban problems.[69]

As Miami spread out, the metropolitan growth machine led by the Chamber of Commerce channeled black demands into prescribed patterns of urban renewal. Robert Fairbanks's description of Dallas fits Miami: "Since the booster rhetoric of the city emphasized ordered growth above all else, government addressed urban social problems most expeditiously when they threatened to promote disorder." While the issue of black access to beaches and parks in Miami and nearby cities had been propelled in part by fears of the impact of disorder on tourism during the 1940s and 1950s, Sunbelt leaders ignored the fate of city parks after they were integrated. As white residents moved to the suburbs, Miami's parks became merely sports fields or ghostly unused spaces, while Overtown was decimated.[70]

Second, the nation's dialogue over race, as Daniel Rogers has observed, became fractured and fragmented, opaque and tangential, even though blacks made electoral advances and black culture entered the mainstream through such TV programs as *Roots*. In the 1970s, attention to black history in Miami began with the inspired work of Dorothy Fields, who founded the Black Archives. Yet it remained difficult to initiate sustained dialogue regarding race that addressed the spatial and economic dynamics of the city and region, and neglect of the urban core and its public spaces persisted. "The civic landscape of the South looks the way it does because of both persistent inequality etched and erected in public spaces and dogged efforts to revise the same terrain," W. Fitzhugh

Brundage has commented. "The enduring presence of white memory in the South's public spaces and black resistance to it, in short, is a central theme of the southern past." The business community connected to the Chamber of Commerce and local media barons remained tethered to visions of Miami as a center of commerce and to continuing policies that marginalized the poor.[71]

Urban renewal, highway building, and neglect of the black community had a devastating effect on both Miami's downtown and its public parks, which became dangerous, poorly programmed, and often unused. Prime waterfront parks were set up to be closed or redefined as commercial entertainment venues and revenue producers for favored corporate interest groups. Most notable by 1977 was the fate of Bicentennial Park, which had been transformed from industrialized dock space into a 28-acre public park designed by the renowned architectural firm EDSA. However, there was no police protection at the park and few residents living nearby. In addition, the design of the park cut it off from street life. As a result, Bicentennial Park quickly became the site of several violent incidents, and few people ventured into it after that. Thus, black assertions of the civil right to public space were largely ignored within the context of a landscape characterized by suburbanization and shopping malls and what historians have characterized as an emergent neoliberal market mechanism of land use that disparaged government planning or saw it merely as a facilitator of the market forces that had become increasingly prevalent by the 1980s.[72]

The desegregation of parks was part of a broader economic and political reality that featured white flight from urban downtowns. Atlanta had gone through a desegregation process in the 1950s that focused, in part, on the use of public space. According to Kevin Kruse, "Little by little, Atlanta's public spaces were . . . desegregated—peacefully, publicly, progressively. And with every successful desegregation, Atlanta's reputation as the 'city too busy to hate' grew as well." Yet this image was largely a myth. Kruse shows that "as public spaces desegregated, whites abandoned them, effectively re-segregating those places in the process. In the end, court-ordered desegregation of public spaces brought a new division in which the public world was increasingly abandoned to blacks and a new private one was created for whites." The anger of working-class whites against wealthy elites who were seldom directly affected by desegregation fostered racially based conservatism. In Miami, the opposite happened. As integration became the law of the land in the 1960s, blacks gradually abandoned their own waterfront park on Virginia Key and dispersed to other places. For most local blacks, Virginia Key Beach receded as a community center.[73]

The need for improved housing in slum neighborhoods, campaigns for school integration and voting rights, and demands for equal access to recreational facilities continued to evolve, but only in very modest ways in Dade County by the 1960s.[74] Instead, urban renewal became a major focus of public policy. A 1960 housing survey "showed about 13,000 of the city's 120,000 housing units were deteriorated and another 4,500 were dilapidated." By 1962, the city had developed a plan to demolish buildings in three blighted areas: the central district, Coconut Grove, and Liberty City. Although white developers were the prime movers behind these plans, some wealthy African Americans colluded in the demise of black neighborhoods.[75] Well into the 1960s, white developers and their allies promoted the eradication of the central negro district using the tool of eminent domain. Blacks whose homes were seized were moved up to the Liberty City area. The strategy was to condemn unsafe buildings, using concern over safety, to promote "negro removal" and "higher use" of the land. White developer Luther Brooks, the man behind the development of Islandia in Biscayne Bay, a major slumlord, and a political fixture in Overtown, openly advocated moving blacks out of downtown. Black leaders "looked askance at" this plan, according to *Miami Herald* reporter Juanita Greene. "For the last 20 years," said Rev. John Culmer of St. Agnes Episcopal Church, "there has been talk of moving the downtown Negro district and the people here have been against it." Henry Arrington, a friend of Martin Luther King and a member of the Miami Housing Authority, said he would never endorse such a project. To do so "would imply . . . the perpetuation of segregation."[76]

Yet Brooks was not reviled in the black community. He was both a benefactor and a partner with several leading blacks, according to historian Nathan Connolly.[77] *Miami Times* reporter Stanley Sweeting, a black writer, commented in the late 1950s on a startling series of articles the *Miami Herald* published on the relationship between slumlords and politicians. He professed little knowledge about Luther Brooks's well-known rental agency and wondered why he was being singled out when other slumlords had done less to upgrade housing. Sweeting emphasized that in 1958 Brooks had "led a one-man fight against the Metro Commission . . . for more recreational facilities for Negro children." Shortly thereafter, the city commission met secretly to deal with the question of a pool. Commissioner B. E. Hearn, who lived only two blocks from the Manor Park Pool, remarked that integrating the pools would soon lead to intermarriage. Father Gibson replied, "We're here to swim, not to get married." The commission finally agreed to build a pool in the Liberty City area. Overall, the mixed picture of deference to Brooks as a white benefactor and the emerging political consciousness of the civil rights movement by blacks for blacks became more central.[78]

CORE and the Miami Sit-In Movement, 1959–1960

Dr. John O. Brown, Leonard and Annsheila Turkel, Jack and Barbara Gordon, A. D. Moore, and other blacks and whites connected to CORE in Miami initiated a series of sit-ins in Miami in 1959–1960. These biracial demonstrations at McCrory's, Woolworth's, and Grant's stores in late April 1959 took place before the 1960 sit-ins in Greensboro, North Carolina.

When he was interviewed for the *Eyes on the Prize* documentary series, ophthalmologist Dr. John O. Brown recalled the campaign. "We were looking for an organization that would involve the people from the streets, the grassroots movement. After investigating, we found the answer to be in the organization called CORE, the Congress of Racial Equality, and we immediately started our sit-ins." Unlike the subsequent student sit-ins in Greensboro, "ours involved grown-ups and people, mainly professionals. . . . Another interesting point was that over half the individuals who were involved in these sit-ins were White." In Miami, "We didn't meet the resistance . . . found in the Deep South. . . . Miami was the glitzy city, and its basic industry was tourism. Everybody came to Miami to have a good time, and the city fathers did not want to see any trouble spots here. We wanted a trouble-free area. We could not project [to] the nation an area where we were having racial violence. They did everything in the world to keep everything quiet."

Brown recalled that Overtown "was not a thriving business community. There were a number of little mom and pop businesses there." But "most of the businesses that existed in Overtown were owned by whites," including Jews. "The only Black hotel in Miami, at that time, was the Mary Elizabeth Hotel. . . . I guess about the only real business that was owned by Blacks was a soft drink company. . . . As far as professionals were concerned, we had about six Black lawyers. We had about sixteen Black doctors. We had one accountant that I can recall. We had a number of school teachers. But other than that the industry was construction and domestics." Nonetheless, black residents remained devoted to Overtown, Brown explained:

> Well, the segregation brought people together, and most everybody knew everybody else. At that time you could walk around at 3 and 4 o'clock in the morning. You didn't lock your cars. You didn't lock your house doors, anything. And this was a good time community. I mean, everybody came to Miami to have a good time. And if you were Black in the United States and you were anybody in the middle to upper middle class, you came to Miami in the wintertime.[79]

Miami's dependence on the tourist trade, including the black tourist trade, meant that racial segregation was in a more liminal place in Miami than elsewhere in the South, more subject to cross-pressures.

A. D. Moore described his initial attraction to CORE in 1959 and his subsequent role as treasurer, activist, and friend of Martin Luther King, a frequent visitor to Miami. His stories focus on the organization's campaign of direct action. "They had a series of meetings for training you how to be nonviolent. How to act, how to conduct yourself, how to dress, what to say if you're approached. You always had a spokesman if you're on a demonstration and somebody comes up and asks you a question. You direct them to the person, there's always somebody in charge. . . . You needed uniformity in what's being said." The group's interracial composition startled some whites:

> For example, our first sit-in was at McCrory's dime store on Flagler Street. . . . Barbara [Gordon, a white woman,] was in charge. . . . One guy came up and said, "Who is the Negro in charge of this affair?" Barbara said, "I'm the Negro," and Barbara looked just like you, you know. (Laughs) That was very funny. She was real good, real good. . . . Outstanding person. The first meetings were loaded

with [white] Palm Island people. . . . It was surprising. The civil rights movement was one of the great lessons for me because until then, and where I came from, I had never met white people, some of whom were more interested in rights for negroes than many negroes. We had many black people that didn't even know what we were doing. You wouldn't believe this. On our demonstrations here in Miami, for every black person, we had two whites, or more. That's right. . . . I hate to see it, I hate to think it, but it's true. There were many people who cried when Martin Luther King died who paid him no attention while he lived. . . . And I'm talking about black folks.[80]

Moore was particularly struck by the fact that "not a single church in my community" sponsored people to participate in the March on Washington. "The white churches in this community paid all of the money. Our participants . . . would ask me, 'What are you all going to do next?'" And that was somebody black as these shoes. I'd said, "What do you mean, you all? What, are you a Mexican or something?' . . . Or, 'I couldn't be in that, I couldn't be nonviolent.' You've been nonviolent your whole life. Everybody in your family has been mistreated and you haven't done a thing about it. That is nothing but nonviolence, isn't it? You haven't done a thing!"[81]

Moore appreciated the moderation of Miami mayor Robert King High. "He advised the police in this city, 'Don't let nobody interfere with those people who are demonstrating.' . . . And that's the way it went. They were not cuffing us. They didn't allow anybody to come around calling us names, pushing us around, or anything." In other cities, "the first person to mess over the civil rights workers were the police. But not here."[82] The tourism industry, led by Mitchell Wolfson of WTVZ and PR wizard Hank Meyer, clearly sought to deflect racial trouble that might discourage visitors. Mayor High negotiated with black leaders in the spring of 1960 to desegregate lunch counters, including Rev. Gibson of the NAACP, who joined representatives from CORE and the Greater Miami Ministerial Alliance, acting as the Committee for Human Dignity.[83] The *Miami Times* also recognized the contribution of Governor LeRoy Collins. In a televised address, "the governor said it was morally wrong for business places to deny Negroes sitting at lunch counters while soliciting their trade in other departments. He suggested that inter-racial committees be appointed to work out inter-racial problems." Endorsing that idea, the mayor appointed a committee with five blacks and six whites.[84]

Miami-area civil rights activists, like those in other cities, were ambivalent about involving the leaders of national organizations, especially one as charismatic as Martin Luther King. Some shared the perspective expressed by Spencer Pompey that "we got to solve this thing locally." Others were happy with the publicity that King's presence brought but were disappointed when he soon departed. A few longtime activists, such as A. D. Moore, were among King's most devoted followers. Others, however, resented the fact that he seemed to be given the credit for what grassroots efforts had accomplished. The most serious problem in the dynamic between local activists and national leadership was that the agreements won through high-level demonstrations and negotiations had to be implemented in day-to-day actions on the ground, and for that crucial task local activists were entirely responsible.

To some, it seemed that segregation was just slowly slipping away. Miami was often compared to Atlanta, which also had a reputation for interracial negotiation rather than confrontation. The *Miami News* quoted Mayor William Hartsfield's comment that "Atlanta's a different city from the balance of the South. We can't afford any narrow mindedness here." The article remarked that Atlanta, like Miami, had integrated its municipal golf courses and "a suit is now pending to abolish segregation in parks and recreation facilities. The city contends that segregation is no longer enforced in those areas, but Negroes have disputed the claim." In this way, as well as in the reality of white flight from downtown, Atlanta resembled Miami.[85]

By the 1960s, vast changes had taken place in the Miami area. Beginning two decades earlier, new highways and air conditioning had led to white flight to the suburbs. The construction of I-95 and I-395 in downtown Miami was traumatic for the African American community. In a blatant example of environmental racism, these freeways sliced right through the heart of Overtown, decimating its population and cultural life. In addition, while urban renewal served the interests of investors, it did not appreciably benefit poor blacks. Nathan Connolly has examined the collusion between white and black leaders in presenting eminent domain as a strategy for slum clearance that just happened to benefit downtown businessmen. Many blacks felt deceived by promises of alternative housing that were never fulfilled. Public purpose in the use of eminent domain perpetuated black poverty and compounded the increasing neglect of public spaces.[86]

Miami did not experience the same type of violence that marred other parts of the South in the early 1960s. Black and white residents occasionally showed their solidarity against racial oppression. After the Birmingham bombings, 2,000 mourners followed a 25-block path through downtown Miami. "Representatives of the three major faiths and of civic and patriotic groups joined in." Participants included white city commissioner Alice Wainwright; Rabbi Solomon Schiff; CORE leaders A. D. Moore, John O. Brown, and Theodore Gibson; and Mayor High. Many marchers wore black armbands and lapel buttons calling for "Freedom Now."[87]

In 1962, the *Miami Herald* reported that "things are so much better for us than they were 20 or 30 years ago—Miami is a better place to live than any other Southern city." According to the paper, Kelsey Pharr was often cited the "No. 1 citizen" for his quiet philanthropy and encouragement; Pharr financed a college education for many young people and worked in interracial relations. The reporter, Roberta Applegate, emphasized the "wise leadership on both sides that makes Miami outstanding." Paying tribute to local whites, Dr. Ira Davis disagreed with many northern friends who told him that Miami was progressive because of the large number of northerners. "I tell them the Southerners are responsible. After all, they can say, 'Heck, I'm a cracker, too.' They are the ones who have done the most." Some blacks expressed ambivalence about the value of sit-ins, Applegate reported. Pharmacist Elmer Ward noted that "all of us are part of one fabric, a part of American life." He, like many others, preferred a combination of "some persuasion, some pushing, and some legal contests." Many blacks looked a little askance at sit-in demonstrators but were also likely to say, "I glory in their spunk."[88]

Violence, Backlash, and the Erosion of Public Space, 1963–1976

The social and political tensions that surfaced in many parts of the nation in the period 1964–1968 found a unique expression in Miami. Blacks had been dealing with white resistance from the founding of the

Figure 11. Martin Luther King urged the Johnson administration to consider prompt withdrawal from the war in Vietnam in a speech at Miami's premier black resort, the Hampton House, on April 13, 1966. King also gave an early version of his "I Have a Dream" speech here before making his famous address in Washington in August 1963. From the Hampton House, King frequently retreated to Virginia Key Beach and went out on boats to fish and relax with friends when he was in Miami. Source: Associated Press/Toby Massey; ©1966 The Associated Press.

city, so whether Miami is an example of southern exceptionalism or the times had caught up with Miami's multicultural and touristic economy is debatable.

Miamians watched as Martin Luther King became involved in the riots in St. Augustine in the summer of 1964. Wade-ins on segregated beaches began there on June 17. Over the next several weeks, additional wade-ins took place in St. Augustine; the manager of the Monson Motor Lodge poured acid on demonstrators who were attempting to desegregate his pool; and white mobs attacked blacks. After Martin Luther King arrived, demonstrations were held at the old slave market. The issue attracted national attention at a time when Congress was debating the Civil Rights Act. The act became national law shortly thereafter.[89] By

1965, riots and social disorder had become a defining concern for King and Miami blacks.

In April 1966, King spoke to a Southern Christian Leadership Conference meeting at Miami's black resort, the Hampton House. Addressing the specific situation of black and poor Miamians, he warned that competition for jobs between blacks and Cubans "could generate explosive tension." He proposed bringing a "breadbasket program" to Miami to fight for more jobs for blacks and to upgrade the jobs they held. "Miami must come to grips with the social dilemma it faces," he said. Pointing to the economic dimension of racial inequality, he asked, "What good is it to have the right to sit at an integrated lunch counter if you don't have the money to buy a hamburger?. . . . We are so busy trying to win a war that can't be won in Viet Nam that we are going to lose a war against poverty at home."[90] King returned in May to address a Unitarian group and a religious group at the University of Miami, but some saw his presence as an effort to assist Robert King High, who was running for governor against the incumbent. Editor and columnist Bill Baggs commented that "in Florida . . . the racial issue raises many suspicions and fears and doubts in the heads of many people. It is an issue which does not belong in our politics."[91]

White backlash in Miami was expressed most cogently in 1968 by city police chief Walter Headley, a 20-year veteran. "Community relations and all that sort of thing has failed," Headley told a reporter for the *Nation*. "We have done everything we could, sending speakers out and meeting with Negro leaders, but it has amounted to nothing." He became "the hero of the nation's law and order circuit." In December 1967, Headley had "called in all my commanding officers and told them to change some things. I said we should use dogs to accompany men on the beat. I said I wanted the force in high-crime areas to carry shotguns. I said I wanted to concentrate men in these high-crime areas, and that I wanted them to use the stop-and-frisk law more." Word of this crackdown reached the press, and suddenly he found he had struck a deep, responsive chord throughout the country. He received, by his count, 8,000 letters and telegrams, only 22 of which expressed disapproval. He subsequently applauded Chicago's Mayor Daley, who called for his police to "shoot to kill" arsonists.[92]

Early in August 1968, a rally called to protest the lack of black representation at the Republican National Convention being held in Miami turned violent. The incident was precipitated by African Americans' anger over police repression. Three blacks were killed in violence that wracked Liberty City for several days. The county sheriff took the fact that so few Liberty City residents had been involved in the violence "as a good sign our community relations program is working." Ralph Abernathy said that the real causes were "deeper—unemployment, poor housing conditions, and acute problems within the ghetto." Ignoring residents' criticisms of white politicians, black leaders blamed outside agitators.[93]

Bill Baggs pondered the violence in relation to the history of race relations in Miami.

> In the 1940s . . . the Negro of Miami lived in a fenced society. He got off Flagler Street by dusk, he rode on the back of the bus, and the warm and lively beaches were not available to him. In a little more than a decade later, a measure of change could be noted when John F. Kennedy met with religious leaders in the East Room of the White House. Mr. Kennedy told the gentlemen attending that the last thing he wanted was to send in federal troops into a city. He said that the cities and states in the South could make this change, however traumatic, on their own. And he said that you could look to Miami as an example. . . . By this time, Miami or really Dade County, had opened up the beaches, had provided a seat in the front of the bus if Negroes wanted it, the department stores had desegregated, and the governments had announced a policy of fair and equal employment practices. We in Miami are now into the stubborn and complicated work of housing and jobs and defacto segregation in education. We are really ahead of most of the country, and perhaps that's why we are in trouble, because now the work becomes so complicated. The wreckers who spawned an evening of violence last night did not one whit to advance the legitimate ambitions of the Negro here. . . . It has been the ugliest of press agentry.[94]

It took the *Miami Times* to squarely define the issue: "It seems rather trivial to us whether the disturbance was started by 'outside agitators' or not. What does matter is that the seeds of discontent, despair, hunger, unemployment, police brutality, and many others were allowed to exist in this great 'liberal' community."[95]

Miami and Miami Beach were vastly different places in 1968 from what they had been in the days of Carl Fisher and E. G. Sewell. Downtown Miami was increasingly a ghost town sliced through with new highways as office workers fled to their suburban homes at night. Miami Beach had an aura of sleaziness. Today, what many see in Miami hinges on its image as an Eden for tourists, a modern paradise under the sun. However, the vision of the Miami area has long been shaped by narrowly defined notions of growth, an absorption with novel spectacles, and a magical tourist economy. As early as the 1960s, though, outside observers perceived this aura as unreal, even phony. At the time of the Republican National Convention in 1968, *New York Times* columnist Russell Baker described Miami Beach as "a ghetto of middle class fun lovers—the well-to-do, the successful and the whites who feel entitled to get away from it all periodically and wallow in a bout of hedonism isolated from the care and nuisance of reality."[96] Norman Mailer portrayed Miami as "materialism baking in the sun, then stepping back to air-conditioned caverns where ice could nestle in the fur."[97]

By 1972, when the Republican convention convened again in Miami Beach, the police had developed a sophisticated crowd control plan for thwarting black protestors and radicals making antiwar demands. Nixon, who was a part-time resident of Key Biscayne, attended a Republican Party rally at the recently constructed Miami Marine Stadium on Virginia Key. At one point the featured black singer, Sammy Davis Jr., rushed onto the stage and hugged Nixon from behind in a scene that made front-page news across the nation. The pragmatic Nixon turned it into a major public relations coup, declaring: "I want to make this pledge to Sammy. I want to make it to everybody here, whether you happen to be black or white, or young or old, and all those who are listening. I believe in the American dream. Sammy Davis believes in it." As historian Warren Susman has noted, however, the very idea of the "American dream" is an invention of postwar political rhetoric born in an era of exuberant national identity.[98] That dream harbored dangerous ambiguities about race and class as much as it protected politicized illusions about equality and patriotism.

Figure 12. Singer Sammy Davis Jr. hugs President Richard Nixon at Miami Marine Stadium in a famous shot during the Republican National Convention, August 1972. Source: Associated Press/Jim Palmer; © 1972 The Associated Press.

The confusing role of race and place are recalled rather succinctly in Sammy Davis's smiling hug. Over the next forty years, both the stadium and the skyline would change dramatically, and the city's surplus of construction cranes became a harbinger of the future. Miami continues to promote itself as a "magic city," charmed by a culture of speed, spectacle, and status. Blacks made substantial economic and political gains in South Florida but justifiably expressed resentment at the unequal help the federal government gave Cubans even as whites feared the withdrawal of their former privileges. Yet the racially charged reaction cut in multiple ways. The state was characterized by political fluidity during the three decades from the time Republican Claude Kirk was elected as governor in 1966 to the time when Jeb Bush solidified Republican dominance in 1998. In a sign of the state's rightward turn, LeRoy Collins was defeated in his run for the U.S. Senate in 1968 by Edward Gurney, a racially conservative Republican. Collins had walked with King in Selma in 1965, and during his campaign the press presented pictures that seemed to show Collins leading the march. In 1970, however, two racial liberals were elected to statewide offices: Lawton Chiles to the U.S. Senate and Reubin Askew to the governorship. In 1974, Chiles remarked, "Now, while race is still there, you have all candidates saying that we 'are seeking the black vote.' So it differs completely from the way it used to be. Now it would hurt you as a candidate to say that you weren't seeking them or if you made some derogatory remarks."[99]

Locally, too, some blacks advanced politically. M. Athalie Range, a Miami funeral director who led the local Parent-Teacher Association's protests of conditions for black pupils, became the first African American to serve on the Miami City Commission in 1965. In 1971, after two terms, Governor Reubin Askew appointed her to head the newly created Department of Community Affairs in the state capital. There she oversaw one of the nation's most progressive planning agencies with more than 200 employees in her charge. She was followed on the commission by Rev. Gibson, who was succeeded by Rev. Edward Graham in 1972 after Gibson moved to serve on the Metro Commission. Despite, or perhaps because of, its success, the NAACP soon lost its preeminence. A *Miami News* reporter captured the association's loss of power and purpose in 1976. "Today, its mission mostly accomplished," the NAACP was seen in "disarray with the fight against job and housing discrimination continuing." The area's four branches—Miami, Homestead, Opa-Locka, and Liberty City—"have long lost their national funding because of their inactivity." A black Metro Commissioner and NAACP supporter said, "We're struggling to keep the organization going. It's a shame. People tend to get complacent. Things worked better when society was tougher on us. It's difficult to get the young people interested. They won't feed the goose that laid the golden egg."[100]

After other beaches were desegregated, Virginia Key Beach was neglected. In the early 1960s, Dade County planners remarked that Virginia Key Beach "should be for the total public, which includes the entire metropolitan area." Calling Virginia Key "the last untapped frontier in the city of Miami," they argued "its use should be judiciously determined." It was a large and largely underutilized island. Although it was not an industrial site, as had been envisioned before 1945, the island became something of a strange, poorly planned hybrid. The wastewater treatment plant on the northeast quadrant of the island emitted noxious smells across a wide area. The island also housed educational and research institutions and, by 1963, the Miami Marine Stadium. Reflecting the lack of imagination and the absence of continuing oversight in planning public spaces in the city, Virginia Key also served as a dumping ground for environmental refuse. Neglect and poor planning were not anomalies but were part of a broad pattern of environmental racism throughout the nation.[101]

The social condition of African Americans living in Miami and the obfuscation of serious questions over racial politics and land use make the island of Virginia Key an important emblem of our times. It is a reminder of our lost context of the role that race has played in our eroding sense of place. Attempts to revive the "black beach" that were initiated back in 1999 and continue and the challenge of redesigning the marine stadium area in 2015 illustrate not just the enduring impact of racism or even the reassertion of African American identity but also the problematic issues of memory ignored, government neglect, and endless deference to private development initiatives. Efforts to preserve and revive these spaces continue to challenge us to find ways to galvanize the public, elected officials, and private donors and to develop more firmly the concept of our civil right to public space.

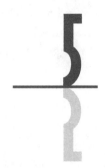

Public Land by the Sea

Developing Virginia Key, 1945–1976

Rickie Sanders has suggested that "public spaces represent how we as a community live and what we value; they are also representative of how we live."[1] This is clearly illustrated in Miami. In 1945, when political and business leaders looked out onto Biscayne Bay and considered the future of the waterfront, especially Virginia Key, most contemplated the possibility of using it for a modern seaport and airport that would make Miami a key connecting point between Latin America and the United States and serve as an economic engine for the region. Few other opinions were heard. The politics of land development in Miami were complex and multilayered, marked by disputes between different political jurisdictions and competing visions of the future. Few were conscious of the value of the natural world, the mangrove hammocks or the wildlife, the need for public access to open space, or the fragility of the land and water.

Some of Miami's most important environmentalists, such as David Fairchild and Charles Torrey Simpson, were passing away. Marjory Stoneman Douglas, Dr. Arthur Marshall, and writer Philip Wylie remained strong environmental advocates but often focused their attention on the Everglades or, for good reason, on issues such as sewage treatment. The Dade County Conservation Council, which had formed in 1933, was inactive. Most residents understood that developer Carl Fisher had manufactured many islands between Miami and Miami Beach for wealthy homeowners. Visions of yet more filled land danced in the heads of many local boomers. Virginia Key was largely perceived as a swampy wilderness that was ready to be remanufactured. In the coming years, oceanographic education, commercial entertainment, yacht racing, and film and TV production dominated the island, turning much of it into commodified space and obscuring any concern for the stewardship of its unique ecosystem.

What had been set aside as public land became ordered in a way that was distinct to the political culture of South Florida yet reflected the prevailing national trend toward the privatization of public space. In densely populated New York City, Gerald Kayden has shown, the incentive zoning law passed in 1961 allowed developers to build higher buildings in exchange for providing small public spaces, most of which are inhospitable.

Americans were increasingly living in a theme park world by the late 1950s, as Disneyland and Seaquarium begat numerous imitations in cities across the nation. Small-scale attractions were being eclipsed. In the next decade, many white Americans began questioning urban liberalism and began to seek greater security and fulfillment within their air-conditioned homes and in new forms of mass consumption and entertainment. Mike Davis wrote in 1992 that "the universal consequence of the crusade to secure the city is the destruction of any truly democratic urban space. The American city is being systematically turned inward. The 'public' spaces of the new megastructures and supermalls have supplanted the traditional streets and disciplined their spontaneity."[2] This chapter explores how those trends worked themselves out in Miami and affected Virginia Key.

The postwar period was the heyday of beach and pool culture and motor boating. Water skiing and boat racing attracted upwardly mobile men and their families. Surfing in California and Hawaii drew the young. At the same time, fascination with the ocean grew: Rachel Carson's *The Sea around Us* (1951) was a nonfiction bestseller, and Jacques Cousteau's ocean explorations drew rapt audiences. On *Wild Kingdom*, a long-running TV series sponsored by Mutual of Omaha that began in 1963, as Alexander Wilson has pointed out, "animals had to be captured before they could be saved." Nature became a contained experience. *Flipper*, a movie and then a TV series intended primarily for a juvenile audience, was filmed, in part, on Virginia Key. The show featured a single dad who was a park ranger, and his two sons, Sandy and Bud. But the star was their pet dolphin, Flipper, who was so bright as to be telepathic and exhibited unswerving loyalty to his humans. Every week's adventure involved a dramatic waterfront confrontation between human-and-dolphin team and the embodied forces of nature. The program's theme song, with lyrics by William Dunham set to music by Henry Vars, expresses and reinforces the prevailing attitude toward the ocean:

> Everyone loves the king of the sea,
> Ever so kind and gentle is he . . .
> They call him Flipper, Flipper, faster than lightning,
> No-one, you see, is smarter than he.

Taken together, these cultural productions helped redefine the relationship of modern technological humans to the natural world and the changing landscapes around them.[3]

Yet in the 1960s, powerful advocates proposed legislation that fostered increased sensitivity to the environment, in particular to sea life. The Endangered Species Protection Act, which was signed into law in 1966 and amended in 1973, and the 1972 Marine Mammal Protection Act began to raise questions of biotic rights. U.S. Supreme Court Justice William O. Douglas published *A Wilderness Bill of Rights* in 1965, which defended public access to the natural world. Historian Lynn White's 1967 essay, "The Historical Roots of Our Ecological Crisis," suggested that Judeo-Christian ideology had inculcated the assumption that nature existed purely for human benefit and questioned whether human dominion over nature was an adequate framework. "By destroying a pagan animism, Christianity made it possible to exploit nature in a mood of indifference to the feelings of natural objects," White argued. Ecologist Garrett Hardin published "The Tragedy of the Commons" in *Science* magazine in 1968, contending that a society actuated by individual self-interest was unable to fully appreciate and conserve the limited range of resources in the natural world as the world's population exploded.[4]

Eloquent opposition to development came from an environmentally conscious African American who lived and fished on Biscayne Bay all his life. Launcelot Jones had grown up on Porgy Key, located between

Elliott Key and Key Largo. He was the son of a former slave from North Carolina, Israel Lafayette "Parson" Jones, and his Bahamian-born wife, Mozelle. Parson Jones had bought Porgy Key for $300 in 1897 from his wages as a stevedore. He was a regular visitor to Miami and a founder of Mount Zion Baptist Church. After his parents' deaths, Launcelot continued to live on Porgy Key, working as a fishing guide and leaving the island only after Hurricane Andrew ruined his home in 1992. He died in 1997 at the age of 99. Crucially, he refused to sell his beloved land to developers and deeded it to the government to form the basis of Biscayne National Park. Jones declared: "Some people would have liked to make this place the No. 2 Miami Beach, but I think it's good for people to have somewhere that they can go to leave the hustle and bustle behind and get out into the quietude of nature."[5]

When Virginia Key Beach "for coloreds" was opened for business back in 1945, the *Miami News* lavished praise on Commissioner Charles Crandon and the Interracial Committee and presented it as a "good augury for the solution of other vexing problems which sometimes agitate feeling among the races that live here side by side, and which must learn to live in mutual understanding and harmony, as indeed it is altogether possible to do." The project should have "been brought off many years ago," the paper admitted; "it represents the kind of fair play and equal opportunity which can be extended to the negro within the framework of the South's social traditions, and its desirability is therefore beyond argument."[6]

Yet the black beach remained a small section of a largely deserted island. Visions for its future derived in part from the furious prewar competition among developers for potential federal grants and the financial schemes of local officials. The future of the island became an open question after World War II. What governmental body would control it? How could it best be used? What would surround the beach in the coming years?

The failure to follow through with any coherent planning process centered on the public interest is the central theme in the postwar history of Virginia Key. The lack of a coherent constituency focused on public land, the ability of favored financial interest groups to propose profitable schemes for the industrial and commercial use of the waterfront, and the lack of a sustained vision for integrated, publicly accessible, and affordable beaches ultimately set Miami's waterfront parks up for failure. The fate of Virginia Key is a stark example of how the politics of public land became caught up in the rush to develop air-conditioned shopping malls and sports venues and how the branding and promotion of place grew alongside the desire for spectacle. What was later called growth politics or neoliberalism was played out in Miami in ways that were not seen in other American cities. The African American community's relationship to a portion of Virginia Key and its stewardship over the land fell victim to political inertia. No controlling public body or shared vision shaped the future of the island.[7]

Miami's experience in defining the uses of its largest public park, located several miles offshore from downtown, can be viewed as part of a broader national pattern. Scholars have recently linked issues of homelessness and social control with the growing power of corporate capital over what has historically been defined as public land. Building on the work of many other scholars, David Harvey writes that "increasingly, Richard Sennett notes, the 'right to the city' became more and more of a bourgeois prerogative. Social control and surveillance of who 'the public' is (or is not) proceeded accordingly. The validation of the new public spaces . . . was heavily dependent upon the control of private functions and activities that abutted upon them."[8]

Waterfront Visions, Park Systems, and the Neglect of Virginia Key

Defining Miami's waterfront and its parks was primarily the province of the city and county commissions. Decisions were promoted by planning departments in both entities, by city and county managers, and, most prominently, the county's Port Authority, the Chamber of Commerce, and other private interest groups. Public officials periodically had to implore the state's Internal Improvement Fund to transfer title of state-controlled land to local governments. In time, decisions over land use generated a changing array of bureaucratic entities within local governments, the employment of consultants, infrequent commentary in the press, and a lack of continuity in decision making. Few environmental advocates focused on the waterfront, and hardly any nonprofit advocacy groups addressed island-related issues. Although Dade County had a vibrant park system, the city of Miami did not. One conference with representatives of the Playgrounds and Recreation Association of America did attempt to draw up a plan for the city park system back in 1929, but little came of it.[9]

The challenge of planning the public waterfront raised complex questions. What private interests were interested in developing it? In what ways were the city or county parks systems involved? In 1939, Charles Crandon had argued that Virginia Key bay bottom should not be sold to private interests. The *Miami News,* reflecting his opinion, editorialized: "The public interest, in the mind of the governor as well as every other decent citizen, must be paramount."[10] But how was the public interest defined and defended? What forms of public input were or were not heard? Did the development of Virginia Key center on the purportedly benevolent intentions of one individual, County Commissioner Crandon? Was that then or can that ever be enough?

Power grows when groups master and evaluate complex development proposals, but the interminable decision-making process in Miami led to public cynicism. "Harbor development has become a highly controversial issue," the *Miami News* reported in 1943, "with currents and crosscurrents building bars between city and county authorities and public opinion caught in eddies or pressure-group activities."[11] Confusion reigned in the public mind. While boosters sought to foster a far more industrialized waterfront, a few observers wondered about the direction the city was taking.

One serviceman's wife wrote a letter to the editor of the *Miami News* as she was leaving town in 1945 that asked a number of pointed questions. "How about fair treatment of negroes? And don't point out the new Virginia Key bathing beach to me: let me point out the slums they live in, to you! . . . How about cleaning up Biscayne Bay and solving the sewage problem?" She disliked the poor transportation system, the lack of a decent library, and Miami's obsession with Pan-Americanism, "which despite any protests to the contrary is just one more way for money hungry Miamians to grab all they can from 'Pan-American tourists.'" Finally, she advised, "Miamians, settle down to being an American city on a yearly basis! Concentrate on making this a real comfortable home-like place, free of all the glitter of a tourists' mecca, and rich in all that counts." Virginia Key was one test case of planning ahead for what counted in Miami.[12]

Crandon had long considered linking the development of Virginia Key and Key Biscayne. In January 1945, when he had first proposed the "negro beach," he had also proposed an aquarium on the island. He advocated a bond issue to help fund a $2 million aquarium on Virginia Key that he said would bring 850,000 visitors to the area. He was engaged in conversations with the University of Miami about building a marine laboratory and also envisioned a facility for the federal Bureau of Fisheries.[13]

In September 1947, Florida Power and Light, the state's provider of electricity, sponsored a symposium to discuss the development of the key that underscored racial rivalries and the white power structure's sense of entitlement. If Virginia Key could be developed for blacks, the implicit logic went, then it could be also developed for whites. The executive director of the city's planning board, Frank Stearns, acknowledged that Virginia Key "might be likened to a blank slate which is yet to be completely shaped." He thought the small area on the south section of the key that the county controlled was being "put to especially good use in the form of a needed Negro bathing beach" but he also thought that an aquarium would be appropriate nearby. The upshot of the symposium was a decision to emphasize the key's economic potential. Little attention was paid to its natural beauty or to conserving the island.[14]

The intention of these kinds of meetings was to hedge in the black beach with a white wall of development that could both serve whites and remind blacks of the invisible lines separating the races. In the next few years, a host of schemes was proposed for Virginia Key, while a few prominent environmental advocates disparaged the misuse of public land. The combination left many blacks both proud of their own public waterfront park and frustrated at their lack of equal treatment, notably when compared to Crandon Park, which was described as one of country's most beautiful beaches.

Miami had long been focused on the downtown Bayfront Park as a premier destination for residents and tourists. It had been altered for military use during World War II, and a small "social hall" that remained became the core of a convention center. A new bandstand was built in the park. As Miami's parking problem became more acute in 1948, private interests proposed taking land from Bayfront Park for a parking lot and, as compensation, dredging and filling a smaller area to the east for new parkland. The proposal was eventually killed and parking garages were developed instead. But many Miamians seemed to regard their parks, like their buildings, as disposable and even movable. Despite strong dissent by some park advocates, a library was constructed in Bayfront Park at the foot of Flagler Street in 1949 that blocked views of the bay. The public uproar was so intense that the city asked the legislature to protect itself from such future building schemes. The legislature passed a law that forbade the construction of any further buildings in Bayfront Park and prohibited the moving of any buildings into the park. The law empowered Florida courts "to enjoin any attempt to violate" the law. There was concern that the park was being nibbled away.[15]

After a devastating hurricane hit southeast Florida in the fall of 1945, Dade County constructed a few facilities, including a concession stand, at Virginia Key Beach to mitigate the impact of the destruction. But these were seen as inadequate, and the *Miami Times* complained, "Promise was made that the beach would be properly developed." It was two more years before a causeway was built that connected the key to the mainland, finally providing black Miamians with road access to their waterfront. Before then, a ferry transported hundreds of African Americans at a time to the area, but getting a place on the ferry was difficult. In June 1947, more than 1,100 picnickers "crowded the sandy beach on Sunday and many more were left on the docks because of inadequate boating facilities to shuttle the throng to and from the beach. Some people who bought tickets at the dock at 10:30 am did not get a seat on a boat until 2:30." In that same year, President Harry Truman dedicated Everglades National Park, and the Rickenbacker Causeway was finally completed, both of which attracted more tourism to the area. It was not likely a mere coincidence that black Miamians were finally connected to the key just when Crandon Park for whites opened nearby. Sadly, a hurricane ravaged Virginia Key in the fall of 1950, and the park was closed "indefinitely."[16]

Some black Miamians feared that their beach could be taken away. When a parking area was being built just south of the park toward the Rickenbacker Causeway, A. D. Barnes, the supervisor of Dade County parks, was forced to assure a reporter for the *Miami Times* that "he knew of no underhand effort to take Virginia Beach from Negroes." But, the reporter continued, "much skepticism was felt when it was learned that the du Pont interests are seeking a six months['] option on land on

Virginia Key where they plan to construct a $2,000,000 privately oper-
ated aquarium."[17]

Debating How to Use the Urban Wilderness

In 1951, a five-person citizens' committee submitted a report to the Miami City Commission concerning the development of Virginia Key. The
committee was apparently convened to determine whether Virginia Key
should be the location of a proposed "Pan American Trade Center." Instead, according to the *Miami Daily News*, the committee made "sweeping suggestions for developing the cross-Bay area." The order of their
recommendations reveals as much about public optimism regarding development as it does about the racial undertones of development plans
in Miami. The committee proposed that Virginia Key be "1. Enlarged by
1,100 acres to accommodate a new public bathing beach for whites, plus
a landing strip for private airplanes; 2. Developed into one of the nation's
foremost park, playground, boating and yachting centers; 3. Joined by
the bridge or underpass with Highway A-1-A in Miami Beach via Fisher's
Island and connect[ed] with the existing road on Biscayne Key; and 4.
Continued as a site for Negro bathing facilities and that a portion of the
land next to this area be set aside for the construction of a Negro hotel or
motel." In rejecting the idea that the island be used as a site for a world's
fair or trade mart, the committee said the "project was not attractive,
and the location indicated it would present perplexing traffic and other
problems."[18]

One writer who had become a passionate advocate for the public waterfront in the postwar days was the *Miami Herald*'s editor, John Pennekamp. He had a deep and abiding love for the natural beauties of the
bay, but he observed accurately:

> Virginia Key is pretty much like a habitual imbiber's headache—
> it's sure to pop up every so often. The county has a tougher policy
> about disposing of public lands than does the city, which is regarded
> as fair game at any time. Financially harassed, the city always is
> ready to listen to the voice that promises money. . . . Next to the
> sun, the waters of the ocean and the bay are the greatest assets we
> have. In fact, they are inseparable in evaluating the area's primary

worth. The people's right to see and enjoy their waters certainly transcends that of any developer who, lacking a civic consciousness and pride, would ride roughshod to his purpose.[19]

The rival *Miami Daily News* also proclaimed its support for saving the bay for the public and protecting it from poorly planned development. Following one developer's proposal for private use of the island, an editorial proclaimed that "the Bay, like the Key, belongs to the people; neither should be sold at any price. The county owns a small section of the Key at the extreme south end. This includes Virginia Beach for Negroes, which [the developer] proposes to cut off." It concluded that "Biscayne Bay has been the continued delight to those who have lived on the shore from the days of the discovering Spaniards until profit-seeing eyes began to move in on its multihued waters. What was once the boast and prided possession of this community is now restricted by man-made projects. Even what is left is under threat. . . . This new move to acquire Virginia Key is a companion piece with the efforts made to strip the people of what little property they have, and which once lost will be irreplaceable."[20] Few writers had written so directly about the loss of public land to development schemes and the links between use of public space and broader social issues.

Continuing debate took place over a proposed causeway from Elliott Key all the way through Virginia Key to Miami Beach and another connecting Key Biscayne to Miami Beach. A state engineering report said the bridge would cost more than $31 million. Income from tolls would pay only half that amount at the beginning; the state would have to subsidize the operation. In 1957, the leader of the Interama project, a major trade mart connecting North and South American businesses that E. G. Sewell had originally proposed, said he would be willing to shift its location from Miami to Virginia Key. Dr. W. H. Walker commented on a plan by the city and county "to use 659 acres of public land (459 city and 200 county) on the Key for the project." By 1958, Interama, three causeways, and the development of Virginia Key had become linked together in a grand development fantasy. Traffic Consultants Wilbur Smith and Associates found that including three causeways and one tunnel would make the plan financially feasible, but this grand vision of connectivity came too late, for the county commission had declined to float the necessary bonds. When the Rouse Company again proposed Interama in 1972, *Miami News* editor Bill Baggs backed the plan. After it failed again, both the site on Virginia Key and Oleta State Park in the northern coast of the county became the projected home of Florida International University. Park advocates in the early 1970s had called for the use of the land on Virginia Key as a central park. Dr. Arthur Marshall commented that "any time anyone wants to build something, they say they want to put it out there." Park advocate Dan Paul added that it "looks to me like they're planning a fourth rate Disney World." Harvey Ruvin, chair of the Urban Affairs Committee of the Audubon Society, commented caustically that "there are no other large cities on this planet that do not have a large park within their boundaries."[21]

In 1957, civic leader Ray Sterling, backed by a civil engineer, presented a plan to the city for a port on the upper end of Virginia Key near the sewage treatment plant. Sterling, an advocate of metropolitan government, which voters were considering at the time, placed two objectionable facilities next to each other, ignoring the existence of the colored beach nearby. As late as April 1959, *Herald* reporter Juanita Greene posited that Virginia Key could be the "key" to solving the seaport problem. The proposal sought to fill in the shallow northern portion, create several large slips, and send ship traffic to the key instead of to Miami's "front yard." The issue was finally sorted out when a Dade County port coordinating committee finally backed a location on Dodge Island for the port, ruling out Virginia Key. Crandon, who voted with the majority, nonetheless said that the Virginia Key location was "more practical than Dodge Island because it provided more room for expansion, would not require 'further spoiling' of the bay, would not interfere with any residential areas, and would not necessarily require the construction of a railroad line."[22] The huge Port of Miami was built on Dodge Island in a way that would have appalled E. G. Sewell, who had earlier deplored the fact that such construction obscured views of the bay.

When he retired from the county commission in 1948, Charles Crandon recounted his accomplishments. "It hasn't been so many years ago that Dade County did not own ONE FOOT of public park or recreational area, and not ONE FOOT of bathing beach." Now "Dade County today has one of the finest park systems in the country and FOUR AND ONE-HALF Miles of PUBLIC BATHING BEACHES," including a park on Virginia Key "for the colored population." Crandon Park, which had opened the previous year, contained 1,500 acres and a two-mile-long beach. No tax funds had been used to buy the park or construct the Rickenbacker Causeway, he assured voters. They had been funded by bonds that would be repaid entirely from "tolls collected from those who use the causeway."[23]

The Dade County park system developed separately from the city park system. Yet by the late 1950s, residents' enjoyment of city parks was diminished by overcrowding. Dr. Reinhold Wolff, head of the University of Miami's Bureau of Business and Economic Research, asserted: "The county must do something to help the $400 million tourist industry. If it doesn't do it for residents, it must do something for the tourists." He blamed the apathy of public officials and the public itself.[24]

The importance of preserving natural areas on Virginia Key was occasionally brought forward. The Tropical Audubon Society promoted the idea of a bird sanctuary on the island in 1956. The corresponding secretary of the society reported: "We have counted more than 100 egrets and herons feeding there at one time. Other winged visitors include roseate spoonbills, white pelicans, ibis, willits, red-breasted mergansers, blue-winged teal, grebes, gulls, lesser scaups, loons, terns and dowitchers." Commissioners asked attorneys what it would take to designate county property "for birds only." A large new beach area on the eastern portion of the key also was seriously considered at that time; dredging nearby areas and putting bulkheads on the mudflats would not impinge on either the black beach or the water treatment plant. However, in 1990, the area became the Bill Sadowski Critical Wildlife Area. Mayor Xavier Suarez promoted this land use. It was expanded in 1993 and is one of the few places in the Miami area that was protected from development.[25]

Public officials and entrepreneurs treated Virginia Key as if it were the solution to several unrelated problems. Interest in privatized development mingled with attempts to solve environmental problems, often uncomfortably. A convention center, an aquarium, the University of Miami Marine School, and resort hotels all emerged as possibilities after the key was connected to the mainland. At the same time, environmental issues attracted political attention. Flooding in Hialeah, the establishment of Everglades National Park, and concerns about pollution and salt-water intrusion were environmental issues with state or national resonance in the late 1940s.[26]

Occasionally, commentators pointed out the connection between environmental and social problems. In 1949, Philip Wylie related the pollution of Biscayne Bay from raw sewage to the conditions in Miami's black slums in an article published in *Look* magazine that was reprinted in the *Miami News*. "Many Florida towns and cities contain a jam-packed Negro slum of such squalor as to constitute a huge 'culture medium' for all infectious diseases. . . . Mosquitoes, flies, parasites and germs do not know about Jim Crow; but all White Florida—like the Deep South everywhere—behaves as if these menacing lower forms of life were well aware of the color line. This past autumn, an inspection group studying the slums of Miami . . . stated that less than four per cent of the wretched hovels in the segregated Negro area could be classified even as 'fair to poor.' So 96 per cent were rated lower than that. Newspapers carried the account of these conditions, but the slum in the sun is unchanged."[27]

Miami was dumping 47,000,000 gallons of raw sewage into the bay every day by the early 1950s. The solution was a sewage treatment plant on Virginia Key and a sewer pipe that sent the resulting sludge three miles out to sea. Wylie remarked that the proposal would result in 6 percent of the raw sewage coming ashore from the planned outfall; forty gallons of sewage a day per foot of beach is a lot, however diluted it might be. In 1952, voters passed a $16,000,000 bond issue to construct an underwater sewer line across Biscayne Bay to a large treatment plant on Virginia Key and an underwater outfall sewer line a mile further out in the ocean. It would be an up-to-date facility similar to those in Houston, Dallas, and Los Angeles. Additional millions would be used for interceptor sewers and pumping stations. The treatment plant would separate solids from liquids, aerate and reduce the bulk by oxidation, and then use chlorine and other chemicals to kill the bacteria in the residue. Placing it in close proximity to the "colored beach" meant that the beachgoers had to endure noxious odors. This plan would never have been made if Virginia Key Beach had been a beach for whites.[28]

One reporter who ventured to the site of the sewage treatment plant described his experience as a "safari." Virginia Key was "not an island—just a high spot in the ocean where trees grow between high tides." The construction workers took the newsmen to the site in "the manner that Stanley used to find Livingston in Africa." They journeyed across swampland to an interior lake that was "clear and filled with fish which somehow local anglers have managed to miss." At that point, they had been unable to get a bulldozer to the site. It was difficult to keep labor in these conditions, the foreman said, which were the "ruggedest he had experienced."[29]

In late 1956, the *Miami News* reported that "since the installation of Miami's new sewage treatment plant on Virginia Key, the pollution of the bay has decreased appreciably." Yet the paper pointed out that only a small part of the metropolitan area was connected to sewers; more than 90 percent of the population was served by septic tanks. The scale of the problem suggested the need for a new metropolitan government to address such issues. Reporter Jane Wood summarized scientific reports about the impact of sewage treatment on the area and the need to avoid greater reliance on septic tanks. "Bay pollution is now coming under control," she reported. But raw sewage spills would occasionally continue to force the closing of beaches.[30]

A gloriously beautiful island next to the state's largest city, Virginia Key offered a golden opportunity for recreation, scientific investigation and education, and for environmental preservation. Most of the island was public land, but Miami leaders did not make—or follow through with—any coherent plan for its long-term public use or for the conservation of its unique natural attributes. In 1951, the University of Miami's Dr. F. Walton Smith finally obtained a six-acre site on Virginia Key for the Marine School, which conducted education and research. The Seaquarium on Virginia Key was the largest marine theme park in the world when it opened in 1955. These facilities originally were perceived to serve a public purpose. Yet limited ability of officials to conceptualize or sustain the preservation of the natural world as a public place contributed to the increasing loss of public space over time.[31]

Philip Wylie lamented that Florida "contains, as do all [states], too many men who are willing—for a quick buck (or a short-term million)—to turn any landscape, however irreplaceable and hence priceless, into a stretch of terrains as bald, repellent, and uninhabitable as the face of the moon." Pointing to the connections among Florida's ecosystems, he prophesied a disaster that has materialized since he wrote.

If farmers and cattlemen insist on having their way, land drainage may eventually so lower the already-failing water tables of the peninsula that the seas, intruding through porous limestone, may "salt" the wells that are the only sources of fresh water for many major cities and thousands of small communities. . . . Greater Miami's wells have already been repeatedly moved inland, owing to the steady, underground incursion of salt water.

Wylie decried the area's ceaseless development. "Almost invariably, the individual who buys this virgin Florida land for a home—or the developer who starts a community—has only one reaction to the 'land of flowers': bulldoze. So hundreds of thousands of acres of Florida have been and are being bulldozed to bare oolite cobblestones. Then, they are set about with homes and streets. Afterwards, dirt has to be brought in, irrigation systems have to be installed, lawns must be planted, and the tediously familiar trees of conventional landscaping are finally set out.[32]

A few proposals were intended to serve African Americans. One New York entrepreneur proposed a hotel for "Negroes" in 1957, envisioning an eight-story, 200-room structure on a ten-acre site. The board of directors of the corporation included black celebrities Cab Calloway and Lena Horne and "many prominent Miamians." But the city commission refused to lease the land for a private project.[33] In 1961, Syracuse entrepreneur Harold Aronson proposed an integrated convention center and resort hotel. "A substantial segment of the Negro population and other minority racial groups of the United States has achieved an economic status higher than that of any comparable group in the world," his proposal began. "The sponsors of 'The Colonnades' . . . recognize the fact that many inter-racial groups conventions represent economic and cultural tastes at present largely unsatisfied with facilities open to their patronage." After looking at three other possible sites where, "in view of the residential nature of adjacent properties, it is doubtful that any extended negotiations could have been fruitful," Virginia Key was selected. This "attraction" would draw "completely new tourist incomes" to Miami. It would not compete with other establishments: "Obviously, such a development must be designed to serve those not presently attracted by existing facilities available to them." Significantly, several of Miami's black leaders were "opposed to the facility because it might impede integration in the area." To *Jet* magazine, Virginia Key beach itself represented "Jim Crow." The magazine reported, perhaps too optimistically, that "city officials . . . are being bombarded with protests from Negro leaders saying it's not needed since Negroes now frequent Miami Beach hotels and facilities."[34]

Columnist John Pennekamp asked a pointed question that could have been asked of many white entrepreneurs over the years under similar circumstances but often was not: "If the promoters conscientiously believe that this area needs an integrated hotel and that it will be financially profitable why don't they go into the market and buy the land they require from private owners? Why take it from the people?" The economics of such deals were then laid out. The "percentage of the receipts in lieu of tax" was one widely used gimmick, affording a "high degree of real estate tax freedom to the promoter." There was also a "release from much of the risk that goes with private investment. Contracts between public agencies and private interests usually carry a renegotiations clause as a safeguard if they are found to be too harsh. Such provisions frequently exist in contracts between private parties too, the difference being that in the latter case adjustments are made on a sound business basis. In public-private contracts self-serving pressures have a way of intruding themselves into the renegotiations." Pennekamp added that "all over the country there is a drive on to end the ruthless destruction of natural resources and the slipping away of publicly owned lands." The federal government was conducting such an effort under its effort to save "our diminishing shorelines." A recent study by the state of Florida had shown that of 8,426 miles of shoreline, the longest in the nation, only 26 miles was in public ownership. The argument about the value of such lands being on the tax rolls was rebutted with the argument that "the eventual tax return proves to be a relative pittance when compared with the resource of which the public is deprived."[35]

The most audacious plan, which came dangerously close to completion, was promoted by oil magnate Daniel Ludwig, who sought to build a huge refinery in the South Bay. This plan provoked intense opposition and unprecedented organizational efforts by environmentalists, who formed the Safe Progress Association. This project and proposals for more bridges and new islands made of fill were halted. Public attention was finally drawn to the natural attributes of the bay. With the help of Representative Dante Fascell, Herbert Hoover Jr., and Secretary of the Interior Stewart Udall, Biscayne National Monument (later National

Park) was created. At the same time, Dodge Island, a new cruise and cargo ship complex just north of Virginia Key, was finished in 1965.[36]

By the early 1960s, Metro planners had declared that land uses on Virginia Key "should be for the total public, which includes the entire metropolitan area." Calling Virginia Key "the last untapped frontier in the city of Miami," they said that "its use should be judiciously determined." It was a large and largely underutilized island, although by then the wastewater treatment plant on the northeast quadrant of the island was emitting noxious smells across a wide area. The proximity of the sewage treatment plant and the black beach resembles the environmental racism of "dumping in Dixie" scholars and activists have described in recent years.[37] Both African Americans and wastewater were regarded as unwanted refuse and removed from proximity to affluent white neighborhoods. In a parody of planning, the island had become a strange hybrid: educational institutions and entertainment sites were located there as well.

In 1960, a national report highlighted the growing problem of encroachment on parklands and waters. "The chief . . . offenders are highways; private, commercial and industrial enterprises; schools; and varied public and quasi-public agency purposes such as fire stations, armories, parking lots, hospitals." Despite the opposition of some county and city officials, it was "cheaper to grab open park lands than to acquire other land." Nevertheless, a culture that valued spectacular technology and sought to contain nature continued to shape the island. A few local organizations stood up to preserve parks and natural areas. The Tropical Audubon Society, the Friends of the Everglades, garden clubs, and the Dade County Conservation Council were able to block some development schemes, but they had little success in promoting alternative values.[38]

A hodgepodge of proposals for Virginia Key came to naught, but their variety indicates the lack of a coherent overall vision that would reconcile complex political pressures. A member of the city parks staff suggested that people be allowed to camp along the causeway beyond the Miami Marine Stadium in order to "see how lonely and empty the place is and [in order to] patronize it more." A group of developers sought to build an "international hotel that will be expanded to include a park, beach, marina, executive craft airport, heliport, and an 18-hole, championship golf course." The fact that the land was public property was not forgotten. Yet the uses to which the city sought to put it indicate that government officials, too, were captivated by the notion of large-scale, profit-producing projects. At the same time that they offered to lease the remaining land on Virginia Key to the state for a public park, they were studying a proposal to build a $2.5 million amusement center on sixty acres adjoining the marine stadium that would have included two restaurants, eighteen major rides, and a "kiddie land." There is no record of African Americans' responses to these ideas, which would have seriously impinged on the black beach.[39]

Scientific study of the oceans continued to develop on Virginia Key. The Florida Marine Research Institute soon became a leading research facility in fisheries and oceanography. Promoters sought to capitalize on its reputation by setting up a 162-acre oceanographic park, including an education center, three museums, a restaurant, and a golf course. Exhibits would show how continents move, why the tides rise and fall, how waves are formed, and how fish and marine mammals communicate. One exhibit would be devoted to submarine warfare. The marine research institute opposed making this a commercial venture because "it would have to depart from the educational aspects and concentrate on what the public will pay for. All our efforts to probe deeper and deeper into the oceans are being subsidized by blue-chip corporations with huge amounts of money." An article in a local magazine proclaimed that "governments of many of the world's nations are encouraging their best intellectual talent in the search for marine food resources, minerals, knowledge of ocean currents that vitally affect climates, fish populations and other facets of the marine world." An aquarium promised to combine science and tourism. The county authorized the Marine Exhibition Corporation to construct what became Seaquarium on fifty-five acres of swamp. Wometco Enterprises Inc. acquired a controlling interest in 1960.[40]

The problem of pollution reentered public debate in the early 1970s after the state indicated that it would allow expansion of the sewage treatment facility. The city and county objected because doubling the plant's capacity would gobble up sixty-five more acres of land. The next year, the issue of unregulated dumping by the city reared its head. The county pollution control officer ordered the city to retrieve as much sludge that had been allowed to drift into the bay as possible. Sludge and trash was floating toward nearby Fisher Island, an exclusive white area. While no one came to grips with these environmental problems, entrepreneurs sought to establish more recreation facilities on the key. Rose Gordon, chair of the Miami Zoning and Planning Board, said she was "appalled" by the idea, which was "the worst planning proposal in recent years." She questioned why this misuse of public land was not being brought before her board for approval: "Private property owners are afforded a public hearing. The same privilege should be granted to the public on all public owned land.[41]

The Containment of Nature

The land on Virginia Key was devoted to an irrational array of incompatible uses, reflecting the lack of comprehensive planning and of concern for the public interest. Although the key still retained some inaccessible, unspoiled natural areas, an unguarded dump filled with toxic materials was growing in the middle of the island. The new Miami Marine Stadium was designed to boost Miami's standing in the intense competition among urban centers located in tropical climates to capitalize on the conjunction of sun and sea. San Diego's Sea World opened in 1965. Located on Mission Bay away from the center city, the facility contained nature, constraining and displaying it to audiences in a safe and supposedly educational manner. Susan Davis explains that Sea World's "spectacular nature is a medium that connects customers to nature, and, in the ordered theme park world, to each other and to themselves. In this way, it both continues and revises the quasi-religious nineteenth century tradition of nature as self-discovery and gives the domination of nature a gentle, civilized face."[42] The same qualities marked the Seaquarium, although the Miami Marine Stadium on Virginia Key epitomized the more modern values of speed, spectacle, and celebrity.

Local leaders worried that "Miami was taking a back seat to other boating hotspots—Los Angeles, San Diego, Seattle and New Orleans—when it comes to providing a safe, fast race course." CBS contracted to broadcast speedboat races and water skiing competitions nationally, which officials regarded as a way to promote tourism. The proposed stadium would be financed by private developers but built on public land. The *Miami Herald* praised the plan, writing that the view from a stadium on Virginia Key westward toward the city of Miami would be "a grand picture—and one that leaves a lasting impression." But the city manager opposed the idea because he "would not be a party to a Teapot Dome scandal," a reference to a notorious incident in the 1920s in which the U.S. secretary of the interior was revealed to have accepted bribes in exchange for leasing federally owned petroleum-producing lands to private oil companies at bargain-basement prices. Officials decided to move forward with a city-owned stadium instead. A study commissioned by the city advocated funding the stadium with a revenue bond issue and creating a race course of 1.67 miles, a floating stage for symphonic attractions, a grandstand with initial seating capacity of 7,000, and boat pits that would be an "aquatic showplace." A deed restriction stated that the land surrounding it could be used "for marine stadium and allied purposes only" or the property would revert from the city back to the county.[43]

The Ralph Munroe Miami Marine Stadium was finally designed by architect Hilario Candela, built for a little more than $2 million and opened to great acclaim on December 27, 1963. Swan boats and fireworks, opera and pop music, waterskiing, and other surprises were featured in the opening "family show." Orchestra leader Guy Lombardo called the new stadium "the best thing that ever happened" to tourism in Florida. There was one story about the possible effects of noxious odors from the wastewater treatment plant about half a mile away, but Miami's optimism triumphed over all—at least in the beginning.[44]

Within a short time, it became clear that the structure was plagued by problems. It had a leaky roof and electrical defects. Commissioner Alice Wainwright remarked that "it is utterly amazing. . . . We never knew we were buying a stadium without a roof. . . . What they have is just a sunshade." Financial difficulties soon became evident as well. The place stood empty for months and was losing substantial amounts of money. Revenue estimates had proven woefully overoptimistic.[45]

In 1966, a headline in the *Miami News* called the marine stadium the "City's Big Headache." The city manager, who had insisted that privately owned facilities not be built on public land, now proposed to lease the stadium to private operators. Oilman George Engle said he would invest about $18 million to turn the stadium and its grounds into a miniature World's Fair. The project, called Spacerama, would include "space exploration displays, the musical fountains of France, the stone inns and shops of Old Bavaria, international floral decorations, French shops and restaurants, the largest clock in the world—a huge timepiece formed of our own native plants and flowers." There would also be a pantomime theater based on the Tivoli gardens in Denmark, a model of "the world of one million years ago," and a 625-foot tower similar to Seattle's Space Needle.[46] Unfortunately for Engle, city officials posed pesky questions; for example, Robert King High asked "whether the proposal would be consistent with the public's interests and what it would mean—in revenue and in tourists—to Miami." Underscoring its general dysfunctionality, however, the Marine Stadium Advisory Board the commission had appointed had not met for a year.[47]

The idea fizzled amid financial disputes, bitter recriminations, and jurisdictional haggling. The city lost more than $115,000 on the stadium in 1965–1966. The official in charge, Jerry Bell, was fired, while requests were made to reduce stadium rental fees to make it more viable. Moreover, neither the state nor the county provided adequate oversight of the deed restriction that stipulated that the land could be used for the marine stadium and allied purposes only and that title would revert to the county if that clause was violated.[48]

In the coming years, the stadium was used as an event venue rather than for boat racing. The Boston Pops orchestra and Mitch Miller's band played at the stadium, and the ballet *Swan Lake* was staged there. Sammy Davis Jr. arrived at his performance "chauffeured in a new black Cadillac provided by the Miami Beach hotel where he stayed overnight," underscoring the changing times. In early 1970, beat poet Allen Ginsberg was forbidden from reading his controversial poetry at the facility, and in 1971, antiwar singer Joan Baez was barred from performing there. The ACLU successfully sued the city in both cases. In 1970 a sunrise Easter service at the stadium featured singer Anita Bryant and Oregon senator Mark Hatfield, who told the audience that the materialism that pervades the life of individuals and the thinking of governments "is a result of the fear of dying. We try to escape death[,] even the thought of death[,] and seek security in this life, as if it were all that is real." At a floating graduation ceremony for the University of Miami, Yitzhak Rabin, then Israel's ambassador to the United States, warned of the dangers of a "gap divid-ing those who literally reach for the moon from those who do not even know how to reach efficiently into their own soil to produce their daily bread." In 1972, Richard Nixon was driven three miles from his home on Key Biscayne to speak to a young audience at the marine stadium shortly before receiving the Republican nomination for a second term at the convention in Miami Beach. His hug from singer Sammy Davis Jr. was flashed across the nation, signaling support from a well-known black en-tertainer. Later that year, the ACLU asserted that the free use of a public facility for a religious observance violated constitutional provisions on the separation of church and state.[49]

In 1992, the marine stadium was partially destroyed by Hurricane Andrew and people wondered if it should be torn down. The question remains unanswered in 2016, underscoring the continued lack of leader-ship, creativity, and oversight regarding public facilities in Miami.

Who's Afraid of Virginia Key?

From 1970 to 1982, the eroding popularity of Virginia Key Beach was a challenge for the county parks department. The integration of water-front parks left the former "colored beach" with a diminished constitu-ency. The problems associated with how to use Miami's downtown wa-terfront and Virginia Key were closely intertwined with cultural trends, growing poverty at the urban core, political decision making, and weak levels of public engagement.

Controversies over park development in the Miami City Commission had focused largely on Bayfront Park. Voters rejected a bond issue for a convention center on the downtown site. In 1970, speaking for the Save the Bay—Save the Park Committee, attorney Dan Paul threatened to sue to stop the expansion of the park with fill dredged from the bay. The group feared that was "nothing but a subterfuge to get the land and then say, 'Isn't it wonderful, now we can put a building on it.' We (the commit-tee) are violently opposed to filling the bay." The city manager, Mel Re-ese, denied that the city had any intention of erecting a large convention center in the park, which Paul termed "a plain, downright lie," explaining that there had been no talk of filling the bay until the convention center was proposed.[50] In 1972, a $39 million city of Miami Parks for People bond issue passed but was opposed by several neighborhood associations, which claimed that the language on the ballot proposition did not state that most of the funds would be used to improve waterfront parks. The case went to the State Supreme Court, which ruled in the city's favor. Many people were bitter because much of the funding went to buy waterfront land and very little was allocated for neighborhood parks in poor black areas.[51]

A failed attempt to develop public land on city-owned Watson Island in the 1970s also illustrates the larger set of political problems in Miami. City and county officials agreed that this 65-acre island just 800 feet from downtown Miami should become a cultural center that housed an art museum, a science museum, and a new public library. The *Miami News* opposed the idea, warning "if our open spaces disappear we may realize we've lost the most valuable acreage we had, but then it will be too late." The *Herald* opposed locating the library on the island because it was not convenient for patrons, a perspective the library director shared. WTVJ news anchor Ralph Renick also spoke against the complex. In an on-air editorial, he asserted: "We need a simple strip of grass to sit upon . . . somewhere for a moment to contemplate what we do all the rest of the time back in the midst of the concrete. . . . Plopping a government building complex there would destroy it." The idea soon died.[52]

Three years later, the developer of downtown Miami's Omni International Complex proposed that a theme park be located on Watson Island or in Bayfront Park. Development ideas for Watson Island proliferated after the city commission directed the manager to send letters asking developers to submit proposals for an amusement park that was tentatively called Miami Miamigo. Mayor Maurice Ferre and Commissioner Rose Gordon were delighted when Abram Pritzker of Chicago expressed interest. The wealthy magnate accepted a 45-day option, without competing bids, for the $40 million project, which would include $20 million in revenue bonds. Attorney Dan Paul criticized the action because of the lack of competitive bidding, which flew "squarely in the face of the Florida constitutional prohibition against a city using its borrowing power to aid a private corporation." The city agreed to put up $100,000 for a scale model if Pritzker did the same after he told them the financial backers wanted to see one.[53]

Pritzger returned with greater demands and negotiated favorable provisions in an agreement with the city. The city would pay up to $45 million by floating revenue bonds and lease the 30-acre amusement center to Pritzker for up to forty years. Ferre opposed the offer, and commissioners began to raise numerous questions about the deal. One commissioner suggested an alternate site on the mainland that would be developed jointly by the city and county, but business leader Alvah Chapman Jr., publisher of the *Miami Herald* and chair of the Chamber of Commerce's New World Action Committee, said that a government-run theme park "would be a disaster." After the Pritzker negotiations failed, the government negotiated with Diplomat World Enterprises, but that contract became mired in controversy after the city attorney, George Knox, an African American, said that he had been excluded from contract negotiations. In addition, Knox said, his review of the contract indicated "that the wording in some sections is so loose that the manager could make several major decisions the commission usually reserves to itself."[54]

Frustrated by the seeming impossibility of making decisions amid conflicting interests in the waterfront, the public began to support calls for comprehensive planning in the late 1970s. The *Miami News* advocated a master plan for the future use of the city-owned shoreline and asserted that "until such a comprehensive plan is adopted, there should be a moratorium on any changes affecting that city property." The city owned only about 4.2 miles of the 23.7 miles of frontage on the Miami River and Biscayne Bay, excluding the land on Virginia Key and Watson Island. Although pressure from the marine industry and developers was building to lease land for dock space and shopping centers, inertia prevailed, and no waterfront plan emerged.[55]

As blacks were gaining access to Miami's public spaces, the parks themselves were coming under assault from the politics of neglect, urban renewal, and privatization. In 1960, Bill Baggs wrote a column expressing his fury about Miami's neglect of its parks, although he never mentioned that access to parks was racially unequal. "In every older city of importance in the world, the park is beyond the reach of a private use. But not here." Private interests were intruding into Haulover Park, Crandon Park, and Bayfront Park. Baggs declared that "the popular sentiment of thinking ahead and refusing to trade off public lands, keeping the lands and designating them for park purposes are all indications of a grown-up civic attitude." Miami did not yet have that attitude. "We have not altogether got out of our frontier ways and we have not come to know that parks are as vital to the life of a city as sanitation or electricity."[56]

As expressways cut through Miami in the 1960s, they impinged heavily on city parks. City manager Melvin Reese "used aerial photographs . . . to show the Miami City Commission that the new East-West Expressway and the North-South Expressway threaten to destroy or seriously damage five public parks within the city limits of Miami." He pointed to the racial dimension of the problem. Dixie Park was being slashed in half. "The running track, softball diamond and little league diamonds are in the path of the highway engineers. This is particularly bad because Dixie Park is one of the few areas available to the mass Negro population for recreation." Lummus Park on the Miami River was losing an acre and a half with the construction of I-95. Increasing federal dollars and political pressure from newly empowered black politicians such as Athalie Range brought a modicum of increased funding for parks for black Miamians. Some called for parks to be built under the expressways. Range asked for small neighborhood parks to be created on vacant lots. "We hope the parks and playgrounds fare as well" as parking lots, the *Miami Daily News* proclaimed.[57]

Lifestyle editor Terry Johnson King made several trips to Virginia Key in the 1970s. In 1972, shortly before Christmas, she drove to the beach and discovered that it was almost completely deserted. She was alone at the beach, even though three miles away at Crandon Park were "families thigh-to-thigh, wrestling for position on the crowded beach." Why, she wondered, was Virginia Key Beach such a "paragon of privacy?" She answered that it was "mostly habit and a matter of history, it seems. Virginia Key started with a reputation that would put that famed city of Secaucus, New Jersey, to shame; for nobody likes to think about where the refuse goes, and most of Miami's goes to the dumps on the west end of the key." The account that followed reversed the actual chronological order of events but suggested the racist association of sewage and waste with blackness. "Because it was known as the garbage dump, Miami's less-than-enlightened city fathers also declared it a Negro beach in the 1950s, before word of civil and human rights got to the South." When she returned in 1976, she discovered a "closed" sign, as the beach was open only on weekends. A recent Dade County grand jury report had criticized the Metro Dade Parks and Recreation Department for shortchanging "an unending list of dilapidated facilities" as newer parks were built at the expense of maintaining older ones. "There's no excuse for Virginia Beach or any other Metro park being kept closed to the public which makes the parks possible in the first instance. The padlocks ought to be taken from the fences immediately."[58]

It is difficult to determine when and how the beach ceased to be a prime location for the African American community. In the mid-1960s, Virginia Key Beach was still a highly popular location, attracting Martin Luther King among so many others. Yet even then it was beginning to decline. The beaches at Crandon Park were integrated and alternative entertainment venues had been created on the key. Places were not built to last in Miami, and the cultural history of the park was clearly slipping from public consciousness.

Garth Reeves remembered the circumstances that devalued the former black beach. Officials "said, 'Well, they can go anywhere now, we don't have to spend any money. We spent $400,000 on Virginia Beach last year. We don't have to spend this money this year.' So they took the money out of the budget. They let the beach go down, just let the beach go down. Just stopped taking care of it."[59] Athalie Range said that by 1975, Virginia Key Beach had begun "to deteriorate and nobody was doing anything about it. People began going over to Crandon. But [Crandon] was never the same. Because the folks you'd meet at Virginia [Key] beach were your good friends, your neighbors, your church people." As she saw it, the county's intentional failure to maintain the park ensured that the black community's beach at Virginia Key was gradually being forgotten as a historically significant spot.[60]

By the mid-1970s, younger African Americans regarded the "colored beach" as a relic of the bad old days and stayed away. Some thought of it as a stain that needed to be cleaned by forgetting, rather than as a victory that deserved commemorating. Many progressives disparaged the beach as tokenism, which it certainly was. But it had functioned as an important community center, signified a dramatic departure in tactics, and was part of the continuous struggle for access to public facilities in the Miami area.

The issue of keeping Virginia Key Beach open became contentious. In February 1975, several dozen protesters expressed their dismay that the beach was closed on winter weekdays and would soon be closed permanently. "Who's Afraid of Virginia Beach?" read a sign placed on the fence that kept the public out. Officials alleged that the park was "never well attended . . . not when segregated or now." While a hiring freeze prevented the county from filling vacancies at other parks, Virginia Key beach had a ten-person staff on weekdays when there were rarely more than fifteen people there. A 20-year-old lifeguard trainee, Lawrence White, joined others in collecting 1,000 signatures on petitions and tallied the number of cars and people turned away: 75 cars and 120 people between 10 am and noon, they said. "It's not just a black beach," asserted White; "it's a community beach now." Another protestor alleged that if they opened a concession stand and a merry-go-round—which had earlier existed at the park—then the park would pay for itself. Beachgoers formed a Committee for the Preservation of Virginia Key Beach and Park and issued a clear statement: "The beaches belong to the public and this order constitutes a direct affront to the democratic rights of citizens and taxpayers in Dade County."[61]

Miami Herald columnist Bea Hines commented: "It's ridiculous to those of us who grew up here and remember the good times, the beach parties, the long walks along the shores, and the dreams of faraway places, that our beach has reportedly become a haunt for undesirables. Back then, going to Virginia Key Beach was the next best thing to Christmas. . . . It was our beach and we were proud of it." Hines described her nostalgic walk back to the beach. "The swaying palm trees whispering in the breeze had an eerie appearance. I walked over to the 'dancing circle,' a concrete platform where we used to go to dance to the music of a jukebox nailed to a post and saw that the sand had all but covered it. I turned and walked away. The times have changed. People have changed. My children have no special feelings about Virginia Key Beach. To them, a beach is a beach."[62]

The meaning of the earlier struggle for the beach became lost in the politics of the moment. That has been a recurrent condition in Miami. Past struggles have been forgotten amid preoccupations with the newest entrepreneurial initiatives or public cost-cutting. Any sustained vision for the public interest was strikingly absent from press coverage and in the rhetoric and plans of politicians, bureaucrats, and public advocacy groups. The significance of building a movement for civil rights was lost in the illusion some harbored that the struggle for access to the land was over. The eternal vigilance on which democracy depends requires both public memory and the defense of public spaces and mandates frequent reanalysis of contemporary threats in relation to earlier concerns.

The Erosion of a "World-Class" Urban Paradise

Tourism, the Environmental Movement, and Planning Related to Virginia Key Beach, 1982–1998

I fear that environmental campaigns that have captured public imagination—such as the worthy battles to save the wilderness, rainforests, and dolphins—have helped foster the impression that this crisis is primarily about distant places and creatures rather than about the natural systems that support our communities and the larger human civilization. This focus on a "nature" remote from our daily lives has reinforced a dualism within our culture— which imagines a nature separate from the places where we live our lives and make it difficult to perceive our situation clearly.

Dianne Dumanoski (1998)

In 1982, Miami officials promoted Virginia Key as the perfect site for the 1992 World Exposition. Intended to celebrate the 500th anniversary of the arrival of Christopher Columbus, the World Expo was projected to attract 50 million visitors, inject $3 billion into the Miami economy, and create some 80,000 jobs. The public relations coup would put Miami on the world map, promoters promised. In typical fashion, city boosters were long on grand schemes and short on follow-through. For example, the grandiose notion of the New World Center in Bicentennial Park on the downtown waterfront, which was created in 1976, had rapidly turned into a derelict park. The city's reputation for world-class waterfront planning was less than stellar. City planners were unprepared for such an event, and the site that was eventually chosen was Seville, Spain. In a press release announcing its decision, the U.S. Commerce Department called Miami's bid "deficient." The bid failed to take into account the neglected state of the island and reflected the impoverished state of the public sphere in the Miami area.

The lobbying effort to hold the fair on Virginia Key took place the same year that portions of the island were formally transferred from Miami-Dade County to the city of Miami. The agreement stated explicitly that the 80-acre Virginia Key Beach was to be used for "public park purposes only" or it would revert back to the county. Yet soon after that, the beach was closed. In 1999, when several of us questioned the county administrators about their oversight process, we discovered that it had been nonexistent.[1]

The doomed bid encapsulated the Miami style of planning: a high-risk bet on entertainment as a way to replenish the city's depleted finances. The proposal to stage a spectacle on an abandoned island was another in a long line of panaceas for Miami's waterfront, indicating a pattern of willful forgetting and disregard of public spaces that was endemic among South Florida's political leaders and power structure. When the proposal for the fair was cobbled together, there was no mention of the black beach or reference to the social or natural history of the island. A map of the proposed development shows international, national, state, local, and corporate pavilions; a "fiesta square"; and a "Great Hall of the Americas," all located on the sands that had once served black Miamians as a place of their own. The proposal elicited objections from environmentalists because it would have destroyed about thirteen acres of mangroves. Promoters stated that "we intend to work with environmental groups to preserve or restore mangroves and sea grasses." Yet at the time, , the beach's social history was not part of the environment in the minds of both promoters and environmentalists.[2] City planners and private developers did not take into account the significance of Virginia Key Beach to Miami's civil rights movement. Building visually compelling global attractions, creating facilities for the elite, and becoming a world-class city were the topics of the era. The black community's civil right to public space was not a compelling concern.

Miami in Disarray

From 1982 to 1999, the city's vision for Virginia Key Beach focused on a globally branded theme park that never materialized. During this period Miami was the most violent and volatile city in the nation. The image of Miami as an urban paradise imploded when race riots began on May 17, 1980, after police officers involved in the brutal death of black insurance salesman and veteran Arthur McDuffie were acquitted. No riots had been so violent since the conflagrations that followed the assassination of Martin Luther King.[3]

Miami was also the epicenter of urban disorder as a result of massive immigration. Some 125,000 Cubans arrived unexpectedly via the Mariel boatlift in 1980. More than 60,000 Haitians fled their country's brutal regime, and more than 1,000 were incarcerated in the Krome Detention Center in southern Dade County. Federal authorities applied a double standard, admitting Cubans—black and white—who were imagined to be refugees from communism while placing Haitians, who were non-white, under suspicion.[4]

Since the 1960s, the national media had represented Miami as at best tawdry and at worst disorderly. A November 1981 cover story on southeast Florida began: "An epidemic of violent crime, a plague of illicit drugs and a tidal wave of refugees have slammed into South Florida with the destructive power of a hurricane. Those three forces, and a number of lesser ills, threaten to turn one of the nation's most prosperous, congenial and naturally gorgeous regions into a paradise lost." It enumerated the signs of impending catastrophe: "In the past five years, 220,000 guns have been sold in Dade County—an average of more than seven guns for every new household. . . . It is easier to buy a pistol than an automobile in Florida, where the gun lobby has frustrated virtually all attempts at handgun controls." The situation of African Americans was particularly alarming: "Stuck on the bottom rung of South Florida's economic ladder, they have always resented the more prosperous Cuban minority. With the arrival of the Marielitos, blacks feared that they would lose out in the scramble for the few low-skill jobs available in the region. Even in Liberty City, the black enclave in North Miami where 18 people died in last year's riot, the Latin influence is apparent. White store owners who abandoned their businesses are being replaced by Latin landlords." Politicians had avoided coming to terms with these profound economic and social problems. "Community boundaries dart haphazardly: they were often drawn by developers who wanted to run their towns as well as build them." Dade County had "27 separate and often rival municipal governments. . . . The result is that the region confronts major crises that could break the will of many communities, while being cursed with a political system that hardly functions well in the best of times."[5]

Planning for the future was limited by narrow political agendas instead of coming to terms with the problems of the region. The city's political and economic culture was shaped by such male-dominated groups as the Greater Miami Chamber of Commerce, the Convention and Tourist Bureau, the Latin Builders Association, and the more informal Non-Group. Thus, Miami remained a trade and tourist center, although major firms in the fields of law, international banking, and architecture and major corporate headquarters made it a hemispheric capital city unlike any other in the South. Its leaders boldly called it the "New World City." In 1980 the city of Miami engaged sculptor Isamu Noguchi to redesign Bayfront Park. Although Noguchi envisioned the space as a "village green," the plan involved demolishing the library and tearing down the bandstand that famed bandleader Caesar LaMonaca had used since the 1920s. Bayfront Park, which had new amphitheaters (one sponsored by AT&T) and a laser light tower, also featured a gargantuan water sculpture that was eventually discovered to be too expensive to operate. *Miami Today* columnist Michael Lewis concluded: "That's how Miami handles assets. It spends big to buy, build or acquire them, then lets them rot."[6]

Two scholars have recently assessed the fate of Miami's public spaces. In *Miami: Mistress of the Americas*, Jan Nijman argues that "urban public space serve as a city's living room—where different people come together to enjoy each other within an inviting environment." But "most Miamians reject this notion, instead valuing private spaces." He suggests that the torrid climate, social polarization, and transience have led people to devalue public spaces. Significantly, he discovered that in five waterfront census tracts abutting the causeway to Virginia Key, 70 percent of residents have primary homes elsewhere.[7]

According to architectural historian Gray Read,

Four genres of events characterized public space in the modern city of Miami: spectacle, civic life, shopping and sport. All are types of performance that define places for those who act and those who watch. The drama revolves around who acts, who watches and how they relate to one another. For example, spectacles present the actions of a few people to a crowd who are separated by a clear threshold such as a proscenium arch. On the other hand, civic life is reciprocal, people seeing each other and being seen in a public realm traditionally defined by a dignified architecture. A civic performance can be simply dressing nicely to go downtown, as most people did in the 50s and 60s. Shopping is a part of civic life that includes displays in shop windows as well as discussions and actions by shoppers so the show happens on both sides of the glass. Finally, sport is physical performance, whether anyone is watching or not. Architectural design sets up all of these situations, placing actors and spectators in strategic spatial relationships with one another.[8]

While each of these genres provide performance space that illustrates the plasticity between public and private spaces, this interesting analysis overlooks the complex and long, drawn-out political struggle in Miami to define and control racialized public spaces within bureaucratic structures. These all become part of the larger set of problems Dolores Hayden has identified: "As the production of built space increases in intensity and scale during the later twentieth century, the politics of space becomes more difficult to map."[9] Neither Read nor Nijman adequately examines the fundamental factors involved in the politics of land use in Miami: the shrouded power of politically connected entrepreneurs, inadequate government planning, the lack of attention to cultural memory, and the fact that constituents do not have input into how public spaces are designed and cared for.

Like Virginia Key, other public places in Miami were woefully neglected. Bobby Maduro Stadium, a locally popular training camp for professional baseball athletes, was allowed to decay and finally sold for housing. The James L. Knight Convention Center, located downtown on the Miami River, a joint venture with the Hyatt Regency Hotel, the University of Miami, and the city that linked meeting, performance, and convention spaces, never found a substantial market. To this day, it "lingers underused as the city tries to sell its asset," according to editor Michael Lewis. A convention center on the waterfront in Coconut Grove blocked the view of the water and became defunct; until recently, it functioned only as a movie studio. It is now becoming a new waterfront park, although the process has been mired in controversy. The Miami Arena, which the city built in 1985 as a new home for the Miami Heat, was abandoned, sold, and leveled little more than a decade later because the city had scrimped on costs, wealthy fans wanted luxury skyboxes, and the team sought to increase revenue.[10] The opposing yet codependent forces of attention and neglect, development and erasure, have long shaped Miami's waterfront.

County Commissioner Harvey Ruvin attempted to secure environmental legislation that would affect the entire bay in the 1970s and 1980s. He was involved in the passage of the Florida's Growth Management Act of 1985 and other legislation that set up the Environmentally Endangered Lands Program. He sought to create a "uniform set of standards that kept people from orienting their development in a way that shamed the bay," for example by "putting their Dempsy dumpsters right on the bay at the back part of the building and not landscaping." But the idea of comprehensive regional planning was regarded as too radical; "I was called a communist," he remembers. "'You're going to tell people how to use their property?' Well, I'm sorry, zoning is a privilege. It's not a right. And that one piece interrelates with everything else and therefore it has to be considered in its development capacity. You have to consider what the impacts are gonna be." Ruvin argued that funds earmarked for environmentally endangered lands should not be "only spent for pristine, natural, environmental . . . more rural areas and things like that. My argument was if that's your standard then you're ruling out anything in any part of urbanized Florida and what you should be looking at is its relative[ly] pristine nature [compared] to its surroundings."[11]

By the 1980s, Miami's tourism industry was beset by intense competition from Disney World and the panoply of central Florida theme parks that redefined tourism as a new world of corporate-dominated entertainment zones. Susan Davis writes:

The theme park specializes in experiential homogeneity. Replacing the petty carnival and midway entrepreneurs with the corporation's own centrally produced and managed attractions, Disney

and his followers gained control over profits, the quality of concessions, and—just as important to advertisers and sponsors—image
and style. This totalizing effort is captured in the industry phrase
"to theme." Surface stylistic characteristics are highly coordinated
in "theming," but more important, the meanings the park contains are centrally produced to be as non-conflictual as possible.
Paradoxically, this overall uniformity is expressed as a rich variety of artifacts, cultures, histories, styles, texts, architectures, and
performances.[12]

Many cities rushed to convert their older downtown districts into entertainment zones and gentrified neighborhoods. Global cities were becoming increasingly "ephemeral," Joel Kotkin has argued. "An economy
oriented to entertainment, tourism and 'creative' functions is ill suited
to provide upward mobility for more than a small slice of its population.
Focused largely on boosting culture and constructing spectacular buildings, urban governments may tend to neglect more mundane industries,
basic education, or infrastructure. Following such a course, they are likely
to evolve ever more into 'dual cities,' made up of a cosmopolitan elite and
a large class of those, usually at low wages, who service their needs."[13]

At the same time that Miami was struggling to maintain its share of
the tourist market, it was suffering from an increase in street crime, a
significant exodus of Anglos, and intense traffic congestion. Although
the economy began to pick up in the mid-1980s, Garth Reeves, editor of
the *Miami Times*, remarked that "everyone is moving on. And here we are
standing by the corner watching the parade go by."[14]

Placelessness in a Theme Park World

Tourism and the pleasure industries were moving to a new organizational and conceptual level of dehistoricized placelessness, reflecting the
entrepreneurial values of the day and promotional experts' dominance
of media. This trend was epitomized in Miami by the powerful cruise
line industry, where destinations became secondary to the highly organized mass spectacle of the experience on the ship. Miami leaders felt
compelled to immerse the city in this wider economic stream, with little

sense of the value of public land or local history beyond their tie-in to commercial purposes.[15]

Benjamin Barber writes that "branding and privatization turn out to work in tandem. As identity moves away from public categories rooted in religion and nationality and toward commercial categories associated with brands and consumables, identity itself is privatized (though hardly individualized!). To brand a public institution is effectively to privatize it. Over the last twenty years, institutions from sports stadiums to colleges have been renamed, branded, and effectively both privatized and commercialized."[16]

Virginia Key and the entire Miami waterfront have long been developed in a disconnected way without any overall consistent planning effort. This connects to broader cultural trends that have tied the city's fragmented identity to increasingly global capital flows. The work of William Cronon and Tim Cresswell, among others, reminds us that the impact of modern transience or fluidity are experienced in a magnified way in tourist-dominated urban settings. Jan Nijman finds Miami to be mostly characterized by transience in which "public spaces are, in principle, for locals, much the same ways that a living room is principally meant for those living in the home." The impact of so much transience and so many part-time residents on the public waterfront commodifies it while reinforcing the value of placelessness within what he calls an "urban perpetuum mobile."[17]

Yet how that fluidity becomes fused to the politics of waterfront development is shaped by public perceptions that politicians and the news media create. Although public land comes in many shapes and serves many purposes, it often has a value beyond promoting economic growth. It can provide a sense of solidity and continuity of identity in the historical struggle to forge a more politically inclusive and responsive city, region, or nation, and it can commemorate shared sacrifices and memories of past injustice and triumph. Yet over time, these more intangible factors often become lost because the news media serve those who are able to pay for advertising and public relations. Governments often neglect parks in their efforts to fund such essential public services as schools and police and fire departments. Yet public space has a clear impact on public health, it enhances surrounding real estate value, and it offers a sense of peace, continuity of identity, and resonance with the natural world.[18]

During the Reagan and George W. Bush administrations, positive associations with notions of the public that were related to service, work, and even civic engagement were undermined. Grand public relations stunts such as celebrating the Statue of Liberty or promoting concern for the homeless by people clasping "Hands Across America" on May 26, 1986, were substitutes for genuine engagement. Military adventures and the idea that government should be run like a business were prevalent. Anne Gorsuch, Reagan's director of the Environmental Protection Agency, and James Watt, Reagan's secretary of the interior, promoted the rapid privatization of the public resources.[19]

South Florida's emerging role as a cruise ship capital and home of the art deco district of South Beach and the emerging identification of the region with hip multiculturalism and drugs, professional sports venues, and fashionable style left it vulnerable to narrowly defined corporate promotional appeals. Individual leisure styles became ever more valued. But boosterism could not address the problems of violence, including the nationally publicized murder of tourists in 1993, and a high rate of homelessness, which of course affected the city's parks.[20]

By 1999, Miami had the highest poverty rate in the nation. The city's government had just gone through bankruptcy and an embarrassing spate of corruption scandals. The fate of Virginia Key became part of various attempts to sell off public land for a variety of commercial ventures. Miami's dominant political culture continually put its environmental assets at risk, devaluing its public spaces and forgetting the complex needs of its citizenry.[21]

Buffeted by racial and ethnic divisions, dazzled by shopping malls and celebrity fads, and imbued with a culture of cynicism, most Miami-area residents in the 1980s and 1990s were unable to grasp the fate of the natural world and the public spaces around them. The sad state of the Everglades and complex systems of water management, the massive scale of suburban sprawl and sorry state of public transportation, and the growing financial mismanagement of the city of Miami all seemed overwhelming, sustaining a sense of futility about shaping the urban environment. In her assessment of the state of local civic life, sociologist Rosabeth Moss Kanter argued that Miami's abysmal lack of a sense of community derived from its lack of social cohesion and from political immaturity. Geographer Jan Nijman observed in 1997 that "it is striking how many people claim they are here temporarily, even if they have no firm future plan to relocate."[22]

Roberta Brandes Gratz's sad observations of the state of the nation apply to Miami: "We do not communicate, relate or connect as a people. And we have few public places left to do that even when we choose to do so. We have eliminated public places from the physical and mental geography of the country. Without the variety of common grounds on which a diverse people mix and mingle in an unplanned manner, the health of the commonweal is undermined. The national landscape no longer differentiates between places. The look of anywhere prevails. And if people don't know and feel where they are, they don't know who they are. . . . We despair but we accept these physical changes as inevitable; allow those who benefit financially and professionally to rationalize its continuance."[23]

Humor heightened public cynicism. *Miami Herald* columnist Dave Barry's spoof of Miami's history ended with several nuggets: "Bayfront Park has been transformed, after years of planning and expenditure, from a downtown waterfront property occupied by vagrants into a downtown waterfront property occupied by vagrants and a fountain that never seems to be working. . . . Downtown Miami is also the site of the Miami Arena, which was completed by the city in 1988 at a cost to taxpayers of $52.5 million; thanks to the foresight and planning that went into this facility, it is expected to continue to meet Miami's arena needs until well into next week."[24]

Yet pressures to transform Miami into a "world-class city" remained strong. Following a national trend, targeted funding for a variety of public purposes were actually used to further particular business interests. Business Improvement Districts (BIDs) provided tax advantages designed to help downtown merchants compete with suburban malls. Managed areas with tight security and attractive streetscapes promoted tourism. In 1985, Miami's BID created Bayside Marketplace; the agreement that other parkland would be provided as compensation for the lost waterfront parkland was never fulfilled. Not until the housing boom that marked the new millennium would people flock back to the city to live. Yet in stark contrast to other tourist locations, notably Hawai'i,

Miami gave developers wide latitude without adequately assessing impact fees or ensuring sustainable designs.[25]

Administrators leased the city's publicly owned waterfront to private
entrepreneurs. Mayor Maurice Ferre tried to revive the downtown but
often deferred to the grand designs of big-name architects and planners
and accepted the terms private ventures set. Officials saw the public waterfront as a commodity to be leased at below-market rents for schemes
that promised to stimulate the local economy. Hotels, casino boats, port
facilities, retail operations, and theme park attractions were promoted
with little sense of how they fit into an integrated waterfront. Miami's
regional rail transportation system was among the most poorly planned
in the nation. Its chief urban rival in Florida, Orlando, had become the
largest theme park city in the world following the advent of Disney World
and other attractions, while Miami was generally seen as a crime-ridden,
violent, corrupt, and alien place. Ironically, the nationally broadcast TV
series *Miami Vice* (1984–1990) was instrumental in reviving South Beach
as a major tourist attraction with a hip postmodern aura.[26]

Themed cities under the control of consortiums of private investors
developed an array of new modes of attracting visitors. Tourism that focused on culture, recreation, and entertainment boomed in some cities.
According to Sharon Zukin, Las Vegas, Los Angeles, and Miami showed
the way to an economic development strategy based on the "sale and consumption of pleasure," the location of objects in space that was generally
driven by private land deals. The example of Miami also underscores the
contention of Michael Sorkin and Susan Davis that "as cities restructure
themselves along touristic principals, the theme park extends outward,
undermining older city forms and recasting urban areas as 'variations on
a theme park.' Public meeting spaces become subsumed under private
controls and public debate grows dimmer."[27]

Public parks have not been able to rival the spectacles produced in
large stadiums or on TV. Recent theorists have been critical of the notion of parks as a counterspace of zones of freedom, self-determination,
and choice because they remain pervaded by commercial values. More
measurably popular than "passive" parks, sports arenas promote drama
that melds human elements into grand tableaux of color and light, action, and vast crowds of enthusiastic fans. When combined with exciting
architectural forms and tie-ins with television promotions, retail outlets,

and even the lure of nostalgia, sports spectacles function as compelling community rituals.[28] Advocates for urban waterfront parks in Miami were no match for these larger cultural forces.

The Environmental Movement and the Management of Growth

The lack of consistent follow-through regarding comprehensive planning for Virginia Key was not appreciably altered by the environmental and growth management movements of the late 1960s through the 1980s. Although Congress never passed a national land use planning law, federal legislation such as the Clean Water Act (1972) and the National Environmental Protection Act (1970) created environmental regulations and funding sources that brought greater scrutiny and some coherence to the development of barrier islands such as Virginia Key. However, the authority of environmental agencies was limited and jurisdictional control over Virginia Key was divided between city, county, state, and federal authorities. The result was years of inaction, lack of regulatory oversight, and neglect.[29]

During the twentieth century, state and federal actions altered the region's hydrology by building a set of canals to siphon off groundwater during flood season. This changed water levels in the Everglades system to the point where they were sometimes inadequate. This rapidly became a life-and-death issue for South Floridians. More than 3 million people lived in the area east of the Everglades, and the need to alternately control seasonal flooding and release more water in the dry season, the growth of new subdivisions, and the hidden costs of infrastructure required politicians to make economic choices that often were not transparent. Programs to help house or employ the poor, for example, were underfunded in order to pay for suburban infrastructure. Growth was skewed toward the needs of developers whose lobbyists well understood where public dollars were located.

Building on the establishment of Everglades National Park in 1947, the environmental movement came into political favor throughout Florida in the late 1960s. Activists were able to stop plans to build a barge canal in the northern part of the state and a proposal for a major jetport that would have destroyed Big Cypress Swamp. In the 1970s and 1980s, Governors Reubin Askew and Bob Graham instituted measures that limited development and established reporting mechanisms through two new state-level departments: the Department of Environmental Regulation and the Department of Community Affairs. These were established to gather, comment on, and to some degree regulate comprehensive development master plans in all the state's cities and counties. Speaking before a Dade County audience in 1971, Askew decried the mishandling of a host of environmental issues. He pointed to the loss of freshwater springs in Biscayne Bay and expressed concern about the possibility of a water shortage in the future. The health of Biscayne Bay was increasingly recognized as essential to the sustainability of the entire metropolitan region.[30]

In 1971, in a first step toward controlling growth, Dade County commissioner Harvey Ruvin called for a six-month moratorium on building permits for new multi-unit structures on Key Biscayne. Ruvin, an attorney who was then vice-president of the Tropical Audubon Society, became a consultant to the Key Biscayne Taxpayers' Association, a group that was trying to limit the development of accommodations for tourists and tighten zoning regulations. He advised the association to ask the county to make a land use plan, but before such a plan could be completed, real estate developers filed for many new zoning permits. In response, Ruvin drafted an ordinance to delay them and set up public hearings on proposed developments. Ruvin later recalled that when the county commission failed to pass his ordinance,

> I came back immediately with an initiatory petition that they had to approve. . . . Well, with this whole network of Key Biscayne, Audubon, we went out and got signatures. I recall we got 18,000 signatures; we needed 12,000. You had to get them in 30 days, too. We forced it on the ballot. The building industry went bananas. . . . You know, this is communism; this is gonna kill construction; this is a terrible thing for the economy. They raised a ton of money. I was fortunate because the Fairness Doctrine was in place, and I got a great deal of [television] time to combat what they were doing. The argument that I had was so logical. It was saying, hey, if we're doing a study, why waste the money on study if it could be forestalled? The public voted for it 2 to 1, 2½ to 1.[31]

This victory emboldened environmental advocates.

In 1972, Dade County's metro government began to institute more comprehensive land use planning. Several reformers, including Harvey Ruvin and John B. Orr Jr., were elected to the commission after a petition campaign led by an activist group called the Committee for Sane Growth. A new comprehensive master plan soon followed. Remarkably, a set of citizen task forces wrote an environmental protection guide and a metropolitan development guide. In 1974, Luther Carter discerned "a political majority behind concepts of land use and growth control that answer to humanistic, aesthetic, and ecological considerations as well as to economic interests."[32] Environmental interest groups gained significant political power in the 1970s and 1980s.

This culminated in the Growth Management Act of 1985, a state law that required localities to submit zoning and land use classifications to the state Department of Community Affairs for review to ensure consistency. Understaffing resulted in ineffective oversight, however, and few questions were raised about the veracity of the reports local governments issued. In Miami, the reporting process meant conjuring up some rather unique notions of park uses. The city designated underwater parcels, health clinics, rooftops, Neighborhood Enhancement Team offices, police stables, and other clearly nonpark areas as parkland. There were few limits on how public space could be redefined or rezoned. Later, the Growth Management Act was largely gutted in the 2011 legislative session under the powerful influence of developers and the leadership of Governor Rick Scott.[33]

To address land acquisition and treat problems of the quantity and quality of water as a public health issue, local environmental groups lobbied state legislators. But most of their efforts focused on the Everglades. In Miami, Fairchild Tropical Botanic Garden and other private parks designed by nationally renowned landscape architects such as William Lyman Phillips, a protégé of Fredrick Law Olmsted, were prioritized. However, environmentalists failed to pay equal attention to urban public parks.[34] Other activists were drawn to issues of civil rights and historic preservation—for good reason—but often ignored issues related to urban parks. Local parks were largely underfunded, and set up for failure by administrators who saw suburban back yards as more important to families than public parkland.[35]

Miami was the home of the major private university in the state and to celebrated writers and environmental activists, and the city's scientists and activists worked to promote environmentally sensitive notions of the public interest. Newspapermen Ernest Coe and Bill Baggs, public health writer Philip Wylie, and authors Marjory Stoneman Douglas and Robert Frost joined numerous grassroots environmental groups. After Biscayne National Monument (later Biscayne National Park) was established in 1968 and a number of marine life "dead zones" were identified in the bay as a result of discharges of warm water from the nuclear power plant at Turkey Point (which was established in the early 1970s), the interdependence of Biscayne Bay and water issues throughout the region became an important concern.[36]

Yet powerful economic interests continued to influence local development policy regarding Miami's beaches in the 1970s and 1980s. The relationship between public access to beaches and the erosion of the shoreline in Miami Beach is a clear example. Instead of welcoming federal dollars to widen the beaches, many hotel owners opposed such measures because of the increased public access to their beachfronts wider beaches would bring. Nonetheless, the Army Corps of Engineers built miles of "renourished" but artificially created beachfront for the public on Miami Beach during the 1970s, although private interests continued to contest public access. After Virginia Key Beach was reinvigorated in the new century and although consciousness of global warming raised new questions about intervening on a barrier island, the U.S. Army Corps of Engineers spent millions on expanding the beach in response to the increasing political clout of African Americans.[37]

Parks across the nation were increasingly being perceived as revenue centers rather than as open spaces that should be free for public use. Miami-Dade County's park system had developed under the powerful, visionary leadership of A. D. Barnes, who began the county parks department in 1933 and continued to lead it for decades. By the 1980s, Dade County parks superintendent Chuck Pezoldt and other officials saw parks as revenue generators and sought to significantly increase fees the public paid. Fees were raised at Crandon Park on Key Biscayne east of Virginia Key, Haulover Beach to the north, and Matheson Hammock Park further south.[38]

Environmentalists and park advocates, led by attorney Dan Paul, achieved striking results with the passage of the Parks for People bond issue in 1972. Yet its eventual outcome underscores the difficulty of preserving waterfront park space in the face of powerful economic pressures to privatize it. Mayor Maurice Ferre was unable to complete a waterfront park that would have included access to the Miami River; the project languishes to this day.[39]

The 1987 City of Miami Master Plan, which was overseen by city planner Jack Luft, enunciated a set of principles that seemed environmentally and politically sound, such as the concepts that "natural forces shall be allowed to shape natural edges" and "all access to and use of the island shall serve recreational needs." Yet some language left doors wide open for reinterpretation: the plan said that "commercial uses shall be water related or dependent" and that "commercial uses shall be confined to the water's edge to promote public access, use and enjoyment of the water." The subsequent actions of the city's planning department signaled a desire to change deed restrictions and facilitate commercialization without improving or protecting public lands.[40]

Transferred, Marginalized, and Forgotten

The pressures from private developers and the jurisdictional disputes that created obstacles to public oversight led to bureaucratic inertia regarding planning and the maintenance of public land along Miami's waterfront. On December 4, 1979, the Board of County Commissioners approved an agreement to exchange ten properties with the city of Miami, one of which was on Virginia Key. Miami wanted to include county-owned land in a planned 1,400-acre park on the key. The city parks department's assistant director and the county's capital improvements coordinator concurred that the park should be a "nature oriented" and "marine-oriented" park. A youth camp, something environmentalist Mabel Miller had advocated for a long time, and an environmental and park maintenance training center could be located there. But city staff opposed the idea because it would yield little or no financial return and the youth camp was not created. Virginia Key Beach was formally transferred from Miami-Dade County to the city of Miami in 1982 as part of this land swap. The deed stated that "the property is restricted to public park purposes only to be kept open to the public, providing maintenance and a level of service equal to or exceeding that which was provided by the County." Any changes had to follow a 1982 master plan that had been approved by the Board of County Commissioners.[41]

Several other touchy issues involving Virginia Key arose at that time. Officials were especially agitated about nude sunbathers who congregated in a secluded area just north of the public beach, formerly the "black beach." The city shut down this portion of the beach in 1985, after naturists found a place at Haulover Beach and the state Supreme Court ruled that selective locations should be made available for nude sun bathing on public land.[42]

In the aftermath of the failure to win the World Expo in 1982, the city agreed to pay Synterra, Ltd., a Philadelphia planning firm, $135,000 to develop a plan for a 600-acre nature park on the key. The city received matching state funding. However, Parks director Carl Kern said it was not "cost effective" to maintain such a park without a master plan. In 1983, city manager Howard Gary suggested paying for the Synterra proposal with a $55 million bond issue for upgrading all city parks. But in 1984, voters rejected a $25 million bond issue that would have included a park on Virginia Key. The next year, a proposal to develop a marina, a theme park, shops, and restaurants on Virginia Key stalled because of inadequate political and financial support.[43] Officials remained uncertain about what could be done with Virginia Key. Turning it into a money-making asset had proven impossible. From 1982 to 2000, the historic Virginia Key Beach Park was effectively closed to the public. It was used occasionally as a police shooting range, a place for a dog kennel, a movie set, and a rental facility for events. The condition of the buildings deteriorated and memories about its role in Miami's history faded as well.

Public Parkland for Sale, Price Negotiable

In the 1980s and 1990s, the city was beset by ugly political warfare, corruption scandals, and economic woes that proved to be the groundwork for setting up waterfront parks for private development. Bayside, a waterfront shopping and dining mall, had been created in Miami's historic Bayfront Park following a 1985 agreement with the Rouse Company. The contract provided that 7 percent of the profits generated from Bayside would go to the city to buy replacement waterfront land, but that proviso was never fully carried out. Indeed, after a drop in profits in 2008, the rent Bayside paid to the city was cut in half by an updated agreement. By then, Rouse had been bought out by the ominously named shopping mall behemoth General Growth. An audit also raised serious questions about whether the company was paying the required amount into a Bayside Minority Foundation to assist minority-owned business operations in the area.[44]

In 1995, in the wake of the devastation Hurricane Andrew had wrought in city parks three years before, the *Miami Herald* reported that the city was "contemplating three multimillion dollar waterfront projects that would allow commercial entities to move into public park land and pay city coffers a combined $2.5 million or more each year in rent." First, Parrot Jungle, a private theme park, sought to take parkland on nearby Watson Island. Second, an ecology oriented campground and RV park was to be created on Virginia Key, and third, the Port of Miami was projected to expand, bringing cruise ship terminals to Bicentennial Park. But the city could not support such proposals. According to City Commissioner Victor De Yurre, the city of Miami government did "not have the money to do these kinds of projects. We have to work with the private sector. They make money and we make money and everybody benefits." University of Miami professor Aristides Millas strongly disagreed, contending that "open space is nature in the city. The history of Miami is to develop and overdevelop. Everything is for sale." He added that "people used to be able to go to Watson Island and picnic and watch the cruise ships go by. That doesn't happen anymore." Attorney Dan Paul commented that city administrators "always say, 'These parks are run down, and people have stopped using them so why don't we cut them up or sell them to a developer?' It's insane." City administrators contended that because of the acute problems of homelessness and crime, the city no longer could control its parks but that combined private investment estimated at $240 million would bring vitality back to the waterfront.[45]

In March 1995, the city requested proposals for a 500-site campground on 152 acres of Virginia Key. While the plan was alleged to be environmentally friendly, it was clearly designed to provide badly needed revenue. At the same time, with this proposal, the city was seeking to lift deed restrictions on the use of public parkland. Jack Luft told the *Miami New Times* that the island was already "a highly disturbed environment. . . . It's been dredged, bulldozed, killed." He saw the plan as an "extraordinary opportunity" to turn a burden into an asset. Luft described what Virginia Key offered to those who would be able to afford to go there. "Imagine getting off work on a Friday afternoon. If you're going to drive to a recreational campground in a natural environment, simply getting back and forth will take most of the weekend. With Virginia Key, you're there in five minutes. You can call ahead and have your trailer taken out of storage. You get there in the evening, maybe bring a bottle of wine and a good book. And now you have your whole weekend to spend in this wonderful, natural environment."[46]

Interestingly, the only commissioner who voted against the commercialization of the key was its sole African American, Miller Dawkins, who said that he wanted "children and grandchildren to know what open space looks like." Eventually the proposal was defeated in a 1995 referendum that was required for commercial development on waterfront parkland. Mabel Miller and her group Friends of Virginia Key worked with the Tropical Audubon Society to spearhead the opposition and mobilize voters. Miller was particularly wary of the proposed water theme park: "Water parks don't do well in winter. . . . If it goes down, the developer cries poverty and says, 'We have to build a resort, we can't make money.' Then they can change anything they want."[47]

From 1988 to 2003, the city park system, even under the caring and sensitive leadership of director Alberto Ruder, was hampered by the lack of funding and political backing from commissioners who constantly deferred to demands for funds from firefighters, police, and other emergency services. The Parks and Recreation Department had little formal control over Virginia Key. City development officials tended to run roughshod over the department as they tried to sell off the parks as unused and inefficient spaces. One city agency advertisement appealed to investors to develop large swaths of Virginia Key even though the deed restrictions had not been changed. Dena Bianchino, in particular, moved back and forth between working for the city administration and for private developers, notably The Related Group, which was headed by Jorge Perez, a former city planner turned billionaire.[48]

The problem of homelessness affected Virginia Key indirectly. In 1997, the U.S. district court decision in *Pottinger v. Miami* mandated that Miami city police alter its procedures for dislodging the homeless from parks and stop disposing of their personal effects, which the court found to be a violation of their constitutional rights. The homeless now had a defensible civil right to public space.[49]

The deepening economic crisis that afflicted Miami, the profound cynicism of citizens about local government, policies that favored the private management of public property, and the mantra of public/private "partnerships" created a major challenge for the small group of activists who sought to preserve Virginia Key. By the late 1990s, most environmental activists were windsurfers, bird enthusiasts, or Sierra Club or Tropical Audubon Society activists. Eventually, however, they found common ground in the goals of enforcing deed restrictions on the commercialization of public land and involving the people in the planning process.

Waterfront Liquidation

By the 1990s, a complex array of political and economic developments had undermined the value of Virginia Key Beach as a public park. Maintenance was not done, the city had failed to enforce deed restrictions, and the beach was closed to the public without any public announcement. Decades after the integration of public accommodations had been established by law, the former black beach had become largely forlorn and deserted. The city of Miami had forgotten its history in its rush to make abandoned land generate revenue by converting the park into a high-end eco-resort. Virginia Key soon became part of a broader struggle waged by a fragile new multicultural coalition to reclaim and redefine public space along Miami's waterfront. Doing historical research and championing the clearly worded yet officially overlooked enforcement of deed restrictions became strategies coalitions used to preserve the land.

Beginning in the 1970s, Friends of Virginia Key, a group of environmentalists led by nature educator Mabel Miller, fought both to preserve the natural attributes of the island and to get public officials to enforce existing deed restrictions, but the group did not have enough political influence to shape a future plan for the beach or the island itself. Time and integration had eroded African Americans' positive associations with the beach and worked against projects that sought to preserve this public space. Black Miamians had built a sense of group identity at the beach even before they publically asserted they had a right to be there.

As geographer Don Mitchell has observed, "By claiming space in public, by creating public spaces, social groups themselves become public." Virginia Key had served as a site for African Americans to nurture group solidarity. As integration opened up other parks, however, many blacks began to look back with some disdain on Virginia Key Beach as inferior to white facilities. To some, it had even become an embarrassment.

By the late 1990s, the purpose of public land had been redefined in terms of the revenue it produced. The Department of Development, which at the time was led by planners Jack Luft, Dianne Johnson, and Dena Bianchino, had eclipsed the Parks and Recreation Department in terms of ability to shape public policy. This vision for the privatization of public land was promoted by the City Manager Donald Warshaw, Mayor Joe Carollo, and a majority of the city commissioners. However, in the 1990s, the city had to provide a comprehensive development master plan and evaluation and appraisal reports in order to comply with the state's Growth Management Act of 1985. City planners manipulated data to show that they had the requisite 1.3 acres of parkland per thousand residents. By early 2000, as one commentator noted, parkland could include a waste dump, a boat ramp, a shopping mall, a sewer plant, and a cemetery. Journalist Jacob Bernstein remarked that "in 1972 the U.S. Department of the Interior deeded 4.46 acres of waterfront property [in Coconut Grove] to the City of Miami for public parks and recreation. The feds gave the land, which housed a hangar and seaplane dock, to the city for free. They reserved the right to reclaim the property if it was not used as intended. Today much of the 'park' serves as a parking lot for the popular eatery Monty's (whose original owner, convicted felon Monty Trainer, was a frequent visitor to city hall)." Commissioner Johnnie Winton and many others were generally unaware of existing deed restrictions and assumed that Bicentennial Park and Virginia Key had been excluded from the new list of city properties that could be sold because city officials had long planned to sell them for private development anyway. Other commissioners saw the move to lease public land as evidence that city administrators were "hiding their plans for future development from the state in the same way they hide it from the city commission." Wallis Tinnie, an African American woman, protested that "it is not the park that they value so little; it is the people. . . . They have decided how much they think those people deserve or need." Tinnie asserted that the city had abandoned its public properties because once people stop visiting them it is much easier to sell them off. Park advocate Dan Paul summed up the situation: "The public's parkland and open spaces are being slowly eroded and taken away without their realizing, and by the time it finally dawns on them it will be too late. There will be concrete everywhere."[50]

The attempt to lift deed restrictions, change zoning categories, and offer new leases to develop Virginia Key was announced in April 1997 by Jack Luft, an experienced urban planner with a keen understanding of the politics of land development. The key had passed environmental tests for development, he alleged. At the time, the city was looking for comprehensive development ideas. One brochure titled "Miami: Changing at the Speed of Magic," sought developers for the entire Marine Stadium Basin and the beach area. The next year, city manager Donald Warshaw sought changes in deed restrictions from Miami-Dade County so the city could develop the neglected lands into commercial properties.[51] However, the city could not proceed without the approval of the county and the state's Internal Improvement Board.

Miami's public waterfront was under siege. It had increasingly become the site of a culture of spectacle and corporate dominance. Bayfront Park, with its free concerts and beautiful gardens, had been replaced by the Bayside shopping mall and casino gambling boat concessions. The view of the water was blocked. Commercialization significantly limited Bayfront Park's public character.[52]

A Cultural Shift?

By the end of the twentieth century, what had once been a drumbeat that promoted the virtues of taking public land for commercial ventures on Miami's waterfront had become more like a steamroller. City administrators assumed that the public seldom went to parks in the tropical climate; that parks were unsafe and were largely inhabited by the homeless; and that reviving public spaces required massive amounts of money that were unavailable in a bankrupt city. A few vocal critics opposed the privatization of public waterfront parkland in the late 1990s, but they were seldom a match for the city's growth machine, an alliance between politicians searching for campaign cash, the unashamedly compliant media, sports entrepreneurs, and corporations. All were focused on the potential revenue that could be generated from vulnerable public land.

Waterfront parkland was fast eroding, though that tide remained largely beyond public view. In 1996, the Miami Heat and Carnival Cruise Line owner Mickey Arison won a campaign to obtain waterfront land for a new arena for his basketball team. In 1997 and 1998, the Port of Miami sought to take over much of Bicentennial Park for new cruise line berths. Adding insult to injury, the city commission allowed commercial development of the beautiful parcel of land between two waterfront parks in Coconut Grove. Although the weakness of local government in promoting or overseeing development of new parks was glaring, the mainstream press seldom mentioned it.[53]

Miami's identity now centered on a sun-drenched spectacle surrounded by an aura of violence. Cuban migrants were finally acquiring political influence that was commensurate with their numbers. Many native Miamians were uncomfortable about the social, economic, and political impact of the Cuban community, and some moved out of town. Many African Americans were angry because these new arrivals received so many federal benefits and exercised such political influence and thought that these gains had come at their expense. Most people adjusted to the diversity, finding excitement in the variety of languages heard on the streets of Miami.[54]

The TV show *Miami Vice* symbolized much of the region's identity by the 1980s and 1990s. Associations with the region had moved beyond its earlier identification with Arthur Godfrey and Jackie Gleason, Flipper, the Rat Pack, and radio talk show host Larry King. Miami Beach, with its art deco buildings, music scene, high fashion, and food, had become hip. The aestheticizing of the area that became associated with South Beach spilled over to the rest of the city. This new look and allure helped make Miami a popular destination for tourists from the northern United States, Europe, and Latin America once again. Yet in this mix, beyond selective concerns about historic preservation and the fate of the Everglades, only a few groups were promoting the quality of public space and their efforts were seldom reported in the mass media. In his best-selling book *Miami: City of the Future* (1987), T. D. Allman wrote: "The reason Crockett and Tubbs [the stars of *Miami Vice*] were so alluring was their lack of definition. They didn't have wives or children like the rest of us; they didn't live in houses; they didn't pay bills. True, they shot it out with murderers and drug dealers. Yet they nonetheless had all those things—exotic cars, exotic clothes, exotic women—that, in real life, people in their position usually can get only by smugglings drugs, or worse."[55] Miami tourist attractions were uniquely exotic. Who worried that they were being outpaced by the wholesome appeal of Disney? Since the 1970s, central Florida had rivaled Las Vegas as the largest entertainment zone in the nation.

At the same time, Miami was growing into a major international banking center. Its airports and seaports were huge economic engines. So, increasingly, were its universities and its cultural scene. Foreign trade amounted to about $4 billion a year by the early 1980s. Allman observed that Miamians "never wait for the customers to show up. Instead they first build their railroads, their hotels, their shopping malls, their skyscraper condominiums. Then they set out, with all the ballyhoo they can muster[,] to create a demand for what they have supplied."[56]

In 1996, the fight over a new arena for the Miami Heat spurred activists opposed to it to form a new nonprofit organization, the Urban Environment League (UEL) of Greater Miami. Initiated by architectural critic Jorge Espinel and Elizabeth Plater-Zyberk, a dean of the University of Miami School of Architecture and a major figure in the new urbanist movement, the UEL brought together architects, planners, historians, and residents interested in good urban design and others interested in transparent government processes and the preservation of public parkland. I recall reading a small item in the newspaper announcing a demonstration against taking the public waterfront land for a new arena for the Heat. I arrived at the waterfront site with my ten-year-old daughter Paula to hold up signs alongside county mayoral candidate Alex Penelas, who based much of his campaign against taking waterfront land. I met Espinel and Dan Paul and was attracted to the organization because it stressed the need for public planning of public space and championed smart growth as an approach to housing and other urban problems. The UEL's fight against the arena failed in 1996, yet the UEL remained a fledgling organization that was forced to focus many of its efforts on trying to enlist a broader public in the task of confronting a selective range of the region's long-standing and seemingly intractable problems.

The UEL organized an evening march and demonstration through the deserted streets of downtown Miami in April 1998. It sought to draw attention to the need to revitalize the area and bring people back downtown at night. A couple of hundred people followed Miami's St. Agnes Marching Band, an African American group formed in the 1930s, which played Dixieland music, from the Cultural Plaza to Lummus Park on the Miami River and then to the Lyric Theater in Overtown and back down Flagler Street. Local historians spoke, pointing to the closed gates at Lummus Park, which encompassed the city's oldest buildings (Fort Dallas and the Wagner House, which had been moved there from other locations) and the constraining racial boundaries of Overtown. Under the slogan "Better Than a Theme Park—Miami: the Real City," the march gained some attention in the local press.[57]

The effort to reverse the closing of public parks and the derelict state of downtown Miami remained daunting, and the UEL was up against a formidable opponent in Assistant City Manager Dena Bianchino. The *Miami Herald* quoted Bianchino as saying: "We have a lot of parks in the city that are very beautiful, but they're not being used and we want to bring development to these areas." A feature story published in 1998, "Bayfront Dreams," reflected the prevailing attitude of most public officials. "Seeking to capitalize on Miami's underutilized real estate portfolio, city leaders are again trying to develop two of its most neglected waterfront properties: Watson Island and Bicentennial Park. This is a great thing for Miami," Bianchino maintained. "It will bring more people to the waterfront than ever before." Critics in the UEL posed pointed questions. Attorney Neal McAliley said that the city had "squandered most of its waterfront. . . . In the quest for recurring revenue, the city is risking the wasting of its most precious physical assets, the waterfront. The city should view the waterfront as an asset that . . . can be used as public space that leverages surrounding areas."[58] The terms of this face-off were becoming clear as UEL spokespersons refused to defer to private interests and public purposes.

In early April 1997, *Miami Herald* columnist and best-selling novelist Carl Hiaasen wrote a column decrying the fate of Virginia Key. "The cash-starved city of Miami is again trying to deliver Virginia Key to favored developers and concessionaires," he warned. "Under the pretense of 'revitalization,' nine parcels currently marked for conservation are proposed for rezoning. The result could be hotels, marinas, shops and even houses." Overall, the "stewardship of Virginia Key has been one of bungling, neglect and political favoritism. Practically everything the city touched has turned to failure. The Miami Marine Stadium has been a wreck since Hurricane Andrew. The beach and park on the Atlantic side—refurbished a few years ago at great expense—is now closed, supposedly because of budget crisis. It's as if Miami purposely abandoned Virginia Key and let it crumble, in order to stir support for development." Hiaasen pointed out the political favoritism the city had shown to the Miami Rowing Club, which had leased a prime waterfront location on Virginia Key for the previous twenty years at an annual rent of $100. The club constructed an 11,000-square-foot clubhouse, swimming pool, banquet hall, and bar, and in 1987 it reported that it had collected $147,000 from rental fees. One of the club's lifetime members was former city manager Cesar Odio. Another city commissioner and later mayor, Joe Carollo, provided security for the facility through his own security firm. Hiaasen called rezoning "just the first step toward another giveaway" and warned that "you don't need to be downwind from the sewer plant to smell the truth."[59]

Forging Our Civil Right to
Public Space, 1999–2015

After the loss of prime waterfront land to the Miami Heat basketball team in 1996 for what became the American Airlines Arena, I grew determined to learn what lay behind what I perceived as an unconscionable land grab. Scrutinizing news coverage and interviewing several participants in the debate, I moved beyond my disengaged and cynical attitude toward Miami as a culture of spectacle to assess a set of vital contemporary issues that concerned me both personally and professionally. That meant crossing the invisible, perhaps mythical lines between history and journalism, objectivity and advocacy. I found that the Heat's promotional perspective dominated TV and print coverage of the controversy. When park advocate Dan Paul was given any air time, he came across as fervent and smart but rather caustic and ineffective, a brilliant lone wolf. One UEL press conference called by Heat opponents attracted just one reporter and garnered no coverage. I interviewed both arena critics and public officials, including Paul, Elizabeth Plater-Zyberk, and Miami city commissioner Johnnie Winton, to try to understand why there was an inadequate planning tradition or viable park constituency in Miami. Something was lacking in advocates' efforts to address decision making related to the waterfront; the problem was not as simple as saying that politicians had been bought off by developers.

This final chapter is a hybrid narrative that both recounts history as objectively as possible and analyzes my own memories about the struggle I was engaged in from early 1999 on. I learned much about activism in Miami from reading government documents, conducting interviews, watching the press closely, speaking out at meetings, and serving as president of the Urban Environment League. I spearheaded the formation of the Bicentennial Park/Waterfront Renewal Committee, which succeeded in stopping the Marlins from taking Bicentennial Park—though at a high cost. I taught several teacher-training courses focused on planning, oral history, and local government and was a member of the Kendall Community Council. My civic engagement was propelled by my sense of personal responsibility but was compatible with my academic positon as director of the university's public history program. I discovered that through doing research, taking the initiative to build coalitions of advocates, creating dramatic events, constructing positive relationships with city officials and the press, and drafting and lobbying for legislation, advocates for public space could have an impact on major development issues related to Virginia Key and the waterfront.

My form of civic engagement and my role as a minor public personality was a far cry from my previous life as an historian who examines the past from a removed perch. No longer content merely to describe Miami's culture of spectacle and abysmal lack of comprehensive planning, I confronted its effects directly. I never worried about the supposed discrepancy between what some saw to be the objective assessment of a scholar and the work of policy advocacy; as I saw it, that functional division was part of Miami's problem. Academics seldom become involved in such matters because of the heavy demands made on their time and the fact that universities generally dissuade faculty from engaging in public life to any significant degree.

Instead of espousing a particular plan for Virginia Key, I focused on advocating an open public process of decision making in order to create a more integrated waterfront. I wrote pieces in the Urban Environment League's newsletter, *The Urban Forum*, penned op-ed columns that were published in the *Miami Herald*, and was often quoted in the local press. It was such a different world from academia, yet in many ways it was far more satisfying. At the same time, I have periodically felt the need to step away from the tasks of the moment to gain perspective. The combination of official indifference toward any coherent public design and planning process and insider entrepreneurialism continues to dominate events to this day, assuming different disguises but almost always seeking public land for private gain.[1]

Generating Civic Engagement

Silence about the past inexorably shrouds public consciousness as time and tides wash away the memories of something as amorphous as a beach. There was also little clarity of perspective in the history of the broader planning process for Virginia Key. The two movements that sought to increase public access to Virginia Key Beach, the first in 1945 and the second since 1999, have been decidedly small-scale and largely local phenomena. Yet they reveal the political pitfalls in the planning process when professional planners often show little sensitivity to the complexities of politics and seldom seek effective public input. Harry Boyte and Sara Evans have inquired into processes "through which [the people] may broaden their sense of the possible, make alliances with others, develop the practical skills and knowledge to maintain democratic organization." The long-term struggle to preserve and revitalize Virginia Key offers some insights that are applicable far beyond this locale.[2]

It has recently become fashionable for universities seeking to wrap themselves in the public legitimacy often associated with service learning to engage with civic life. Institutions such as the University of Minnesota, the University of Pennsylvania, and the University of Michigan are scrambling to become more relevant to their communities. Yet most seek to be identified as "global universities," and few have been particularly creative about finding new forms of public involvement in local and regional planning. How can the public expand democracy so its members can help design local land use more effectively? I discovered that, as Boyte has written in his primer for activists, "A broad, bipartisan citizen group skilled at tackling tough public problems shows how attention to the cultural and values dimensions of issues can generate new power and energy."[3]

First as an historian, then as an activist, I found that local and national reform movements form, fragment, and morph over time. Goals and ideological perspectives inevitably become attenuated, allies divide, and leaders move on to new interests or have to focus on their jobs or family concerns. Opponents pose new challenges and associate their cause with new coalitions and political candidates or become compromised. Often newer attractions and issues take over. In many cases, the original impetus becomes deflated or channeled into vastly different patterns of what passes for reform, financial demands, or bureaucratic interests. Memories dissipate and the historical record is forgotten. Above all, the dominant economic and political power structure absorbs small elements of change and reasserts itself.

The fate of Virginia Key and other public waterfront spaces in Miami is an important example of this cycle within a larger, deeply racialized urban canvas. We began the attempt to create a master plan for the beach and then for the entire island in 1999 and in 2010 a community consensus appeared to emerge, but there is still no clear resolution of the issues the plan involves. I hope that this account will help sustain and renew the vigilance needed to retain and reuse public spaces in our time. Years ago I asked environmentalist Lloyd Miller what he thought was the most important quality in his work as one of the original advocates for Biscayne National Park. He answered, "Not brilliance but pure bulldog perseverance."[4]

Local government initiatives to increase civic involvement in planning the creative uses of Miami's public land have generally lacked continuity in the face of a politically timid news media, inadequate historical analysis, stunted or decontextualized memories, marginalized advocacy organizations, corrupted governmental processes, and the dominance of private development interests. In terms of racial politics, land use, and any larger sense of social equity in Miami, the result has been an endemic loss of bureaucratic knowledge of existing ordinances and past agreements, deference toward the corporate flavor of the day that results in decisions to lease public land or build gargantuan sports stadiums at immense public expense, and profound public cynicism about the ability to have any effect on the system. All too often, this combination leads to the steady erosion of any creative or continuous use of and identification with public parkland or natural areas. Government officials become preoccupied with providing funding for grant initiatives and emergency services and ignore their responsibility as stewards of open spaces. Public land becomes "empty space, a space of abstract freedom but no enduring connection." In this cynical age, our sense of common purpose has been all but lost.[5]

Yet this condition began to change noticeably by the 1980s and 1990s as the environmental movement sank deeper roots into local communities, nurturing a host of new models of well-planned city parks and broadening participation in planning and landscape design. In cities such as New York, Chicago, Philadelphia, Seattle, and Chattanooga, movements to create or preserve parks, community gardens, and community centers brought out diverse constituencies that created a sense of community from their championship of common spaces. The Trust for Public Land and the Project for Public Spaces became highly effective consultants and brokers in stimulating new ways of using public land for public benefit.[6]

Miami's waterfront parkland was perhaps the most vulnerable in the nation, as numerous commercial enterprises sought to take advantage of its derelict condition with the support of cash-strapped public officials. Peter Harnik said in 2000 that "Miami has less open space than any big city in the country," warning that the situation in Miami "may be a harbinger . . . of what the future holds for many American cities."[7] The upsurge of interest in Miami's waterfront parks in the late 1990s was led by an interracial environmental coalition. It was stimulated by dramatic struggles over the future of Virginia Key and several downtown parks, including the Miami Circle and Bicentennial Park. I helped give historical focus and some leadership to that effort, though many others were also central actors. We had learned enough about the process of losing public land in Miami and became fed up with what we saw as a pattern of collusion between government officials and greedy entrepreneurs. Both our success and its limits became evident as activists created a new organization to oversee Virginia Key Beach and addressed a new set of problems related to controlling and defining public space in Miami.

The ragtag movement that saved Virginia Key beach from commercial development in 1999 morphed into the Historic Virginia Key Beach Park Trust, which was chartered by the city of Miami in 2000. It became a nonprofit city entity with a board of directors, a burgeoning staff, and a mission that was separate from that of the regular city and county park systems yet was funded in large part by the city, the county, and federal grants. Its political clout derived in part from newly ascendant African

American public officials, notably county and city commissioners Arthur Teele, Barbara Carey-Shuler, and Athalie Range and U.S. representative Carrie Meek.

Yet few officials in the eight-year administration of Mayor Manny Diaz, who was elected in 2002, held the trust to clear standards of accountability or seriously questioned its funding needs until the economic crash of 2009, when city officials again sought what had long been the goal of many—extensive private development in the park and throughout the island. The strong pressures brought to bear upon the trust to vastly expand its financial base in order to create an extensive Civil Rights Museum subtly shifted its priorities from the need to save the land, preserve memories, and showcase the environmental and the civil rights struggle in Miami toward financial concerns and a burgeoning bureaucracy of its own. The 2009 financial crisis that swept the nation wiped away most of the park's city funding. Then, in a form of political vengeance against what was perceived to be financial mismanagement by the African American staff, the park became the chief victim of previous success.

Entrepreneurial forces were never asleep, especially after the city began to create a master plan for the entire island in 2005. Developers continued to seek extensive commercial uses of public land, often in league with selected city officials and planning consultants. Many had long sought to build hotels, shopping plazas, and theme parks on the island. City administrators had tried to remove the deed restrictions and commercialize both the beach and the area around the Miami Marine Stadium without real public input into the decision-making process. The future use of the key remains murky, even after a dramatic upsurge of public involvement, led in part by the UEL, redefined the planning process, proved effective enough to overturn a commercially dominated city plan, and produced a consensus master plan that was passed by a unanimous vote of the city commission on July 22, 2010. Yet even a key plank in that plan that called for a Virginia Key Planning Oversight Board was essentially shelved for years. It was finally passed by the city commission on December 10, 2015.

This historical narrative, like the public memory of the long planning process for Virginia Key, builds upon but involves more than what are uncomfortably called "racial issues." Indeed, it illuminates the pernicious effects of dominant neoliberal assumptions about usurping public space for entrepreneurially defined needs under the guise of more economically viable public land use. Because of limited press coverage and public debate, the relatively weak leadership of nonprofit advocacy organizations, inattentive political leadership, and the energy of private entrepreneurs, the continuous contestation over public space has yielded limited results. The inability of officials to effectively manage public spaces makes them more vulnerable to appropriation by private ventures spawned by economic downturns and political intrigue and remains a challenge for civic activists. The lack of creative public control of the development process is appalling.

A Questionable Purpose

The threat to Miami's public waterfront by the late 1990s came not only from the drive to commercialize it but also from the loss of the commitment of the public to its parks. The growing visibility of homelessness and a lack of security, maintenance, and programming kept people away from parks. In an air-conditioned, mall-obsessed, and TV-dominated culture, few regarded parks as significant community landmarks. The few who sought to preserve historic buildings treated them as ends in themselves, disregarding their connection to public space and the larger issues of political economy involved. Often, as Richard Francaviglia has observed, "heritage landscapes are sold, but the price is often a complete reinterpretation of the past."[8]

In recent decades, big-city mayors around the nation have devised new strategies to privatize, revitalize, and market urban public spaces. But, as Sharon Zukin has remarked, "these strategies leave little room for examining who gains and who loses from upscale development." In the fast-paced, touristic world of South Florida, authenticity usually amounted to the exhibition of, performance of, and competition between bodies in manufactured spaces. Places became ephemeral byproducts of collective spectacle, while dialogue about the public's need for recreational areas in the natural world remained marginalized. This way of managing public spaces emphasizes public-private partnerships as a means of saving public money and does not make local governments responsible for holding corporate entities responsible for their actions.

Gated communities, park conservancies, and Business Improvement Districts (BIDs) are powerful instruments that have been used to alter the funding and management of parks. "The general aim of BIDs is to put public places within cities on the same footing as the private places outside them—shopping centers and strip malls," policy analyst Jerry Mitchell has found. Planned unit developments (PUDS) have allowed suburban developers to build more densely, although according to Alexander Garvin they "have provided little open space that is clearly marked for the general public." The creative reuse of abandoned federal and city properties, such as New York's Highline Park and San Francisco's Presidio, has demonstrated that broad public involvement in park planning can not only transform public spaces but can also go a long way toward reviving older neglected urban neighborhoods and rekindling pride in local spaces. New York's waterfront, especially in Battery Park, is an example of the positive changes that are taking place around the nation's urban waterfronts. Yet the dominant trend, epitomized by the ubiquitous Rouse Company's "festival marketplace," has transformed public space into chain store–dominated shopping malls with views of the water or more grandiose spectacles for the wealthy, as the struggle over a luxurious space needle in Miami's downtown public waterfront called Skyrise has shown in recent years.[9] Miami's Bayside Marketplace has become one more unoriginal waterfront mall that is always looking for a new element of spectacle.

There was some hope in Miami that better planning could be instituted that would act as a counterweight to the private deals that had long been dominant in the city. The 1972 Decade of Progress bond issue that had built the Metrorail enlarged the county's infrastructure, but city dwellers resented the fact that it benefited a small group of well-heeled suburban residents. In 1996, however, the Trust for Public Land helped sponsor a major bond issue for parks that won overwhelming voter support in the county. The Save Our Parks bond issue included a charter amendment penned by lawyer Dan Paul to limit commercial activity in public parks. The trust followed this victory with a Greenway Plan for the Miami River that envisioned walkways on both its northern and southern banks.[10]

Yet, as we have seen, during the late 1990s, the city of Miami, in a misguided attempt to address its desperate financial condition, made

surreptitious plans to develop waterfront parkland for revenue-enhanc-
ing purposes, as I later learned in an interview with county archaeolo-
gist Bob Carr. Efforts by Miami-Dade County and the city of Miami to
refocus planning efforts on long-derelict spaces, from its poor neighborhoods to long-ignored waterfront public spaces such as Virginia Key,
were often stymied by complex fights over jurisdiction. By late 1998,
given the conflicting interests of the cities of Miami and Key Biscayne,
financial interests on Virginia Key such as the owners of Seaquarium,
and state and county environmental regulatory bodies, it appeared that
political consensus was improbable. The future of Virginia Key became a
test of whether Miami leaders could create an inclusive and transparent
planning process that would challenge the status quo or whether any set
of forces would be able to redirect the growth machine.

Planning for Virginia Key remained largely in limbo. The situation
worked to the advantage of private entities such as the owners of the aging Seaquarium, who sought adjacent public land for parking and added
attractions. The city of Key Biscayne remained concerned about traffic
on Virginia Key and wanted to be able to use island land for ball fields
and a high school because they had not adequately planned for them
on their own island. Environmentalists and sailboard advocates, notably
the Tropical Audubon Society, the Sierra Club, the redoubtable Mabel
Miller and her Friends of Virginia Key, and the South Florida Sailboard
Association, remained the chief advocates for preserving the beaches as
public parkland. They contended against an array of commercial forces
that both openly and covertly sought space for RV campgrounds, hotels,
restaurants, water theme parks, and the redevelopment of the marine
stadium basin and other areas of the island.

Both private enterprises and public officials put pressure on public
parks to become revenue producers. County Parks and Recreation assistant director Howard Gregg recounted that he had "seen the pendulum
swing" from "more resource-based stewardship"—the professional management of historical, cultural, and biological resources—to "a real drive
to generate revenue." In the face of the "budget crisis," he explained,
he and his colleagues cut corners: "Because we are so proud of the park
system and wanting it to continue to be operating . . . for people in the
county, you find yourself doing things that were a little bit out of the
historical norm for managing park systems." Private developers and

planners who shared these officials' perspective tended to regard parks not as natural sanctuaries to be enjoyed but as sites for packaged entertainment. Jack Luft articulated that attitude:

> We have to face the fact that the first choice for a family on a Sunday afternoon is not a quiet walk by the waterfront. People want something more. We are a society that insists on being entertained. . . . When Central Park was designed, people were living on top of each other—Manhattan had more people per square mile than Bombay. The park was a place for people to restore themselves once they got out of the sweatshops. Today, parks in South Florida, now that we've manufactured a suburban environment, have to meet different needs. . . . The overriding objective for us has been to use public lands to achieve broad public purposes.

Although Luft did not specify what those purposes were, he was clearly interested in turning public parks into profit-making ventures.[11]

The concept of the "broad public purpose" of parks had been interpreted to mean serving the interests of private promoters seeking sweetheart deals for the use—or misuse—of the city's public spaces using the rationale that a small proportion of the profits would go into the public coffers. Yet the ambiguities of this language also created a window of opportunity for park advocates to show how public planning might yield an alternative approach to these places.[12]

The Growing Power and Continued Poverty of Miami's Black Community

How would the fate of Miami's waterfront be linked to the interests of African Americans? When concerns began surfacing about preserving Virginia Key as a public park in the late 1990s, environmental activists knew little about its civil rights history or its cultural significance for previous generations of black Miamians. What gradually became clear, however, was that the perspectives of a coalition of African Americans and environmentalists of various ethnic backgrounds could no longer be ignored in public debate over the future of the city.

In the latter part of the twentieth century, African Americans had attained a measure of political power in the Miami area. By the 1980s, black leaders Arthur Teele and Barbara Carey-Shuler were elected to the city and county commissions, respectively, and Mayor Ferre selected a black city manager, Howard Gary. Although Cubans came to dominate the political scene, African Americans were able to hold a share of county commission seats because an order by federal judge Clyde Adkins assured that county commission districts would be defined by geography. Black tourism had also become a recognized economic factor in the region. Anglo and Cuban residents discovered this the hard way. In 1992, when the Cuban political leadership snubbed South African leader Nelson Mandela because he had made positive comments about Fidel Castro, black tourists boycotted Miami for months. In later years the Hip Hop Festival, the African American Film Festival, the Black Entertainment Television awards ceremony and other music and arts events became a huge draw for people of African descent.[13]

Equally important, Miami's black community had become more organized and assertive about its history. Archivist Dorothy Fields founded the Black Archives Research and Study Center in 1977; her subsequent efforts focused on preserving the Lyric Theater and creating the Overtown Folklife Village, an ongoing project. Scholars such as Raymond Mohl and Paul George helped uncover the complex history of the black community during segregation. The state's Law Mandating the Teaching of African and African American History, which was passed in May 1994 and was amended in 2002, required the teaching of "the history of African Americans, including the history of African peoples before the political conflicts that led to the development of slavery, the passage to America, the enslavement experience, abolition, and the contributions of Africans to society." But the story of the black experience in the Miami area remained fragmentary and incomplete until the publication of Marvin Dunn's *Black Miami in the Twentieth Century* in 1999. Dunn also engaged in civic life; with his Florida International University students, he started a community garden project in Overtown next to I-395, an area that had been decimated when the highway was built.[14]

Despite these changes, reports continued to underscore the degraded social condition of the inner city. In 1995, the planning department found that "the City of Miami is the most densely populated metropolis in the state of Florida." Federal statistics indicated that in 1990 42.2 percent of Miamians under the age of eighteen lived below the poverty level. "With the decline in household income for City residents . . . private recreation options are beyond the scope of the typical family budget [and] the role of public recreational opportunities (facilities) intensifies," the report stated. "The importance of recreation and open space to the welfare of City residents is growing." Yet little was done to rectify this situation. Numerous reports continued to detail the city's desperate state. A Brookings Institution study focused on income disparities between urbanites and suburbanites and between white households and those of African Americans, Puerto Ricans, Nicaraguans, and Haitians. Among the challenges that contributed "to the region's troubling income trends and inhibit its ability to retain and build the middle class" were the low level of formal education of the city's residents, the low wages Miami employers paid, and the exodus of middle-class people from the city center. The report concluded that "Miami's decentralized growth patterns isolate low-income residents from opportunity. Basic necessities consume a large portion of poor residents' income. Limited use of mainstream financial institutions and government support programs impedes the wealth-building capacity of low-income households."[15]

The contradiction between the political power African American leaders had attained and the chronic impoverishment and malign neglect that afflicted the black community was bound to produce unrest. Fortunately for the future of Virginia Key Beach, black Miamians soon became actively involved in deciding its fate.

Racial Politics and the Preservation of Miami's Public Waterfront

In January 1999, the historic site at the mouth of the Miami River known as the Miami Circle and Virginia Key emerged almost simultaneously as major local issues, although the discovery of the archaic circle dominated the media. Waterfront park space was emerging as a contentious issue.

The prior fall, another critical piece of land between the Barnacle State Historical Site and the city's Peacock Park, the site of the area's first hotel, was conveyed to private owners for wealthy housing called Cloister by the Bay after a heated local debate. The land would have made a magnificent waterfront park, one of the elements that was part of the 1985 agreement that created Bayside Marketplace. Yet the city commission clearly preferred the revenue potential of an upscale housing development over the possibility of a broad waterfront park in that area.

Shortly thereafter, an astounding 2,000-year-old artifact was discovered at the mouth of the Miami River where a large apartment building was slated to rise. The site was allegedly built by Tequesta Indians. It became a major multicultural symbol of the need to stop development in historically significant places in Miami. Street demonstrations by members of the Dade Heritage Trust in league with Native Americans and the UEL led the state to take over the unique site.[16]

In January 1999, as the new president of the Urban Environment League, despite some personal hesitation, I became personally involved in both the Miami Circle as well as the emerging Virginia Key issue. Mabel Miller's urging influenced my decision. The presidency soon took over much of my life. At a meeting of the Ad Hoc Virginia Key Task Force, the group charged with planning future uses for selected portions of the island, I heard a presentation by Ecoexperience Development Inc. president Wendall Collins, who sat on the state's commission on ecotourism. It turned out that Ecoexperience was owned by Arthur Hertz, who was also the CEO of Wometco, a major local media and entertainment corporation, and the owner of the Seaquarium on Virginia Key. As Collins extolled the wonders of eco-resorts and described the upscale accommodations he planned to build in the park, I worried that development would destroy the very ecology it marketed to tourists. The small audience of environmentalists decried the lack of attention to retaining the beach as a natural area.[17]

After listening to them make eloquent pleas, I sensed that they were not gaining any traction with the task force. I stood up and said, "What is being overlooked is the historical significance of the park to the African American community. Why shouldn't the whole park be designated to honor the civil rights struggle in Miami? That would be a perfectly valid reason to deny the privatization of that land." I had just read Marvin Dunn's book *Black Miami in the Twentieth Century* and was acutely aware that galvanizing a black constituency was probably the only way to save the land from development. The confluence of environmentalism and civil rights made perfect sense to me.

The city had set up an Ad Hoc Virginia Key Task Force, to determine the future of the "black beach." The dominant member, Jim Courbier, who was influential with local politicians, immediately dismissed this suggestion and said that a commemorative plaque could be installed instead. Many in the audience took offense at this trivialization of a significant issue. Everyone, including me, was startled by my spontaneous suggestion. No one had seriously considered the notion of having the park commemorate the civil rights struggle through which the black beach was established. The city's historic preservation officer said she had never heard of parkland receiving historic designation. As events unfolded, Virginia Key Beach's historical association with the black community proved to be strategically important in saving the land as a park.[18]

Over the next several days I drafted a document titled "Principles and Possibilities for the Future of Virginia Key" and presented them at the next meeting of the task force on February 3, 1999. The sixteen principles of the document advocated abiding by deed restrictions, creating a civil rights park, and reopening the land to the public. I also promoted a public design workshop to determine the shape of the park. Several members of the task force scoffed at the idea, saying that it would cost too much to hire professional planners to set up and guide such a public process.

Activist Nancy Lee loaned me a carton of documents that reflected several years of hard work on her part, including letters to and from local and state officials and the detailed reports the complex growth management process required the city to submit when it wanted to change its land use plans. My historian's interest was peaked and I sought to understand the more complex past of this forlorn place. Surprisingly, two middle-class white people collaborated with each other to create a plan for a civil rights park at the site. Nancy and her husband, Bob Weinreb, both windsurfers and avid park advocates, had done extensive research on Virginia Key on their own initiative.

Nancy suggested using the outdoor FDR Memorial in Washington, D.C., as a model for the beach and sketched an open-air site overlooking Bear Cut. This vision reminded me of Yad Vashem, the memorial to Holocaust victims I had seen in Israel during a recent visit. However, Nancy and I understood very well that any attempt to transform the land into a civil rights park would be a failure unless the effort was led by African Americans. To this end, with the support of Dorothy Fields, I spoke in front of an oral history panel of African Americans at the downtown public library, where I listened to older people's memories of the beach and called for a public workshop to redesign the park. I was saddened when more than a few African Americans said that they wanted to forget this symbol of segregation and second-class citizenship, although I was surprised to hear such comments from my friend and fellow historian Whittington Johnson, a longtime resident of the city and the first African American member of the University of Miami faculty.[19] Preserving and enhancing the black beach required not only convincing the task force of its feasibility but also figuring out how its complex meanings could be interpreted by and for African Americans of quite different generations.

At subsequent meetings of the task force, city staff continued to promote what they saw as economically viable uses of the land. These plans would require removing deed restrictions to allow commercial development by an eco-resort. They would not have fostered any creative or historically sensitive solutions for either the old "black beach" or the nearby Miami Marine Stadium. We needed to move quickly to outline an alternative vison for a civil rights park and promote it to public officials at several levels of government. As a first step, I persuaded the board of directors of the Urban Environment League to support the idea.

We rapidly enlisted prominent African American leaders in the campaign to save the historic beach. One of the first people I contacted, Dinizulu Gene Tinnie, had worked with us on the Miami Circle demonstration shortly before. Tinnie, a calm and thoughtful man, an artist, a writer, and a profound thinker, later described how that campaign led to the forging of the coalition that went on to save Virginia Key. He noted that "the discovery by archaeologists of the 2,000-year-old Miami Circle at the mouth of the Miami River gave rise to an immense groundswell of local, national, and international interest and concern, as the site faced the threat of destruction in the name of development. This concern, in turn, gave rise to the idea that the Circle might do for Miami in the 2000s what Miamians themselves could not do throughout the 1900s, which was to bring the whole community together around a common cause and purpose, without the usual divisions of class, culture, language, and ethnicity." The convergence of interest in preserving the past and preserving open space gave rise to renewed sense of common purpose in preserving Virginia Key Beach. "In an unexpected way and an unexpected place," Tinnie continued, "this is precisely what began to happen when several groups and individuals involved with the struggle to save the Circle learned, thanks to the Public Parks Coalition of the Urban Environment League (UEL), that another historic site, with much more recent but no less significant meaning to the community, was facing a similar threat. Quietly behind the scenes, a proposal for exclusive private development on historic Virginia Key Beach was making its way toward approval by the Miami City Commission. The far-reaching and ominous implications of that proposal brought together groups as diverse as a windsurfers' club, environmentalists, public parks activists, Key Biscayne residents, and concerned citizens in the African American community for whom the beach was especially significant because of its decades of history as a segregated park for 'Colored Only.'"[20]

Looking back on these events, Tinnie reflected: "One of the strategies that we have to have is looking at our sacred sites, places that have been consecrated by, labored by, the struggle. As I talked about this to people I would find that every time I mentioned Virginia Key I'd see people with this look upon their face. There are too many people with too many fond memories, too many people who have been baptized out there, had their honeymoons out there, had their first love affair out there. . . . That was a place that brought together an entire black community. It was the only place we could go. . . . All the different neighborhoods all the different social classes, the churchgoers, the heathens if you will, because you've heard the phrase over and over again, it was the only place we could go."[21]

Enid Pinkney also became an outspoken advocate of saving the beach. An African American educator and former president of the predominantly white Dade Heritage Trust, Enid had a beautiful smile and a positive attitude. She was a passionate advocate of historic preservation. She wrote Mayor Joe Carollo:

> As a person who was born in Miami and had to live under segregated laws, in a segregated community and world, Virginia Beach was the only beach that I was allowed to go to by law. Virginia Beach is a part of Miami history, and I feel that it should remain as a public beach. Many African Americans made sacrifices and put much time and effort into asking for and getting a beach where African Americans could have an experience at the beach. Keeping Virginia Beach as a public beach could be a memorial to those brave

African Americans who stood up for the right to enjoy God's ocean, sand, and sun in a beach setting.[22]

Support from the black community made a critical difference. Tinnie played a crucial role, writing columns that tracked the issue for the *Miami Times*; the paper's publisher, Garth Reeves, had been among the demonstrators who desegregated Crandon Park in the late 1950s. In his articles, Tinnie criticized the "back room" decision making in meetings that are technically open to the public but are rarely announced. He expressed concern about the lack of participatory democracy in Miami. When Tinnie showed up to speak in favor of the civil rights park at a task force meeting, a furious Courbier declared: "This is never going to fly." But events proved him wrong.

The scope of analysis of the Virginia Key Task Force was narrow. It did not investigate the site's history, and it subscribed to no clear principles for park management or definitions of the "broad public purposes" that parks should serve. Its activities were handled by city staff, who were experts at marginalizing public input. For its part, the UEL board endorsed a resolution I wrote to reopen the park and promote a public design process, stating that "the rights of citizens are eroded when they have inadequate access to public parkland" and concluding that "in the event that the City of Miami fails to enhance the public land, we request that the County consider reversion of the title to the land back to its control or to state control so that the public can benefit from it."[23] When several of us met with county officials to ask about their oversight of the deed restrictions, we learned that had never been done.

The narrow breadth of the vision of the official City's Virginia Key Task Force aroused anger among park advocates. On February 18, 1999, I sent an angry letter to its chair, Dr. Virginia Newell, a marine biologist who was assistant dean of the University of Miami's Rosenstiel School. Newell was a well-meaning person caught in a difficult political position between city staff and the growing anger of environmentalists who had joined forces with African Americans. My letter criticized the committee for its lack of black representation and its lack of transparency and accountability. The proposal for an African American Civil Right Memorial Park "was blatantly ignored by a committee that is totally unrepresentative of the diversity of the city of Miami. The heritage of the African

American community has been given short shrift, again, in considering what to do with public land. What an affront to those engaged in the heroic struggle for civil disobedience at Haulover Beach in 1945, those who demanded access to waterfront beach which had for so long been denied to people of color. This is an issue that should interest people of all backgrounds because the struggle for civil rights continues, is central to all our lives, and is broadening its scope in this day and age to include such issues as the right to adequate public space for all our people." Subsequently, for reasons that remain unknown to me to this day, the Ad Hoc Task Force dissolved.[24]

To its credit, the press published numerous articles describing the impact of the advocacy group that we called the Public Parks Coalition. The *Sun Sentinel*'s Jay Weaver quoted Mayor Carollo: "Since these are the best properties in Miami, we want to make sure we're going to get world-class developments." Assistant city manager Dena Bianchino, who had moved back and forth between working for the city and working for private developers, stated that "we are going to be marketing internationally and we're going to be more open in terms of uses. We realize we're not the private sector. There are a lot of creative people out there." Presumably that meant deferring to private entrepreneurs in altering the public space. Jon Ullman, local head of the Sierra Club, summed up the critics' viewpoint: the city commission "doesn't understand the value of preserving public lands like this. They always think for the moment, not of the big picture."[25]

In fact, the city administration had been surreptitiously promoting commercial development of the Virginia Key Park site and the Miami Marine Stadium site. A glossy brochure titled "Miami: Changing at the Speed of Magic" featured beautiful views of a "Tropical Urban Island." The "Old County Park" was mentioned, but its historical link to the African American community and the deed restrictions on its development were pointedly ignored.[26]

A diverse group of people, including members of the Sierra Club, the UEL, and Friends of the Everglades, particularly Nancy Lee, Bob Weinreb, Blanca Mesa, and Gene Tinnie, spent dozens of hours preparing a proposal to present to the city's Waterfront Advisory Board, chaired by John Brennan, on March 10, 1999. As Tinnie recalled, "When it came to light that Virginia Key Beach was very much in the pipeline for private development," we began to articulate an alternative. "To say, 'Well, no, we cannot be satisfied with a monument that says, this was once a black beach.' There are much greater social and environmental issues at stake here. . . . This was [a] city owned, citizen owned—we like to emphasize that—piece of property. We did not want to be self-appointed watch-dogs . . . on the outside that they could listen to or dismiss as they saw fit."[27]

Although a growing list of prominent African Americans testified to the historical importance of the beach, the task force's recommendation shrouded the issue in obscurity. It advocated a Virginia Key Foundation "for oversight of the holistic financial and environmental reconstruction of the park." Buried beneath the formal language was tacit permission to lease part of the park for an eco-campground. Yet by March 1999 the Ad Hoc Task Force was losing its legitimacy. The Waterfront Board was confused about which proposal the task force favored. Its chair, John Brennan, held up the Public Parks Coalitions' civil rights park proposal and asked, "Is this the city's proposal?" Produced by Nancy Lee, it was beautifully illustrated and well organized and included copies of the deed restrictions. This presentation gave our side significant credibility.

Advocates for the civil rights park learned how to use the press to get more exposure for the issues related to Virginia Key. We learned never to rely on the mainstream press, whether print or TV, to get our story out. We persuaded a cable news station to air a segment on the beach. One especially helpful outlet was the *Miami New Times*, a brash weekly paper whose editor, Jim Mullin, loved a good fight over public space, especially if the *Miami Herald* was not covering the issue. It published a story called "Saviors of Virginia Key," which praised our struggle to "reclaim Miami's forgotten past." Mullin wrote:

> The once segregated Virginia Beach may not hold the archaeologi-
> cal import that rallied thousands to save the mysterious Miami
> Circle, but with the same newfound respect for history, it has in-
> spired its own circle of impassioned advocates. As this movement
> has gained momentum, the wider planning process for Virginia
> Key has virtually ground to a halt, an unexpected turn of events
> that has pleased environmentalists and park advocates who long
> fought to protect the island from commercial development. For

those who have sought to exploit the Key as a revenue source for the financially beleaguered city of Miami, the injection of race relations into the debate has changed everything.

City staff "now found themselves in the precarious position of appearing bigoted if they raised objections," Mullin remarked. "And in an ironic twist to a tale that is full of them, all this drama surrounding the fate of Virginia Key has been orchestrated not by concerned black Miamians, but by a small cadre of white activists."[28]

New awareness of the past was coming to the rescue of the beach. *Miami New Times* reporter Kirk Nielsen wrote, "Today the long-closed beach on Virginia Key is a symbol of racial segregation, the black struggle against it, and the need to preserve history." Athalie Range told reporter Teresa Mears writing in the *San Francisco Chronicle* that "the struggle, the civil rights issues that have been part of Miami for now over 50 years, need to be remembered. . . . I can think of no better way to remember it than by opening this park and doing what needs to be done to bring the citizens back." Rick Bragg wrote a long article in the *New York Times* that focused on the memories of African Americans instead of on the relative value of developing the park into an eco-campground. "Now, as developers eye this small key of largely palm and sand with intentions of turning it into an upscale resort area, the older black residents of Miami-Dade are shaking their heads once again." A monument related to the black experience was "really due." Athalie Range said, "It is only human nature that black residents would push for the monument at a time when developers want to turn it into a playground for people who can afford waterfront cottages." Drawing on black Miamians' memories of the beach, she commented, "We forget about these things and when it comes to a point when someone wants to do something else, you remember."[29]

Gene Tinnie and other park advocates held an oral history session to gather and videotape memories of Virginia Key Beach on April 3, 1999. The *Miami Times*, reporting on the session, provided some background: "The debate rages on several levels, around such issues as the fragile natural environment, the lack of citizens' participation in the decision making, the contentious matter of the park being closed to the public, and especially the politics of handing over public land for private development." Garth Reeves declared that "we want our beach back," although he and others affirmed that it would serve not just African Americans but all Miamians.[30]

Attracting the interest of 83-year-old former city commissioner Athalie Range proved pivotal. Quiet and unassuming, humorous, smart, and kind, Range had a commanding stature within the black community. She was the first African American woman elected to the city commission and then was the first head of Florida's Department of Community Affairs. For decades, she had run the most prominent black funeral home in Miami. In a later interview, she told me that Virginia Key was "important to me as a citizen of the community. I like to think of Miami as I have always known it. And as a very small child, I remember Virginia Beach as the only beach where blacks would go to have some entertainment or refreshment as far as water sports were concerned, and this came about because of the terrible segregation that we've always had here in Miami."[31]

Determined black and white women, including Nancy Lee, Mabel Miller, Athalie Range, Enid Pinkney, Eugenia Thomas, and Blanca Mesa, were showing how to change the system by working from the bottom up instead of from the distance of an academic perch or bureaucratic office. They attended all the important lower-level meetings and never personalized a problem with city staffers. We all came to appreciate that officials needed to know our faces and gain some trust in our motives, even if they disagreed with us. After the Public Parks Coalition made a bold, thoughtful, and complete presentation, the Waterfront Board endorsed its proposal. Our group had researched the historical record and produced a clear and concise proposal that cited past ordinances and presented evidence of longtime official neglect, including the fact that the city was supposed to have a Parks Advisory Board. With the help of parks director Alberto Ruder, I subsequently drafted an ordinance for such a board, lobbied for it with commissioners, saw it enacted, and became its first chair.[32]

The next step was a full-court press to convince the city commission, the mayor, and the city manager. A small delegation, including Athalie Range, Gene Tinnie, Nancy Lee, Bob Weinreb, and myself, met in May with the lone but powerful and brilliant African American city commissioner, Arthur Teele, in his office at the DuPont Plaza Hotel, which overlooked the Miami Circle site. Teele, who seemed sympathetic, decried the city's rampant corruption and warned us that lobbyists were lined up to develop hotels on Virginia Key. Sadly, in 2005, he was later implicated (but cleared) in scandals and committed suicide in the lobby of the *Miami Herald*. A small delegation also met with City Manager Donald Warshaw. When he denied that he had requested that existing deed restrictions on the park be lifted, Nancy Lee showed him a copy of his own letter to the county manager, proving that he had just lied to us. Our research was beginning to pay off. Near the end of the meeting, Enid Pinkney told the manager with vivid language that the truth needed to be told about race relations in Miami's history.[33]

In the spring of 1999, Mayor Joe Carollo cleverly outflanked the Public Parks Coalition's effort to open Virginia Key Beach by opening an adjacent parcel of beachfront land. The *Miami Herald* prominently pictured Mayor Carollo romping in the surf with black kids from the city, a publicity stunt in his reelection campaign. Most of us thought it was a cynical ploy to deflect attention from the historic black beach. Eventually the debate on whether to allow the eco-resort or to construct a civil rights memorial park went to the city commission. The city staff selected Alison Austin, a black woman, to extol the virtues of eco-campgrounds. The *Herald* editorial board finally came through with a statement strongly supporting our cause: "Nothing could be more fitting or astute than for commissioners today to agree to turn the beach on the southern portion of Virginia Key into a park free of development, mindful of history, and open to the public." The city commission eventually voted for the recommendations of the Public Parks Coalition to move forward with a process to redesign the park as a historical and environmental space and eventually create a trust to oversee the park.[34]

The Public Design Workshop

Thus, we had persuaded the city administration to allow another task force to move forward with the idea of planning a civil rights park. Due to the powerful advocacy of Commissioner Teele, the city appropriated $25,000 to help pay for a charrette, or design workshop, for the public. This was held in January 2000 at the University of Miami's Rosenstiel School. The charrette sent an important message about new forms of civic involvement. Dozens of community members, both black and white, came to the event to think boldly about what they wanted for the site. Numerous architects donated their time, led by Clyde Judson, the African American vice-president of the UEL. Juan Bueno, of the Florida International University School of Design, came up with the idea of an Aqua Necklace of parks and waterways around Biscayne Bay, a brilliant extension of Frederick Law Olmsted's design of Boston's Emerald Necklace. The Virginia Key Park would recreate the carousel, concession stand, nature trails, and railroad that had previously existed there and create nature trails and a civil rights historical museum.

Charrettes have a long history as an intense design process that involves residents or stakeholders of a defined area, planners, and architects in constructing numerous possible designs and seeking consensus. They have been practiced across the nation for many years, and professionals are available to run them. My main criticism of them, based on my experience in Miami, is that they do not gather enough oral histories from residents beforehand to appreciate the depth and scope of neighborhood history and the complex visions and social needs of current residents.[35]

Tinnie recalled: "The beauty of [the Virginia Key charrette] was that not only did many of the leaders, county commissioners, Congresswoman Meek's representatives show up there to kind of underscore how important it was and how supportive they were, but a lot of us went into that process a little bit wary. . . . Well, if everybody [was] not heard on an equal basis, wouldn't the guys with the big money and interests and the lawyers carry the thing? To everybody's surprise, that's not what really happened. While a lot of us went in there with some visions of what this could be, what came out of it was a real consensus. Everybody got a chance to hear other ideas, other concerns. . . . This charrette was not going to answer all questions, but it provided an outlet to raise the right questions and set the groundwork for the next detailed plan. . . . We are looking at restoring and preserving the historic site the way it used to be." In addition to the new civil rights museum, the charrette envisioned "a regional linkage of Virginia Key to other waterfront parks" and "to other historic sites like Overtown and the New African American Research Cultural Center in Broward. So that as you go to Virginia Key . . . you become aware of these other places and even the transportation links to them. We are looking at the environmental nature trails, wildlife observation platforms and so forth so that it actually does become this natural experience that's not so intrusive and disturbing. That's the bright vision for the future."[36]

In early 2000, the Florida Marlins' attempt to take over sixteen acres of Bicentennial Park for a new downtown waterfront stadium took center stage. Opponents, again led by the UEL, used a variety of strategies to thwart this plan, and the Marlins' campaign ultimately failed. I wrote an op-ed piece for the *Miami Herald* about the park being neglected, and set up for failure to be handed over for a stadium; further misuse of the waterfront in my view. "Recently I took a walk through Bicentennial Park, the gates were open, and there were a dozen or so homeless people camped out in that vast expanse of prime waterfront land. Conditions were deplorable. The grass had not been cut for months, and garbage was strewn throughout. In many places the infrastructure needs to be brought up to code. These dangerous and embarrassing conditions must be rectified as soon as possible." Just prior to writing this piece, I had joined a group from Miami led by the Trust for Public Land that had visited Chattanooga and seen the far-reaching efforts that had made there to enhance the city's parks and waterfront area. A stadium taking over much of the downtown waterfront because of official neglect and lack of planning was a basic moral issue for me.[37]

Jim Mullin, editor of the *Miami New Times*, faced the issue of the stadium in the park squarely. He began: "The seeming lack of opposition to this scheme must bring comfort to [Marlins owner John] Henry and the public-relations juggernaut he's about to [let] loose on South Florida. A slumbering citizenry and complacent media fit nicely with the analysis he undoubtedly has already done, analysis that would lead him to conclude this about the city's political establishment." Mullin then imagined Henry must be thinking:

> Hey, if they can rip apart downtown's signature park [referring to Bayfront Park] to toss up a cheesy tourist trap like Bayside Marketplace; and if they can ignore the fact that residents spent $23 million to purchase the waterfront property to the north specifically for [Bicentennial Park], then let it sit fallow until they could sell it for the benefit of a greedy corporate pig like me; and if they can take Bicentennial Park and ruin it by gouging out a racetrack and

then leaving the place to rot; and if they can let beautiful Virginia Key go to seed, but only after numerous failed attempts to sell it to the highest bidder; and if they can do the same with Watson Island but succeed in selling it to commercial interests—if they can do all that and actually get away with it, then they sure as hell can arrange things so I can build a baseball stadium in that junk heap on the water.[38]

Dan Paul, Robert Weinreb, and Jorge Espinel all made pointed comments about the stupidity of placing the stadium on the only available open waterfront space in the downtown area. I summed up the reasons behind the park's failure. "This is a textbook case of the incompetence of the City of Miami. It gets to the larger issue of oversight. The public is being robbed of their parks."[39] Our voice was finally being heard.

The UEL held "Walks of Renewal" through Bicentennial Park in early January to raise awareness of the history of that long-neglected park. Several months later, Gene Tinnie told reporter Teresa Mears that planners and private developers were "disenfranchising the public from what is ours." I described Miami as "a city without memory. . . . I personally see parks, even in hot Miami, as a place for recentering neighborhoods. I think parks have a greater symbolic value and a real role to play in bringing people together." Over the course of the next year, we held two design workshops that generated alternative visions for the park and got them published in the *Herald*.[40]

I wrote one op-ed piece in direct opposition to the *Miami Herald*'s editorial page editor Tom Fiedler, who had argued that a sports stadium would enhance the sense of community.

Miami's history has long been strewn with empty rhetoric confusing crowds with community. From the founding of the city to the present, we have allowed our culture of spectacle and promotion to run this town with scant regard to residents' needs. . . . We need to forge a consensus in planning for the renewal of our downtown rather than face non-negotiable demands for prime real estate so the wealthy can look out on the bay. . . . In 1886, so the story goes, all the residents of the Biscayne Bay region gathered on the porch of the Bay View House to celebrate Christmas. (Imagine such a gathering of all our community today in one spot.) Yet, like Fiedler's baseball community in 2000, the 1886 picture is a convenient fiction. In fact, there were numerous Bahamian workers and native people not included in the picture, nor, in the minds of many, were they considered part of the community. A vital community is built on the premise that all are considered in overall planning efforts.[41]

After 350 people turned out for a city-sponsored charrette in March 2001, we were able to convince numerous public officials that placing the stadium in the park was not good use of that valuable space. Unfortunately, we had not anticipated that the Miami Museum of Science (later renamed the Patricia and Phillip Frost Museum of Science) and the Miami Art Museum (later renamed the Perez Art Museum of Miami) would smartly and strategically dominate the design tables with their own advocates and eventually convince City Commissioner Johnny Winton of the wisdom of "giving" the museums eight acres of prime land instead of redesigning the park as a park, even though the museum plan was clearly not what the majority of participants had wanted. (We had the whole charrette videotaped to document the process.) I discovered that this modern instrument of urban democracy could be channeled by smart and politically influential folks.[42]

The Creation of the Historic Virginia Key Beach Park Trust

The Virginia Key charrette that took place on January 14–16, 2000, was a major success in defining plans for a park that both was environmentally sensitive and reused historic structures. It brought out well over 100 people and created pride in the community.

The city commission subsequently passed an ordinance creating the Historic Virginia Key Beach Park Trust to oversee fund-raising and plan the revitalization of the old "colored beach." Athalie Range served as its chair until her death in November 2006; Gene Tinnie was vice-chair. Joined by white environmentalist Richard Townsend, African Americans, notably Gene Tinnie, Enid Pinkney, Eugenia Thomas, Mark Walters, Maude Newbold, and Bernice Sawyer, devoted countless hours of their time to preserve and enhance the site. Representative Carrie Meek proved instrumental in securing millions of dollars of federal funds for beach restoration, and U.S. senator Bob Graham's office explored the

Map 2. Final conceptual land use plan—Virginia Key Island, 2003 master plan

feasibility of making the park part of Biscayne National Park, along with the Miami Circle site. Contrary to earlier expectations, Virginia Key gained state designation as a historic site and its own substantial city budget. Through the enormous efforts of dedicated people over several years, the park was saved from commercial development. The politicization of cultural memory was an essential part of a strategy that challenged the exclusive development ethos of city officials. We formed a broad constituency, and we were able to implement a new, more democratic public planning process. Most important, environmentalists and historic preservationists, both black and white, worked together effectively. By 2003, a coherent and thoughtful master plan for the park had emerged. Yet, as it became painfully clear, our civil right to public space can be won and then easily lost. Successes cannot be considered permanent as long as politicians' ambitions and business interests remain dominant.

The newly created Historic Virginia Key Beach Park Trust received substantial funding from the federal government to fix the old groins to diminish beach erosion, while we envisioned that city and county funding would initiate and staff a civil rights museum and other park amenities. A documentary film was begun and oral history testimonies were collected. The staff burgeoned—some say out of control. Its budget grew to $1.3 million a year before the great recession of 2008–2009. Park director David Shorter was paid more than $160,000 for a yearly salary.[43]

Internationally prominent museum consultants were hired to flesh out a grand proposal for a civil rights museum, including a large building that was projected to cost at least $40 million. In 2005, the National Park Service asked me to complete a feasibility study of the historic site as a potential addition to the national park system. That status puts federal power behind the preservation of endangered places with national significance. My study came to the conclusion that the site should be included in the national park system, although my recommendations were ignored for inexplicable reasons. Later I heard that Virginia Key Park staff might have tried to scuttle National Park Service status for fear of losing control of the site and their jobs; it also seems likely that the lack of advocacy by Florida's congressional delegation and the reluctance of local politicians concerned about giving away their property to the federal government were responsible. However, many members of the trust have long sought a partnership with the National Park Service to ensure that the park will be preserved and maintained.

On February 22, 2008, opening ceremonies finally took place for the revived Virginia Key Park. It was a wonderful day, full of promise. Thousands of people were there, having fun by the beach and listening to remarks from public officials, although not, significantly, from the mayor or the local commissioner. Some of the usual political posturing took place, but speakers made memorable remarks. Reverend Dr. Joseph Lowery of the Coalition for the People's Agenda, a veteran of the Southern Christian Leadership Conference and one of the last surviving colleagues of Martin Luther King (he later spoke at the inauguration of President Barack Obama), convulsed the crowd with laughter. "I'm sure when Mrs. Range said she wanted to reopen this park, people told her she was crazy," Lowery said from the small stage beneath a canopy festooned with red, black, and green. "But there's bad crazy, and there's good crazy. This here is good crazy." County Commissioner Barbara Jordan remarked: "My family had to bring me here from Florida City if I wanted to enjoy the beach as a kid. But I was so excited, and enjoyed it so much. Those memories come floating back today, but they come floating back in a happy way, because I know that I'm not limited, I'm not a second-rate citizen."[44]

Planning as a Democratic Art Form: Forging a Master Plan for the Key

The creative planning of urban development and public spaces more specifically remains a democratic art form that reflects the tensions and evolving contours of power in our era. The challenges involved in doing it better over time continue to be daunting. Many, though not all, professional planners lack historical context and often have little patience with the public process, seeing it as a formality rather than as a new and evolving tool for civic involvement. Politically adept leadership is needed to refine this process, though it seldom emanates from politicians and administrators themselves, who remain preoccupied with financially more powerful interests possessing deep pockets to fund political campaigns.

In 2004, county manager George Burgess described public involvement in planning as "all about talking to people, communicating with people repeatedly, making sure as you talk to them that hopefully you are conveying to them your strengths and weaknesses. . . . Hopefully, as time goes on and you change the culture, you change the perception, you continue to talk and you continue to listen."[45] Ironically, in one of Burgess's biggest decisions, he failed to involve the public at all. In 2009, the county and city of Miami commissions funded a new Marlins' stadium following a deal, which Burgess had negotiated at the instigation of Miami mayor Manny Diaz and county mayor Carlos Alvarez, that reputedly will cost taxpayers well over $2.4 billion over forty years. No public vote on the proposal was allowed for this form of corporate welfare. Burgess later resigned after incumbent county mayor Carlos Alvarez lost a recall election due to voter anger over the bad deal. The campaign contributions and side deals in deference to politicians' demands had been a major factor in the original victory. However, Norman Braman, a billionaire opponent of the stadium deal, became a major funder and force in the county mayor's ouster. What became clear to me and others was that citizen-advocate groups that choose to get involved in the planning process must do so early; do extensive research; and be tenacious, collaborative, and creative in using the media and seeking broader public input. These strategies are necessary because of widespread public apathy and confusion about the issues and the often overwhelming power and unlimited financial resources of those seeking to appropriate public land for private purposes.[46]

Another example: In a forum I organized in 2004, columnist Beth Dunlop commented on the overall state of growth management in South Florida. "You think, wait a minute . . . this is a state that theoretically has these enlightened growth management laws and these layers of government, regional planning controls, even hurricane evacuation controls that should keep fifty-story buildings off a really small island. Yet where does all this go and what happens in the face of developers who come in and immediately are pleading hardships, saying, 'We can't make a go of it unless we build fifty stories'? The bait-and-switch is an old trick." Citing the enormously large Flagstone property that was slated to be built after voters actually approved a development plan for Watson Island, she said: "This perplexes me everywhere I go. There's a setback, the Dan Paul ordinance, that would keep those buildings way away from the bay. There wouldn't be enough land from the channel, and the voters did approve that. That is a law that's on the books. It's like some of the old blue laws. They just sort of put it aside." That property, which allowed development of wealthy residential and boating interests on public waterfront land, passed a public referendum in 2001 but has languished since then. The developer had difficulty getting financing and often failed to pay required funds to the city. The upshot has been a set of lawsuits by area neighbors and increasing public cynicism at the secretive political culture of the city administration.[47]

Numerous cities and national advocacy groups have responded to such challenges by building organizations and websites, holding public meetings, and expressing diverse social needs for recreation, psychic renewal, and authentic connections with the natural world. The Trust for Public Land and the Project for Public Spaces have implemented the ideas of William S. Whyte, Jane Jacobs, and other early environmentalists. These organizations have often done effective work in reviving interest in restoring public open spaces and have developed considerable expertise in figuring out how to fund them, although they often shy away from political controversy. More nonprofit advocacy groups that are well funded are clearly needed to closely monitor the public interest in development-related issues throughout the process rather than as an afterthought. What changed the landscape in the case of the ousting of the county mayor after the Marlins deal was primarily the money and maneuvering of the billionaire Norman Braman and the efforts of one lone commissioner, future Mayor Tomás Regalado. The public should have been better organized through groups such as the UEL, but that group has never had any staff that would enable it to speak out more effectively.

In 2002, I thought it was time to give up the presidency of the UEL and spend more time on teaching and scholarship and with my family. I was newly married to Irene Secada, a political consultant who had been extremely helpful to the UEL in the struggle against the Marlins. It appeared that Virginia Key Beach was secure under the leadership of Range and Tinnie. Other waterfront park issues had gained the attention of the UEL. In 2004, the art and science museums, which had sought as many acres as possible in our 2001 charrette, worked with the county administration to obtain several hundred million dollars to build their museums in the park. Many of us believed from our first charrette that a smaller museum footprint in the park was more appropriate, that the museums should be located inland, and that two large museums would destroy the park's role as a potentially "natural" setting. The issue became contentious within the UEL. Two members of the board, including its chair, were staunch supporters of the museums and the funding through what many of us considered to be a vaguely worded bond issue. The county generated a large and complex bond issue that provided support for infrastructure development and capital funding for a variety of cultural institutions, including $15 million for a museum for Virginia Key beach and two museums in Bicentennial Park. The bond issue won in 2004 and the museums are now being completed in the park. Whether a conservancy should control and enhance the rest of the park space is the topic of an ongoing debate.[48]

In 2001, underscoring the urgent need for comprehensive planning of parks and public space, the UEL, the city's Parks Advisory Board that I then chaired, and other organizations called for a master plan for the park system of the entire city and another master plan for Virginia Key. Under the administration of Mayor Manny Diaz, the city eventually responded with processes for both and another one for Bicentennial Park. The master plan for the city, which Goody Clancy constructed, called for parks within short walking distance of all residents. Some of the recommendations reflected a public survey that demonstrated strong support among citizens. The report concluded, "Miami needs more parks."[49]

Yet master plans that garner public attention such as the Goody Clancy plan are often ignored. In 2005, Miami-Dade County Public School System sought to take over a portion of Haulover Park, the site of Lawson Thomas's 1945 demonstration, for a new school, and was dissuaded only by a loud public outcry. The city made another attempt to abrogate the deed restrictions on Virginia Key in 2004 through an elaborate land swap deal with the County that failed due especially to tenacious lobbying by the Sierra Club.[50]

In 2005, after prodding from the city's Parks Department director and the Parks Advisory Board as well as the UEL, Miami finally decided to inaugurate a master plan process for the entire island of Virginia Key. It eventually hired the prominent firm EDSA, Inc., of Fort Lauderdale for what turned out to be about $1 million to complete the plan. The entire effort was characterized by secret political agendas, constant delays, contentious public meetings, and official recommendations that systematically ignored public input. City documents stated that the proposed plan "should emphasize the opportunities for mixed-use waterfront development, including the redevelopment of the properties along the Marine Stadium, integrate and recommend improvements to the existing Sewage Treatment Plant, integrate and preserve the historic Virginia Key Beach Park, and make recommendations for future island-wide improvements and the protection of the remaining public beaches, parks and conservation areas."[51] It was almost two years before EDSA held a single public meeting. In March 2007 a *Miami Herald* editorial decried the city's pattern of avoiding public input.

> Instead of first holding public hearings or charrettes to learn what residents wanted on the publicly owned land and then using that information to develop a responsive master plan, the city did just the opposite. An architectural firm was hired to write several possible scenarios for the island without first hearing from city taxpayers and other stakeholders. Only when these scenarios were finished was the public invited into the process, at a meeting Thursday night where a single presentation drawn from the three scenarios was presented. That's just plain wrong. . . . Whatever motives are behind this backward process and its uninspiring results, they need a transparency that so far is missing.[52]

In February 2007, a UEL dinner that I organized to honor the recently deceased Athalie Range and veteran environmental activist Mabel Miller sought to push the city's consultants to listen to the public input. EDSA had met only with carefully selected stakeholders, not with park users and constituents throughout the county. The UEL event drew more than 100 people, including some prominent officials, but the consultants did not show up.

A cover story in the *Sun Post* emphasized the noncommercial value of the park. "Only 128 acres of the types of ecosystem found in Virginia Key—composed of mangroves, coastal hammocks and a dune area—exist in all the United States. Hence it is categorized as 'endangered vegetation,' with six native plant species also listed as endangered."[53]

Gene Tinnie's eloquent argument for preserving the island seamlessly fused the perspectives of the environmental and civil rights movements. "The people want Virginia Key to be an open, mostly natural space, with a beautiful beach and recreational facilities that enhance our awareness of the nature around us and of the history that has made us who we are today. The sewage treatment plant and the former waste dump with its lingering questions are encroachments on this vision with which we simply have to live, as they are products of the past which we cannot control. The future is another matter." Unlimited growth and urban sprawl was no longer regarded as positively as it was before. "It is no longer assumed that progress consists of building something on every square foot of available land. Nor is it acceptable that decisions that affect all of us should be driven by only a few of us, and those, mostly, who have no real stake in either the community's past or its future. Certainly the economic downturn in 2008 has served to confirm many of these misgivings and to strengthen citizens' resolve to seek a better way." Tinnie deplored the "agenda of 'privatizing everything'" that was underlain by "the exacerbated disparities and radical shifts of wealth" that occurred in the Reagan and Bush era. "Undoing all the damage caused by . . . effectively almost gutting the public sector . . . is a huge challenge, but I still dare to believe that we are up to it." Land use issues, he argued, "represent the core consciousness of the community today, especially in urban settings where these issues play out with very direct consequences to the quality of life of most of us."[54]

By the fall of 2009, the national economic collapse had had a direct impact on Virginia Key. The executive director of the Historic Virginia Key Beach Park Trust was earning a relatively high salary, and the trust employed another dozen or so people. Their ability to get grants had not met city administrators' expectations. There was a lack of accountability and oversight of its operations by city administrators. The trust's predominantly African American makeup was doubtless an important political factor. City administrators did not want to create racial tension by overtly challenging the operations of the trust but continued to see the park as a potential moneymaker for private interests, using the language of making it "sustainable."[55]

When I heard from several sources that Larry Spring, the African American chief financial officer of the city of Miami, was trying to persuade board members to support large commercial development on the Historic Virginia Key Beach Park in order to obtain much-needed revenue, I wrote to him directly.

It appears to me that the City Administration is quietly threatening the Trust that County Bond money could not be accessed to help build their Civil Rights Museum unless revenue from a hotel is factored into the equation. Further, it promotes the notion that this proposal should appear to come from members of the Trust rather than from the administration. I would ask you to cease and desist your role in altering the public purpose of the beach that has long been fought for by many members of the community—black and white.

Miami has a long and sad history of ignoring deed restrictions in the public interest and of using a variety of tactics to denigrate or erode public land and transfer it to private interests. . . . Instead of creating an open public process and finding creative solutions within an overall Master Plan to promote public use of public land, this City Administration is using sleight of hand and backroom pressure tactics to do the bidding of private developers. The city has also long sought to use African American spokesmen to deliver the message that development was necessary, indeed inevitable for this beach. You should be aware that your actions are thus part of a longstanding cynical pattern to erode the purpose and use of public land in the city of Miami. . . .

Miami's pattern of bowing to developers rather than respecting and enhancing the value of its historic public spaces is also part of a national pattern: similar incidents are taking place around the nation as civil war battlefields and other locations are being threatened by shopping malls and other forms of commercial development, permanently altering the character of historically significant locations. The public has been aroused against such unwarranted development time and again and will do so in relation to Virginia Key Park if further attempt to promote such development take place.

I argued that the fiscal crisis of the city was "being used as an excuse and battering ram to change the purpose of Virginia Key Beach Park by initiating a rush to development behind closed doors. Why should public parkland be the victim of the poor financial management of the city administration? Miami has a long tradition of allowing one limited commercial interest to gets its nose under the tent of public land and then turning around to find the entire character of the place permanently altered. Our civil rights to public space are clearly under attack."[56]

Andres Viglucci of the *Miami Herald* supported the preservation of Virginia Key and noted the recurring pattern of threats to the island: "Virginia Key Beach . . . was revived after a 10-year campaign led by the late Athalie Range, the city's first black commissioner, spurred by plans the city floated to turn it over to private development. Trust leaders say they now fear the same concept may be in the offing again, as city administrators urge them to explore 'partnering' with developers to establish . . . profit-making ventures."[57]

Finally, after much public pressure, a large public design workshop for the island's master plan was held at Columbus High School in May 2007. Yet the Marine Stadium had been omitted from the drawings for the public to consider, something that activist Blanca Mesa brought to EDSA's attention by drawing it in herself. A growing public antipathy toward the inside agenda that the EDSA consultants were promoting increasingly alienated many activists interested in the public, environmental, and recreational character of the island. Two years later, in May 2009, EDSA finally unveiled its plan. Instead of enhancing environmental features and providing nature trails, bike paths, and public access to the waterfront, the plan focused on creating a major sports complex in the old landfill area of the island and developing the marine stadium basin into a commercially viable facility.[58] Activists began to organize meetings to come up with an alternative plan that reflected public input achieving major victories in May and June 2009 when the City's Waterfront Board and Planning Advisory Board roundly rejected the EDSA master plan with scathing critiques. A slightly revised city plan was presented by EDSA in late September but the commission agreed to delay any final vote in order to get more public input. Seeking to organize that public input, the UEL held a well-attended design workshop on September 27 and came up with a series of specific alternative recommendations. We called for a welcome center, retention and upgrade of the marine stadium, no major sports complex in the old landfill site, bike trails on the north beach area, deference to the master plan for Historic Virginia Key

Beach, and minimal commercial intrusion in the marine stadium basin. A central plank also called for a new controlling authority to specifically oversee the future of the entire island.[59]

Although we had forced the city to scale back its plans considerably, we needed more time to complete an alternative plan. We then forged a tenuous Virginia Key Coalition between powerful advocates of a revived Marine Stadium and others who had greater interest in the natural features of the island at large. The following spring, the UEL-led coalition, in conjunction with Marine Stadium's Don Worth, UM architecture professor and preservationist Jorge Hernandez, Hilario Candela (the original architect of the stadium), and students at the University of Miami's School of Architecture, gathered to present a very different vision of the island from the EDSA plan. It was much more friendly to open space, called for less commercial development and more small-scale recreational uses of the island, and the revival of the Marine Stadium, which had remained derelict and neglected by the city since Hurricane Andrew had devastated it in August 1992. I worried that little attention was being paid to remedying the financial problems of Historic Virginia Key Beach Park Trust and the rest of the island; preserving the Miami Marine Stadium was receiving much greater emphasis. Yet the political momentum was on the side of the stadium at that time.

Finally, in July 2010, the efforts of the UEL and its many partners—including the Tropical Audubon Society, Miami Neighborhoods United, the Sierra Club, the Miami Rowing Club, and the Urban Paradise Guild—produced what passed for a public consensus (generally they are all manufactured) after many compromises. A *Miami Herald* editorial welcomed the result: "Fresh off the drawing board, the revised Virginia Key master plan finally reflects the public's—not developers'—best interests. It has been blessed by environmental groups and other stakeholders who roundly criticized previous attempts to inject more cement than green into the island makeover. When the City Commission takes up the plan . . . it should heed its own advisory groups, which have given it a thumbs up."[60]

What had changed? First, the city had a new administration. Former mayor Manny Diaz favored using a significant portion of the 1,000 acres for a conference center, extensive sports fields within a large athletic center, and twelve parking garages but did not support rehabilitating the marine stadium. Newly elected mayor Tomás Regalado said he favored "kinder and gentler" uses of the key's natural environment. So did the public, whose voice was finally organized and held some sway. The new plan reflected hundreds of hours of public testimony. It included the restoration of beaches and hammocks, the creation of bike paths and hiking trails, and revitalization of the marine stadium, but it eliminated large-scale development. The *Miami Herald* concluded that "the plan . . . now has its priorities straight: protecting the island's fragile environment while providing diverse opportunities for people to enjoy its many assets.[61]

The commission unanimously passed the new plan in July 2010. Our elation was tempered by Commissioner Marc Sarnoff's warning that such master plans often mean little in coming years as pressures change. He turned out to be prophetic because much of the master plan was ignored by commissioners and city administrators in the years that followed. What remains particularly interesting to me, as both a longtime participant and an observer, is the assessment by the *Miami Herald*'s chief reporter on urban design issues, Andres Viglucci. As the Virginia Key master plan was about to come before the commission, he wrote a relatively even-handed piece, but his final report on its adoption was buried in the back page of the local section and largely reflected official sources. He largely ignored the participation of the Historic Virginia Key Beach Park Trust, the UEL, and other advocacy organizations. The public had little understanding of the context of the island's history or the scope of efforts to ensure public access to the largest open space in the most populous city in Florida.[62]

Since 2010, much of the whole north point area of the island has been developed into a series of mountain bike trails. The old fish house called Jimbo's has been torn down and a vastly expanded public high school, Mast Academy, has been constructed along the causeway. Yet the development of the Marine Stadium has languished. Historic Virginia Key Beach Park Trust, with minimal staff and little city funding, continues to attract events as a prime revenue source.

Historic Virginia Key Beach Park, indeed, the entire island, continues to be impacted by burgeoning yet constantly changing forms of commercial encroachment that benefit wealthy and connected interests at the expense of the public. Sensitivity to the natural world or any sense of historical identity continues to be cavalierly subsumed under the latest development schemes. Even though a planning oversight board for the island was explicitly spelled out in the 2010 master plan and unanimously approved by the city commission, no such body was created by city commissioners until a vote towards that end was promoted by Commissioner Francis Suarez on December 10, 2015 with drafting help from UEL board members.

However, the latest example of this long-term pattern of deference to developers follows the debacle involving schemes to develop the Miami Marine Stadium from 2010 through May 2015. The historically significant stadium and the land around it impact the entire island's future. While the laudable goal of preserving the architecturally significant stadium became popular with the public and politicians, efforts to raise the necessary funds to do so—over $30 million—became mired in a series of insider financial schemes involving the leading advocacy group, Friends of the Miami Marine Stadium. Garnering national attention, several million dollars in County funds, and the support of Mayor Tomas Regalado and commissioners, the revival effort preoccupied leaders, to the exclusion of almost all else related to the island. Then, in December 2014, after an apparently successful publicity campaign culminating in TV and front-page *Miami Herald* coverage of famed Miami singer Gloria Estefan's effort to bring attention to the revival of the stadium, the Friends of Miami Marine Stadium were exposed in the press to be part of a scheme to make millions in fees for insiders. Their efforts to revitalize the stadium collapsed in scandal.[63]

As it turned out, however, promoters had long been dealing with a shadowy marine (and educational) promoter named Manny Alonso Puch, who had championed an upscale marine exhibition hall next to the stadium during the 2010 master plan process. Since the spring of 2014, the city has attempted to bring a major boat show to the island—and away from Miami Beach, where it had previously been held—through a license agreement with the National Marine Manufacturers Association in a manner that circumvented the need to get voter approval for such a use of public waterfront space. Yet by May 2015, it had become clear that what many thought was a week-long temporary boat show had a broad set of land use consequences for the entire island. The impact of the boat show would last for months and have far broader consequences than was ever presented in the 2010 master plan. First, city administrators decided to float a $16 million bond issue (not subject to voter approval) to fund extensive infrastructure in what they called a "flex park" (cleverly adapted from the master plan). That would result in acres of tents to display the boats (and perhaps additional shows in the future). In exchange, the association would pay $1.1 million a year and 50 percent of the income from sales of food and beverages to the city.

After that, awareness of the impact of the Miami Boat Show on the entire island increased. The show would take up at least seventeen acres of the public waterfront land for boat show tents that required many months of construction, it would have an impact on parking, access and the use of the Historic Virginia Key Beach Park, and it would clearly thwart public access to the waterfront and stave off potential funding to revive the marine stadium. There were also later attempts by the city administration to alter the online master plan in order to facilitate requests for proposals from marine industry developers to create hundreds of boat slips in the basin, something that was never contemplated by the master plan. Parking demands and potential traffic congestion spawned by the boat show (which will begin in February 2016) so riled the nearby village of Key Biscayne that it initiated lawsuits against the city of Miami and the Miami Boat Show for their lack of transparency and for potentially clogging the only route into and out of their island of 12,000 residents. The city commission voted for the boat show unanimously on May 28, 2015, ignoring its own master plan and creating the penultimate example of commercial takeover of public space on this long-abused island.[64] In the end, the board of the Historic Virginia Key Beach Park Trust was silent and did not oppose the boat show in May 2015, perhaps because its members had been inadequately informed about its impact or because they did not want to upset the economic-political establishment that supported the trust's continued existence.

Within this broader context, the Historic Virginia Key Beach Park Trust has been unable to decide how to spend upward of $15 million in county bond funds that voters originally approved in 2004 for a civil rights museum with the theme of "Free to Be." Trust officials are caught in the awkward situation of receiving capital dollars from a large financial proposal by a Canadian consulting firm that had little knowledge of the local political terrain. Plans for the museum building (originally estimated at $40 million) have languished for years without resolution or action because the trust has needed to show it had adequate operating revenue or an alternative plan, which trust members have been slow to complete.

The assault on the public waterfront often seems endless; politicians, city administrators, and even the public seem to have little memory of the past. To complicate the demands for Miami's downtown public waterfront, in the summer of 2014, the Miami-Dade County Commission approved plans for a Cuban exile history museum to be built on another prime parcel of public land. It was projected to be built on a three-acre piece of land in downtown Miami called Parcel B (along the water near the American Airlines Arena, a large ship slip, and Bicentennial Park, now renamed Museum Park). This "free land" was alleged to be worth well over $100 million. Yet back in 1996, when the Miami Heat created an advertising campaign to win a referendum to secure park land from the county in a complex deal for what became the American Airlines Arena, it promoted the concept that Parcel B would become parkland. This was a key element in its successful strategy to obtain voter approval of county funding and use of the land. However, the county has long neglected the task of transforming this land into any viable park. Instead, because of the team's political clout, the Miami Heat has used Parcel B for parking and staging.

Only one Cuban American commissioner, Xavier Suarez, voted against the proposal to convey the land for a Cuban exile history museum. African American commissioner Dennis Moss was also the conspicuous ethnic exception; he voted for the Cuban Exile Museum with the expressed expectation of support from commissioners for funding a black history museum (in association with the Black Archives) at an equally prominent waterfront site. Moss noted the long-standing prosperity gap between blacks and Cubans in Miami and mentioned the hundreds of millions of tax dollars the county had given to support two local museums—one for art and one for science—that were later named after several of Miami's wealthiest patrons. Moss asked for county dollars to fully fund the black museum on the waterfront as a form of social and historical justice, ignoring the precious quality of waterfront parkland. It should be noted that neither he nor the staff of the Black Archives spoke with members of the Historic Virginia Key Beach Park Trust about a proposal for what might be considered to be a rival civil rights/black history museum. The lack of overall strategic political leadership for waterfront development and the absence of coordination to promote historical museums in Miami-Dade County has led to narrowly focused ethnic competition for institutions on public waterfront space. What a sad development when there are other viable locations.[65]

Another push for prime waterfront land came in 2014 from a major league soccer group led by celebrity player David Beckham. After failing to secure a site for a soccer stadium at the Port of Miami, the Beckham group sought to build it on land that was part of Museum Park (formerly Bicentennial Park) and to fill in part of a large and historical public boat slip just north of the American Airlines Arena. County mayor Carlos Gimenez was in favor of the downtown site, as was, at first, Miami mayor Tomás Regalado. The TV media and Mayor Gimenez all fawned over the soccer star and his appearances in Miami and his plans both received broad exposure. Yet a public outcry against taking the prime waterfront land slowly became better organized. Pressure against the deal came from multiple sources, including new downtown residents, nearby museum advocates, planners, architects, and former mayor Diaz. Behind the scenes, that pressure also included a meeting I and fellow UEL Board member Grace Solares had with Mayor Regalado. We gave numerous reasons why the mayor should switch his position. We may have helped convince him to change his mind and oppose the stadium. The deal at that location died. And after other protracted negotiations, it now appears that the stadium will be built, ironically enough, in Overtown, near the Miami River.[66]

To me, the overlapping issues of social justice and cultural memory for people of African American heritage, for Cuban Americans, and, indeed, for all residents reflects the rather stark power of money and lobbyists to influence land development. The challenges seem never ending. As this book goes to press, two developments underscore the oscillating sense of hope and despair public space activists feel about the future of Virginia Key and greater access to Miami's waterfront for the benefit of the public. It so often seems that the language of "financial benefits" for powerful interest groups has supplanted the language of the public waterfront. On the one hand, the city of Miami administration and the city and county commissions have totally ignored the 2010 master plan and instead promote and facilitate a gargantuan Miami Boat Show facility surrounding the Marine Stadium. They have transformed the area into a far more intensive commercial venue than either the public or city commissioners ever agreed to. Both the environmental impact and the impact on Historic Virginia Key Beach Park will be considerable. The park will be transformed into a parking lot for boat show and allied construction activities for weeks on end. Many have felt the city administration of Miami, which has pushed an $18 million bond issue for loosely considered infrastructure under the label of a "flex park," has set up the entire basin area to accommodate an endless array of conventions and other commercial ventures. Such a future was clearly opposed in the 2010 master plan. To its credit, the *Miami Herald* editorial board noted in December 2015 that the city administration "has not acted as a responsible steward of this invaluable waterfront property that belongs to the residents of Miami." In the end, the county commission also acceded to a fait accompli to allow the boat show to move forward even in the face of lawsuits from the city of Key Biscayne. Eight hundred thousand square feet of semi-permanent tents are being erected and slips for 830 boats will take over much of the Marine Stadium Basin, effectively closing off public use in exchange for a reputed $600 million in general economic stimulus to the local economy.[67]

On the other hand, there is some hope for better planning of the island in the future. After the November 2015 election of Ken Russell, a new city commissioner for waterfront District Two, another commissioner, Francis Suarez, took the lead in working closely with members of the UEL to draft and get the city commission to pass a new ordinance (on first reading) that finally creates a Virginia Key Advisory Board with broad membership and power to review future development and land use changes on the island. Constant public vigilance is needed in the future, as is the assistance of a variety of advocacy organizations. The city also made an attempt to—finally—seek professionals to rehabilitate the Marine Stadium, although many doubted that the city would be able to afford the estimated $35 million cost or ultimately see the long-term economic viability in its revival.

Overall, the lack of integrated waterfront planning remains a major detriment to the future economic viability—not to mention the identity—of Miami, which continues to squander its major asset while failing to preserve or enhance what little is left of its natural environment. What hope is there at the end of this book? I attempt to sketch some ideas to consider in the afterword.

Afterword

The Real Miami; Better Than a Theme Park

Everybody needs beauty as well as bread, places to play in and pray in, where nature may heal and give strength to body and soul alike.

John Muir, 1912

The power of nature is the power of life in association. Nothing stands alone.

Terry Tempest Williams, 2004

If you don't know where you are, you don't know who you are.

Wendell Berry, 1992

Stimulating public participation in growth management and land conservation is a major challenge of contemporary urban life. The politics of land use planning must be redirected from serving private interests toward achieving broad social goals: constructing and preserving healthy jobs and neighborhoods, caring about the beauty of the natural world beyond the myriad glittering surfaces that surround and submerge us, appreciating the continuity of place over time, and enhancing the uses of public space. It requires forging long-term plans for sustaining ourselves and our cities through the process of climate change.

This book has examined the changing fate of African Americans as their history intersected with the erosion of waterfront public space in Miami, particularly as embodied in a fragile island off the coast. The story centers on continuing economic injustices that are perpetrated by corporations and perpetuated by community leaders, the enduring structure of discriminatory real estate policies, and failed local steward-ship of public lands. Yet in a few critical moments, people have chal-lenged the legacy of racial exclusion and segregation, imagined visionary possibilities, and demonstrated more inclusive civic uses of public space. Sadly, those plans and pressures have been unable to improve the lives of tens of thousands of poor residents of the area—black, white, and brown—by giving them access to natural places. Virginia Key is only a few miles from downtown Miami, but the social distance between the city and the island is difficult to cross.

Poverty remains entrenched in inner-city Miami, and planning and redevelopment programs have sometimes been even more destructive than neglect. Many local problems emanate from the disjuncture be-tween local ethnic, racial, and class realities and state and national poli-cies. Politicians spend much more time planning boondoggles, such as a new baseball stadium, than they do addressing poverty. Others defer to dreams of a creative class focused on art and technology, often ignoring deeply entrenched social needs that are all too often divorced from the natural world. Given the ephemeral character of political platforms, per-vasive public cynicism, and the weakness of both bureaucratic memory and environmental advocacy groups, the result is, at best, inconsistent concern for the economic condition of ordinary people and the viabil-ity of public spaces. This neglect is not accidental. The prevailing power structure produces an inexorable erosion of public space, new patterns of poverty, fortress enclaves, and profound skepticism about governance. Similar trends are visible in other cities, but Miami seems to be a potent harbinger of the future. Although we often feel powerless, it is our future to make.[1]

Miami's experience reflects the inequality produced by the pervasive confusion between corporate capitalism and democracy, the conun-drums involved in land use decisions, and boosters' manipulation of our sense of community. The problem was most cogently defined decades ago by David Potter in *People of Plenty*[2] and has been summarized by Jack-son Lears: "The extraordinary availability of natural resources as well as the advanced technology, fluid society, and enterprising spirit . . . al-lowed Americans to transform these resources into the raw materials of economic development; the result of that development . . . was a huge and growing pile of mass produced things. That was American abundance. Americans were a people of plenty because they had lots of stuff."[3] We appear to be waking up in the aftermath of that experience in a sharply bifurcated society that privileges a few and consigns the many to insecure, low-wage jobs and an increasingly alienated existence.

We have lived through a prolonged Cold War; hot wars in Vietnam, Afghanistan, and Iraq; and racial violence in cities. The world is now dominated by global capitalism, burgeoning plutocracy, and neoliberal policies. Yet too many academics discuss abstract, theoretical questions in language that is incomprehensible to nonspecialists. By adopting more publicly oriented goals and experimenting with practical applications, such as greater economic equity, more creative synergy between government and business, and a reawakened relationship with nature, scholars and others can help open up political debate, dislodge partisan gridlock, and expose and even subvert oligarchic power structures. We can work collaboratively to produce what David Harvey has called "spaces of hope" by thinking holistically about new ways to stimulate investment and job creation through more inclusive forms of democracy and continuing to focus on both our sense of community and our relationship to the natural world.[4]

This book about Miami began with an examination of patterns of discrimination, emerging campaigns for the ability to exercise a civil right to public waterfront space, and the preservation of historic sites, but it expanded its focus to include civic participation in reshaping our relationship to the environment. Activists who live in cities that resemble theme parks have become aware of the interconnected problems that result from deference to gigantic entertainment complexes as economic panaceas. Politicians and the largely passive public who have hailed the next big idea, the next Interama, have learned that despite repeated revisions of this model from 1939 to 1974, what they are left with in the end is a dump for toxic and infectious waste. We should know better than to be seduced by the pretty pictures and designs for what so often are white elephants whose detritus litters our few remaining public spaces. We should forge more viable urban visions on a human scale around the values of health, exercise, and recreation in natural settings and the attractions of a simpler mode of living instead of focusing on huge air-conditioned venues for novel spectacles. Tourism as the be-all and end-all of a local economy can be a fatal snare.[5]

Tourism, according to Dennis Judd and Susan Fainstein, "marks the culture of the place that is visited." It "provides people with a reflected image of themselves, which then leads them to conform to that image. It also does so by providing a globalized space within the local community; when local residents use this space, they become, in effect, tourists. . . . The main spatial effect of urban tourism is to produce spaces that are prettified, that do not feature people involved in manual labor (except when engaged in historical reenactments or entertainment), that exclude visible evidence of poverty, and that give people opportunities for entertainment and officially sanctioned fun."[6]

Moving away from the monoculture of tourism that is so often associated with Miami—although this model is very different from the view of those who regard it as "Your-Ami" rather than their own—means seeing ourselves as empowered actors in a history that goes beyond tourism and the economics of global finance and trade. Our stories and our collective wisdom must be heard, collected, and organized, must become fully functioning parts of a broader democratic mosaic that can be translated into concrete plans for greater equality. That requires us to reinvent the relationship between cities, democracy, and the natural world to benefit all people. The gargantuan sports and gambling complexes we are inveigled into building for private owners often assisted with taxpayers' dollars do not improve the quality of life for most residents or even fill the public coffers with tax revenue.[7]

We have learned that environmental activism requires more than the fixation of fashionable elites with capturing the sublimity of nature and preserving pristine wilderness far from urban dwellers. A broader mosaic of people can look beyond the landscapes of modernity and postmodernity toward holistic forms of integration and civic management within the natural world. That means more than simply preserving nature in urban-oriented locations; it means finding new ways to act within and learn from nature. Secretary of the Interior Bruce Babbitt declared that the "imperative for good land use planning is public involvement and active participation from all levels of government" and called for Americans "to take renewed interest in defending our heritage—the freedom

and glory of wide open spaces." For an Arizonan, the association of freedom with the mythic landscape of the West comes naturally. But more is
required than preserving natural and historical places.[8]

The real challenge is to more fully appreciate the synergy among nature, public planning, and a new economy that Terry Tempest Williams
has called the Open Space of Democracy, in which we learn from nature
how to preserve and enhance it while changing ourselves in ways we can
barely imagine: "It is easy to believe we the people have no say, that the
powers in Washington will roll over our local, on-the-ground concerns
with their corporate energy ties and thumper trucks. It is easy to believe
that the American will is only focused on how to get rich, how to be entertained, and how to distract itself from the hard choices we have before
us as a nation." But attending to our relationship with the natural world
and opening spaces for public discussion and thoughtful consideration
of our priorities is possible. In the process, we will have to overcome
the current fragmentation of our own consciousness, what Benjamin
Barber and others see as our infantilization through the endless lure of
commodities that we consume in utter ignorance of their conditions of
production and the context in which we acquire them.[9]

In 1976, during the nation's bicentennial, Harvey Molotch called for a
"counter-coalition" against the urban growth machine that would come
together around issues of equality and environmental concerns to build
new bases of social power. Yet the fluidity and contradictions of global
capitalism, which consolidates incessantly while simultaneously rhetorically championing individual freedom, coupled with the growing power
of corporate-dominated mass media and the fragmentation of critics has
allowed a dangerously backward-looking neoliberalism to move into the
ascendancy and remain all too powerful. That trend continues, despite
the financial crisis, the stock market collapse, the bank bailout, and ob-
scenely expensive and ineffective wars initiated during the administration of George W. Bush.[10] Our irrational deference to the urban growth
machine and our fascination with technology and postmodern spectacles must be reconsidered. We have heard cries against the devastating
effects of overbuilding and environmental destruction before. In Florida,
John Kunkle Smalls's 1929 book *From Eden to the Sahara: Florida's Tragedy* sounded an alarm that few heard or heeded. Philip Wylie, Marjory
Stoneman Douglas, Bill Baggs, and John Pennekamp all made fervent

appeals to alert Floridians to the impact of the modern juggernaut. Instead of relying on elites to champion environmental values, we must construct broad coalitions on a foundation of coherent messages that connect the quality of everyday life with conditions in both the natural world and the communities we live in.[11]

The shape of postmodern power facing us is dauntingly gargantuan, yet insidiously seductive. "Postmodern, postindustrial capitalism is about consuming experience not goods, about creating insatiable desire that must be fulfilled in front of an approving audience," historian Hal Rothman wrote about Las Vegas. Who could resist our all-too-human desire for exuberant fun and a chance at winning the jackpot? Once unleashed, such desires only generate hunger for more. That's what Las Vegas, Orlando, and Atlantic City are all about. Rothman, Robert Venturi, and other observers have explored the fascination generated by these places.[12] Gambling resorts should not become the model for the livable cities of the future, especially given the challenges we face in terms of energy, housing, employment, education, and technology. Experiments in other cities have already failed. Waterfront festival marketplaces designed by the James Rouse Company can be reproduced only a few times before cities become stale copies of single brand, having cheapened or even eviscerated their distinctive histories in the process.

Basing local and regional economies on gambling and tourism reinforces a culture of speed, spectacle, and status built upon chance and placelessness. Such foolish short-sightedness mirrors the sense of futility that some people experience when they think about their work, their entertainment, and their disconnection from the land. Wendell Berry has posed deeper questions about the basic cultural premises of a competitive society: "The ideal of competition always implies, and in fact requires, that any community must be divided into a class of winners and a class of losers. . . . The danger of the ideal of competition is that it neither proposes nor implies any limits. . . . The human economy is pitted without limit against nature." Pleasure industries dominate the modern landscape in ways that reinforce the futility of even attempting to change the economic structures from which they benefit. "More and more," Berry adds, "we take for granted that work must be destitute of pleasure. More and more, we assume that if we want to be pleased we must wait until evening, or the weekend, or vacation, or retirement."[13]

In a competitive environment, a sense of place is perceived to be the province of older elites. Nowhere is this truer than in Miami. Berry's colleague, Wallace Stegner, explored the problem of place: "Some are born in their place, some find it, some realize after long searching that the place they left is the one they have been searching for. But whatever their relation to it, it is made a place only by slow accrual, like a coral reef." We should adapt ourselves to a simpler, more locally grounded life within our global, electronically connected world, one that values tolerance, equality, and continuing education about the fascinating natural world we live in.[14]

In my experience, new modes of civic activism in Miami have shown the potential that lies in converging models of consciousness that build constituencies and envision a life of work and pleasure that is entwined with the natural world. Achieving that future will require new respect for nature, planning, and the history we have made on the land. "The challenge that lies ahead," Patrick Hurley writes, "is finding effective ways to link the preservation of built and natural landscape more coherently in terms of interpretation and comprehensive urban planning."[15]

We must not be naïve about the opposition this movement will encounter. Highly paid professionals use politically charged language to distort common assumptions about healthier uses of our environment. One example is Republican Party strategist Frank Luntz, who has invented such titles as "Healthy Forests Initiative" for a program that in practice allows private lumber companies to decimate national forest land. The corporate-dominated and well-funded right wing has a seemingly limitless ability to dress up their agenda in propaganda. To counter their message and their power, we must build a grassroots effort to construct a better world from the ground up.[16]

More pointed public debates at the local, state, and national levels must explore the diverse physical, historical, and cultural elements that make for livable places. Drawing upon the stories and real-life concerns of ordinary people that intersect with issues related to urban design, structural economic change, continuing forms of discrimination, shifting demographics, and the politics of growth and recession will require new tools of communication. The commercial media have largely abdicated their responsibility for public education and dialogue because they are financially dependent on revenue from companies that advertise

empty commodities and because they disseminate politically self-serving ideological positions. Government-supported and nonprofit media
remain lame and marginalized; at best, they stage formulaic debates
that explore only two sides of an issue and fail to allow access to those
who would reformulate the questions at hand in more provocative and
open ways. The new social media are good at mobilizing existing affinity groups, but they often fragment the dialogue and fuel the power of
special interests.

I remain convinced that evolving a new urban ecological ethos requires us to confront and transform the educational-media-entertain-
ment complex that now controls information. It means challenging the
tax structure that allows unlimited write-offs for advertisements that divide us from one another and from the land. Speeding through the landscape while fiddling obsessively with the latest gadgets offered at bargain
prices produces an obliviousness that can be fatal. We must create a new
focus on the public domain that will enable us to collaboratively redesign
and redevelop the land we live on. We must also demand greater equity
in public funding for projects that sustain a more profound sense of community as part of—rather than apart from—nature. And that requires
going beyond a simplistic deference to public-private partnerships, as
Miami-Dade Commissioner Xavier Suarez recently noted. "The problem
is that there are public projects susceptible to some form of privatization
and others for which privatization merely means that a classic public
good (e.g., a highway or a beach) goes from being truly 'public' (i.e., free
to all residents) to being unaffordable to the working and middle class."[17]

Our society's grave political and economic woes have no quick fixes.
Our own cultural proclivities are part of the problem. But the bankruptcy
of those in power has been amply demonstrated. Developing solutions
will require us to elect a new generation of democratic leaders, to know
the scope of urban possibilities, to ground our actions in commitment to
the place and the people around us, and to act in concrete ways to engage
more and more folks in common efforts. We must listen to other people's
stories and become part of one another's lives through newly designed
communal spaces for conversation and dialogue.

The concept of recentering our focus on the natural world and on
human-scale development has had many champions, including Henry
David Thoreau, George Perkins Marsh, and John Muir in the nineteenth

century; Aldo Leopold, Jane Jacobs, and Rachel Carson in the postwar period; and Bill McKibben, Richard Louv, and others who are addressing twenty-first-century dilemmas. Aldo Leopold wrote that "harmony with land is like harmony with a friend; you cannot cherish his right hand and chop off his left. . . . The land is one organism. Its parts, like our own parts, compete with each other and co-operate with each other. The competitions are as much a part of the inner workings as the co-operations. You can regulate them—cautiously—but not abolish them."[18] An ecological understanding of the land makes us aware of how we compete or cooperate with other organisms and the processes that sustain them.

"More than anything," write Richard Louv and Howard Frumkin, "we need a vision of healthy, wholesome places, a vision that extends from densely settled cities to remote rural spreads, from the present to the future, from the most fortunate among us to the least fortunate, from the youngest child to the oldest adult. Conservation of land is central to this vision. Such places will promote our health, enhance our well-being, nourish our spirits, and steward the beauty and resources of the natural world."[19] This vision is inspiring, to be sure, but how are we to get from here to there?

The most penetrating local perspective comes from Gene Tinnie, the African American activist who has long been a leader in the campaign to preserve Historic Virginia Key Beach.

In the 21st century, two things will be recognized that will change the paradigms of our traditional thinking. One is that all political questions will need to be reduced to the single question of Land Use; the old parameters of income, social class, race and ethnicity, education levels as determinants of political decisions (politics is nothing more or less than that art and science of determining who gets what, where, when, how and why) are outdated, divisive, and dysfunctional for today's needs. The second sea change in thinking is directly related to this one, which is that history and land are one and the same thing. No human history has ever occurred anywhere but on a land base. (Even our adventures at sea or in space must take place aboard structures manufactured from land-based materials, with land-based methods). Because land is the embodiment of its natural history (volcanic eruptions, glacial movements, sedimentary rock, wave action, etc.), and humans—whether we admit it or not—are a part of nature ("we're all made from stardust"), not apart from nature, then human and natural history are fused.[20]

Deeply informed by the African American experience in Miami and by the struggle to prevent the erosion of public space, Tinnie understands that the land is the ultimate resource that social power depends on. "We need a new story about race and place in America," Carl Anthony says. "This new story is not only about toxic waste dumps and hazardous materials; it is about the fundamental right of a people to have a relation with all of creation."[21]

Beyond the ideas of urban synergy propounded by scholars such as Richard Florida, reintegrating our future with the natural world means reinventing growth and spatial dynamics to benefit all while wasting less, reusing more, and being conscious of where the goods we consume come from and how they are produced. Today Miami has heard new messages from citywide organizations that assert dramatically different visions; Take Back the Land, Catalyst Miami, Seeds of the City, the Miami Workers Center, Emerge Miami, Earth Learning, and the Cleo Institute are but a few examples.[22]

Nationally, historic preservationists are widening their field through the whole place movement. Although Virginia Key is fated to be underwater within this century because of climate change, it remains a unique location that can illustrate how public planning and history, recreation and nature can be fused to define new public spaces of hope, solidarity, and pleasure. Seeing how entire groups of people have been overlooked and reintegrating them into these spaces offers exciting lessons about our diversity and our ability to learn from the mangroves and hurricanes, the ibis and the manatee.

Through my years of political activism and scholarly reflection, I have come to understand that civic involvement is a lifelong commitment that takes different forms at different times. At the moment, I want to pay more attention to the quality of life enjoyed by my daughter, a young adult with multiple intellectual disabilities yet a uniquely feisty and beautiful soul. I have learned so much from her over the years. Her curiosity, love of animals, and determination have been inspirations for me.

And speaking out on behalf of the environment at crowded meetings in public buildings in downtown Miami is not the same as being immersed in the natural world, which often eludes me. But enabling those labeled "disabled" to have access to Virginia Key, to continuing education, and to work skills—like enabling African Americans to have their own beach on the island—demands collective action.

Several years ago, I worked with others to found an organization called Nature Links for Lifelong Learning that serves young adults with developmental delays and disabilities. It was originally located at the wonderful waterfront site near City Hall in Coconut Grove called Shake A Leg Miami. Through Nature Links for Lifelong Learning, children have experienced nature through sailing and park cleanups, internships at the local zoo, and a myriad of other skill-building activities. In a manner that brings my own work full circle, we have sought to create Nature Links for Lifelong Learning as a component of the Historic Virginia Key Beach Park Trust, along with other partners such as the cities of Miami, Pinecrest, and South Miami and the Patricia and Phillip Frost Museum of Science. Nature Links will provide this overlooked constituency with opportunities to create an organic garden; learn about sea life, the weather, nutrition, and the body; help with habitat restoration; and learn culinary arts by working at the historic concession stand and at other locations. Using nature as the subject, site, and medium for learning for those with disabilities may well become a model for other groups. Our civil rights to public space and our sensitivity to the human rights of everyone are forged through our deeper appreciation of the natural world.[23] As Gene Tinnie put it, "Our planning for folks with developmental disabilities is a part of the larger need to address the entire population of folks with ALL disabilities," whether those disabilities are developmental or are inflicted by society. "That understanding should not divert our focus; on the contrary, it should sharpen it."[24]

"In the 21st century," Tinnie adds, "sound thinking requires us to reconsider and reverse conventional ways of thinking and doing things. For example, separate discussions of and movements for civil rights, women's rights, LGBT rights, and the rights of the disabled are rapidly becoming obsolete. African American history is a core element of American history, not a separate field. The history of Hispanic people in America, like that of the African Diaspora, directs our attention to the global forces that have converged in this place over time. Learning the history of the Holocaust and other genocides, civil wars, and armed conflicts is vital for a people who would learn to make peace among themselves. We need to know human history and make progress toward universal human rights."

Accommodating the particular needs of disabled persons is not new. "In postwar Europe," Tinnie added, "when the terrible toll of suffering and disability that remained in the wake of war was visible among the survivors, public and private accommodations alike took these disabilities into account. The principle was to build an environment that serves everyone. Those with developmental delays are active subjects, not objects that require special adjustments. Disabled persons can provide insight into what works for them and for others, including the visually impaired and the wheelchair bound. Programs such as Nature Links are designed to meet specific needs, but their effects can be more inclusive. We all have challenges and need to be more open to others. This project is another variation of "Think globally, act locally."[25]

Looking back at the contours of segregation in Miami's past and the measures that continued to constrict access to space and the ability to see the spatial boundaries around how we live, work, and play today underscores how far we have come. Yet we have much further to go in order to generate a democracy that offers hope, health, and equality to all. We must move beyond cynicism, build coalitions, and become proactive. Public awareness about the ramifications of climate change and other serious environmental threats is essential. Public involvement in planning exciting new civic spaces through forums and modes of communication that facilitate listening to the diverse voices around us, stimulating entrepreneurial talents, and cultivating a revived interest in the natural world, healthy styles of living, and community wellness can point the way to a better future. Even in Miami.

Notes

Acknowledgments

1. See Gregory W. Bush, "'Playground of the USA': Miami and the Promotion of Spectacle," in "Orange Empires," edited by William Deverell, Greg Hise, and David C. Sloan, special issue, *Pacific Historical Review* 68 (May 1999): 153–72.

2. See Gregory W. Bush, "Special Resource Study: Report to Congress," National Park Service, 2008, http://parkplanning.nps.gov/document.cfm?parkID=423&proje ctID=12493&documentID=39793. See also Gregory Bush, "Virginia Key Beach Park Natural Resource Study: Historic Context & Significance Research & National Significance: Public Recreation as a Civil Right," unpublished study, University of Miami.

Introduction: The Struggle for the Civil Right to Public Space in Miami

1. Douglas Hanks, "Gimenez Pushes Privatization of County's Transit Future," *Miami Herald*, September 25, 2015, http://www.miamiherald.com/news/local/community/miami-dade/article36625737.html#storylink=cpy.

2. United States Census, "Miami-Dade County, Florida," State & County Quick-Facts, http://quickfacts.census.gov/qfd/states/12/12086.html.

3. See Gregory W. Bush, "Special Resource Study: Report to Congress," National Park Service, 2008, http://parkplanning.nps.gov/document.cfm?parkID=423&proje ctID=12493&documentID=39793. See also Gregory Bush, "Virginia Key Beach Park Natural Resource Study: Historic Context & Significance Research & National Significance: Public Recreation as a Civil Right," unpublished study, University of Miami.

4. Dan Gaby, *The Miami River and Its Tributaries* (Miami: Historical Association of South Florida, 1995), 18–22.

5. Quoted in National Oceanic and Atmospheric Administration (NOAA), *Biscayne Bay: Environmental History and Annotated Bibliography* (Silver Spring, Md.: NOAA, 2000), 31.

6. Eileen M. Smith, "Black Churchgoers, Environmental Activism, and the Preservation of Nature in Miami, Florida," dissertation abstract, January 1, 2003, FIU: Digital Commons, Florida International University, http://digitalcommons.fiu.edu/dissertations/AAI3126427.

7. Johnny Winton, interview with Gregory Bush, 2000, in author's possession. See also Harvey J. Graff, *The Dallas Myth: The Making and Unmaking of an American City* (Minneapolis: University of Minnesota Press, 2008), 6; Tom Wolfe, "Art and Real Estate: The Secret of Urban Renewal," address delivered at Miami's Freedom Tower, October 7, 2007 (notes in author's possession); and Richard Florida, "The Rise of the Creative Class," *Washington Monthly*, May 2002, http://www.washingtonmonthly.com/features/2001/0205.florida.html. For a critique of Florida, see Alex Macguilles, "The Ruse of the Creative Class," *American Prospect* (January 2010), http://prospect.org/cs/articles?article=the_rise_of_the_creative)_class.

8. See Victor M. Valle and Rodolfo D. Torres, *Latino Metropolis* (Minneapolis: University of Minnesota Press, 2000), chapter 4.

9. See, most notably, Richard Louv, *Last Child in the Woods: Saving Our Children from Nature-Deficit Disorder* (Chapel Hill, N.C.: Algonquin Books of Chapel Hill, 2008).

10. Paula Park, "Parks and Profits: Believe It or Not, Miami's Planning Czar Jack Luft Says He Can Make Virginia Key Both Lovely and Lucrative," *Miami New Times*, October 23, 1997; Jacob Bernstein, "Take Me Out to . . . the Parking Lot?" *Miami New Times*, January 27, 2000, http://www.miaminewtimes.com/2000-01-27/news/take-me-out-to-the-parking-lot/.

11. Kenneth Goings and Raymond Mohl, "Toward a New African American Urban History," *Journal of Urban History* 21, no. 3 (1995): 288. See also the penetrating film *Claiming Open Spaces*, produced by Austin Allen (New York: Third World Newsreel, 2001). On the recent use of parks to redefine community, see examples of the work of the Trust for Public Land at www.tpl.org; Patricia Leigh Brown, "Born of Disaster, Little Park Helps Redeem a Community," *New York Times*, October 22, 2005; Mike Davis, *City of Quartz* (New York: Vintage Books, 1992), 226–28; Jennifer Wolch, John P. Wilson, and Jed Fernbach, "Parks and Parks Funding in Los Angeles: An Equity Mapping Analysis," *Urban Geography* 26 (2005): 4–35; and Peter Harnik, *Inside City Parks* (Washington, D.C.: Urban Land Institute, 2000), 47–52.

12. Charles Birnbaum, "In Defense of Open Space," *Preservation* 57 (September–October 2005): 38–39. On black tourism, see Sandhya Somashekhar, "Black History Becoming a Star Tourist Attraction," *Washington Post*, August 15, 2005.

13. Don Mitchell, *The Right to the City: Social Justice and the Fight for Public Space* (New York: Guilford Press, 2003), 129.

14. Boyd Shearer, "Narrative," The Daily Aesthetic, http://www.uky.edu/Projects/TDA/narrativ.htm.

15. Robin D. G. Kelley, "'We Are Not What We Seem': Rethinking Working-Class Opposition in the Jim Crow South," *Journal of American History* 80 (June 1993): 84–85, quoted at Shearer, "Narrative."

16. Enid Pinkney, interview with Gregory Bush, 1999, Special Collections Department, Otto G. Richter Library, University of Miami; Wallace Stegner, "The Sense of Place," in *Where the Bluebird Sings to the Lemonade Springs* (1993; repr., New York: Penguin, 1992), 199.

17. Lynn Abrams, *Oral History Theory* (New York: Routledge, 2010), 169.

18. Kim Lacy Rogers, *Righteous Lives: A Narrative of the New Orleans Civil Rights Movement* (New York: New York University Press, 1993), 11.

Chapter 1. Wade-In: Lawson Thomas and the Potent Combination of Direct Action and Negotiation

1. "Negroes Test Beach Rights at Haulover," *Miami Herald*, May 10, 1945, 1.

2. Marvin Dunn, *Black Miami in the Twentieth Century* (Gainesville: University Press of Florida, 1997), 160; Generally the best account is Kirk Nielsen, "A Historic Dip," *Miami New Times*, August 4, 1999.

3. Glenn Garvin, Michael J. Sainton, and Lance Dixon, "Remembering Protest that Led to Opening First Beach for Black Miamians," *Miami Herald*, May 9, 2015.

4. Jacqueline Dowd Hall, "The Long Civil Rights Movement and the Political Uses of the Past," *Journal of American History* 91 (March 2005): 1233–63; Glenda Gilmore, *Defying Dixie: The Radical Roots of Civil Rights, 1919–1950* (New York: W. W. Norton, 2008); Eric Arnessen, "Reconsidering the 'Long Civil Rights Movement,'" *Historically Speaking* 10, no. 2 (2009): 31–34; John Dittmer, *Local People: The Struggle for Civil Rights in Mississippi* (Urbana: University of Illinois Press, 1994); Mary Z. Dudziak, *Cold War Civil Rights: Race and the Image of American Democracy* (Princeton, N.J.: Princeton University Press, 2000), 11.

5. George B. Kirsch, "Municipal Golf and Civil Rights in the United States, 1910–1965," *Journal of African American History* 92, no. 3 (2007): 371. For a broad perspective, see also Jeff Wiltse, *Contested Waters: A Social History of Swimming Pools in America* (Chapel Hill: University of North Carolina Press, 2007).

6. Harry Boyte and Sarah Evans, *Free Spaces: The Sources of Democratic Change in America* (Chicago: University of Chicago Press, 1992); Michel de Certeau, *The Practice of Everyday Life*, vol. 2, *Living and Cooking* (Minneapolis: University of Minnesota Press, 1998), 98–99.

7. Angel David Nieves, "'We Are Too Busy Making History . . . to Write History': African American Women, Constructions of Nation, and the Built Environment in the New South, 1892–1968," in *"We Shall Independent Be": African American Place Making and the Struggle to Claim Space in the United States*, edited by Angel David Nieves and Leslie M. Alexander (Boulder: University Press of Colorado, 2008), 309; Robin D. G. Kelley, "'We Are Not What We Seem': Rethinking Black Working-Class Opposition in the Jim Crow South," *Journal of American History* 80 (June 1993): 77. See also Andrew Hurley, *Beyond Preservation: Using Public History to Revitalize Inner Cities* (Philadelphia: Temple University Press, 2010); and Ned Kaufman, *Place, Race, and Story: Essays on the Past and Future of Historic Preservation* (New York: Routledge, 2009).

8. Mike Davis, *Ecology of Fear: Los Angeles and the Imagination of Disaster* (New

York: Random House, 1998); Harvey J. Graff, *The Dallas Myth: The Making and Un-making of an American City* (Minneapolis: University of Minnesota Press, 2008).

9. Quoted in Martin Wachs, "The Evolution of Transportation Policy in Los Angeles: Images of Past Policies and Future Prospects," in *The City: Los Angeles and Urban Theory at the End of the Twentieth Century*, edited by Allen J. Scott and Edward Soja (Berkeley: University of California Press, 1996), 119.

10. Roy Rosenzweig and David Thelen, *The Presence of the Past: Popular Uses of History in American Life* (New York: Columbia University Press, 1998), chapter 6; W. Fitzhugh Brundage, *The Southern Past: A Clash of Race and Memory* (Cambridge, Mass.: Harvard University Press, 2005), 313–14.

11. Dr. Oscar Braynon, oral history interview with Chanelle Rose, 2005, Historic Virginia Key Beach Park Trust.

12. Rachel Carson, *The Sea Around Us* (New York: Oxford University Press, 1991); Anne Morrow Lindbergh, *Gift from the Sea* (1955; repr., New York: Pantheon, 1991). See also Lena Lenck and Gideon Bosker, *The Beach: The History of Paradise on Earth* (New York: Penguin Books, 1998); and Lena Lenck and Gideon Bosker, eds., *Beach: Stories by the Sand and Sea* (New York: Marlowe and Company, 2000).

13. Russ Rymer, *American Beach* (New York: HarperCollins, 1998), 4–5.

14. Rymer, *American Beach*.

15. For local variations, see Irvin D. S. Winsboro, ed., *Old South, New South, or Down South? Florida and the Modern Civil Rights Movement* (Morgantown: University of West Virginia Press, 2009). The most comprehensive and thoughtful book on the topic of African American beaches in the Jim Crow South—which oddly ignores Florida—is Andrew W. Kahrl, *The Land Was Ours: African American Beaches from Jim Crow to the Sunbelt South* (Cambridge: Harvard University Press, 2012).

16. Robert Garcia and Erica Flores Baltodano, *Free the Beach! Public Access, Equal Justice, and the California Coast* (Los Angeles: Center for Law in the Public Interest, 2005), 16.

17. Gilbert R. Mason, *Beaches, Blood, and Ballots: A Black Doctor's Civil Rights Struggle* (Jackson: University Press of Mississippi, 2000); David Colburn, *Racial Change and Community Crisis: St. Augustine, 1877–1980* (Gainesville: University Press of Florida, 1991); Setha Low, Dana Taplin, and Suzanne Scheld, *Rethinking Urban Parks: Public Space and Cultural Diversity* (Austin: University of Texas Press, 2005), 126–48. See also Victoria Wollcott, *Race, Riots, and Roller Coasters: The Struggle over Segregated Recreation in America* (Philadelphia: University of Pennsylvania Press, 2012); and Victor M. Valle, and Rodolfo D. Torres, *Latino Metropolis* (Minneapolis: University of Minnesota Press, 2000), chapters 4–5.

18. Dean A. Sullivan, ed., *Late Innings: A Documentary History of Baseball* (University of Nebraska press), 106, quoting *Race Relations Law Reporter* 2 (June 1957): 714. On Montgomery, see Randall Robinson, "Martin Luther King's Constitution: A Legal History of the Montgomery Bus Boycott," *Yale Law Journal* 98, no. 6 (1989): 999–1067. For an examination of segregated recreational spaces in Lexington, Kentucky, see the website The Daily Aesthetic: Leisure and Recreation in a Southern

City's Segregated Park System, by Boyd Shearer Jr., http://www.uky.edu/Projects/TDA/narrativ.htm.

19. On Willcox Lake, see "W. E. B. Du Bois and the NAACP," Virginia Historical Society, http://www.vahistorical.org/civilrights/naacp.htm.

20. Ernesto Longa, "Lawson Edward Thomas and Miami's Negro Municipal Court," *St. Thomas Law Review* 18 (2005): 126. The case was *State v Wilson*, 25 So. 2d 860, 862 (Fla. 1946).

21. Ellyn Ferguson, "To Him, Overtown Is Not 'Over There,'" *Miami Herald*, February 16, 1983; "Quince to Be Defended by Negro Lawyer: Accused Man to Enter Plea Before Judge on Tuesday," *Daytona Beach Evening News*, August 15, 1947, 1A, quoted in Longa, "Lawson Edward Thomas and Miami's Negro Municipal Court," 126. See also Andrea McDaniels. "Family Courthouse Center Renamed for Black Crusader," *Miami Herald*, October 22, 2000.

22. Lawson Thomas, "The Professions in Miami," *The Crisis*, March 1942, 85.

23. Lawson Thomas, "The Criteria for Professional Leadership," Jacksonville High School teacher seminar, 1947, 4–5, in author's possession, courtesy of Eugenia Thomas.

24. Lawson Thomas, speech to Omega Psi Phi, Tampa, November 9, 1947, 5, in author's possession, courtesy of Eugenia Thomas.

25. Lawson Thomas, speech to Omega Psi Phi, 8–10.

26. Lawson Thomas, "The American Democracy," speech given at Delray Beach, 1947, 8, copy in author's possession, courtesy of Eugenia Thomas.

27. Lawson Thomas, speech to Mt. Olive AME Church, Jacksonville, November 11, 1948, 4–5, in author's possession, courtesy of Eugenia Thomas.

28. Joan Gill Blank, *Key Biscayne: A History of Miami's Tropical Island and the Cape Florida Lighthouse* (Sarasota, Fla.: Pineapple Press, 1996), 148, 157.

29. Luther Carter, *The Florida Experience: Land and Water Policy in a Growth State* (Baltimore, Md.: Johns Hopkins University Press, 1974), chapter 3. See also Jack E. Davis, *An Everglades Providence: Marjory Stoneman Douglas and the American Environmental Century* (Athens: University of Georgia Press, 2009), 61–62. On disputed titles and African Americans' uses of land on the key, see Blank, *Key Biscayne*, 75, 85, 92, 148, 157–61.

30. Kenneth Roberts, *Sun Hunting* (1922; repr., Ithaca, N.Y.: Cornell University Press, 2009); Gregory Bush, "'Playground of the USA': Miami and the Promotion of Spectacle," *Pacific Historical Review* 68 (May 1999): 153–72; T. H. Weigall, *Boom in Paradise* (New York: Alfred H. King, 1932); Paul George, "Brokers, Binders, and Builders: Greater Miami's Boom of the Mid-1920s," *Florida Historical Quarterly* 65 (July 1986): 27–51.

31. Mark Rose, *Castles in the Sand: The Life and Times of Carl Graham Fisher* (Gainesville: University Press of Florida, 2000). See also "Mr. Miami Beach," episode of *The American Experience*, written, produced, and directed by Mark Davis, aired on PBS February 2, 1998. A transcript of this documentary is available at http://www.pbs.org/wgbh/amex/miami/filmmore/transcript/index.html.

32. On Bay Front Park, see Paul George, "Miami's Bay Front Park: A History," http://www.bayfrontparkmiami.com/pages/history/historyessay.html, accessed December 31, 2015. For more background on the early struggle over Miami's downtown waterfront, see Greg Lightfoot, "Judge Worley and FEC Waterfront Access in Miami," unpublished paper in author's possession. For a later view of Miami's waterfront, see the opening segment of Frank Capra's film *It Happened One Night* (1934). Photos of Bay Front Park can be seen at this site at Historical Photos of Bay Front Park, http://www.bayfrontparkmiami.com/pages/history/historyphotos.html.

33. Davis, *An Everglades Providence*, 289. See also Ralph Middleton Munroe, *The Commodore's Story: The Early Days on Biscayne Bay* (1930; repr., Miami: Historical Museum of Southern Florida, 1990); Charles Torrey Simpson, *In Lower Florida Wilds* (New York: G. P. Putman's Sons, 1920); John Kunkle Small, *From Eden to the Sahara: Florida's Tragedy* (1929; repr., Sanford, Fla.: Seminole Soil and Water Conservation District, 2004).

34. On the *Valdemar* and the threat to shipping, see George, "Brokers, Binders, and Builders."

35. Works Progress Administration and Florida State Planning Board, *Planning Your Vacation in Florida: Miami and Dade County, including Miami Beach and Coral Gables* (Northport, N.Y.: Bacon, Percy, and Daggett, 1941), 87.

36. E. G. Sewell, "Shall Miami's Only View of the Ocean Be Sold?" *The Miamian*, September 1924, 4, 14; E. G. Sewell, "The Menace in the Present Harbor Situation," folder "Port of Miami," Pamphlets and Ephemera, Archives & Research Center, HistoryMiami, Miami, Florida (hereafter HistoryMiami). See also "City Manager's Report to City Commission of Five Years of Commission Manager Government for the City of Miami," 1926, 65–68, Arva Moore Parks Collection, Special Collections Department, University of Miami Libraries.

37. See "Biscayne Bay Lands to Be Put on Market," *Miami Herald*, January 9, 1924; "Compromise Is Made on Virginia Key Fill," *Miami Herald*, February 16, 1924, "Island to Be Larger," *Miami Herald*, May 2, 1926; "Miami Adopts Revised Plan for Harbor," *Miami Herald*, August 11, 1928.

38. "South Causeway over Bay Sought," *Miami Herald*, April 22, 1934.

39. "Bay Bottom Land Transfer Deferred," *Miami Herald*, November 5, 1937.

40. "City May Buy Virginia Key," *Miami Herald*, February 10, 1938.

41. "Causeway Plan in New Attack," *Miami Herald*, September 2, 1938; "City in New Try to Save Harbor Plan," *Miami Herald*, September 15, 1938; "New Port Plan Goes By Plane to Washington," *Miami Herald*, September 18, 1938.

42. Jeanne Bellamy, "Ten Men Hold the Fate of Virginia Key Project," *Miami Herald*, May 28, 1939.

43. "Men Are Beating the Depression on Key," *Miami Herald*, March 18, 1934.

44. On Merrick and Douglas, see Arva Moore Parks, *Miami: The Magic City* (Miami: Community Media, 2008); and Davis, *Everglades Providence*.

45. George Merrick, "Planning the Greater Miami for Tomorrow," speech to the Miami Realty Board on Monday, May 17, 1937, and at the Miami Bayfront Park Friday

May 28, 1937, 10–11, George Merrick Collection, Archives & Research Center, HistoryMiami. See also Raymond Mohl, "The Pattern of Race Relations in Miami since the 1920s," in *The African American Heritage of Florida*, edited by David R. Colburn and Jane L. Landers (Gainesville: University Press of Florida, 1995), 329; Ruth M. L. Bowe assisted by Patrice Williams, "Grants Town and the Historical Development of Over-the-Hill," typescript, journals.sfu.ca/cob/index.php/files/article/download/73/42; and Michael Craton and Gail Saunders, *Islanders in the Stream: A History of the Bahamian People*, vol. 2 (Athens: University of Georgia Press, 1998).

46. See the oral history interview of Charles Crandon with Harvey and Mary Napier, May 11, 1976, Archives & Research Center, HistoryMiami, transcript in author's possession.

47. A. D. Barnes, *History of Dade County Park System, 1929–1969: The First Forty Years* (Miami: n.p. 1986), 85.

48. Blank, *Key Biscayne*, 157; Charles Crandon, *Country Bumpkin* (Miami: Johnson Press, 1975), 62–68.

49. Charles Crandon, interview with Harvey and Mary Napier, May 11, 1976.

50. Virginia Beach, attachment to County Manager M. R. Stierheim's memo to mayor and commissioners, March 16, 1982, copy in author's possession.

51. "Proposed Areas on Ocean Front: Two Dade County Dreams for Park Development Site," *Miami Herald*, May 12, 1940, 2; "See Causeway Key to Growth," *Miami Herald*, November 29, 1940; "Key Plans Waits War Measures," *Miami Herald*, May 22, 1940; "Bear Cut Span Also Approved," *Miami Herald*, December 4, 1940, 1; "Action Slated This Congress," *Miami Herald*, March 7, 1941, 1; "Key Project Wins Approval," *Miami Herald*, April 17, 1942; "Navy Favors Key Project," *Miami Herald*, August 5, 1941.

52. "Clear the Atmosphere," *Miami Herald*, January 21, 1942; "Virginia Key," *Miami Herald*, May 25, 1942; "Virginia Key Job to Be Halted," *Miami Herald*, September 1, 1943, 1.

53. *Dade County's Recreation Parks: A Report to the People of Dade County Florida on the Present Extent and State of Development of the Several County Recreational Park Units Together with Recommendations for Future Development of the Park System* (Miami: Dade County Park Department, 1941), 2–16, in author's possession.

54. Richard Lingeman, *Don't You Know There's a War On? The American Homefront 1941–1945* (New York: Putnam, 1970), 85; "Playground Program Planned for Negro Children of Miami," *Miami News*, June 2, 1943, Agnew Welsh Scrapbooks, Miami-Dade Public Library System. See also Harry Porter, "The Lanham Act," *History of Education Journal* 3, no. 1 (1951): 1–6.

55. County Commission Minutes, March 14, 1944, 1, County Commission Meeting Archives Microfilm, Miami-Dade County Clerk's Office.

56. "Interracial Group Meets," *Miami Daily News*, August 27, 1944, Agnew Welsh Scrapbooks, Miami-Dade County Public Library System.

57. "Crandon Tells Virginia Key Beach Plans," *Miami Herald*, January 28, 1945, 4; Ernie Hill, "Virginia Key Airport: Plans Action through Pepper," *Miami Herald*, February 9, 1945, 1; Carl Ogle, "Round Table Demands Port Authority Push Virginia Key," *Miami Herald*, February 23, 1945.

Chapter 2. Beyond Colored Town: The Changing Boundaries of Race Relations and African American Community Life in Miami, 1896–1945

1. Irwin D. S. Winsboro, ed., *Old South, New South, or Down South? Florida and the Modern Civil Rights Movement* (Morgantown: University of West Virginia Press, 2009), 6; Isabel Wilkerson, *The Warmth of Other Suns: The Epic Story of America's Great Migration* (New York: Random House, 2010), 60–62.

2. Dorothy Fields, "Tracing Overtown's Vernacular Architecture," *Journal of Decorative and Propaganda Arts* 23 (1998): 325.

3. Raymond Mohl with Matilda "Bobbi" Graff and Shirley M. Zoloth, *South of the South: Jewish Activists and the Civil Rights Movement in Miami, 1945–1960* (Gainesville: University Press of Florida, 2004).

4. Paul George, "Colored Town: Miami's Black Community, 1896–1930," *Florida Historical Quarterly* 46 (April 1978): 432–47; Marvin Dunn, *Black Miami in the Twentieth Century* (Gainesville: University of Florida Press, 1998); Chanelle Rose, *The Struggle for Black Freedom in Miami: Civil Rights and America's Tourist Paradise, 1896–1968* (Baton Rouge: Louisiana State University Press, 2015); Thomas Castillo, "Big City Days: Race and Labor in Early Miami, 1914–1935" (PhD diss., Florida International University, 2000); Alex Lichtenstein, "'Putting Labor's House in Order': The Transportation Workers Union and Anti-Communism in Miami during the 1940s," *Labor History* 39 (February 1998): 7–23; Sheila Croucher, *Imagining Miami: Ethnic Politics in a Postmodern World* (Charlottesville: University Press of Virginia, 1997); Melanie Shell-Weiss, *Coming to Miami: A Social History* (Gainesville: University Press of Florida, 2009), chapters 2 and 3.

5. Nancy Hewitt, *Southern Discomfort: Women's Activism in Tampa, Florida 1880s–1920s* (Urbana: University of Illinois Press, 2001), 9, 41.

6. Paul Ortiz, *Emancipation Betrayed: The Hidden History of Black Organizing and White Violence in Florida from Reconstruction to the Bloody Election of 1920* (Berkeley: University of California Press, 2005), xv; Winsboro, *Old South, New South, or Down South?*.

7. James Nimmo, interview with Gregory Bush and students, 1984, in author's possession; Ned Kaufman, *Place, Race, and Story: Essays on the Past and Future of Historic Preservation* (New York: Routledge, 2009); Jane Jacobs, *The Death and Life of Great American Cities* (New York: Random House, 1961).

8. Hugo L. Black III, "Richard Fitzpatrick's South Florida, 1822–1840," Part 2, "Fitzpatrick's Miami River Plantation," *Tequesta* 41 (1981): 33–68; Thelma Peters, *Biscayne Bay Country* (Miami: Banyan Books, 1981); Thelma Peters, *Lemon City: Pioneering on Biscayne Bay, 1850–1925* (Miami: Banyan Books, 1976), chapter 13.

9. John Sewell, *Memoirs and History of Miami* (1933; repr., Miami: Arva Parks & Co, 1988), 75; Isador Cohen, *Historical Sketches and Sidelights of Miami* (Miami: Privately printed, 1925). See also Cecilia Tichi, *Shifting Gears: Technology, Literature, Culture in Modernist America* (Chapel Hill: University of North Carolina Press, 1996); and David Nye, *Electrifying America: Social Meanings of a New Technology* (Cambridge, Mass.: MIT Press, 1990).

10. Sewell, *Memoirs and History of Miami*, 27–28; David Nye, "Technology, Nature, and American Origin Stories," *Environmental History* 8, no. 1 (2004): 8–24. The election that resulted in the city's incorporation involved 368 voters, 206 white and 162 black; Arva Moore Parks, *Miami: The Magic City* (Miami: Community Media, 2008), 76–77, 85. According to Thomas Fleischmann, "Less than three years later, on May 10, 1899, black votes were again used to win the county seat back from Juno by a count of 690 to 468"; Thomas Fleischman, "Black Miamians in *The Miami Metropolis*, 1896–1900," *Tequesta* 52 (1992): 29. The *Miami Metropolis* openly acknowledged the importance of black voters in the southern half of Dade County: "Everything went off smooth from morning until night and all worked in harmony for the general good, and for once the color line was obliterated and every one of the black and tan vote counted. White men were riding through the streets with the colored fellows, and there was a full determination that the colored fellow should vote just as he wished, which fortunately was for Miami, and that his vote should be counted." "It Is Miami's," *Miami Metropolis*, May 12, 1899, 29, quoted in Fleischman, "Black Miamians," 29.

11. Don Doyle, *New Men, New Cities, New South: Atlanta, Nashville, Charleston, Mobile, 1860–1910* (Chapel Hill: University of North Carolina Press, 1990), chapters 10–11; Thomas Tweed, "An Emerging Protestant Establishment: Religious Affiliation and Public Power on the Urban Frontier in Miami, 1896–1904," *Church History* 64, no. 3 (September 1995): 412–37.

12. On the development of clubs and lodges, see Cohen, *Historical Sketches and Sidelights of Miami*, chapter 5. The allusion to "crackers" is in "Our Business Interests," *Miami Metropolis*, May 15, 1896, 1, 6. See also Mary Barr Munroe, "Pioneer Women of Dade County," *Tequesta* 3 (1943): 49–56; and "A Housekeeper's Club," *Harper's Bazaar* 25 (April 16, 1892), 310–11.

13. Joe M. Richardson, "Florida Black Codes," *Florida Historical Quarterly* 47 (April 1969): 365–79; Jerrell H. Shofner, "Custom, Law and History: The Enduring Influence of Florida's 'Black Codes,'" *Florida Historical Quarterly* 55 (January 1977): 277–98. See also David Colburn and Jane Landers, eds., *The African American Heritage of Florida* (Gainesville: University Press of Florida, 1995); and Ortiz, *Emancipation Betrayed*.

14. Thelma Peters, *Miami 1909* (Miami: Banyan Books, 1984), 117–18; "Ransom Christmas, 1902," *Update* 7, no. 4 (1980): 8–10. See also Paul George, "Criminal Justice in Miami, 1896–1930" (PhD diss., Florida State University, 1975); and Paul George, "Policing Miami's Black Community, 1896–1930," *Florida Historical Quarterly* 57 (April 1979): 434–50.

15. "Ourselves," *Miami Metropolis*, May 15, 1896, 5; Sewall, *Memoirs and History of Miami*, quoted in Jeanne Bellamy, "Newspapers of America's Last Frontier," *Tequesta* 12 (1952), 8. See also George, "Policing Miami's Black Community."

16. C. R. Ferguson, "Police Chief Ferguson Explains Purse Snatching," *Miami Herald*, March 14, 1912. See also Paul George, "Colored Town: Miami's Black Community, 1896–1930," *Florida Historical Quarterly* 47 (April 1978): 432–47; George, "Policing Miami's Black Community"; Paul George, "Miami's City Marshall and Law Enforcement

in a New Community, 1896–1907," *Tequesta* 44 (1984): 39–40; Sewell, *Memoirs and History of Miami*.

17. "The Colored School at Coconut Grove," *Miami Metropolis*, April 28, 1899, quoted in Thomas Fleischman, "Image and Reality: Perceptions of Early Black Miami by the Miami Metropolis, 1896–1900" (MA thesis, University of Miami, 1987), 57. See also Fleischmann, "Black Miamians in *The Miami Metropolis*, 1896–1900," *Tequesta* 52 (1992): 21–38.

18. "Railroad Company Will Comply with Law," *Miami Metropolis*, October 4, 1907, 1.

19. Samuel Proctor, *Napoleon Bonaparte Broward: Florida's Fighting Democrat* (1950; repr., Gainesville: University Press of Florida, 1993), 174, 252. See also Jerrell H. Shofner, "Custom, Law and History: The Enduring Influence of Florida's 'Black Codes,'" *Florida Historical Quarterly* 55 (January 1977): 277–98; and Joe M. Richardson, "Florida's Back Codes," *Florida Historical Quarterly* 47 (April 1969): 365–79.

20. "Senator Beard's Platform," *Miami Metropolis*, October 18, 1907. Reports of violence among blacks and mocking humor were also often used in the local press; see Fleischman, "Image and Reality," 43–44.

21. "Anti-Prohibitionists Carried the County in Yesterday's 'Wet' and 'Dry' Election by Small Margin of Only Four Votes," *Miami Metropolis*, October 18, 1907.

22. "Require Mayor to Close the Segregated District," *Miami Metropolis*, February 12, 1917, 2. See also "Segregation of Races Assured by Candidates at Meeting in Highland Park," *Miami Metropolis*, June 22, 1917, 3.

23. "Request for Military Organization and Presence in Reserve Form," *Miami Metropolis*, July 2, 1897.

24. Donna Thomas, "'Camp Hell': Miami during the Spanish-American War," *Florida Historical Quarterly* 57, no. 2 (1978): 141–56; Parks, *Miami*, 102; George, "Policing Miami's Black Community."

25. Jack E. Davis, *An Everglades Providence: Marjory Stoneman Douglas and the American Environmental Century* (Athens: University of Georgia Press, 2009), 239–40; Marjory Stoneman Douglas, "Frank Bryant Stoneman," *Tequesta* 2 (November 1944): 3–12.

26. Dr. J. L. White, "Local Tragedies—Their Challenge," 22 March 1925, in author's possession.

27. "Klan Circus Praised," *Miami Herald*, January 2, 1926, 4; "Miami Night Life Loses 'Hot Spots,'" *New York Times*, November 22, 1937, 2, quoted in John Stuart, "Constructing Identity: Building and Place in New Deal South Florida," in *The New Deal in South Florida*, edited by John A Stuart and John F. Stack Jr. (Gainesville: University Press of Florida, 2008), 56; "Miami Club Raided by Group in Klan Regalia Closed for One Night," *Evening Standard* (St. Petersburg), November 17, 1937.

28. "Accuses Miami Police of Medieval Torture," *New York Times*, May 8, 1928; "Miami Police 'Terrorism' Is Revealed in Negro Death Probe Involving Quigg," *Miami News*, March 2, 1928; George, "Policing Miami's Black Community."

29. "More Than Thousand Bahama Islanders Reach Miami during Year," *Miami*

Metropolis, June 12, 1909. See also Whittington B. Johnson, *Post-Emancipation Race Relations in the Bahamas* (Gainesville: University Press of Florida, 2006); and Katharine Beard, "Bahamian Immigrants," in *Multicultural America: An Encyclopedia of the Newest Americans*, edited by Ronald H. Baylor, vol. 4 (Santa Barbara: ABC-CLIO, 2011), 90.

30. George, "Criminal Justice in Miami," 111–59, 165; Raymond Mohl, "Black Immigrants: Bahamians in Early Twentieth-Century Miami," *Florida Historical Quarterly* 65 (January 1987): 271–97; Shell-Weiss, *Coming to Miami*, 50–52, 72. See also Jacob Bernstein, "Black in Blue," *Miami New Times*, November 13, 1997, accessed November 16, 2005, http://www.miaminewtimes.com/1997-11-13/news/black-in-blue/; and Raymond Mohl, "The Pattern of Race Relations in Miami since the 1920s," in *The African American Heritage of Florida*, edited by David Colburn and Jane Landers (Gainesville: University of Florida Press, 1995), 326–65.

31. "Accuses Miami Police of Medieval Torture," *New York Times*, May 8, 1928; Matilda "Bobbi" Graff, interview with Gregory Bush, 1992, in author's possession; Mohl, "Black Immigrants," 277; Yolanda Cooper Baker, interview with Gregory Bush, 2000, in author's possession.

32. Raymond A. Mohl and George E. Pozzetta, "From Migration to Multiculturalism: A History of Florida Immigration," in *The New History of Florida*, edited by Michael Gannon (Gainesville: University Press of Florida, 2012), 400.

33. "Color Line to Be Maintained in Magic City Asserts Trade Union Bodies," *Miami Metropolis*, December 25, 1914, 3. See also Thomas Castillo, "Chauffeuring in a White Man's Town: Black Service Work, Movement, and Segregation in Early Miami," in *Florida's Labor and Working-Class Past: Three Centuries of Work in the Sunshine State*, edited by Robert Cassanello and Melanie Shell-Weiss (Gainesville: University Press of Florida, 2009), 143–67; Thomas Castillo, "Miami's Hidden Labor History," *Florida Historical Quarterly* 82, no. 4 (2004): 438–67; and "Race Difficulty Smoothed Out in Joint Conference," *Miami Daily Metropolis*, July 17, 1917, 1.

34. "Police Asked to Protect Negroes in Colored Town," *Miami Metropolis*, 20 August 1915, 7.

35. "Segregation of Races in Miami to Receive Careful Consideration," *Miami Herald*, August 20, 1915; "Want 20th Street Colored Town Moved Away," *Miami Metropolis*, August 27, 1915; "Color Line to Be Drawn, Council Committee Will Work With Civic Clubs and Negro Organization," *Miami Herald*, August 27, 1915, 5; "Color Line Established to Satisfaction of All," *Miami Metropolis*, October 22, 1915, 2.

36. "Shall Mob Law Rule in Miami?" *Miami Metropolis*, July 30, 1915, 4. See also "Rowdy Chauffer Attacks Negro for Driving His Auto," *Miami Metropolis*, June 8, 1917, 8.

37. "Negroes Not to Use Violence to Gain Privileges," *Miami Metropolis*, July 14, 1917, 2; "Police Have Been Unable So Far to Apprehend Rowdies Who Dynamited Negro Lodge Hall," *Miami Daily Metropolis*, July 16, 1917, 1.

38. "To Enlist Negroes for Service as Stevedores," *Miami Metropolis*, September 4, 1917, 8; "Protest Against Enticing Labor Out of County," *Miami Daily News*, August 15, 1918, 2.

39. "Committee Appointed by Mayor to Settle 'Color Line' Dispute, Meets at City Hall to Hear Complaints," *Miami Herald*, May 26, 1920, 1.

40. "300 Armed Men Rushed to Colored Town Following Explosion of Dynamite Bombs," *Miami Herald*, June 30, 1920; "Tar and Feather . . . Masked Men Apply Coat Then Dump P.S. Irwin in Front of Urmey Hotel," *Miami Herald*, July 18, 1921. Two weeks earlier, the pastor of a Baptist church in Coconut Grove was kidnapped, whipped, and ordered to leave town. He complied, sailing to Nassau. See Shell-Weiss, *Coming to Miami*, 91–92.

41. Davis, *Everglades Providence*, 238–40.

42. "So-Called 'Blue Laws' Are Not Being Enforced," *Miami Metropolis*, May 10, 1920.

43. Ibid.

44. Dade County School Board Minutes, January 19, 1921, 1003, quoted in Doug Andrews, "Black Education in Miami, 1921–1941," *Tequesta* 59 (1999): 46.

45. George, "Colored Town," 437. See also "White Supremacy," *Miami Herald*, 27 October 1921.

46. See the oral history interview with the Stirrup sisters done by Arva Parks, private collection of Arva Moore Parks, Miami. See also "Kelsey L. Pharr, Negro Undertaker," January 11, 1939, interviewed by Bertha Comstock for the Federal Writers' Project, http://lcweb2.loc.gov/mss/wpalh1/10/1012/10120109/10120109.pdf.

47. "Kelsey L. Pharr, Negro Undertaker."

48. Michel-Rolph Trouillot, *Silencing the Past: Power and the Production of History* (Boston: Beacon Press, 1995), 48.

49. Garth Reeves Sr., interview with Dorothy Fields, October 14, 1977, Black Archives Historic Lyric Theater Cultural Arts Complex, Miami, Florida. For an example of sensationalistic reporting of black crime, see "Literally Cut to Pieces by One of His Own Race," *Miami Herald*, October 27, 1912.

50. "Avert Race Riots by Aiding in Work to Uplift Blacks," *Miami Metropolis*, August 15, 1919, 4.

51. Ortiz, *Emancipation Betrayed*, 205–7.

52. "White Primary Said Bulwark of Supremacy," *Miami News*, October 14, 1928. See a biography of John S. Beard in H. G. Cutler, *The History of Florida: Past and Present, Historical and Biographical*, vol. 3 (Chicago: Lewis Publishing Co., 1923), 52, http://files.usgwarchives.net/fl/leon/bios/b6300001.txt.

53. Ortiz, *Emancipation Betrayed*, 126.

54. Fred Brown, interview with Chanelle Rose, 2005, Historic Virginia Key Beach Park Trust, Miami; George, "Colored Town."

55. Mrs. Henry Gould Ralston, "Miami Will Be What Her Promoters Make It," *Miami Herald*, August 7, 1913, 13.

56. "Give the Negroes a Park," *Miami News*, April 19, 1916.

57. "Buy Two Public Parks for Negroes of Miami," *Miami Metropolis*, August 21, 1916.

58. "What of That Park for Colored Town?" *Miami News*, August 1, 1919, 2.

59. "Negroes Will Clean Up Their Own Park and Hold Barbecue," *Miami News*, August 22, 1921.

60. Thomas Pancoast to Carl Fisher, September 23, 1920, Carl Fisher Papers, Archives & Research Center, HistoryMiami.

61. Carl Fisher to Thomas Pancoast, September 28, 1920, Carl Fisher Papers, Archives & Research Center, HistoryMiami.

62. On Dana Dorsey, see Dunn, *Black Miami*, 78–81. See also Dorothy Fields, "Tracing Overtown's Vernacular Architecture," *Journal of Decorative and Propaganda Arts* 23 (1998): 322–33.

63. "The Task for the Future—A Program for 1919," in *Annual Report of the National Association for the Advancement of Colored People for the Years 1917 and 1918* (New York, 1919), reprinted in Thomas R. Frazier, ed., *Afro-American History: Primary Sources* (Chicago: Dorsey Press, 1988), 214. See also Harvard Sitkoff, *A New Deal for Blacks: The Emergence of Civil Rights as a National Issue: The Depression Decade* (New York: Oxford University Press, 1978), 33. On Rosewood, see David R. Colburn, "Rosewood and America in the Early Twentieth Century," *Florida Historical Quarterly* 76, no. 2 (1997): 175–192; and Winsboro, *Old South, New South, or Down South?*, 6, 224.

64. See Rose, *The Struggle for Black Freedom in Miami*.

65. Ortiz, *Emancipation Betrayed*, 92.

66. "Miami Negroes Remember Day of Emancipation," *Miami Herald*, January 2, 1918. On the Jones family, see Kim A. O'Connell, "The Keepers of the Keys," *National Parks*, May–June 2003, 30–33.

67. James Nimmo, interview with Kip Vought, November 8, 1990, Special Collections, Otto G. Richter Library, University of Miami.

68. Alain Locke, *The New Negro: An Interpretation* (New York: A. and C. Boni, 1925). See also Alain Locke, "An Evaluation of the New Negro," *Opportunity* 1 (August 1923): 231.

69. Kip Vought, "Racial Stirrings in Colored Town: The UNIA in Miami during the 1920s," *Tequesta* 45 (2000): 59. Dr. Holly was a prominent figure in Miami's black community. He had been educated in Barbados, Cambridge, and New York City. He set up a practice in Nassau and traveled around the islands before moving to South Florida and establishing several clinics at the turn of the century. Targeted by the KKK for his radical activities, he was run out of town on several occasions but continued to practice medicine.

70. Ibid., 61.

71. *Negro World*, March 27, 1926. On the Overseas Club, see Robert Hill, *The Marcus Garvey and United Negro Improvement Association Papers, September 1920–August 1921* (Berkeley: University of California Press, 1984), 250.

72. James Nimmo, oral history interview with Gregory Bush, 1984, in author's possession; Vought, "Racial Stirrings in Colored Town: The UNIA in Miami during the 1920s," *Tequesta* 45 (2000): 67; *Miami Herald*, March 9, 1928. See also "'Princess' Dies Following Attack," *St. Petersburg Times*, March 10, 1928. On the UNIA and Princess Koffey, see also Claudrena N. Harold, *The Rise and Fall of the Garvey Movement in*

the Urban South 1918–1942 (New York: Routledge, 2007), chapter 3. See also Robert Hill, ed., *The Marcus Garvey and Universal Negro Improvement Association Papers*, vol. 7 (Berkeley: University of California Press, 1990), 166–171.

73. See Kenneth E. Burnham, *God Comes to America: Father Divine and the Peace Mission Movement* (Boston: Lambeth Press, 1979); and Robert Weisbrot, *Father Divine and the Struggle for Racial Equality* (Urbana: University of Illinois Press, 1983).

74. For general background, see Kate Ramsey, *The Spirit and the Law: Vodou and Power in Haiti* (Chicago: University of Chicago Press, 2011).

75. Cleomie Ward Bloomfield, "Ninth Street Was Most Important Street in Colored Town," unpublished manuscript, Black Archives Historic Lyric Theater Cultural Arts Complex, Miami; Willie Mae Rolphe Murray, "Education in Miami," *The Crisis*, March 1942, 91–94. The African Orthodox Church broke away from the Episcopal Church in 1921. Some of its leaders were associated with the UNIA.

76. Garth Reeves Sr., interview with Andrea Benitez, March 2, 2006, Miami Oral Histories, http://miami.fiu.edu/moh/interviews/reeves/reeves.htm.

77. Garth Reeves Sr., interview with Julian Pleasants, August 19, 1999, http://ufdcimages.uflib.ufl.edu/UF/00/00/55/26/00001/FNP40.pdf.

78. "Aid for Unemployed Falls Behind Here," *Miami Herald*, December 1, 1932.

79. Mohl, "The Pattern of Race Relations in Miami," 328–29.

80. Raymond Mohl, "Trouble in Paradise: Race and Housing in Miami during the New Deal Era," *Prologue: Journal of the National Archives* 19 (Spring 1987): 9–10. White residents in the Nor'West League were also putting pressure on blacks to limit their residential expansion.

81. On Father John Culmer, see "The Reverend John Edwin Culmer, 1891–1963," The Church Awakens: African-Americans and the Struggle for Justice, http://www.episcopalarchives.org/Afro-Anglican_history/exhibit/leadership/culmer.php. The two-week *Miami Herald* housing exposé was published in the period September 6–20, 1934.

82. John Gramling to Horatio B. Hackett, October 17, 1934, Boxes 297–310, Records of the Public Housing Administration, RG 196, National Archives and Records Administration, Washington, D.C., quoted in Mohl, "Trouble in Paradise," 11. See also John A. Stuart, "Liberty Square: Florida's First Public Housing Project," in *The New Deal in South Florida*, edited by John A Stuart and John F. Stack Jr. (Gainesville: University Press of Florida, 2008), 190–91.

83. Stuart, "Liberty Square," 206. See also Paul George and Thomas Peterson, "Liberty Square: 1933–1987, The Origins and Evolution of a Public Housing Project," *Tequesta* 48 (1988): 53–68.

84. Raymond Mohl, "The Origins of Miami's Liberty Square," *Florida Environmental and Urban Issues* 12 (July 1985): 11; E. G. Sewell to Harry Hopkins, June 18, 1934, Records of the Federal Emergency Relief Administration, RG 69.3, National Archives and Records Administration, Washington, D.C. See also Stuart, "Liberty Square"; and George and Peterson, "Liberty Square."

85. Resolution No. 627, August 1935, Board of County Commissioners Minutes, Book of Resolutions, Book 10, 56–47, Miami-Dade County Clerk's Office.

86. "Miami Night Life Loses 'Hot Spots,'" *New York Times*, November 22, 1937, 2, quoted in Stuart, "Constructing Identity," 56.

87. Stetson Kennedy, interview with Gregory Bush, May 19, 1997, in author's possession.

88. Works Progress Administration and Florida State Planning Board, *Planning Your Vacation in Florida: Miami and Dade County, including Miami Beach and Coral Gables* (Northport, N.Y.: Bacon, Percy, and Daggett, 1941), 4–5. For the valuable work of Stetson Kennedy, see his *Palmetto Country* (1942) and *Southern Exposure* (1946) and the website http://www.stetsonkennedy.com/. See also Studs Terkel, "Stetson Kennedy, 77," in Terkel, *Coming of Age* (New York: New Press, 1995), 391–400. Zora Neale Hurston worked with Kennedy on the Florida project. See Stetson Kennedy, "Way Down Upon . . . Gathering Tales of Folklife in Suwannee Country," *FHC Forum* 17 (Spring/Summer 1993): 22–27; and "The W.P.A. Florida Writers Project: A Personal View," *FEH Forum* 12 (Spring 1989): 1–4. For more on the Federal Writers' Project in Florida, see "Florida Writings from the Federal Writers' Project," American Memory, The Library of Congress, http://memory.loc.gov/ammem/collections/florida/ffbib. html; and James A. Findlay and Margaret Bing, "Touring Florida through the Federal Writers' Project," *Journal of Decorative and Propaganda Arts* (1998), https://www. broward.org/library/bienes/lii10213.htm.

89. City of Miami, "Better Housing, Healthier Children, Happier Families," 1940, Special Collections, University of Miami, in author's possession.

90. "WPA Recreation in Florida," May 11, 1938, 1–2, RG69, Records of the Works Projects Administration, National Archives and Records Administration, Washington, D.C.

91. Shell-Weiss, *Coming to Miami*, 106–8.

92. Mark Foster, *Castles in the Sand: The Life and Times of Carl Fisher* (Gainesville: University Press of Florida, 2000), 160; "Votes to Stop Negro Jitneys," *Miami Herald*, March 3, 1938; Stetson Kennedy, *Jim Crow Guide: The Way It Was* (1958; repr., Boca Raton: Florida Atlantic University Press, 1990), 227; Fred Brown, interview with Chanelle Rose, Historic Virginia Key Beach Park Trust.

93. "PWA Official Here to Inspect Project," *Miami Herald*, December 27, 1935; "Work to Commence on Housing Project," *Miami Herald*, January 11, 1936. See also John A. Stuart, "Constructing Identity: Building and Place in New Deal South Florida," in *The New Deal in South Florida*, edited by John A Stuart and John F. Stack Jr. (Gainesville: University Press of Florida, 2008), 31–70.

94. Enid Pinkney, interview with Gregory Bush, June 24, 1999; Athalie Range, interview with Gregory Bush, 1999, both in Special Collections, Otto G. Richter Library, University of Miami.

95. Enid Pinkney, interview with Chanelle Rose, 2005; Garth Reeves Sr., interview with Chanelle Rose, 2005; and David White, interview with Chanelle Rose, 2005, all at Historic Virginia Key Beach Park Trust; Athalie Range, interview with Gregory Bush, 1999. See also Kirk Neilsen, "A Historic Dip," *Miami New Times*, April 8, 1999.

96. Shell-Weiss, *Coming to Miami*, chapters 3–5.

97. For the origin of the moniker "Magic City," see E. V. Blackman, *Miami and Dade County, Florida: Its Settlement, Progress, and Achievement* (Chuluota, Fla.: Mickler House, 1921). The term was used for other urban centers as well.

98. Rose, "Neither Southern nor Northern," chapter 2.

99. Shell-Weiss, *Coming to Miami*, 87, 115–17; Rose, "Neither Southern nor Northern," 55–57.

100. Mary Davis, "Personal Experiences and Memories of Inter-Group Relations in Miami 1940–1960," private collection of Arva Moore Parks, in author's possession.

101. Rose, "Neither Southern nor Northern," 47, 90–93, 99–100, 213; Miami Pictorial Number, special issue, *The Crisis*, March 1942, 74; *The Crisis*, June 1939, 185; Roberta Hughes Wright, Wilbur B. Hughes, and Gina Renee Misiroglu, *Lay Down Body: Living History in African American Cemeteries* (Detroit, Mich.: Visible Ink Press, 1995), 148; Maxine D. Jones and Kevin M. McCarthy, *African Americans in Florida* (Sarasota: Pineapple Press, 1993), 164; "Reverend John Edwin Culmer"; biographical note based on an interview with Leomie S. Culmer (widow of John E. Culmer), *Episcopal Clerical Directory* (New York: Church Hymnal Corporation, 1962); and Collections of Leomie Culmer on the Reverend John Edwin Culmer, AR2007,077, Episcopal Society for Cultural and Racial Unity (ESCRU) Archive, Archives of the Episcopal Church, Austin, Texas.

102. "Klan Parades, Burns Crosses to Frighten Off Negro Voters," *Miami Herald*, May 2, 1939, 1; "Miami Klan Tries to Scare Negro Vote," *Life*, May 15, 1939, 27–28; "Florida: Black Ballots," *Time*, May 15, 1939, 19. See also "Negro Voters Ask Protection," *Miami Daily News*, May 1, 1939, 1; and Patricia Raub, "True to Life: *Life* Magazine's Coverage of African Americans, 1936–40," *Prospects* 25 (October 2000): 607–40. On Sam Solomon, see "Conference Speaker," *The Crisis*, June 1939, 185. On the 1920 elections, see Ortiz, *Emancipation Betrayed*, 216.

103. Raymond Arsenault, *The Sound of Freedom: Marian Anderson, the Lincoln Memorial, and the Concert that Awakened America* (New York: Bloomsbury Press, 2009).

104. Mercedes H. Byron, "Negro Looks at Miami," *The Crisis*, March 1942, 84.

105. Stetson Kennedy, *Southern Exposure* (1946; repr., Boca Raton: Florida Atlantic University Press, 1991), 59–60. See also Ben Green, *Before His Time: The Untold Story of Harry T. Moore, America's First Civil Rights Martyr* (New York: Free Press, 1999), 52; Nathan Daniel Beau Connolly, "By Eminent Domain: Race and Capital in the Building of an American South Florida" (PhD diss., University of Michigan, 2008), 248.

106. Gary Mormino, "Midas Returns: Miami Goes to War, 1941–1945," *Tequesta* 57 (1997): 5–51, http://digitalcollections.fiu.edu/tequesta/files/1997/97_1_01.pdf.

107. Ibid., 7, 31–34.

108. Kennedy, *Jim Crow Guide*, 181; Kennedy, *Southern Exposure*, 58–60.

109. "City Seeking to Condemn Park Acreage," *Miami Herald*, September 8, 1943, Agnew Welsh Scrapbooks, Miami-Dade Public Library System.

110. Fred Brown, interview with Chanelle Rose, 2005, Historic Virginia Key Beach Park Trust. See also Ellen J. Uguccioni, "Black Police Precinct and Courthouse, 1009 NW 5th Avenue," City of Miami Designation Report, September 17, 2002, http://

www.historicpreservationmiami.com/pdfs/Black%20Police%20Precinct.pdf. See also Sidney Poitier's account of his relationship with the Miami police in *This Life* (New York: Ballantine Books, 1981). On the KKK as part of the police force, see Matilda "Bobbi" Graff, oral history interview with Gregory Bush, 1992, Special Collections, Otto G. Richter Library, Miami University, in author's possession.

111. Lillian Smith, *Strange Fruit* (1944; repr., New York: Harcourt, Brace, Jovanovich, 1992); Gunnar Myrdal, *An American Dilemma: The Negro Problem and Modern Democracy* (New York: Harper and Row, 1944); Wallace Stegner, *One Nation* (Boston: Houghton Mifflin, 1945), 209.

112. Steven Lawson, *Running for Freedom: Civil Rights and Black Politics in America since 1941* (New York: McGraw Hill, 1997), 28.

113. Lizabeth Cohen, *A Consumers' Republic*: *The Politics of Mass Consumption in Postwar America* (New York: Alfred Knopf, 2003), 90, 93, 100.

114. James Farmer, oral history interview with Harri Baker, October 1969, 17, Lyndon Baines Johnson Library Oral History Collection, University of Texas, Austin, Texas, http://www.lbjlib.utexas.edu/johnson/archives.hom/oralhistory.hom/Farmer/farmer1.pdf. See also Carleton Mabee, "Evolution of Non-Violence," *The Nation*, August 12, 1961.

115. Matilda "Bobbi" Graf, interview with Gregory Bush, 1992; Alex Lichtenstein, "'Scientific Unionism' and the "Negro Question': Communists and the Transport Workers Union in Miami, 1944–1949," in *Southern Labor in Transition, 1940–1995*, edited by Robert Zeiger (Knoxville: University of Tennessee Press, 1997), 58–84.

Chapter 3. Island Pleasures: Memories of African American Life at Virginia Key Beach

1. Robin D. G. Kelley, "'We Are Not What We Seem': Rethinking Working-Class Opposition in the Jim Crow South," *Journal of American History* 80 (June 1993): 84–85, quoted at Boyd Shearer, "Narrative," The Daily Aesthetic, http://www.uky.edu/Projects/TDA/narrativ.htm.

2. Shearer, "Narrative."

3. Raymond Mohl, "'South of the South?' Jews, Blacks and the Civil Rights Movement in Miami, 1945–1960," *Journal of American Ethnic History* 18 (Winter 1999): 3–36.

4. W. Fitzhugh Brundage, *The Southern Past: A Clash of Race and Memory* (Cambridge, Mass.: Harvard University Press, 2005), 6.

5. Catesby Leigh and Pete Collins, "Recalling Martin Luther King's Pleasure Trips to Miami: Civil Rights Leader Frequently Slipped into Town for Rest and Relaxation," *Miami News*, January 16, 1988.

6. See Vicki Crawford, Jacqueline Anne Rouse, and Barbara Woods, eds., *Women in the Civil Rights Movement: Trailblazers & Torchbearers, 1941–1965* (Bloomington: Indiana University Press, 1990).

7. "Park It on Virginia Key," *Miami Herald*, July 7, 1999; Rick Bragg, "Developers Covet a Florida Island Beach that Was Born of Racism," *New York Times*, March 28, 1999, 19; "Preserve Virginia Key," *Miami Times*, March 4, 1999, 6A.

8. David Harvey, *Spaces of Hope* (Berkeley: University of California Press, 2000); Thomas Bender, *The Unfinished City* (New York: New Press, 2002), 234; Sharon Zukin, *Landscapes of Power: From Detroit to Disney World* (Berkeley: University of California Press, 1991), 12; Jane Jacobs, *The Death and Life of Great American Cities* (New York: Random House, 1961), chapter 5; William H. Whyte, *The Social Life of Small Urban Spaces* (New York: Project for Public Spaces, 1980).

9. Hal Rothman, *Neon Metropolis: How Las Vegas Started the Twenty-First Century* (New York: Routledge, 2003), 115. See also Frank Vanclay, Matthew Higgins, and Adam Blackshaw, eds., *Making Sense of Place: Exporting Concepts and Expressions of Place through Different Senses and Lenses* (Canberra: National Museum of Australia, 2008).

10. Peggy Bartlett, ed., *Urban Place: Reconnecting with the Natural World* (Cambridge: MIT Press, 2005); Zukin, *Landscapes of Power*, chapter 1.

11. David Lowenthal, *Possessed by the Past: The Heritage Crusade and the Spoils of History* (New York: Free Press, 1996), 91, 21, 84.

12. Andrew W. Kahrl, *The Land Was Ours: African American Beaches from Jim Crow to the Sunbelt South* (Cambridge: Harvard University Press, 2012), 257. See also Jeff Wiltse, *Contested Waters: A Social History of Swimming Pools in America* (Chapel Hill: University of North Carolina Press, 2007). See also Nikola Naumov, "Heritage Tourism in Urban Areas: Contemporary Complexities and Challenges," *Illuminare: A Student Journal in Recreation, Parks, and Leisure Studies* 12, no. 1 (2014): 68–76.

13. Andrew Hurley, *Beyond Preservation: Using Public History to Revitalize Inner Cities* (Philadelphia: Temple University Press, 2010); Ned Kaufman, *Place, Race, and Story: Essays on the Past and Future of Historic Preservation* (New York: Routledge, 2009).

14. Michael Frisch, *A Shared Authority: Essays on the Craft and Meaning of Oral and Public History* (Albany: State University of New York Press, 1990), xxii; Lynn Abrams, *Oral History Theory* (New York: Routledge, 2010), 155; Jan Walmsley, "Life History Interviews with People with Learning Disabilities," in *The Oral History Reader*, edited by Robert Perks and Alistair Thomson (New York: Routledge, 1998), 184–97; Richard Louv, *Last Child in the Woods: Saving Our Children from Nature-Deficit Disorder* (Chapel Hill, N.C.: Algonquin Books, 2008).

15. Fred Brown, interview with Chanelle Rose, 2005, Historic Virginia Key Beach Park Trust.

16. Garth Reeves, interview with Chanelle Rose, 2005, Historic Virginia Key Beach Park Trust.

17. David Shorter, interview with Chanelle Rose, 2005, Historic Virginia Key Beach Park Trust.

18. Fred Brown, interview with Chanelle Rose, 2005, Historic Virginia Key Beach Park Trust; and Dr. Edward Braynon, interview with Chanelle Rose, 2005, Historic Virginia Key Beach Park Trust.

19. Fred Brown, interview with Chanelle Rose, 2005.

20. Dr. Edward Braynon, interview with Chanelle Rose, 2005, in possession of the Historic Virginia Key Beach Park Trust.

21. "Easter Sunrise Service to Be First for Negroes," *Miami Herald*, March 26, 1948, 57; "Negro Easter Sunrise Service," *Miami Herald*, April 10, 1949, Agnew Welsh Scrapbooks, Miami-Dade County Public Library System.

22. Leah Sands, interview with Chanelle Rose, 2005, Historic Virginia Key Park Trust. See also Dorothy Fields, interview with Chanelle Rose, 2005, Historic Virginia Key Beach Park Trust.

23. Sydney Winn, interview with Chanelle Rose, 2005, Historic Virginia Key Beach Park Trust.

24. "Virginia Beach to Get Cabanas," *Miami Times*, April 20, 1948, Agnew Welsh Scrapbooks, Miami-Dade Public Library System.

25. Enid Pinkney, interview with Chanelle Rose, 2005, Historic Virginia Key Beach Park Trust.

26. Dorothy Fields, interview with Chanelle Rose.

27. Garth Reeves, interview with Chanelle Rose.

28. Wilhemina Jennings, interview with Chanelle Rose, 2005, Historic Virginia Key Beach Park Trust.

29. Sydney Winn, interview with Chanelle Rose, 2005, Historic Virginia Key Beach Park Trust.

30. Athalie Range, interview with Chanelle Rose, 2005, Historic Virginia Key Beach Park Trust.

31. Dr. Edward Braynon, interview with Chanelle Rose.

32. Bernice Sawyer, interview with Chanelle Rose, 2005, Historic Virginia Key Beach Park Trust.

33. Leah Sands, interview with Chanelle Rose, 2005, Historic Virginia Key Beach Park Trust, Miami.

34. See Douglas Hanks, "For Hampton House, a Return from History," *Miami Herald*, May 8, 2015.

35. Kirk Nielsen, "A Historic Dip," *Miami New Times*, April 8, 1999.

36. Dorothy Fields, interview with Chanelle Rose.

37. Kenneth T. Williams, interview with Chanelle Rose, 2005, Historic Virginia Key Beach Park Trust.

38. Quoted in Nielsen, "A Historic Dip."

39. Miami-Dade County Department of Parks and Recreation, Virginia Key Beach Park Advertisement, 1950s, archives of Historic Virginia Key Beach Park Trust, Miami.

40. Other black beaches in Florida include Manhattan and Butler's Beach near St. Augustine; see Marsha Dean Phelts, *An American Beach for African Americans* (Gainesville: University Press of Florida, 1997), chapter 1. On American Beach on Amelia Island, see also Russ Rymer, *American Beach: A Saga of Race, Wealth, and Memory* (New York: HarperCollins, 1998); and Mireya Navarro, "Fernandina Beach Journal: A Black Beach Town Fights to Preserve Its History," *New York Times*, April

6, 1998, A14. On Mary McLeod Bethune's New Smyrna Beach, see Rackham Holt, *Mary McLeod Bethune: A Biography* (Garden City, N.Y.: Doubleday, 1964). For a deeper perspective, see Howard Rabinowitz, *Race Relations in the Urban South, 1865–1890* (Urbana: University of Illinois Press, 1980), 190.

41. F. Knebel and B. Kociva, "One Man's Progress . . . and the Fight Ahead," *Look*, April 14, 1959. This article was part of a series titled "The Negro in Florida." On Martin Luther King and his relationship to Miami and Virginia Key Beach, see Pete Collins, "Recalling King's Pleasure Trips to Miami," *Miami News*, February 2, 1988.

Chapter 4. The Shifting Sands of Civil Rights in Southeast Florida, 1945–1976

1. Nicholas Patricios, *Building Marvelous Miami* (Gainesville: University Press of Florida, 1994), chapters 4–5.

2. Garth Reeves Sr., interview with Andrea Benitez, March 2, 2006, Miami Oral Histories, http://miami.fiu.edu/moh/interviews/reeves/reeves.htm.

3. "A Great Idea," *Miami News*, August 22, 1944.

4. Thelma Gibson, interview with Gregory Bush, October 26, 1999, in author's possession. See also Christine Ardalan, *Warm Hearts and Caring Hands: South Florida Nursing from Frontier to Metropolis, 1880–2000* (Miami: Centennial Press, 2005); and Carita Swanson Vonk, *Theodore R. Gibson: Priest, Prophet and Politician* (Miami: Little River Press, 1997).

5. Enid Pinkney, "Growing Up in Overtown," in *Miami: The American Crossroad*, edited by Arva Parks and Gregory Bush (New York: Simon and Schuster, 1996), 117–18.

6. Thelma Gibson, interview with Gregory Bush, October 26, 1999, in author's possession.

7. David Colburn, *Yellow Dog Democrat to Red State Republican: Florida and Its Politics since 1940* (Gainesville: University Press of Florida, 2007); Tom Wagy, *Governor LeRoy Collins of Florida: Spokesman of the New South* (Birmingham: University of Alabama Press, 1985). For recent critiques of Collins as a moderate, see Irvin D. S. Winsboro, *Old South, New South, or Down South? Florida and the Modern Civil Rights Movement* (West Virginia University Press, 2009), 12.

8. "Babylon, U.S.A. Gets Set for Its Hundred Days," *Life*, December 29, 1957, 31–42; Isaac Bashevis Singer, introduction to Richard Nagler, *My Love Affair with Miami Beach* (New York: Simon & Schuster, 1991), v–viii; "Florida Ho!," *Newsweek*, July 4, 1949, 36.

9. Chanelle Rose, "Tourism and the Hispanicization of Race in Jim Crow Miami, 1945–1965," *Journal of Social History* 45, no. 3 (2011): 1–22. See also Chanelle Rose, *The Struggle for Black Freedom in Miami: Civil Rights and America's Tourist Paradise, 1896–1968* (Baton Rouge: Louisiana State University Press, 2015).

10. Stetson Kennedy, *Southern Exposure* (1946; repr., Boca Raton: Florida Atlantic University Press, 1991), 59, 345.

11. Raymond Mohl, "Elizabeth Virrick and the 'Concrete Monsters': Housing Reform in Postwar Miami," *Tequesta* 61 (2001): 5–37. See also Alex Lichtenstein, "Putting Labor's House in Order: the Transport Workers Union and labor anti-Communism in Miami during the 1940s," Labor History 39 (1998): 7–23.

12. John Carlton, "Probe of Communists Here Seen as House Group Studies Exposé," *Miami Daily News*, February 21, 1948, 1.

13. *Miami Herald*, February 10, 1948.

14. Ben Green, *Before His Time: The Untold Story of Harry T. Moore, America's First Civil Rights Martyr* (New York: Free Press, 1999); Isabel Wilkerson, *The Warmth of Other Suns: The Epic Story of America's Great Migration* (New York: Random House, 2010), 319–27. See also Jacqueline Dowd Hall, "The Long Civil Rights Movement and the Political Uses of the Past," *Journal of American History* 91 (March 2005): 1233–63; Steven Lawson, *Civil Rights Crossroads: Nation, Community, and the Black Freedom Struggle* (Lexington: University Press of Kentucky, 2003); Glenda Gilmore, *Defying Dixie: The Radical Roots of Civil Rights, 1919–1950* (New York: W. W. Norton, 2008); Mary Dudziak, *Cold War Civil Rights: Race and the Image of American Democracy* (Princeton, N.J.: Princeton University Press, 2000); Raymond Mohl with Matilda "Bobbi" Graff and Shirley M. Zoloth, *South of the South: Jewish Activists and the Civil Rights Movement in Miami, 1945–1960* (Gainesville: University Press of Florida, 2004); Eric Arnesen, "Reconsidering the 'Long Civil Rights Movement,'" *Historically Speaking* 10 (April 2009): 31–34.

15. Stetson Kennedy, "Miami: Anteroom to Fascism," *The Nation*, December 22, 1951, 546–47; Frank Donner, "The Miami Formula: An Expose of Grass Roots McCarthyism," *The Nation*, January 22, 1955, 65–71; Gregory Bush, "We Must Picture an 'Octopus': Anticommunism, Desegregation and Local News in Miami, 1945–1960," *Tequesta* 65 (2005): 49–63.

16. David Kraslow, "Communist Paper Sponsored Concerts Held at Beach Center," *Miami Herald*, February 15, 1953; Al Spears as told to Damon Runyon Jr., "I Was a Miami Red," *Miami Herald*, June 7, 1954, 1; "Plan for 'Model' Village in Area Upset by Patriot," *Miami Herald*, June 11, 1954, 1.

17. Matilda Graff, "The Historic Continuity of the Civil Rights Movement," reprinted in Raymond Mohl with Matilda "Bobbi" Graff and Shirley M. Zoloth, *South of the South: Jewish Activists and the Civil Rights Movement in Miami, 1945–1960* (Gainesville: University Press of Florida, 2004), 63–122; Matilda "Bobbi" Graff, interview with Gregory Bush, 1992, Special Collections, Otto G. Richter Library, Miami University; Max Schlafrock, interview with Gregory Bush, December 5, 1992, in author's possession; *Investigation of Communist Activities in the State of Florida: Hearings Before the Committee on Un-American Activities, Eighty-Third Congress*, Parts 1 and 2 (Washington, D.C.: Government Printing Office, 1955), November 29 and 30 and December 2, 1954.

18. Louis Harap, "Nightmare in Miami," *Jewish Life* 9 (December 1954), 4–9. See also Leslie B. Bain, "Red Hunt in Miami: Who Formed the Posse?" *The Nation*, August 7, 1954, 110–12.

19. Harap, "Nightmare in Miami," 5–6; "Two More Balky Witnesses Get Year," *Miami Herald*, September 16, 1954. See also William G. Crawford Jr., "Judge Vincent Giblin: The Life and Times of a South Florida Attorney and Judge," *Tequesta* 70 (2010): 96–99.

20. Haines Colbert, "Pastor Defends Reds in Flock," *Miami Daily News*, June 28, 1954.

21. "Church Pastor and Church Secretary Cited for Contempt," *Sarasota Herald-Tribune*, October 7, 1954; Harap, "Nightmare in Miami," 5–6.

22. Harap, "Nightmare in Miami," 4, 8.

23. The state legislature's investigations of links between alleged communists, civil rights organizations, and homosexuals were only recently released to the public; see "Veil Lifts on 'Red Scare' Panel," *Miami Herald*, June 14, 1993. For background, see Steven F. Lawson, "The Florida Legislative Investigation Committee and the Constitutional Readjustment of Race Relations, 1956–1963," in *An Uncertain Tradition*, edited by Kermit L. Hall and James W. Ely Jr. (Athens: University of Georgia Press, 1989), 296–99.

24. Matilda "Bobbi" Graff, interview with Gregory Bush, October 14, 1992, in author's possession.

25. Jacob Bernstein, "Black in Blue," *Miami New Times*, November 13, 1997. For the *Smith v. Allwright* decision, see https://www.oyez.org/cases/1940-1955/321us649.

26. "Negroes Ask Stadium Seats," *Miami News*, December 18, 1946; "Citizens Protest Orange Bowl Discrimination," *Miami News*, December 21, 1946, both in Agnew Welsh Scrapbooks, Miami-Dade Public Library System. See also Charles H. Martin, "Integrating New Year's Day: The Racial Politics of College Bowl Games in the American South," *Journal of Sport History* 24 (Fall 1997): 368.

27. "Negroes Ask Use of Beach Golf Course," *Miami Herald*, April 22, 1949.

28. Kirk Neilsen, "In the Rough: A Half-Century before Tiger Woods Era, Black Miamians Fought a Losing Battle to Hit the Links," *Miami New Times*, February 24, 2000. See also Garth Reeves Sr., interview with Julian Pleasants, August 19, 1999, 10, http://ufdcimages.uflib.ufl.edu/UF/00/00/55/26/00001/FNP40.pdf; "The Golf Question," *Miami Times*, April 23, 1949; and "Speed Negro Golf Course Building," *Miami News*, April 13, 1949, Agnew Welsh Scrapbooks, Miami-Dade Public Library System. The deciding case by the U.S. Supreme Court was *Holmes et al. v. Atlanta* 223 F. 2d 93 (5th Cir. 1955).

29. "Whites Form Group to Raise Fund for Negro Center," *Miami Herald*, February 9, 1947; "Miami Beach Committee Raises $100 for Center," *Miami Times*, April 8, 1947 (Agnew Welsh Collection); Warren M. Banner, *An Appraisal of Progress, 1943–1953* (Miami: Department of Research and Community Projects: National Urban League, 1953), 6. For an overview of recreational facilities in the county in the mid-1950s, see "A Plan for Future Action: A Report by the Citizens Study Committee on Recreation and Group Work," Community Chest of Dade County, Welfare Planning Council of Dade County, Miami, Florida, March 1954, Special Collections, Otto Richter Library, University of Miami.

30. Enid Pinkney, interview with Gregory Bush, 2000, Special Collections, Otto G. Richter Library, University of Miami.

31. Ibid. Albert Pick owned the largest hotel in Miami; the Pinkney family lived in the servants' quarters there. On Pick's life and business, see "Albert Pick, Jr.," Accuracy Project, http://www.accuracyproject.org/cbe-Pick,Albert.html.

32. "Concert Race Issue Avoided," *Miami Herald*, January 25, 1953, 14A; Doris Reno, "First Marian Anderson Concert in Miami Rare, Delightful Event," *Miami Herald*, January 26, 1952, 3B; "Mixed Miami Throng Hears Miss Anderson," *New York Times*, January 27, 1952; Allan Keier, *Marian Anderson: A Singer's Journey* (New York: Scribner's, 2000), 259; Melanie Shell-Weiss, *Coming to Miami: A Social History* (Gainesville: University Press of Florida, 2009), 154.

33. Russ Marchner, "Beaches Are Opened to Negroes in Delray," *Miami Herald*, May 16, 1956, 1; "Cross Burned at Delray Beach," *Miami Herald*, May 17, 1956, 1; "Four Negroes Appear at Municipal Beach," *Miami Herald*, May 18, 1956; "'Breakdown' Closes Delray Beach Pool," *Miami Herald*, May 20, 1956; "Delray Shore Cleared to Prevent Violence," *Miami Herald*, May 21, 1956; "New Facilities Due for Negroes' Beach," *Miami Herald*, May 22, 1956; Russ Marchner, "Delray Forbids Mingling," *Miami Herald*, May 24, 1956, 1; "Delray Votes Segregation Law," *Miami Herald*, May 24, 1956, 1; "4 Negroes Seek WPB Course Use," *Miami Herald*, May 27, 1956, section B; "2 Negroes Held in Bus Seating Row," *Miami Herald*, May 28, 1956, 1; "Negro Drivers Urged on Buses," *Miami Herald*, May 30, 1956; "Tallahassee Drops Charges in Bus Row," *Miami Herald*, May 31, 1956, 1; "Bus Boycott Spreads in State Capital," *Miami Herald*, June 1, 1956, 1; "Board Rejects Bus Integration," *Miami Herald*, June 5, 1956, 1; "Governor Shuns Bus Boycott," *Miami Herald*, June 5, 1956, 1.

34. For further information, see "The Tallahassee Bus Boycott Begins, 1956," Florida Memory, May 26, 2013, http://www.floridamemory.com/blog/2013/05/26/tallahassee-bus-boycott/, accessed December 29, 2015.

35. "City Faced by Boycott of Buses," *Miami Herald*, June 8, 1956, 1; Russ Marchner, "Delray Moves to Exclude Negro Section from City," *Miami Herald*, June 6, 1956, 1; "NAACP Files Suit to End Segregation in County's Schools," *Miami Herald*, June 13, 1956, 1; Bert Collier, "Another Negro Disobeying Bus Rule Arrested," *Miami Herald*, June 13, 1956, 1. See also Carita Swanson Vonk, *Theodore R. Gibson: Priest, Prophet and Politician* (Miami: Little River Press, 1997), 69; Marvin Dunn, *Black Miami in the Twentieth Century* (Gainesville: University Press of Florida, 1997), 4; and Shell-Weiss, *Coming to Miami*, 154–56.

36. See Anthony Badger, "The South Confronts the Court: The Southern Manifesto of 1956," *Journal of Policy History* 20 (2008):126–42.

37. Zola Swarthout, "Negro Beach Planned," *Miami Herald*, June 13, 1956; "White, Negro Youths Trade Shots in WPB," *Miami Herald*, June 17, 1956; "Face Arrest in Shooting at WPB," *Miami Herald*, June 18, 1956; "Negro Beach Planned: Martin County Officials Act," *Miami Herald*, June 13, 1956; "Pool, Golf Sites Eyed," *Miami Herald*, June 21, 1956; Russ Marchner, "Riviera Continues Beach Segregation," *Miami Herald*, June 23, 1956.

38. "Ervin Lays Out Segregation Path," *Miami Herald*, June 13, 1956, 1; "Inter-Racial Council Aim: No Pressure or Court Action," *Miami Herald*, June 14, 1956; Duane Jones, "Racial Relations on 'Right Track,'" *Miami Herald*, June 21, 1956. The group was formally known as the Fort Lauderdale Council on Human Relations.

39. "Council Vows to Hold Line for Segregation," *Miami Herald*, June 26, 1956, B1; "Integration Issue Blamed on Reds," *Miami Herald*, June 26, 1956; "Integration Foes

Form Unit in State," *Miami Herald*, June 27, 1956; "Caution Urged for Negroes," *Miami Herald*, June 28, 1956, 1.

40. Hendrick J. Berns, "Collins Aid Available in Delray Row," *Miami Herald*, June 28, 1956; "Top Negroes Vetoed Deal, Mayor States," *Miami Herald*, June 29, 1956, 1; Hendrick J. Berns, "Delray Negroes Still Hope for Solution but Faith Vanishing," *Miami Herald*, June 29, 1956; "Delray Sits Tight on Seething Problem of Negroes on Beach," *Miami Herald*, June [?], 1956; "Officials Promised to Build Pool," *Miami Herald*, June 27, 1956; Hendrick J. Berns, "Troubled Delray: What Is Answer?" *Miami Herald*, June 24, 1956; Hendrick J. Berns, "Timetable Tells the Story of Delray Beach vs. Negro," *Miami Herald*, June 25, 1956.

41. "Delray Plan Held No Answer to Racial Issue over Black Beach," *Miami News*, June 6, 1956; WTVJ, "Incident at Delray Beach," July 1956, Lynn and Louis Wolfson II Florida Moving Images Archive, Miami Dade College, Miami.

42. Russ Marchner, "Negro, White Leaders Weld Accord in Delray," *Miami Herald*, July 3, 1956, 1; George Vickery, "TV Newsman Makes News by Bringing Peace to City Torn by Racial Conflict," *The Quill*, September 1956, 15–16.

43. Vickery, "TV Newsman Makes News"; Russ Marchner, "Negro, White Leaders Weld Accord in Delray," 1; Steve Liewer, "Divisive Beach United Blacks," *Sun-Sentinel*, February 27, 1994. Thanks to Douglas Gomery for bringing this source to my attention.

44. Irwin D. S. Winsboro, ed., *Old South, New South, or Down South? Florida and the Modern Civil Rights Movement* (Morgantown: University of West Virginia Press, 2009); Gary Mormino, *Land of Sunshine, State of Dreams: A Social History of Modern Florida* (Gainesville: University Press of Florida, 2005), chapter 9; Michael D. Sprout, "A Beach Too Far," *Sarasota Magazine*, June 2005, https://sarasotamagazine.com/2005/06/01/a-beach-too-far/; S. Brent Spain, "Florida Beach Access: Nothing but Wet Sand?," *Journal of Land Use & Environmental Law* 115 (1999), http://archive.law.fsu.edu/journals/landuse/vol151/spain1.htm. See also Martha Dean Phelts, *An American Beach for African Americans* (Gainesville: University Press of Florida, 1997).

45. Spencer Pompey, interview with Gregory Bush, July 9, 1999, Delray Beach, in author's possession.

46. "Beaches Hold Segregation," *Miami News*, June 19, 1954; Mormino, *Land of Sunshine, State of Dreams*, 314; Peter Cary, "When Fort Lauderdale Had a Negro Beach," *Miami Herald*, September 16, 1985. The most comprehensive treatment is William G. Crawford Jr., "The Long Hard Fight for Equal Rights: The History of Broward County's Colored Beach and the Fort Lauderdale Beach 'Wade-Ins' of the Summer of 1961," *Tequesta* 67 (2007): 19–49.

47. "Parks Decision New Challenge," *Miami News*, November 8, 1955. The Supreme Court ruled in 1955 that it was illegal to provide segregated beaches in Maryland (*Mayor and City Council of Baltimore v. Dawson*, 350 U.S. 877 [1955]). See also Monika Stodolska, Kimberly Shinew, Myron Floyd, and Gordon J. Walker, *Race, Ethnicity and Leisure* (Champaign, Ill.: Human Kinetics, 2014), 42.

48. Mormino, *Land of Sunshine, State of Dreams*, 309–16.

49. Dunn, *Black Miami*, 185.

50. "3 Major Candidates in Miami: Collins, Warren, Lowry Campaigning in Miami," *Miami Herald*, May 3, 1956, 1, 13A. See also Charles Hesser, "Adlai Invades Miami in Final Bid for Support," *Miami News*, September 24, 1956; John Bartlow Martin, *Adlai Stevenson and the World* (New York: Anchor Books, 1978), 296. For a retrospective view of Hadley's campaign, see Glenda Wright, "Hadley's Machine Winds Down," *Miami News*, February 9, 1981. The interposition struggle is discussed in LeRoy Collins, interview with Jack Bass and Walter De Vries, May 19, 1974, Southern Oral History Program, Southern Historical Collection, Special Collections, Louis Round Wilson Library, Chapel Hill, North Carolina, http://ufdc.ufl.edu/UF00005580/00001/17j.

51. Charles F. Hesser, "House OK Expected on Last Ditch Segregation Bill," *Miami News*, April 7, 1957; "On Last Resort Bill," *Miami News*, May 14, 1957.

52. John Boyles, "Collins Fears Race Tensions May Hurt Industrial Growth," *Miami Herald*, September 7, 1956, Agnew Welsh Scrapbooks, Miami-Dade Public Library System.

53. Ruth Perry, "Along Freedom's Road," *Miami Times*, March 15, 1958, 7. Hoover quoted in Richard Gid Powers, *Secrecy and Power: The Life of J. Edgar Hoover* (New York: Free Press, 1987), 31.

54. Ruth Perry, "Along Freedom's Road," *Miami Times*, February 22, 1958, 11; Elliott J. Prieze, "Legislative Communist Investigation Flops," *Miami Times*, March 1, 1958.

55. Robert Boyd, "Miami's NAACP Chief Cleared," *Miami Herald*, March 26, 1963, 1. See also Lawson, "The Florida Legislative Investigation Committee and the Constitutional Readjustment of Race Relations."

56. Perry, "Along Freedom's Road," *Miami Times*, February 22, 1958. See also Judith G. Poucher, "Raising Her Voice: Ruth Perry, Activist and Journalist for the Miami NAACP," *Florida Historical Quarterly* 84 (Spring 2006): 517–40.

57. "Rockpit Death Stirs Cry for Swimming Pool," *Miami Times*, April 25, 1959, 1.

58. Bill Baggs, "Race Progress Botched," *Miami News*, October 30, 1959; "City Pools, Parks Open to Negroes," *Miami News*, October 27, 1959.

59. Merrett Stierheim, interview with Gregory Bush, 2004, Special Collections, Otto G. Richter Library, University of Miami.

60. John Morton, "Pool Integration Revoked by Board," *Miami Herald*, October 28, 1959; Rose Allegato, "Some Go for Dip—Without Incident," *Miami Herald*, October 28, 1959.

61. William Tucker, "Negroes Seek County Opening," *Miami News*, October 30, 1959.

62. "Text of Ruling on Integration," *Miami News*, November 24, 1959.

63. Ibid. Robert Dawson had filed in federal district court challenging racially segregated beaches in Maryland, charging that legally mandated segregation violated the Fourteenth Amendment's equal protection clause. After the federal district judge dismissed Dawson's case, Dawson appealed to the Fourth Circuit Court of Appeals, which based its ruling on the *Brown v. Board of Education* decision and reversed the

district court's finding. See *Mayor and City Council of Baltimore City v. Dawson*, 350 U.S. 877 (1955).

64. "Negroes Integrate Crandon Park," *Miami Times*, November 28, 1959; "Negroes Swim at Crandon," *Miami News*, November 25, 1959.

65. Garth Reeves Sr., interview with Andrea Benitez, March 2, 2007, http://miami.fiu.edu/moh/interviews/reeves/reeves.htm. See also Garth Reeves Sr., interview with Julian Pleasants, August 19, 1999, http://ufdc.ufl.edu/UF00005526/00001.

66. "Text of Ruling on Integration," *Miami News*, November 24, 1959.

67. "Negroes Swim on Miami Beach," *Palm Beach Post*, August 10, 1960; Gilbert R. Mason, *Beaches, Blood, and Ballots: A Black Doctor's Civil Rights Struggle* (Jackson: University Press of Mississippi, 2000), 63, 72.

68. Maria Cristina Garcia, *Havana USA: Cuban Exiles and Cuban Americans in South Florida, 1959–1994* (Berkeley: University of California Press, 1996); Anthony P. Maingot, "Immigration and the Caribbean Basin," Lisandro Perez, "Cuban Miami," and Max J. Castro, "The Politics of Language in Miami," all in *Miami Now! Immigration, Ethnicity, and Social Change*, ed. Guillermo Grenier and Alex Steppick III (Gainesville: University Press of Florida, 1992), 18–40, 83–108, and 109–132, respectively; Sheila Croucher, *Imagining Miami: Ethnic Politics in a Postmodern World* (Charlottesville: University Press of Virginia, 1997).

69. Mathew D. Lassiter, *The Silent Majority: Suburban Politics in the Sunbelt South* (Princeton, N.J.: Princeton University Press, 2006).

70. Robert Fairbanks, *For the City as a Whole*, 147, quoted in Harvey J. Graff, *The Dallas Myth: The Making and Unmaking of an American City* (Minneapolis: University of Minnesota Press, 2008), 173.

71. Daniel Rogers, *Age of Fracture* (Cambridge, Mass.: Harvard University Press, 2011), 143. See also W. Fitzhugh Brundage, *The Southern Past: A Clash of Race and Memory* (Cambridge, Mass.: Harvard University Press, 2005), 6–7.

72. Timothy Weaver, *Blazing the Neoliberal Trail: Urban Political Development in the United States and United Kingdom* (Philadelphia: University of Pennsylvania Press, 2016), 29–30.

73. Kevin Kruse, *White Flight: Atlanta and the Making of Modern Conservatism* (Princeton, N.J.: Princeton University Press, 2005), 106. See also Lassiter, *The Silent Majority*; and Julian Zelizer, "Reflections: Rethinking the History of American Conservatism," *Reviews in American History* 38 (June 2010): 368.

74. "28 Students Enroll at Orchard Villa," *Miami Herald*, September 5, 1959, 1; "Miami Schools Finally Integrated," *Miami Herald*, September 12, 1959, 1; Dunn, *Black Miami*, 230; Shell-Weiss, *Coming to Miami*, 154. See also Bob Simms: An Activist's Life and Legacy, collection description at http://scholar.library.miami.edu/bobsimms/about.html. For recent trends, see David Smiley, "'Re-Segregation' Trend: 60 Years after Ruling, Dozens of Miami-Dade Schools Remain 'Isolated,'" *Miami Herald*, May 19, 2014.

75. Dick Nellius, "Program Aims at Slums: Central Negro Area First Target for Wreckers," *Miami News*, October 16, 1962; Stephen B. Harris, "Slum Group Would

Testify before House Lobby," *Miami News*, April 21, 1950. For a detailed analysis of urban renewal, see Connolly, "By Eminent Domain." The definitive treatment of Miami housing policy can be found in Nathan Connolly, *A World More Concrete: Real Estate and the Remaking of Jim Crow South Florida* (Chicago: University of Chicago Press, 2014).

76. Juanita Greene, "He'd Shift Negro District, Build a New 'Downtown," *Miami Herald*, May 28, 1961, 4F.

77. Connolly, *A World More Concrete*.

78. "L. L. Brooks Leads Fight for Negro Playgrounds," *Miami Times*, June 18, 1960; Stanley Sweeting, "*Herald*'s Slum Clearance Series Gets Reporter's Comments," *Miami Times*, March 29, 1958; "Pool Integration Seen Monday," *Miami Times*, April 15, 1961, 1; "It's Official! Pools Now Open to All," *Miami Times*, April 22, 1961, 1. See also Connolly, "By Eminent Domain," chapter 7.

79. Dr. John O. Brown, interview with Madison Davis Lacy Jr., June 21, 1989, Eyes on the Prize II Interviews, http://digital.wustl.edu/e/eii/eiiweb/bro5427.0540.023drjohnobrown.html.

80. A. D. Moore, interview with Kathy Hersh, May 11, 2001, Media Center, Turner Tech High School, Miami, Community Studies Project, Dade County Public Schools.

81. Ibid.

82. Ibid.

83. "Next Move Planned by Negroes," *Miami News*, April 14, 1960; Shell-Weiss, *Coming to Miami*, 175.

84. "Boycott Is Called Off Here," *Miami Times*, April 16, 1960, 1.

85. "Segregation in Atlanta: Going, Going . . . Gone with the Wind," *Miami News*, August 29, 1961.

86. Nathan Daniel Beau Connolly, "By Eminent Domain: Race and Capital in the Building of an American South Florida" (PhD diss., University of Michigan, 2008), 13–14.

87. George Newman, "Mourners Send $1,000," *Miami News*, September 23, 1963.

88. Roberta Applegate, "Miami's the Best, Say Negroes," *Miami Herald*, February 14, 1962.

89. "King Jailed in St. Augustine," *Miami News*, June 11, 1964.

90. "King Calls Cuban, Negro Job Competition Perilous," *Miami News*, April 13, 1966.

91. Bill Baggs, "Rev. King," *Miami News*, May 18, 1966.

92. George Lardiner Jr., "Epidemic of 'Law and Order,'" *The Nation*, February 19, 1968, 231–34; "Police: Patch of Blue," *Time*, March 15, 1968.

93. Gene Miller and Thirlee Smith, "600 Guardsmen Move into Trouble Area: 3 Slain; Looting Goes On," *Miami Herald*, August 9, 1968, 2; Paul Wyche, "Negro Leaders Blame Outsiders," *Miami News*, August 8, 1968; Paul Wyche, "Before, During After: What Caused Trouble?" *Miami News*, August 10, 1968; Bill Baggs, "The Violent Hucksters," *Miami News*, August 9, 1968; Lardner, "Epidemic of 'Law and Order.'" See also Erick Tscheschlok, "Long Time Coming: Miami's Liberty City Riot of 1968," *Florida Historical Quarterly* 74 (Spring 1996): 440–60.

94. Baggs, "The Violent Hucksters,"

95. Editorial, "Out of Evil Comes Good," *Miami Times*, August 16, 1968.

96. Russell Baker, "Miami Beach and the Politicians: A Place and People in Concert," *New York Times*, August 4, 1968, 1. See also Gregory Bush, "'Playground of the USA': Miami and the Promotion of Spectacle," *Pacific Historical Review* 68 (May 1999): 153–72.

97. Norman Mailer, *Miami and the Siege of Chicago* (New York, Signet, 1968), 14.

98. See Warren Susman, *History as Culture: The Transformation of American Society in the Twentieth Century* (New York: Pantheon Books, 1984). See also Richard Nixon, "Remarks to a Young Voters Rally in Miami, Florida," August 22, 1972, The American Presidency Project, http://www.presidency.ucsb.edu/ws/index.php?pid=3536.

99. LeRoy Collins, interview with Jack Bass and Walter De Vries, May 19, 1974, 26; Lawton Chiles, interview with Jack Bass and Walter De Vries, January 30, 1974; both in Southern Oral History Program, Southern Historical Collection, Special Collections, Louis Round Wilson Library, Chapel Hill, North Carolina.

100. Ian Glass, "NAACP Then, Now: Once-Dynamic Rights Group Now a Victim of Inertia," *Miami News*, October 8, 1976; David Chappell, "The Lost Decade of Civil Rights," *Historically Speaking* 10 (April 2009): 37–41.

101. Errol Schweizer, "Environmental Justice: An Interview with Robert Bullard," *Earth First! Journal* (July 1999), http://www.ejnet.org/ej/bullard.html; Robert Ballard, *Dumping in Dixie: Race, Class, and Environmental Quality*, 3rd ed. (Boulder, Colo.: Westview Press, 2000). Writing in 2005, Congresswoman Maxine Waters remarked, "Environmental justice has broadened its focus beyond pollution and environmental hazards to focus on benefits and amenities. For example, the themes of open space and waterfront access, environmental benefits that historically have been withheld from communities of color, have emerged as major issues in grassroots communities around the country through proactive community planning." "Foreword," in *The Quest for Environmental Justice: Human Rights and the Politics of Pollution*, edited by Robert D. Bullard (San Francisco: Sierra Club Books, 2005), xvi.

Chapter 5. Public Land by the Sea: Developing Virginia Key, 1945–1976

1. Jerold S. Kayden, *Privately Owned Public Space: The New York City Experience* (New York: John Wiley & Sons, 2000); Rickie Sanders, "The Public Space of Urban Communities," in *Public Space and the Ideology of Place in American Culture*, edited by Miles Orvell and Jeffrey Meikle (Amsterdam: Ropopi, 2009), 266.

2. Margot Ammidon, "Edens, Underworlds, and Shrines: Florida's Small Tourist Attractions," *Journal of Decorative and Propaganda Arts* 23 (1998): 239–59; Gary Mormino, *Land of Sunshine, State of Dreams: A Social History of Modern Florida* (Gainesville: University Press of Florida, 2005), chapter 3; Mike Davis, "Fortress Los Angeles: The Militarization of Urban Space," in *Variations on a Theme Park: The New American City and the End of Public Space*, edited by Michael Sorkin (New York: Hill & Wang, 1992), 155.

3. "Rides Crest of Motorboat Boom," *Life*, June 13, 1955, 35–38.

4. Roderick Frazier Nash, *The Rights of Nature* (Madison: University of Wisconsin Press, 1989), 130, 173, 90; Garret Hardin, "The Tragedy of the Commons," *Science* 162, no. 3859 (1968), http://www.sciencemag.org/content/162/3859/1243.full.

5. Kim A. O'Connell, "The Keepers of the Keys," *National Parks*, May–June 2003, 30. See also Susan Shumaker, "Untold Stories from America's National Parks, Israel Lafayette 'Parson' Jones, Sir Lancelot Jones, and Biscayne National Park," http://www-tc.pbs.org/nationalparks/media/pdfs/tnp-abi-untold-stories-pt-03-jones.pdf, accessed January 1, 2016.

6. "Advance," *Miami News*, August 1, 1945.

7. Raymond Arsenault, "The Cooling of the South," *Wilson Quarterly* 8 (Summer 1984): 150–59.

8. David Harvey, "The Political Economy of Public Space," http://davidharvey.org/media/public.pdf.

See also Don Mitchell, *The Right to the City: Social Justice and the Fight for Public Space* (New York: Guilford Press, 2003); Setha Low, Dana Taplin, and Suzanne Scheld, *Rethinking Urban Parks: Public Space and Cultural Diversity* (Austin: University of Texas Press, 2005); Kristine F. Miller, *Designs on the Public: The Private Lives of New York's Public Spaces* (Minneapolis: University of Minnesota Press, 2007).

9. "Park Planning System Sought by City Board," *Miami News*, April 9, 1929.

10. "A Clear Case," *Miami News*, April 14, 1939, 18.

11. "Greater Miami Planning Group to Scan Future," *Miami News*, August 3, 1943.

12. "Critique of Miami," *Miami News*, August 5, 1945.

13. "City, County Plan to Provide Needed Work, Improvements," *Miami News*, September 9, 1945.

14. *Symposium: The Economic Significance of the Keys Opened to Development by the New Rickenbacker Causeway* (Miami: Florida Power & Light Co., 1947).

15. Paul S. George, "Miami's Bayfront Park: A History," http://www.bayfrontpark-miami.com/pages/history/historyessay.html; "Expand Bayfront Park for Big Parking Lot," *Miami Daily News*, April 14, 1948; John Denson, "Bayfront Park Plan or Parking Garages: What's the Answer?" *Miami Herald*, December 13, 1948; John Pennekamp, "Stormy Years of Park," *Miami Herald*, July 22, 1967; "Law Snags Auditorium Expansion," *Miami Herald*, May 27, 1954.

16. "Virginia Beach," *Miami Times*, n.d. (ca. 1946), Agnew Welsh Scrapbooks, vol. 39, 46, Miami-Dade Public Library System; "Transportation to Beach Inadequate," *Miami Times*, June 24, 1947, Agnew Welsh Scrapbooks, Miami-Dade Public Library System; "Crandon Park Picnic Area Opens Today," *Miami News*, October 22, 1950.

17. "Virginia Beach Gets Improvements: Parking Area Being Built," *Miami Times*, July 5, 1947, Agnew Welsh Scrapbooks, Miami-Dade Public Library System.

18. "Develop Virginia Key for Public, City Urged/Ruled Out as a Site for Fair, Trade Mart," *Miami Daily News*, November 1, 1953, 1; "Sift Citizens' Recommendations for Virginia Key, Graces Tract," *Miami News*, November 2, 1953. Black resorts were also proposed for the park; see "Dade Legislators Face 3-Way Battle over Key," *Miami News*, January 10, 1947, 10A.

19. John Pennekamp, "Many Eyes Are Turned toward Development of Virginia Key," *Miami Daily News*, September 10, 1947; John Pennekamp, "Behind the Front Page: Superior Rights to the Beauty of the Bay Belong to Public," June 6, 1947, *Miami Herald*.

20. "Virginia Key Offer Does Not Help Public," *Miami Daily News*, August 5, 1948.

21. "Early Decision Due on Road for Elliott Key," *Miami News*, November 3, 1954; Jack W. Roberts, "To Finance Keys Causeway," *Miami News*, October 25, 1955; Jack W. Roberts, "Interama Originator Finds Virginia Key Acceptable," *Miami News*, July 21, 1957; Paul Einstein, "Keys Linkup Feasible, Traffic Experts Find," *Miami News*, November 20, 1958; "Grand Plan Is Unveiled," *Miami News*, February 14, 1972; "Interama Critics Urge Park at Site," *Miami News*, February 14, 1972; Robert Gonzalez, "Interama: Visions of a Pan-American City," in *Miami Modern Metropolitan: Paradise and Paradox in Midcentury Architecture and Planning*, edited by Allan T. Shulman (Miami Beach: Bass Museum of Art, 2009), 147–51.

22. Ken Heinrich, "New Plan Would Put Port on Virginia Key," *Miami News*, February 19, 1957; Juanita Greene, "Virginia Is the 'Key' to Unlock Seaport Problem, Many Insist," *Miami Herald*, April 28, 1959; Ken Heinrich, "Coordinators Back Modified Port Plan," *Miami News*, October 20, 1956.

23. "Crandon Reports," *Miami News*, April 23, 1948; Jane Wood, "Dade Park System Dresses Up Its New Summer Attractions," *Miami News*, April 18, 1954; "Widely Considered One of the Best Park Systems in the Country," *Miami News*, April 18, 1954; "Crandon Protests Beach Link to Keys," *Miami News*, March 3, 1955.

24. Sanford Schnier, "Let's Go to the Beach, But Where Did It Go?" *Miami News*, September 21, 1958.

25. "Bird Sanctuary on Virginia Key?" *Miami News*, December 2, 1956; Juanita Greene, "Mud Flat to Become Play Area," *Miami Herald*, June 1, 1958.

26. Jack E. Davis, *An Everglades Providence: Marjory Stoneman Douglas and the American Environmental Century* (Athens: University of Georgia Press, 2009); Luther Carter, *The Florida Experience: Land and Water Policy in a Growth State* (Baltimore, Md.: Johns Hopkins University Press, 1974), chapter 4.

27. Philip Wylie, "Florida: Polluted Paradise," *Miami News*, March 19, 1949, 1, 4.

28. Philip Wylie, "The (Sewer) Pipe Dream," *Miami News*, April 1, 1950, 1; "Sewage System Planned to Be Most Modern Kind," *Miami News*, May 18, 1952.

29. Jack Roberts, "Sewage Site Safari Learns 'Awful Truth,'" *Miami News*, n.d., in author's possession.

30. "Entire Community Adds to Pollution," *Miami News*, December 19, 1956; Jane Wood, "Scientists Take Squint at 'Polluted Paradise,'" *Miami News*, April 27, 1955. For more recent concerns, see Lou Ortz, "Sewage Leak Time Bomb in Biscayne Bay," *Miami Today*, July 26, 2012.

31. Jean Yehle, "The History of the Rosenstiel School of Marine & Atmospheric Science: 1940–1950's," Rosenstiel School of Marine & Atmospheric Science, http://www.rsmas.miami.edu/about-rsmas/history/. "Giant Aquarium One of City's Oldest Attractions," *Miami Daily News*, March 21, 1987. In the mid-1970s, an

80,000-square-foot interactive oceanographic museum called Planet Ocean opened across from the Miami Seaquarium. It closed in 1991 and was replaced by Mast Academy, a specialized oceanographic high school of Miami-Dade County Public Schools.

32. Philip Wylie, "Florida Must Face Its Problems or See Its Expansion Slowed Up," *Miami News*, March 6, 1956.

33. Frederick Sherman, "A Lease from City," *Miami Herald*, July 4, 1957.

34. "Mixed Hotel Slated for Miami; Officials Say," *Jet*, March 16, 1961, 23; "New York Beat," *Jet*, December 14, 1961, 64.

35. John Pennekamp, " . . . Has an Old Design," unidentified, undated clipping (*Miami Herald*, 1961), Florida Clippings File Collection, Miami-Dade Public Library System, in author's possession.

36. "Monroe Triumphs on Keys Link Plan," *Miami News*, August 21, 1957; Ken Heinrich, "Authority to Seek Control of New Port," *Miami News*, March 3, 1957; Lloyd Miller, *Biscayne National Park: It Almost Wasn't* (Redland, Fla.: Lemdot Publishing, 2008); Polly Redford, "Small Rebellion in Miami," *Harper's Magazine*, February 1964; Lloyd Miller, interview with Gregory Bush September 11, 2000, Special Collections, Otto G. Richter Library, University of Miami; Davis, *Everglades Providence*, 441–45.

37. Robert Bullard, *Dumping in Dixie: Race, Class, and Environmental Quality* (Boulder, Colo.: Westview Press, 1990); Robert Bullard, ed., *Unequal Protection: Environmental Protection and Communities of Color* (San Francisco: Sierra Club Books, 1994).

38. "County Parks Squeezed Out by 'Progress,'" *Miami News*, November 26, 1960; "Reverse Action on Aquarium," *Miami News*, July 25, 1951; "Ervin Upholds Public Interest," *Miami News*, August 1, 1951; "'Protectors' of Parks Now Legal," *Miami News*, March 11, 1958.

39. "Camping Site by Virginia Key Studied," *Miami News*, November 17, 1964; "Private Projects on Key Opposed," *Miami Herald*, April 20, 1962; Morton Lucoff, "Virginia Key Leaps Hurdle," *Miami News*, May 28, 1964; "'Funland' Studied for Virginia Key," *Miami News*, June 30, 1964.

40. Bill Amlong, "Virginia Key Plans Offered to City," *Miami Herald*, February 28, 1969; "City Commission to Hear Plans for Marine Museum," *Miami News*, February 26, 1969; Morton Lucoff, "Only Fun, Science Plans Urged for Virginia Key," *Miami News*, March 12, 1969; "Virginia Key Master Plan on Agenda," *Miami News*, April 24, 1969.

41. Raul Ramirez, "No Permit Issued for Operation," *Miami Herald*, January 16, 1971; Fred Tasker, "Don't Use Bayfront, City Told," *Miami Herald*, July 27, 1971; "Virginia Key Plan 'Appalls' Zoning Chairman," unidentified clipping, 28 July 1971, Florida Clipping Collection, Miami-Dade Public Library System.

42. Susan Davis, *Spectacular Nature: Corporate Culture and the Sea World Experience* (Berkeley: University of California Press, 1997), 35.

43. Johnny Wilson, "Miami Marine Stadium Plan Gathers Dust for 5 Years," *Miami Herald*, July 30, 1961; Dick Nellius, "Developers Cancel Virginia Key Stadium Plan," *Miami Herald*, April 26, 1962; Charles Whited, "2-Million-Dollar Marine Stadium

Urged on Miami," *Miami Herald*, 3 September 1962; John Blades, "Huge Marine Stadium Proposed for Miami," *Miami Herald*, November 21, 1961.

44. "Opening Will Be a Spectacle" and "New Stadium Wins Praise," both in *Miami Herald*, December 22, 1963.

45. Morton Lucoff, "Alice Wainwright Raises Stadium's Leaky Roof," *Miami News*, April 10, 1964; Dick Knight, "It's New-Plan Time for Marine Stadium," *Miami Herald*, November 8, 1964.

46. Morton Lucoff, "City's Big Headache—Marine Stadium," *Miami News*, July 24, 1966; "$18 Million Fair Proposed," *Miami News*, June 13, 1966.

47. Lucoff, "City's Big Headache."

48. "City Loses a Bundle on Marine Stadium," *Miami Herald*, September 26, 1966; "'Spacerama' Fizzles," *Miami Herald*, June 28, 1966; Steve Rogers, "Reduction Urged in Stadium Fees," *Miami Herald*, August 20, 1966; Mike Power, "Marine Stadium: White Elephant?" *Miami Herald*, October 9, 1967; Morton Lucoff, "Jaycees Seek Hearing on Marine Stadium," *Miami News*, December 11, 1967. On the deed restriction, see Jack Luft, assistant director of development of Miami, to Percy Mallison, director of the Division of State Lands in the Florida Department of Environmental Protection, June 7, 1994, asking for waivers from the confusing state conveyances to the county and city. Letter and response in author's possession.

49. "Sammy Davis Turns on Foot-Stomping Crowd," *Miami Herald*, 28 April 1970; "Float along with Mitch," unidentified newspaper clipping, July 5, 1970, Miami Clipping Files, Miami-Dade Public Library System; "Ginsberg Reads, Lights Stay On," *Miami Herald*, January 3, 1970; Raul Ramirez, "Joan Baez Finds Stage After Rebuff," *Miami Herald*, February 4, 1971; Adon Taft, "Brilliant Sunrise Inspired Easter Worshippers," *Miami Herald*, March 30, 1970; June Kronholz, "U Floats Grads into Work Class," *Miami Herald*, January 24, 1970; William Montabano, "It's Nixon with All But One," *Miami Herald*, August 23, 1972; "Stadium Services Will Remain Free," *Miami Herald*, November 17, 1972.

50. Louis Salome, "Paul: Expanding Beach Excuse for Building," *Miami News*, July 13, 1970.

51. Disputes erupted over the city's political and financial maneuvering regarding purchase of Florida East Coast Railway waterfront land just north of the Miami River that became mired in protracted controversy, notably in relation to land purchases in black neighborhoods and bayfront land. See Courtland T. Milloy, "Challenge to Park Bonding," *Miami Herald*, July 15, 1972; Brue Giles, "Parks Bonds Ballot Upheld without Item-by-Item Vote," *Miami Herald*, October 12, 1972; Theodore Stanger, "Gordon: Audit Park Funding," *Miami Herald*, February 10, 1977; John Arnold, "FEC Purchase Would Gut Park Funds," *Miami Herald*, February 1, 1977; "Bayfront Purchase an Acceptable Risk," *Miami News*, June 23, 1977.

52. Morton Lucoff and Dick Holland, "Culture Center at Watson Island Gets Nod from Ferre, Orr," *Miami News*, November 16, 1973; "Now They're After Watson Island," *Miami Herald*, November 19, 1973; Steve Sink, "Director Says Island Library Means People Won't Drop In," *Miami Herald*, December 13, 1973, 12B; "Let's Save

Watson Island," WTVJ editorial, November 29, 1973, Lynn and Louis Wolfson II Florida Moving Image Archives, Miami Dade College, in author's possession; Frank Greve, "Library, Museum Officials Snub Watson Isle Cult," *Miami Herald*, December 21, 1973; "Orr Trim Watson Plan," *Miami News*, December 27, 1973.

53. Larry Birger, "Build Tivoli in Bayfront, Developer Says," *Miami News*, January 27, 1976; Theodore Stanger, "City Awaits Pritzker's Reply Today on Watson Isle Amusement Park," *Miami Herald*, December 29, 1976; Theodore Stanger, "Amusement Park Offer Is Accepted," *Miami Herald*, December 21, 1976; "Lawyers Blast Watson Option," *Miami Herald*, December 28, 1976; Bill Gjebre, "Miami Awaiting $100,000 for Watson Island," *Miami News*, January 14, 1977.

54. Theodore Stanger, "Watson Clauses Favor Pritzker," *Miami Herald*, February 12, 1977; Andy Rosenblatt, "Theme Park Site Switch Is Proposed," *Miami Herald*, March 2, 1977; Bill Rose, "Miami's Attorney Left Out of Talks on Watson Park," *Miami Herald*, October 2, 1977.

55. "Waterfront Plan Needed in Miami," *Miami News*, May 30, 1978.

56. Bill Baggs, "Keep Parks for Public," *Miami News*, August 29, 1960.

57. Jack Kassewitz, "Progress Prunes Our Parks," *Miami News*, February 18, 1964; "Negro Parks to Be Improved," *Miami News*, December 13, 1965; "A Place for Parks," *Miami Daily News*, January 29, 1969.

58. Terry Johnson King, "The Splendid Isolation That Is Virginia Key," unidentified newspaper clipping, December 18, 1972, in author's possession; "Absurd to Lock a Public Beach," *Miami News*, November 25, 1976, 14A.

59. Garth Reeves, interview with Chanelle Rose, 2005, Historic Virginia Key Beach Park Trust.

60. Kirk Nielsen, "A Historic Dip: Witnesses to the Segregated History of Virginia Beach Tell a Sorry but Inspiring Tale," *Miami New Times*, April 8, 1999. See also Julian M. Pleasants, ed., *Orange Journalism: Voices from Florida Journalism* (Gainesville: University of Florida Press, 2003), 204–5.

61. Gayle Pollard, "Blacks Say They Always Braved Beach," *Miami Herald*, February 19, 1975, 4B.

62. Bea Hines, "A Deserted 'Old World' Beach," *Miami Herald*, February 22, 1975.

Chapter 6. The Erosion of a "World-Class" Urban Paradise: Tourism, the Environmental Movement, and Planning Related to Virginia Key Beach, 1982–1998

Epigraph source: Dianne Dumanoski, "Rethinking Environmentalism," *Conservation Matters*, Autumn 1998, 42.

1. See the video documentary on black public spaces and urban boosterism in the city of Columbus's Flora Festival in 1992: Austin Allen, *Claiming Open Spaces*, first aired on PBS in 1996, now available from Third World Newsreel. See also Allen's statement about this film at Austin Allen, "Dreaming Spaces Anew," Project for Public Spaces, http://www.pps.org/articles/austinallen/.

2. Bill Gjebre, "Virginia Key Urged as 1992 Fair Site," *Miami Daily News*, May 27,

1982. See also "Virginia Key Is Considered for the 1992 World's Fair," *Miami Herald*, May 28, 1982, 2DH; "Planning for the 1992 World Fair at Virginia Key Continues," *Miami Herald*, September 17, 1982; "Expo 500 Threatens Virginia Key with the 1992 World's Fair," *Miami Herald*, October 4, 1982, 1BH.

3. Bruce Porter and Marvin Dunn, *The Miami Riot of 1980: Crossing the Bounds* (Lexington, Mass.: Lexington Books, 1984); Alejandro Portes and Alex Steppick, *Miami: City on the Edge* (Berkeley: University of California Press, 1993); William Wilbanks, *Murder in Miami* (Lanham, Md.: University Press of America), 1984.

4. Jan Nijman, *Miami: Mistress of the Americas* (Philadelphia: University of Pennsylvania Press, 2011), 58–61.

5. James Kelly, "South Florida: Trouble in Paradise," *Time*, November 23, 1981.

6. Paul George, "Miami's Bayfront Park: A History," http://www.bayfrontparkmiami.com/pages/history/historyessay.html. See also a video about Isamu Noguchi's work, "The Sculpture of Spaces," at http://digital.films.com/play/734LJZ; and Michael Lewis, "Miami Should Form Self-Perpetuating Trust to Save Its Assets," *Miami Today*, August 18, 2011, 6.

7. Nijman, *Miami*, 190–93.

8. Gray Read, "Many Miamis: The Theater of Public Space," in *Miami Modern Metropolis: Paradise and Paradox in Midcentury Architecture and Planning*, edited by Allan T. Shuman (Miami Beach: Bass Museum of Art, 2009), 60–81.

9. Dolores Hayden, "Urban Landscape History: The Sense of Place and the Politics of Space," in *Understanding Ordinary Landscapes*, edited by Paul Groth and Todd Bressi (New Haven, Conn.: Yale University Press, 1997), 132.

10. Tyler Bridges, "Knight Center a Costly Dream," *Miami Herald*, July 4, 1999, 1; Candi Calkins, "Developers to Get a Shot at Finding New Use for Grove Center," *Miami Today*, July 29, 1999, 11.

11. Harvey Ruvin, interview with Gregory Bush, July 22, 2004, in author's possession.

12. Susan G. Davis, *Spectacular Nature: Corporate Culture and the Sea World Experience* (Berkeley: University of California Press, 1997), 24–25.

13. Joel Kotkin, *The City: A Global History* (New York: Modern Library, 2005), 154. In "Theme Bonanza," *Miami Herald*, May 12, 1996, J1, Jay Clarke discussed the new attractions at Busch Gardens, Universal Studios, Sea World, and Disney World.

14. Tom Morganthau and Vincent Coppola, "Clouds on the Beach," *Newsweek*, February 11, 1980, 40–41; Stewart Powell, "The Struggle to Regain Paradise Lost," *U.S. News & World Report*, February 24, 1986, 21–22.

15. See Gregory Bush, "From Stateroom to Skybox: The Miami Arena Controversy and the Promotion of Spectacle," paper presented at the annual meeting of the American Studies Association, October 1997, in author's possession. See also Wendell Berry, *What Are People For?* (San Francisco: North Point Press, 1990), 129–44.

16. Benjamin Barber, *Consumed: How Markets Corrupt Children, Infantilize Adults, and Swallow Citizens Whole* (New York: Norton, 2007), 200.

17. Jan Nijman, *Miami: Mistress of the Americas* (Philadelphia: University of

Pennsylvania Press, 2011), 192, 206. On mobility, connections, and placelessness, see Tim Cresswell, *Place: An Introduction*, 2nd ed. (New York: Wiley Blackwell, 2015), chapter 3; William Cronon, "Kennecott Journey: The Paths out of Town," in *Under an Open Sky*, edited by W. Cronon, G. Miles, and J. Gitlin (New York: W. W. Norton, 1992), 28–51; Lucy Lippard, *The Lure of the Local: Senses of Place in a Multicultural Society* (New York: The New Press, 1997); and Yi-Fu Tuan, *Topophilia: A Study of Environmental Attitudes and Values* (New York: Columbia University Press, 1974).

18. On definitions of public land, see Katharyne Mitchell, "The Culture of Urban Space," *Urban Geography* 21 (2000): 443–49; Peter G. Goheen, "Public Space and the Geography of the Modern City," *Progress in Human Geography* 22, no. 4 (1998): 479–96.

19. See the video *The Story of Hands across America* (Karl-Lorimar Video, 1987); and C. Brant Short, *Ronald Reagan and the Public Lands: America's Conservation Debate, 1979–1984* (College Station: Texas A&M University Press, 1989).

20. Porter and Dunn, *The Miami Riot of 1980*; Edwin McDowell, "Florida Tourism Works to Recover from Killings," *New York Times*, November 26, 1993. See also Anne Moncreiff Arrarte, "Selling Paradise," *Miami Herald*, October 16, 1996, 26, 27.See also *Thirty-Year Retrospective: The Status of the Black Community in Miami-Dade County* (Metropolitan Center, Florida International University, n.d.), http://www.miami-dade.gov/economicadvocacytrust/library/disparity-study.pdf.

21. On homelessness in Bicentennial Park in the early 1990s, see William Labbee, "Keep off the Grass," *Miami New Times*, May 22, 1991. On poverty, see federal census data in Alemayehu Bishaw and John Iceland, "Poverty: 1999," *Census 2000 Brief*, May 2003, https://www.census.gov/prod/2003pubs/c2kbr-19.pdf, accessed January 2, 2016.

22. Rosabeth Moss Kanter, *World Class: Thriving Locally in a Global Economy* (New York: Simon and Schuster, 1995); Jan Nijman, "Globalization to a Latin Beat: The Miami Growth Machine," *Annals of the American Academy of Political and Social Science* 551, no. 1 (1997): 175. See also Michael Grunwald, *The Swamp: The Everglades, Florida, and the Politics of Paradise* (New York: Simon and Schuster, 2006); Cynthia Barnett, *Mirage: Florida and the Vanishing Water of the Eastern U.S.* (Ann Arbor: University of Michigan Press, 2007).

23. Roberta Brandes Gratz, "Doing It Wrong to Get It Right," Project for Public Spaces, 2009, http://www.pps.org/reference/roberta/.

24. Dave Barry, "A Hundred Years of Ineptitude," *Tropic Magazine* (*Miami Herald*), March 10, 1996, 11, 23. In earlier years, former president Nixon made his own questionable land deals. See William Amlong, "Bebe and Cik on a Houseboat," *The Nation*, November 12, 1973, 489–93;

25. On the idea of world-class city, see Saskia Sassen, *Territory, Authority, Rights: From Medieval to Global Assemblages* (Princeton, N.J.: Princeton University Press, 2006). On BIDs, see Margaret Kohn, *Brave New Neighborhoods: The Privatization of Public Space* (New York: Routledge, 2004), chapter 4; Jerold S. Kayden, *Privately Owned Public Space: The New York City Experience* (New York: John Wiley & Sons,

2000); James Mak, *Developing a Dream Destination: Tourism and Tourism Policy Planning in Hawai'i* (Honolulu: University of Hawai'i Press, 2008), 69.

26. See M. Barron Stofik, *Saving South Beach* (Gainesville: University Press of Florida, 2005).

27. Hal Rothman, "Shedding Skin and Shifting Shape: Tourism in the Modern West," in *Seeing & Being Seen: Tourism in the American West*, edited by David M. Wrobel and Patrick T. Long (Lawrence: University Press of Kansas, 2001), 100–120; Michael Sorkin, ed., *Variations on a Theme Park: The New American City and the End of Public Space* (New York: Hill and Wang, 1992); Sharon Zukin, *The Culture of Cities* (Boston: Blackwell, 1995), 14. Atlantic City has an even more questionable record in relation to public space. See Bryant Simon, *Boardwalk of Dreams: Atlantic City and the Fate of Urban America* (New York: Oxford University Press, 2004): 214–15.

28. See Mark S. Rosentraub, *Major League Losers: The Real Cost of Sports and Who's Paying for It* (New York: Basic Books, 1997).

29. See Luther Carter, *The Florida Experience: Land and Water Policy in a Growth State* (Baltimore, Md.: Johns Hopkins University Press, 1974), esp. 174–76 on the jetport; Jack Davis, *An Everglades Providence: Marjory Stoneman Douglas and the American Environmental Century* (Athens: University of Georgia Press, 2009); Jack Davis and Raymond Arsenault, eds., *Paradise Lost? The Environmental History of Florida* (Gainesville: University of Florida Press, 2005).

30. Gordon Harvey, "The Politics of Environmental Protection in 1970s Florida," in *Paradise Lost? The Environmental History of Florida*, edited by Jack Davis and Raymond Arsenault (Gainesville: University of Florida Press, 2005), 359; Davis, *An Everglades Providence*, chap. 32; Michael Grunwald, *The Swamp: The Everglades, Florida, and the Politics of Paradise* (New York: Simon and Schuster, 2006).

31. Harvey Ruvin, interview with Gregory Bush, July 22, 2004, in author's possession.

32. Carter, *The Florida Experience*, 174–76, 186. See also Nelson Blake, *Land into Water, Water into Land: A History of Water Management in Florida* (Gainesville: University Press of Florida, 1989).

33. Mary Ellen Klaus, "Florida Lawmakers Wipe Out 30 Years of Growth Management Law," *Tampa Bay Times*, May 7, 2011.

34. Joanna Lombard, "The Memorable Landscapes of William Lyman Phillips," *Journal of Decorative and Propaganda Arts* 23 (1998): 260–87.

35. See Jack E. Davis, "'Conservation Is Now a Dead Word': Marjory Stoneman Douglas and the Transformation of American Environmentalism," in *Paradise Lost? The Environmental History of Florida*, edited by Jack Emerson Davis and Raymond Arsenault (Gainesville: University Press of Florida, 1998), 297–325; Gordon E. Harvey, "'We Must Free Ourselves . . . from the Tattered Fetters of the Booster Mentality': Big Cypress Swamp and the Politics of Environmental Protection in 1970s Florida," in *Paradise Lost?*, 350–74; Jacob Bernstein, "Take Me Out to the . . . Parking Lot?," *Miami New Times*, January 27, 2000, http://www.miaminewtimes.com/news/take-me-out-to-the-parking-lot-6356876, accessed March 6, 2007.

36. Lloyd Miller, *Biscayne National Park: It Almost Wasn't* (Redland, Fla.: Lemdot Publishing, 2008), 76–78. On the Biscayne Bay Aquatic Preserve, see "Biscayne Bay Aquatic Preserves," Florida Department of Environmental Protection, http://www. dep.state.fl.us/coastal/sites/biscayne/, accessed January 2, 2016. The quote is from "Florida's Aquatic Preserves," Florida Department of Environmental Protection, http://www.dep.state.fl.us/coastal/programs/aquatic.htm.

37. Davis, "'Conservation Is Now a Dead Word.'" See also Davis, *Everglades Providence*; Polly Redford, "Small Rebellion in Miami," *Harper's Magazine*, February 1964; Lloyd Miller, interview with Gregory Bush, 1999, Special Collections, Otto Richter Library. For additional information about the history and environmental conditions of Biscayne Bay, see *Biscayne Bay: Environmental History and Annotated Bibliography*, NOAA Technical Memorandum NOS NCCOS CCMA 145, http://www.aoml.noaa. gov/general/lib/bbehdoc.pdf, accessed March 6, 2007. Also see G. L. Wingard et al., "Ecosystem History of Southern and Central Biscayne Bay: Summary Report on Sedimentary Core Analyses," U.S. Geological Survey Open File Report 03-375, September 15, 2003, http://sofia.usgs.gov/publications/ofr/03-375/.

38. Howard Gregg, Assistant Director, Miami-Dade Parks and Recreation Department, interview with Gregory Bush, 2004, Special Collections, Otto G. Richter Library, Miami University.

39. "Proposed City of Miami Parks and Recreational Bond Program," January 20, 1972, Miami-Metro Department of Publicity and Tourism, January 19, 1972, in author's possession. On the Parks for People bond issue and the failure to complete the "baywalk," see John Arnold, "FEC Purchase Would Gut Park Future," *Miami Herald*, February 1, 1977.

40. A. D. Barnes, *History of Dade County Park System, 1929–1969: The First Forty Years* (Miami: Metro-Dade County Parks and Recreation Department, 1986); Howard Gregg, assistant director, Miami-Dade County Parks Department, interview with Gregory Bush, 2001, in author's possession; Maurice Ferre, interview with Gregory Bush, 1999, Special Collections, Otto Richter Library. Also see Jack Luft, assistant director of the city of Miami Department of Development, to Percy Mallison, director, Division of State Lands, Florida Department of Environmental Protection, June 7, 1994, and response by Anna Marie Hartman (Florida Department of Environmental Protection), November 1, 1994, copies of both in author's possession.

41. Elizabeth Wilson, "Agreement Nearing on Virginia Key Land Swap," *Miami Herald*, 4 December 1980; M. R. Stierheim, county manager, to Board of County Commissioners, March 16, 1982, copy in possession of the author.

42. David Baum, "Virginia Key, Part One: Paradise Found," *The Sun Dial* 6 (Spring 2006), http://sffb.com/pdfs/sundial/sd_sp06med.pdf. See also Calvin Godfrey, "Mayor of the Nude Beach," *Miami New Times*, February 28, 2008, http://www.miaminewtimes.com/2008-02-28/news/mayor-of-the-nude-beach/.

43. Brian Blanchard, "Firm Picked to Plan Virginia Key Park," *Miami Herald*, December 12, 1982, 12; Brian Blanchard, "Restaurant Planned for Virginia Key," *Miami Herald*, January 30, 1983, 3; Michael Cottman, "Planners, Fair Boosters, Police Vie for

a Piece of Virginia Key," *Miami Herald*, October 4, 1982, 1B; Sandra Dibble, "$12 Million Plan Would Transform Virginia Key," *Miami Herald*, September 11, 1983, 3; Rick Hirsch, "City May Not Build Virginia Key Beach Park," *Miami Herald*, May 7, 1985, 3D.

44. "Miami Bayside Getting a $93 Million Face Lift," *Chicago Tribune*, November 3, 1986, 4; Yudislaidy Fernandez, "Miami Agrees to Let Strapped Bayside Marketplace Pay Only Half of Unpaid Rent," *Miami Times*, December 18, 2008, http://www.miamitodaynews.com/news/081218/story2.shtml. For the most recent private assault on Bayfront Park, see Douglas Hanks, "Miami Dade Approves $9 Million for Skyrise Miami," *Miami Herald*, December 16, 2014.

45. Joanne Cavanaugh, "Shoring Up the Waterfront," *Miami Herald*, September 28, 1995, B1.

46. Greg Baker, "Treasured Isle," *Miami New Times*, March 23, 1995, http://www.miaminewtimes.com/1995-03-23/news/treasured-isle/, accessed March 6, 2007; James Paddon and Daniel Suman, "The Virginia Key Campground," in *Urban Growth and Sustainable Habitats: Case Studies of Policy Conflicts in South Florida's Coastal Environment*, edited by Daniel Sumna, Manoj Shivlani, and Maria Villabueva (Miami: University of Miami, 1995), 155–68, Dawkins quoted on 159.

47. Greg Baker, "Treasured Island," *Miami New Times*, March 23, 1995. See also Carl Hiaasen, "Virginia Key Camp Deal Really Reeks," *Miami Herald*, November 2, 1995.

48. City of Miami Department of Real Estate Advertisement, "Miami: Changing at the Speed of Magic," in author's possession; Alberto Ruder, interview with Gregory Bush, 2000, Special Collections, Otto G. Richter Library, Miami University.

49. Don Mitchell, *The Right to the City: Social Justice and the Fight for Public Space* (New York: Guilford Press, 2003); *Pottinger v. City of Miami*, 810 F. Supp. 1551 (S.D. Fla. 1992), February 2, 1996. See also Stephen Schnably, "Safe Zones and Invisibility in *Pottinger v. City of Miami*," paper presented at the Law and Society Association, Toronto, June 2, 1995.

50. Bernstein, "Take Me Out to the . . . Parking Lot?"

51. Paula Park, "Parks & Profits: Believe It or Not, Miami's Planning Czar Jack Luft Says He Can Make Virginia Key Both Lovely and Lucrative," *Miami New Times*, 23 October 1997, 13–23; Jeffrey S. Solocheck, "City Cleared to Move Ahead on Developing Virginia Key," *Miami Today*, April 10, 1997; "Miami: Changing at the Speed of Magic." For the deed restrictions, see State of Florida Internal Improvement Fund, Deed No 18730, August 21, 1942, Records Book 2247, 260, as corrected by Deed No 18730-A, February 11, 1953, Records Book 3724, 318, both in author's possession. For requests to lift deed restrictions, see Donald Warshaw, city manager, to Ms. Toni Riordan, Florida Department of Community Affairs, September 3, 1998; and Guillermo Olmedillo, director, Planning, Development and Regulation Department, Miami-Dade County, September 3, 1998, copies in author's possession.

52. Bernstein, "Take Me Out to the . . . Parking Lot?" On the establishment of the Children's Museum on Watson Island, see Kirk Nielsen, "The Children's Museum, Inc.," *Miami New Times*, October 12, 2000, http://www.miaminewtimes.com/news/

the-childrens-museum-inc-6354628, accessed March 6, 2007. On Watson Island, see Kirk Nielsen, "Spoiled Island," *Miami New Times*, September 21, 2000.

53. On the Coconut Grove waterfront development, see Kirk Nielsen, "Cloistering the Commodore," *Miami New Times*, December 17, 1998, http://www.miaminewtimes.com/1998-12-17/news/cloistering-the-commodore/, accessed March 6, 2007; Yolanda Balida, "Grove Land on Bay to Be Developed," *Miami Herald*, December 9, 1998.

54. Maria Cristina Garcia, *Havana USA: Cuban Exiles and Cuban Americans in South Florida, 1959–1994* (Berkeley: University of California Press, 1996); Melanie Shell-Weiss, *Coming to Miami: A Social History* (Gainesville: University Press of Florida, 2009), chapter 8.

55. T. D. Allman, *Miami: City of the Future* (New York: Atlantic Monthly Press, 1987), 105.

56. On Miami as a banking and trade center, see Jan Nijman, *Miami: Mistress of the Americas* (Philadelphia: University of Pennsylvania Press, 2011), 80–89.

57. On the UEL's march in 1998, see Geoffrey Tomb, "Miami Revisited Tour Seeks to Find 'Real City,'" *Miami Herald*, April 23, 1998, 1B.

58. Yolanda Balido, "Bayside Dreams: City Makes New Attempt to Develop Waterfront," *Miami Herald*, December 20, 1998, B1. See also Yolanda Balido, "Forum to Address Protection of Miami's Parks," *Miami Herald*, January 21, 1999.

59. Carl Hiaasen, "'Revitalization' Is a Threat to Virginia Key," *Miami Herald*, April 3, 1997, reprinted in *Kick Ass: Selected Columns of Carl Hiaasen* (Gainesville: University Press of Florida, 1999), 376–70.

Chapter 7. Forging Our Civil Right to Public Space, 1999–2015

1. Amy Chillag, "Preservationist Fights for Public Space," *Sun Sentinel*, 20 May 2001, http://articles.sun-sentinel.com/2001-05-20/news/0105190357_1_miami-circle-civic-activist-space; Gregory Bush, "An Integrated Waterfront?" *The Urban Forum*, October/November 2000, 1–2; Rob Jordan, "Distant Shores," *Biscayne Times*, October 2008, http://rob-jordan.com/articles/waterfront.pdf; Peter Harnik, "Parks under Siege," Trust for Public Land, http://cloud.tpl.org/pubs/ccpe-ParksUnderSiege-Planning2008.pdf, reprinted from *Planning*, October 2008.

2. Harry Boyte and Sara Evans, *Free Spaces: The Sources of Democratic Change in America* (New York: Harper and Row, 1986), 202.

3. Harry C. Boyte, *The Citizen Solution: How You Can Make a Difference* (St. Paul: Minnesota Historical Society, 2008), 89. See the Arts of Citizenship Project at the University of Michigan, http://www.artsofcitizenship.umich.edu/; the Penn Project for Civic Engagement, http://www.gse.upenn.edu/pcel/programs/ppce/; and Augsburg College's Sabo Center for Democracy and Citizenship, http://www.augsburg.edu/sabo/.

4. Lloyd Miller, interview with Gregory Bush, 1999, in author's possession.

5. Richard Sennett, *Flesh and Stone: The Body and the City in Western Civilization* (New York: W. W. Norton, 1994); Richard Sennett, *The Fall of Public Man* (New York:

W. W. Norton, 1976); Peter G. Goheen, "Public Space and the Geography of the Modern City," *Progress in Human Geography* 22, no. 4 (1998): 470–96; Katharyne Mitchell, "The Culture of Urban Space," *Urban Geography* 21 (2000): 443–49.

6. Alexander Garvin and Gayle Berens, *Urban Parks and Open Space* (Washington, D.C.: Urban Land Institute, 1997).

7. Peter Harnik, *Inside City Parks* (Washington, D.C.: Urban Land Institute, 2000), 47–52.

8. Richard Francaviglia, "Selling Heritage Landscapes," in *Preserving Cultural Landscapes in America*, edited by Arnold R. Alamen and Robert Z. Melnick (Baltimore, Md.: Johns Hopkins University Press, 2000), 68; see also David Schuyler and Patricia M. O'Donnell, "The History and Preservation of Urban Parks and Cemeteries," in ibid., 70–93.

9. Sharon Zukin, *The Naked City: The Death and Life of Authentic Urban Places* (New York: Oxford University Press, 2010), 228. Jerry Mitchell, *Business Improvement Districts and the Shape of American Cities* (Albany: State University of New York Press, 2008), 6–7; Alexander Garvin, "Enhancing the Public Realm," in *Urban Parks and Open Space*, edited by Alexander Garvin and Gayle Berens (Washington, D.C.: Urban Land Institute, 1997), 19. On Highline Park, see http://www.thehighline.org/, accessed August 4, 2010. On the Presido, see Peter Holloran, "Seeing the Trees through the Forest: Oaks and History in the Presidio," in *Reclaiming San Francisco: History, Politics, Culture*, edited by James Brook, Chris Carlsson, and Nancy J. Peters (San Francisco: City Lights Books, 1998), 333–51. See also Jerold S. Kayden, *Privately Owned Public Space: The New York City Experience* (New York: John Wiley & Sons, 2000). On New York's waterfront marketplace, see Christine Boyer, "Cities for Sale: Merchandizing History at South Street Seaport," in *Variations on a Theme Park: The New American City and the End of Public Space*, edited by Michael Sorkin (New York: Hill and Wang, 1992), 181–204. See also Setha Low and Neil Smith, eds., *The Politics of Public Space* (New York: Routledge, 2006); and Setha Low, Dana Taplin, and Suzanne Scheld, *Rethinking Urban Parks: Public Space and Cultural Diversity* (Austin: University of Texas Press, 2005). On Skyrise, see Suzy Strutner, "Voters Approve SkyriseMiami, the 'Eiffel Tower' of Thrill Rides," *Huffington Post*, September 4, 2014, http://www.huffingtonpost.com/2014/09/04/skyrise-miami_n_5752244.html; and Douglas Hanks, "Braman, Raquel Regalado Sue to Block Skyrise Miami Subsidy," *Miami Herald*, February 5, 2015.

10. See Miami River Greenway Act Plan, Miami River Commission, 2001, http://www.miamirivercommission.org/PDF/greenway.PDF; and "City Approves Miami River Greenway Plan," The Trust for Public Land, May 21, 2001, http://www.tpl.org/news/press-releases/city-approves-miami-river-greenway.html.

11. Howard Gregg, interview with Gregory Bush, March 8, 2004, Special Collections, Otto G. Richter Library, University of Miami; Paula Park, "Parks and Profits: Believe It or Not, Miami's Planning Czar Jack Luft Says He Can Make Virginia Key Both Lively and Lucrative," *Miami New Times*, October 23, 1997.

12. "A Noisy Fight over Some Quiet Refuges," *Miami Herald*, March 3, 1995, 1A,

12A, quoted in James Paddon and Daniel Suman, "The Virginia Key Campground," in *Urban Growth and Sustainable Habits: Case Studies of Policy Conflicts in South Florida's Coastal Environment*, edited by Daniel Suman, Manoj Shivlani, and Maria Villanueva (Miami: Rosenstiel School of Marine and Atmospheric Science, 1995), 158.

13. Will Anderson, interview with Gregory Bush, n.d., in author's possession; Kitty Cunningham, "Building Bridges in Miami," *Florida Trend*, October 1995, 78–81; Sheila Croucher, *Imagining Miami: Ethnic Politics in a Postmodern World* (Charlottesville: University of Virginia Press, 1997), 53–56; Sheila Croucher, "Miami in the 1990s: 'City of the Future' or 'City on the Edge'?" *Journal of International Migration and Immigration* 3 (June 2002): 223–39.

14. Florida Legislature F.S. 233.061 Sec. (1) (G) (1994) as amended by F.S. 1003.42 (g). Current version online at http://www.leg.state.fl.us/statutes/index.cfm?App_mode=Display_Statute&URL=1000-1099/1003/Sections/1003.42.html, accessed January 2, 2016; Sandhya Somashekhar, "Black History Becoming a Star Tourist Attraction," *Washington Post*, August 15, 2005, A01. See also Melanie Shell-Weiss, *Coming to Miami: A Social History* (Gainesville: University of Florida Press, 2009), chapter 8; Stetson Kennedy, *Southern Exposure* (1946; repr., Boca Raton: Florida Atlantic University Press, 1991); Stetson Kennedy, *Palmetto Country* (New York: Duell, Sloan & Pearce, 1942); Paul George, "Criminal Justice in Miami, 1896–1930" (PhD diss., Florida State University, 1975); Paul George, "Policing Miami's Black Community, 1896–1930," *Florida Historical Quarterly* 57 (April 1979): 434–50; Raymond Mohl, "Black Immigrants: Bahamians in Early Twentieth-Century Miami," *Florida Historical Quarterly* 65 (January 1987): 271–97; Raymond Mohl, "Making a Second Ghetto in Metropolitan Miami, 1940–1960," *Journal of Urban History* 21 (May 1995): 395–427; Raymond Mohl, "'South of the South?' Jews, Blacks, and the Civil Rights Movement in Miami, 1945–1960," *Journal of American Ethnic History* 18 (Winter 1999): 3–36; Raymond Mohl with Matilda "Bobbi" Graff and Shirley M. Zoloth, *South of the South: Jewish Activists and the Civil Rights Movement in Miami, 1945–1960* (Gainesville: University Press of Florida, 2004); and Marvin Dunn, *Black Miami in the Twentieth Century* (Gainesville: University of Florida Press, 1997).

15. "Growing the Middle Class: Connecting All Miami-Dade County Residents to Economic Opportunity; Immigration, Florida, Cities, Jobs and the Economy, Demographics," report, The Brookings Institution, June 2004, http://www.brookings.edu/reports/2004/06cities.aspx.

16. P. Mercer, "Miamians Tangle with Developers Over Curious Tequesta Indian Ruin," *New York Times*, February 15, 1999; Jay Weaver, "Overdevelopment or Opportunity?" *Sun Sentinel*, December 13, 1998, http://articles.sun-sentinel.com/1998-12-13/news/9812120210_1_sierra-club-bayfront-land-attorney, accessed January 3, 2016.

17. Jacob Bernstein, "Who's Afraid of Virginia Key?" *Miami New Times*, March 4, 1999, 9.

18. See also Shaila K. Dewan, "Civil Rights Battlegrounds Enter World of Tourism," *New York Times*, August 10, 2004, 1.

19. Whittington Johnson, interview with Aldo Regalado, 2003, Special Collections, Otto G. Richter Library, University of Miami.

20. Dinizulu Gene Tinnie, "Virginia Key Beach Task Force History and Update," November 1999, in author's possession.

21. Dinizulu Gene Tinnie, interview with Chanelle Rose, October 13, 2000, Special Collections Department, Otto G. Richter Library, University of Miami.

22. Enid Pinkney to Mayor Joe Carollo, February 4, 1999, in author's possession.

23. UEL Virginia Key Resolution, February 19, 2000, in author's possession.

24. Gregory Bush to Dr. Virginia Newell, February 18, 1999, in author's possession.

25. Jay Weaver, "Taking a Stand," *Sun Sentinel*, February 3, 1999, 10A.

26. "Miami: Changing at the Speed of Magic," brochure in author's possession.

27. Dinizulu Gene Tinnie, e-mail to author, August 28, 2009.

28. Jim Mullin, "Saviors of Virginia Key," *Miami New Times*, April 1, 1999.

29. Kirk Nielsen, 'Historic Dip: Witnesses to the Segregated History of Virginia Beach Tell a Sorry but Inspiring Tale," *Miami New Times*, April 8, 1999; Teresa Mears, "Black Pearl," *San Francisco Chronicle*, September 6, 1999, A3; Rick Bragg, "Developers Covet a Florida Island Beach that Was Born of Racism," *New York Times*, March 28, 1999, 19.

30. "Citizens and Waterfront Board Members Hear Virginia Key History," *Miami Times*, April 8, 2000, 2A.

31. M. Athalie Range, interview with Gregory Bush, 1999, Special Collections, Otto G. Richter Library, University of Miami.

32. Amy Chillag, "Preservationist Fights for Public Space," *Sun-Sentinel*, May 20, 2001, http://articles.sun-sentinel.com/2001-05-20/news/0105190357_1_miami-circle-civic-activist-space, accessed January 3, 2016.

33. Teele died on July 27, 2005. See Manuel Roig-Franzia, "Ex-Miami Official Kills Self at Paper's Office," *Washington Post*, July 28, 2005.

34. "Park It on Virginia Key Civil-Rights Memorial," editorial, *Miami Herald*, July 7, 1999, B1. See also Susan Candiotti, "The Racial Legacy of a Miami Beach," CNN.com, May 27, 1999, http://www.cnn.com/SPECIALS/views/y/1999/05/candiotti.beach.may27/.

35. Some examples of charrettes can be found at NCI Charrette System, http://www.charretteinstitute.org/charrette.html; CharretteCenter.net, http://www.charrettecenter.net/charrettecenter.asp?a=spf&pfk=7 Dover, Kohl, & Partners is a local planning firm in South Miami specializing in running charrettes with whom I have worked and for which I have developed much respect. See their website at http://www.doverkohl.com/.

36. Dinizulu Gene Tinnie, interview with Chanelle Rose, October 13, 2000, Special Collections, Otto G. Richter Library, University of Miami.

37. Gregory Bush, "Restore Bicentennial Park," Op ed., *Miami Herald*, October 25, 1999.

38. Jim Mullin, "Just Say No to John Henry," *Miami New Times*, September 20, 1999.

39. Jim Mullin, "Bicentennial Park Rip-Off: Kill This Stupid Idea Now," *Miami New Times*, September 30, 1999, www.miaminewtimes.com/news/mullin-6358170, accessed December 12, 2015.

40. Teresa Mears, "Miami: The No-Park Zone," *Miami Metro Magazine*, January 2000, 45–46.

41. Ibid.

42. Gregory Bush, "Define Public Park," *Miami Herald*, July 19, 2000, 5L.

43. For the enabling legislation for the Historic Virginia Key Beach Park Trust, see "Virginia Key Beach Park, Miami, Florida: Paradise Renewed," http://egov.ci.miami.fl.us/Legistarweb/Attachments/50384.pdf.

44. Joy Ann Reid, "Hundreds Celebrate Virginia Key Beach Re-Dedication," *South Florida Times*, February 2008 [ca. February 23]. See also "Paradise Renewed," special issue of the *Miami Times*, February 20–26, 2008, http://ufdc.ufl.edu/UF00028321/00535/1x, accessed January 2, 2016.

45. "Planning and the Public Voice: Charrettes, Democracy and the Growth Management Process," Democracy in Miami: A Work in Progress, Spring 2004, http://scholar.library.miami.edu/community_forum/growthTranscript.html.

46. For two helpful books along this line, see Bob Graham, *America: The Owner's Manual: Making Government Work for You* (Washington, D.C., CQ Press, 2010); and Harry C. Boyte, *The Citizen Solution* (St. Paul: Minnesota Historical Society, 2008).

47. "Planning and the Public Voice: Charrettes, Democracy and the Growth Management Process." For recent events related to Watson Island, see Eleazar David Melendez, "You Can't Build That! Island Gardens Opponent Claims the Watson Island Project Is Illegal," *Daily Business Review*, March 23, 2015; Erik Bojansky, "Watson Island Forum to Discuss Flagstone Project," *The Real Deal: South Florida Real Estate News*, February 3, 2015, http://therealdeal.com/miami/blog/2015/02/03/watson-island-development-forum-to-discuss-flagstone-project/. See also Fabiola Santago, "Residents Are Fed Up with Runaway Development," *Miami Herald*, April 18, 2015, http://www.causewaychaos.org/media/2015/4/18/fabiola-santiago-residents-are-fed-up-with-runaway-development, accessed December 13, 2015; Andres Viglucci, "13 Years After Agreement for Development, Miami's Watson Island Is Still Barren," *Miami Herald*, June 21, 2014, http://www.miamiherald.com/news/local/community/miami-dade/article1967480.html, accessed December 13, 2015.

48. Gregory Bush, "Bond Issue: 2004: Find Out Who Decides What Gets Funded and Why," *Miami Herald*, May 26, 2004; Kirk Nielsen, "Vote for Culture," *Miami New Times*, November 18, 2004; Gregory Bush, "Become Involved in the Creation, Upkeep of Public Parks, *Miami Herald*, March 3, 2007, 21A.

49. Goody Clancy, *Miami Parks and Public Spaces Master Plan*, May 2007, http://www.miamigov.com/planning/docs/plans/MP/Parks_Master_Plan.pdf.

50. Kelly Josephson, "Plan to Remove Development Restrictions on Miami Marine Stadium Area Deferred," *The Islander News*, 8 August 2004.

51. Oscar Pedro Musibay, "Professor Strives to Preserve History-Rich Virginia Key," *Miami Daily Business Review*, September 29, 2006, A3. See also Gregory Bush, "An Integrated Waterfront?," *The Urban Forum*, October–November 2000, 1–2.

52. "Virginia Key: Process Skipped Resident's Views," *Miami Herald*, March 31, 2007, 22A.

53. Omar Sommereyns, "Key Timing: The Future Remains Uncertain for Long-Neglected Virginia Key. The Time to Save It Is Now, Say Preservationists," *Sun Post* (Miami), March 8, 2007, 18–20.

54. Dinizulu Gene Tinnie, e-mail to author, August 28, 2009.

55. Oscar Pedro Musibay, "Virginia Beach Group Rethinks Museum Plan after Funding Cut," *South Florida Business Journal*, November 6, 2009, http://southflorida.bizjournals.com/southflorida/stories/2009/11/09/story5.html.

56. Gregory Bush to Larry Spring, chief financial officer, city of Miami, August 28, 2009, copy in author's possession.

57. Andres Viglucci, "Miami Could Cut Once-Untouchable Agencies," *Miami Herald*, September 21, 2009.

58. Andres Viglucci, "Virginia Key Revamp on Again," *Miami Herald*, May 20, 2009, D1. See also Andres Viglucci, "Revised City Plan on Table," *Miami Herald*, October 5, 2009, B1.

59. Virginia Key Public Planning Coalition with City of Miami Planning Department, "Virginia Key Master Plan; 2010," May 20, 2009, http://www.miamigov.com/planning/docs/plans/vk/PAB_June2009.pdf.

60. "Virginia Key: A Greener Island. Our Opinion: Revised Virginia Key Blueprint a Win for Public," *Miami Herald*, July 20, 2010.

61. Ibid.; Virginia Key Public Planning Coalition with City of Miami Planning Department, "Virginia Key Master Plan: 2010."

62. Andres Viglucci, "Virginia Key Plan Is Approved," *Miami Herald*, July 23, 2010.

63. David Smiley, "Gloria Estefan Hammers Marine Stadium Group after Failed Redevelopment Bid," *Miami Herald*, December 3, 2014.

64. David Smiley, "City Floats Plan for Stadium" *Miami Herald*, May 2, 2015, B1; David Smiley, "Boat Show Sails Ahead as City Rejects Appeal," *Miami Herald*, May 15, 2015, B1; John Charles Robins, "City Facing List of Choices Swimming around Marine Stadium," *Miami Today*, May 14, 2015, 8; David Smiley, "10 Year Tent Deal Draws Critics," *Miami Herald*, May 28, 2015; David Smiley, "Miami Commission Approves Key Boat Show Agreements," *Miami Herald*, May 28, 2015; David Smiley, "Commission OKs Key Boat Show Agreements," *Miami Herald*, May 29, 2015. One conspicuously bright note was published in the *Miami Herald* the next day by noted lawyer Richard Pettigrew, who castigated the city for all its secret deals and for violating public records laws in making it almost impossible for citizens to sue the city; Richard Pettigrew, "City Keeps Development Deals a Secret," *Miami Herald*, May 29, 2015.

65. Douglas Hanks, "Miami-Dade Commissioners Back Plan for Cuban Exile Museum behind American Airlines Arena," *Miami Herald*, July 17, 2014; Douglas Hanks, "After Backing a Cuban Museum, Miami Dade Commissioner Says It's Time for a Black Museum Too," *Miami Herald*, September 1, 2014; Douglas Hanks, "Black History Museum Endorsed in Miami-Dade," *Miami Herald*, October 7, 2014; Douglas Hanks, "Cuban-Exile Museum May Get Company on Miami Waterfront," *Miami*

Herald, March 16, 2015. See also Michael Murphy, "Successful Strategies for Pitching an Arena Project to Voters," *Sports Business Journal*, January 12–18, 2004, http://www.sportsbusinessdaily.com/Journal/Issues/2004/01/20040112/SBJ-In-Depth/Successful-Strategies-For-Pitching-An-Arena-Project-To-Voters.aspx, accessed December 13, 2015. Murphy wrote that "white voters were most excited about a new family-friendly park on Miami's waterfront, including soccer fields and a new arena, which would bring in concerts and other entertainment events. Recasting the arena as a waterfront park and arena was to be key to our campaign."

66. See "David Beckham Unveils Proposal for Waterfront Miami Soccer Stadium," YouTube video, https://www.youtube.com/watch?v=KR1gx-i8sk8, accessed December 13, 2015. See also Andres Viglucci, "Debate over Soccer Stadium Centers on Park Use," *Miami Herald*, June 1, 2014, http://www.miamiherald.com/news/local/community/miami-dade/article1965326.html, accessed December 13, 2015; and Patricia Mazzei, "Updated: Group of Prominent Architects, Urban Planners Oppose David Beckham's Miami MLS Stadium Plan," *Miami Herald*, May 28, 2014, http://miamiherald.typepad.com/nakedpolitics/2014/05/group-of-prominent-architects-urban-planners-opposes-david-beckhams-miami-mls-stadium-plan.html, accessed December 13, 2015.

67. "City Failed Boat Show, Virginia Key," *Miami Herald*, December 9, 2015, http://www.miamiherald.com/opinion/editorials/article48931415.html; David Smiley, "County Approves Miami International Boat Show Permit on Virginia Key," *Miami Herald*, December 16, 2015, http://www.miamiherald.com/news/local/community/miami-dade/article49962845.html, accessed December 27, 2015.

Afterword: The Real Miami; Better than a Theme Park

1. Setha Low and Neil Smith, eds., *The Politics of Public Space* (New York: Routledge, 2006).

2. David Potter, *People of Plenty* (Chicago: University of Chicago Press, 1954).

3. Jackson Lears, "Reconsidering Abundance: A Plea for Ambiguity," in *Getting and Spending: European and American Consumer Societies in the Twentieth Century*, edited by Susan Strasser, Charles McGovern, and Matthias Judt (Washington, D.C.: Smithsonian Institution and Cambridge University Press, 1998), 449.

4. Will Allen, *The Good Food Revolution* (New York: Gotham, 2012); Barbara Miner, "An Urban Farmer Is Rewarded for His Dream," *New York Times*, September 25, 2008.

5. On the low level of civic participation, see National Conference on Citizenship, "A Tale of Two Cities: Civic Health in Miami and Minneapolis-St. Paul," January 24, 2011, http://ncoc.net/Civic_Engagement_in_Miami_and_MinneapolisSt_Paul.

6. Susan S. Fainstein and Dennis R. Judd, "Cities as Places to Play," in *The Tourist City*, edited by Dennis R. Judd and Susan S. Fainstein (New Haven, Conn.: Yale University Press, 1999), 268–69.

7. Michael Lewis, "Organized Gambling Thrives on Silence of Unorganized Foes," *Miami Today*, 13 October 2011.

8. Bruce Babbitt, *Cities in the Wilderness* (Washington, D.C.: Island Press, 2005);

Yi-Fu Tuan, *Topophilia: A Study of Environmental Attitudes and Values* (New York: Columbia University Press, 1974), 125.

9. Terry Tempest Williams, *The Open Space of Democracy* (Great Barrington, Mass.: Orion Society, 2004), 83; Benjamin R. Barber, *Consumed: How Markets Corrupt Children, Infantilize Adults, and Swallow Citizens Whole* (New York: W. W. Norton, 2007), 51.

10. Andrew E. G. Jonas and David Wilson, eds., *The Urban Growth Machine: Critical Perspectives Two Decades Later* (Albany: State University of New York Press, 1999), 7; David Harvey, *A Brief History of Neoliberalism* (New York: Oxford University Press, 2005), 77–81.

11. John Kunkle Small, *From Eden to the Sahara: Florida's Tragedy* (1929; repr., Sanford, Fla.: Seminole Soil and Water Conservation District, 2004).

12. Hal Rothman, *Neon Metropolis: How Las Vegas Started the Twenty-First Century* (New York: Routledge, 2003), viii; Jackson Lears, *Something for Nothing: Luck in America* (New York: Viking, 2003).

13. Wendell Berry, *What Are People For? Essays* (San Francisco: North Point Press, 1990), 131, 139.

14. Wallace Stegner, *Where the Bluebird Sings to the Lemonade Springs* (New York: Penguin, 2002), 200.

15. Patrick Hurley, *Beyond Preservation: Using Public History to Revitalize Inner Cities* (Philadelphia: Temple University Press, 2010), 144.

16. Jenifer Lee, "A Call for Softer, Greener Language," *New York Times*, March 2, 2003: http://www.nytimes.com/2003/03/02/us/a-call-for-softer-greener-language.html?pagewanted=all, accessed January 2, 2016.

17. Xavier Suarez, "Not a Solution for All of Our Public Problems," *Miami Herald*, March 8, 2015.

18. Aldo Leopold, *A Sand County Almanac with Essays on Conservation from Round River* (New York: Ballantine Books, 1966), 190.

19. Howard Frumkin and Richard Louv, "The Powerful Link between Conserving Land and Conserving Health," Children & Nature Network, http://www.childrenandnature.org/news/detail/the_powerful_link_between_conserving_land_and_preserving_health. See also Roderick Frazier Nash, *The Rights of Nature* (Madison: University of Wisconsin Press, 1989); Richard Louv, *The Nature Principle* (Chapel Hill, N.C.: Algonquin Books, 2011); David Orr, *Earth in Mind: On Education, Environment, and the Human Prospect* (Washington, D.C.: Island Press, 2004).

20. Gene Tinnie, e-mail message to Gregory Bush, August 28, 2009.

21. Carl Anthony, "Reflections on the Purposes and Meanings of African American Environmental History," in *"To Love the Wind and the Rain": African Americans and Environmental History*, edited by Dianne D. Glave and Mark Stoll (Pittsburgh: University of Pittsburgh Press, 2006), 206.

22. Max Rameau, *Take Back the Land* (Miami: Nia Press, 2008)

23. See the Nature Links website: www.naturelinks.net.

24. Gene Tinnie, e-mail message to Gregory Bush, October 6, 2011.

25. Ibid., Although many people claim to have originated this famous phrase, it originated in a 1915 book *Cities in Evolution: An Introduction to the Town Planning Movement and to the Study of Civics* (London: Williams) by Patrick Geddes, a Scottish town planner, and was revived and applied to environmental concerns by an array of activists in the late 1960s and 1970s.

Bibliography

Archives

Arva Moore Parks, Miami
    Private collection
Black Archives Historic Lyric Theater Cultural Arts Complex, Miami, Florida
    Oral history interview transcripts
Eugenia Thomas, Miami
    Private collection of the speeches of Lawson E. Thomas (now in author's posses-
    sion)
HistoryMiami Archives & Research Center
    Carl Fisher Papers
Louis Round Wilson Library, Chapel Hill, North Carolina
    Southern Oral History Program, Southern Historical Collection
Miami Dade College
    Lynn and Louis Wolfson II Florida Moving Image Archives
Miami-Dade County Archives
    Minutes of Dade County Commission
Miami-Dade County Clerk's Office
    County Commission Meeting Archives Microfilm
National Archives and Records Administration, Washington, D.C.
    RG69, Records of the Works Projects Administration
    RG69.3, Records of the Federal Emergency Relief Administration
Miami-Dade County Clerk's Office
    Board of County Commissioners Minutes
    Book of Resolutions
Miami-Dade Public Library System
    Agnew Welsh Scrapbooks

Helen Muir Florida Collection
Otto G. Richter Library, University of Miami
    Special Collections
Special Collections Department, University of Miami Libraries
    Arva Moore Parks Collection, 1896–2005
Historic Virginia Key Park Trust
    Oral history interview transcripts

Newspapers

Biscayne Times
Daytona Beach Evening News
Evening Standard (St. Petersburg)
The Islander News
Miami Daily Business Review
Miami Daily News
Miami Daily Metropolis
Miami Herald
Miami Metropolis
Miami New Times
Miami News
Miami Times
Miami Today
The Miamian
Palm Beach Post
St. Petersburg Times
South Florida Times
Sun Post (Miami Beach, Fla.)
Sun-Sentinel (Fort Lauderdale, Fla.)
Washington Post

Interviews

Anderson, Will. Interview with the author, n.d., in author's possession
Baker, Yolanda Cooper. Interview with the author, 2000, in author's possession.
Braynon, Edward. Interview with Chanelle Rose, 2005, Historic Virginia Key Beach
    Park Trust, Miami.
Braynon, Oscar. Interview with Chanelle Rose, 2005, Historic Virginia Key Beach
    Park Trust, Miami.
Brown, Fred. Interview with Chanelle Rose, 2005, Historic Virginia Key Beach Park
    Trust, Miami.
Brown, Dr. John O. Interview with Madison Davis Lacy Jr., June 21, 1989, Eyes
    on the Prize II Interviews. Transcript at http://digital.wustl.edu/e/eii/eiiweb/
    bro5427.0540.023drjohnobrown.html.
Chiles, Lawton. Interview with Jack Bass and Walter De Vries, January 30, 1974,

Southern Oral History Program, Southern Historical Collection, Special Collections, Louis Round Wilson Library, Chapel Hill, North Carolina.

Collins, LeRoy. Interview with Jack Bass and Walter De Vries, May 19, 1974, Southern Oral History Program, Southern Historical Collection, Special Collections, Louis Round Wilson Library, Chapel Hill, North Carolina. Transcript at http://ufdc.ufl.edu/UF00005580/00001/1j.

Crandon, Charles. Interview with Harvey and Mary Napier, May 11, 1976, Archives & Research Center, HistoryMiami, Miami.

Farmer, James. Interview with Harri Baker, October 1969, Lyndon Baines Johnson Library Oral History Collection, University of Texas, Austin, Texas. Transcript at http://www.lbjlib.utexas.edu/johnson/archives.hom/oralhistory.hom/Farmer/farmer1.pdf.

Fascell, Dante. Interview with Gregory Bush and Michael Krenn, June 1993, Special Collections, Otto G. Richter Library, University of Miami.

Fields, Dorothy. Interview with Chanelle Rose, 2005, Historic Virginia Key Beach Park Trust, Miami.

Gibson, Thelma. Interview with Gregory Bush, October 26, 1999, in author's possession.

Graff, Matilda "Bobbi." Interview with Gregory Bush, 1992, in author's possession.

Graham, Bob. America: The Owner's Manual: Making Government Work for You. Washington, D.C., CQ Press, 2010.

Gregg, Howard. Interview with Gregory Bush, 2004, Special Collections, Otto G. Richter Library, University of Miami.

Jennings, Wilhemina. Interview with Chanelle Rose, 2005, Historic Virginia Key Beach Park Trust, Miami.

Johnson, Whittington. Interview with Aldo Regalado, March 2000, Special Collections, Otto G. Richter Library, University of Miami.

Kennedy, Stetson. Interview with Gregory Bush, May 19, 1997, in author's possession.

Miller, Lloyd. Interview with Gregory Bush, September 11, 2000, Special Collections, Otto G. Richter Library, Miami University.

Moore, A. D. Interview with Kathy Hersh, May 11, 2001, Media Center, Turner Tech High School, Miami, Community Studies Project, Dade County Public Schools.

Nimmo, James. Interview with Gregory Bush and students, 1984, in author's possession.

———. Interview with Kip Vought, November 8, 1990, Special Collections, Otto G. Richter Library, University of Miami.

Pharr, Kelsey L. Interview with Bertha Comstock, January 11, 1939, Federal Writers' Project, http://lcweb2.loc.gov/mss/wpalh1/10/1012/10120109/10120109.pdf.

Pinkney, Enid. Interview with Gregory Bush, 1999, Special Collections, Otto G. Richter Library, University of Miami.

———. Interview with Chanelle Rose, 2005, Historic Virginia Key Beach Park Trust, Miami.

Pompey, Spencer. Interview with Gregory Bush, July 9, 1999, in author's possession.

Range, Athalie. Interview with Gregory Bush, 1999, Special Collections, Otto G. Richter Library, University of Miami.

———. Interview with Chanelle Rose, 2005, Historic Virginia Key Beach Park Trust, Miami.

Reeves, Garth, Sr. Interview with Chanelle Rose, 2005, Historic Virginia Key Beach Park Trust, Miami.

———. Interview with Andrea Benitez, March 2, 2006. Transcript at Miami Oral Histories, http://miami.fiu.edu/moh/interviews/reeves/reeves.htm.

———. Interview with Dorothy Fields, October 14, 1977, Black Archives Historic Lyric Theater Cultural Arts Complex, Miami, Florida.

———. Interview with Julian Pleasants, August 19, 1999. Transcript at http://ufdcimages.uflib.ufl.edu/UF/00/00/55/26/00001/FNP40.pdf.

Ruder, Alberto. Interview with Gregory Bush, 2000, Special Collections, Otto G. Richter Library, University of Miami.

Ruvin, Harvey. Interview with Gregory Bush, July 22, 2004, in author's possession.

Sands, Leah. Interview with Chanelle Rose, 2005, Historic Virginia Key Beach Park Trust, Miami.

Sawyer, Bernice. Interview with Chanelle Rose, 2005, Historic Virginia Key Beach Park Trust, Miami.

Schlafrock, Max. Interview with Gregory Bush, December 5, 1992, in author's possession.

Shorter, David. Interview with Chanelle Rose, 2005, Historic Virginia Key Beach Park Trust, Miami.

Stierheim, Merrett. Interview with Gregory Bush, 2004, Special Collections, Otto G. Richter Library, University of Miami.

Tinnie, Dinizulu Gene. Interview with Chanelle Rose, October 13, 2000, Special Collections, Otto G. Richter Library, University of Miami.

Williams, Kenneth T., interview with Chanelle Rose, 2005, Historic Virginia Key Beach Park Trust.

Winn, Sydney. Interview with Chanelle Rose, 2005, Historic Virginia Key Beach Park Trust, Miami.

Winton, Johnny. Interview with Gregory Bush, 2000, in author's possession.

Published Sources

Abrams, Lynn. *Oral History Theory*. New York: Routledge, 2010.

"Albert Pick, Jr." Accuracy Project, http://www.accuracyproject.org/cbe-Pick,Albert.html.

Allen, Will. *The Good Food Revolution*. New York: Gotham, 2012.

Allman, T. D. *Miami: City of the Future*. New York: Atlantic Monthly Press, 1987.

Amlong, William. "Bebe and Cik on a Houseboat." *The Nation*, November 12, 1973, 489–93.

Ammidon, Margot. "Edens, Underworlds, and Shrines: Florida's Small Tourist Attractions." *Journal of Decorative and Propaganda Arts* 23 (1998): 239–59.

Andrews, Doug. "Black Education in Miami, 1921–1941." *Tequesta* 59 (1999): 31–51.

Anthony, Carl. "Reflections on the Purposes and Meanings of African American Environmental History." In *To Love the Wind and the Rain: African Americans and Environmental History*, edited by Dianne D. Glave and Mark Stoll, 200–210. Pittsburgh: University of Pittsburgh Press, 2006.

Ardalan, Christine. *Warm Hearts and Caring Hands: South Florida Nursing from Frontier to Metropolis, 1880–2000*. Miami: Centennial Press, 2005.

Arnesen, Eric. "Reconsidering the 'Long Civil Rights Movement.'" *Historically Speaking* 10 (April 2009): 31–34.

Arsenault, Raymond. "The Cooling of the South." *Wilson Quarterly* 8 (Summer 1984): 150–59.

———. *The Sound of Freedom: Marian Anderson, the Lincoln Memorial, and the Concert that Awakened America*. New York: Bloomsbury Press, 2009.

Babbitt, Bruce. *Cities in the Wilderness*. Washington, D.C.: Island Press, 2005.

"Babylon, U.S.A. Gets Set for Its Hundred Days." *Life*, December 29, 1957, 31–42.

Bain, Leslie B. "Red Hunt in Miami: Who Formed the Posse?" *The Nation*, August 7, 1954, 110–12.

Ballard, Robert. *Dumping in Dixie: Race, Class, and Environmental Quality*. 3rd ed. Boulder, Colo.: Westview Press, 2000.

Banner, Warren M. *An Appraisal of Progress, 1943–1953*. Department of Research and Community Projects, National Urban League, 1953.

Barber, Benjamin R. *Consumed: How Markets Corrupt Children, Infantilize Adults, and Swallow Citizens Whole*. New York: W. W. Norton, 2007.

Barnes, A. D. *History of Dade County Park System, 1929–1969: The First Forty Years*. Miami: Metro-Dade County Parks and Recreation Department, 1986.

Barnett, Cynthia *Mirage: Florida and the Vanishing Water of the Eastern U.S.* Ann Arbor: University of Michigan Press, 2007.

Bartlett, Peggy, ed. *Urban Place: Reconnecting with the Natural World*. Cambridge: MIT Press, 2005.

Baum, David. "Virginia Key: Paradise Found." *The Sun Dial* 6 (Spring 2006): 1, 4–5. http://sffb.com/pdfs/sundial/sd_sp06med.pdf.

Beard, Katharine. "Bahamian Immigrants." In *Multicultural America: An Encyclopedia of the Newest Americans*, edited by Ronald H. Baylor, vol. 4. Santa Barbara: ABC-CLIO, 2011.

Bender, Thomas. *The Unfinished City*. New York: New Press, 2002.

Berry, Wendell. *What Are People For?* San Francisco: North Point Press, 1990.

Birnbaum, Charles. "In Defense of Open Space." *Preservation* 57 (September–October 2005): 38–39.Reprinted at City Park NOLA, http://www.cityparknola.org/web/index.asp?mode=full&id=34.

Biscayne Bay: Environmental History and Annotated Bibliography. NOAA Technical Memorandum NOS NCCOS CCMA 145. Accessed March 6, 2007, http://www.aoml.noaa.gov/general/lib/bbehdoc.pdf.

Black, Hugo L., III. "Richard Fitzpatrick's South Florida, 1822–1840." Part 2, "Fitzpatrick's Miami River Plantation." *Tequesta* 41 (1981): 33–68.

Blackman, E. V. *Miami and Dade County, Florida: Its Settlement, Progress, and Achievement*. Chuluota, Fla.: Mickler House, 1921.

Blake, Nelson. *Land into Water, Water into Land: A History of Water Management in Florida*. Gainesville: University Press of Florida, 1989.

Blank, Joan Gill. *Key Biscayne: A History of Miami's Tropical Island and the Cape Florida Lighthouse* (Sarasota, Fla.: Pineapple Press, 1996.

Bowe, Ruth M. L., assisted by Patrice Williams. "Grants Town and the Historical Development of Over-the-Hill." Typescript, journals.sfu.ca/cob/index.php/files/article/download/73/42.

Boyer, Christine. "Cities for Sale: Merchandizing History at South Street Seaport." In *Variations on a Theme Park: The New American City and the End of Public Space*, edited by Michael Sorkin, 181–204. New York: Hill and Wang, 1992.

Boyte, Harry C. *The Citizen Solution: How You Can Make a Difference*. St Paul: Minnesota Historical Society, 2008.

Boyte, Harry, and Sara Evans. *Free Spaces: The Sources of Democratic Change in America*. New York: Harper and Row, 1986.

Brown, Peter Hendee. *America's Waterfront Revival: Port Authorities and Urban Redevelopment*. Philadelphia: University of Pennsylvania Press, 2009.

Brundage, W. Fitzhugh. *The Southern Past: A Clash of Race and Memory*. Cambridge, Mass.: Harvard University Press, 2005.

Bullard, Robert. *Dumping in Dixie: Race, Class, and Environmental Quality*. Boulder, Colo.: Westview Press, 1990.

Bullard, Robert, ed. *Unequal Protection: Environmental Justice and Communities of Color*. San Francisco: Sierra Club Books, 1994.

Burnham, Kenneth E. *God Comes to America: Father Divine and the Peace Mission Movement*. Boston: Lambeth Press, 1979.

Bush, Gregory. "From Stateroom to Skybox: The Miami Arena Controversy and the Promotion of Spectacle." Paper presented at the annual meeting of the American Studies Association, October 1997.

———. "An Integrated Waterfront?" *The Urban Forum*, October–November 2000, 1–2.

———. "'Playground of the USA': Miami and the Promotion of Spectacle." *Pacific Historical Review* 68 (May 1999): 153–72.

———. "Special Resource Study: Report to Congress." National Park Service, 2008, http://parkplanning.nps.gov/document.cfm?parkID=423&projectID=12493&documentID=39793.

———. "Virginia Key Beach Park Natural Resource Study: Historic Context & Significance Research & National Significance: Public Recreation as a Civil Right." Unpublished study, University of Miami.

Byron, Mercedes H. "A Negro Looks at Miami." *The Crisis*, March 1942, 84.

Carson, Rachel. *The Sea around Us*. New York: Oxford University Press, 1991.

Carter, Luther. *The Florida Experience: Land and Water Policy in a Growth State*. Baltimore, Md.: Johns Hopkins University Press, 1974.

Castillo, Thomas. "Big City Days: Race and Labor in Early Miami 1914–1935." PhD diss., Florida International University, 2000.

———. "Chauffeuring in a White Man's Town: Black Service Work, Movement, and Segregation in Early Miami." In *Florida's Labor and Working-Class Past: Three Centuries of Work in the Sunshine State*, edited by Robert Cassanello and Melanie Shell-Weiss, 143–67. Gainesville: University Press of Florida, 2009.

———. "Miami's Hidden Labor History." *Florida Historical Quarterly* 82, no. 4 (2004): 438–67.

Chappell, David. "The Lost Decade of Civil Rights." *Historically Speaking* 10 (April 2009): 37–41.

Clancy, Goody. "Parks and Public Spaces Master Plan, 2006." City of Miami, May 2007. http://www.miamigov.com/planning/docs/plans/MP/Parks_Master_Plan.pdf.

Cohen, Isador. *Historical Sketches and Sidelights of Miami*. Miami: Privately printed, 1925.

Cohen, Lizabeth. *A Consumers' Republic: The Politics of Mass Consumption in Postwar America*. New York: Alfred Knopf, 2003.

Colburn, David. *Racial Change and Community Crisis: St. Augustine, 1877–1980*. Gainesville: University Press of Florida, 1991.

———. "Rosewood and America in the Early Twentieth Century." *Florida Historical Quarterly* 76, no. 2 (1997): 175–192.

———. *Yellow Dog Democrat to Red State Republican: Florida and Its Politics since 1940*. Gainesville: University Press of Florida, 2007.

Colburn, David, and Jane Landers, eds. *The African American Heritage of Florida*. Gainesville: University Press of Florida, 1995.

Connolly, Nathan. "By Eminent Domain: Race and Capital in the Building of an American South Florida." PhD diss., University of Michigan, 2008.

———. *A World More Concrete: Real Estate and the Remaking of Jim Crow South Florida*. Chicago: University of Chicago Press, 2014.

Crandon, Charles. *Country Bumpkin*. Miami: Johnson Press, 1975.

Craton, Michael, and Gail Saunders, *Islanders in the Stream: A History of the Bahamian People*. Vol. 2. Athens: University of Georgia Press, 1998.

Crawford, Vicki, Jacqueline Anne Rouse, and Barbara Woods, eds. *Women in the Civil Rights Movement: Trailblazers & Torchbearers, 1941–1965*. Bloomington: Indiana University Press, 1990.

Crawford, William G., Jr. "Judge Vincent Giblin: The Life and Times of a South Florida Attorney and Judge." *Tequesta* 70 (2010): 96–99.

———. "The Long Hard Fight for Equal Rights: The History of Broward County's Colored Beach and the Fort Lauderdale Beach 'Wade-Ins' of the Summer of 1961." *Tequesta* 67 (2007).

Cresswell, Tim. *In Place/Out of Place: Geography, Ideology, and Transgression*. Minneapolis: University of Minnesota Press, 1996.

———. *Place: An Introduction*. 2nd ed. Wiley Blackwell, 2015.

Cronon, William. "A Place for Stories: Nature, History, and Narrative." *Journal of American History* 78 (March 1992): 1347–76.

———. "Kennecott Journey: The Paths out of Town." In *Under an Open Sky*, edited by W. Cronon, G. Miles, and J. Gitlin, 28–51. New York: Norton, 1992.

———. "The Trouble with Wilderness, or, Getting Back to the Wrong Nature." *Environmental History* 1 (January 1996): 7–55.

Croucher, Sheila. *Imagining Miami: Ethnic Politics in a Postmodern World*. Charlottesville: University Press of Virginia, 1997.

———. "Miami in the 1990s: 'City of the Future' or 'City on the Edge'?" *Journal of International Migration and Immigration* 3 (June 2002): 223–39.

Cunningham, Kitty. "Building Bridges in Miami." *Florida Trend*, October 1995, 78–81.

Dade County's Recreation Parks: A Report to the People of Dade County Florida on the Present Extent and State of Development of the Several County Recreational Park Units Together with Recommendations for Future Development of the Park System. Miami: Dade County Park Department, 1941.

Davis, Jack E. *An Everglades Providence: Marjory Stoneman Douglas and the American Environmental Century*. Athens: University of Georgia Press, 2009.

———. "'Conservation Is Now a Dead Word': Marjory Stoneman Douglas and the Transformation of American Environmentalism." In *Paradise Lost? The Environmental History of Florida*, edited by Jack Emerson Davis and Raymond Arsenault, 297–325. Gainesville: University Press of Florida, 1998.

Davis, Mike. *Ecology of Fear: Los Angeles and the Imagination of Disaster*. New York: Random House, 1998.

———. "Fortress Los Angeles: The Militarization of Urban Space." In *Variations on a Theme Park: The New American City and the End of Public Space*, edited by Michael Sorkin, 154–80. New York: Hill & Wang, 1992.

Davis, Susan G. *Spectacular Nature: Corporate Culture and the Sea World Experience*. Berkeley: University of California Press, 1997.

Dittmer, John. *Local People: The Struggle for Civil Rights in Mississippi*. Urbana: University of Illinois Press, 1994.

Douglas, Marjory Stoneman. "Frank Bryant Stoneman." *Tequesta* 2 (November 1944): 3–12.

Dovey, Kim. "On Politics and Urban Space." In *Debating the City: An Anthology*, edited by Jennifer Barrett and Caroline Butler-Bowdon, 53–67. Sydney: Historic Houses Trust, 2001.

Doyle, Don. *New Men, New Cities, New South: Atlanta, Nashville, Charleston, Mobile, 1860–1910*. Chapel Hill: University of North Carolina Press, 1990.

Dudziak, Mary Z. *Cold War Civil Rights: Race and the Image of American Democracy*. Princeton, N.J.: Princeton University Press, 2000.

Dumanoski, Dianne. "Rethinking Environmentalism." *Conservation Matters*, Fall 1998, 4–9.

Dunn, Marvin. *Black Miami in the Twentieth Century*. Gainesville: University Press of Florida, 1997.

Fainstein, Susan S., and Dennis R. Judd. "Cities as Places to Play." In *The Tourist City*, edited by Dennis R. Judd and Susan S. Fainstein, 262–72. New Haven, Conn.: Yale University Press, 1999.

Fields, Dorothy. "Tracing Overtown's Vernacular Architecture." *Journal of Decorative and Propaganda Arts* 23 (1998):322–33.

Findlay, James A., and Margaret Bing. "Touring Florida through the Federal Writers' Project." *Journal of Decorative and Propaganda Arts* (1998), https://www.broward.org/library/bienes/lii10213.htm.

Fleischman, Thomas. "Black Miamians in *The Miami Metropolis,* 1896–1900." *Tequesta* 52 (1992): 21–38.

———. "Image and Reality: Perceptions of Early Black Miami by the Miami Metropolis, 1896–1900." MA thesis, University of Miami, 1987.

"Florida: Black Ballots." *Time*, May 15, 1939, 19.

"Florida Ho!" *Newsweek*, July 4, 1949, 36.

"Florida Writings from the Federal Writers' Project." American Memory, The Library of Congress, http://memory.loc.gov/ammem/collections/florida/ffbib.html.

Florida, Richard. "The Rise of the Creative Class." *Washington Monthly*, May 2002, http://www.washingtonmonthly.com/features/2001/0205.florida.html.

Foster, Mark. *Castles in the Sand: The Life and Times of Carl Fisher*. Gainesville: University Press of Florida, 2000.

Francaviglia, Richard. "Selling Heritage Landscapes." In *Preserving Cultural Landscapes in America*, edited by Arnold R. Alamen and Robert Z. Melnick, 44–69. Baltimore, Md.: Johns Hopkins University Press, 2000.

Frazier, Thomas R., ed. *Afro-American History: Primary Sources*. Chicago: Dorsey Press, 1988.

Frisch, Michael. *A Shared Authority: Essays on the Craft and Meaning of Oral and Public History*. Albany: State University of New York Press, 1990.

Frumkin, Howard, and Richard Louv. "The Powerful Link between Conserving Land and Conserving Health." Children & Nature Network, http://www.childrenand-nature.org/news/detail/the_powerful_link_between_conserving_land_and_preserving_health.

Gaby, Donald C. *The Miami River and Its Tributaries*. Miami: Historical Association of South Florida, 1993.

Garcia, Maria Cristina. *Havana USA: Cuban Exiles and Cuban Americans in South Florida, 1959–1994*. Berkeley: University of California Press, 1996.

Garcia, Robert, and Erica Flores Baltodano. *Free the Beach! Public Access, Equal Justice, and the California Coast*. Los Angeles: Center for Law in the Public Interest, 2005.

Garvin, Alexander. "Enhancing the Public Realm." In *Urban Parks and Open Space*, edited by Alexander Garvin and Gayle Berens, 1–24. Washington, D.C.: Urban Land Institute, 1997.

Garvin, Alexander, and Gayle Berens, eds. *Urban Parks and Open Space*. Washington, D.C.: Urban Land Institute, 1997.

George, Paul. "Brokers, Binders, and Builders: Greater Miami's Boom of the Mid-1920s." *Florida Historical Quarterly* 65 (July 1986): 27–51.

———. "Colored Town: Miami's Black Community, 1896–1930." *Florida Historical Quarterly* 46 (April 1978): 432–47.

———. "Criminal Justice in Miami, 1896–1930." PhD diss., Florida State University, 1975.

———. "Miami's Bayfront Park: A History." http://www.bayfrontparkmiami.com/pages/history/historyessay.html.

———. "Miami's City Marshall and Law Enforcement in a New Community, 1896–1907." *Tequesta* 44 (1984): 32–43.

———. "Policing Miami's Black Community, 1896–1930." *Florida Historical Quarterly* 57 (April 1979): 434–50.

George, Paul, and Thomas Peterson. "Liberty Square: 1933–1987, The Origins and Evolution of a Public Housing Project." *Tequesta* 48 (1988): 53–68.

Gilmore, Glenda. *Defying Dixie: The Radical Roots of Civil Rights, 1919–1950*. New York: W. W. Norton, 2008.

Gitlin, Todd. "Domesticating Nature." *Theory and Society* 8 (September 1979): 291–97.

Goheen, Peter G. "Public Space and the Geography of the Modern City." *Progress in Human Geography* 22, no. 4 (1998): 470–96.

Goings, Kenneth, and Raymond Mohl. "Toward a New African American Urban History." *Journal of Urban History* 21, no. 3 (1995): 283–95.

Gonzalez, Robert. "Interama: Visions of a Pan-American City." In *Miami Modern Metropolis: Paradise and Paradox in Midcentury Architecture and Planning*, edited by Allan T. Shulman, 146–51. Miami Beach: Bass Museum of Art, 2009.

Graff, Harvey J. *The Dallas Myth: The Making and Unmaking of an American City*. Minneapolis: University of Minnesota Press, 2008.

Graff, Matilda. "The Historic Continuity of the Civil Rights Movement." In Raymond Mohl with Matilda "Bobbi" Graff and Shirley M. Zoloth, *South of the South: Jewish Activists and the Civil Rights Movement in Miami, 1945–1960*, 11–62. Gainesville: University Press of Florida, 2004.

Gratz, Roberta Brandes. "Doing It Wrong to Get It Right," Project for Public Spaces, 2009, http://www.pps.org/reference/roberta/.

Green, Ben. *Before His Time: The Untold Story of Harry T. Moore, America's First Civil Rights Martyr*. New York: Free Press, 1999.

Grenier, Guillermo, and Alex Steppick III, eds. *Miami Now! Immigration, Ethnicity, and Social Change*. Gainesville: University Press of Florida, 1992.

Grunwald, Michael. *The Swamp: The Everglades, Florida, and the Politics of Paradise*. New York: Simon and Schuster, 2006.

Hall, Jacqueline Dowd. "The Long Civil Rights Movement and the Political Uses of the Past." *Journal of American History* 91 (March 2005): 1233–63.

Harap, Louis. "Nightmare in Miami." *Jewish Life* 9 (December 1943): 4–9.

Hardin, Garret. "The Tragedy of the Commons." *Science* 162, no. 3859 (1968): 1243–1248. http://www.sciencemag.org/content/162/3859/1243.full.

Harnik, Peter. *Inside City Parks*. Washington, D.C.: Urban Land Institute, 2000.

———. "Parks under Siege." http://cloud.tpl.org/pubs/ccpe-ParksUnderSiege-Planning2008.pdf, reprinted from *Planning*, October 2008.

Harvey, David. *A Brief History of Neoliberalism*. New York: Oxford University Press, 2005.

———. *Spaces of Hope*. Berkeley: University of California Press, 2000.

———. "The Political Economy of Public Space." http://davidharvey.org/media/public.pdf.

Harvey, Gordon. "'We Must Free Ourselves . . . from the Tattered Fetters of the Booster Mentality': Big Cypress Swamp and the Politics of Environmental Protection in 1970s Florida." In *Paradise Lost? The Environmental History of Florida*, edited by Jack Emerson Davis and Raymond Arsenault, 350–74. Gainesville: University Press of Florida, 1998.

Hayden, Dolores. "Urban Landscape History: The Sense of Place and the Politics of Space." In *Understanding Ordinary Landscapes*, edited by Paul Groth and Todd Bressi, 111–33. New Haven, Conn.: Yale University Press, 1997.

Hewitt, Nancy. *Southern Discomfort: Women's Activism in Tampa, Florida 1880s–1920s*. Urbana: University of Illinois Press, 2001.

Hiaasen, Carl. *Kick Ass: Selected Columns of Carl Hiaasen*. Gainesville: University Press of Florida, 1999.

Hill, Robert. *The Marcus Garvey and United Negro Improvement Association Papers, September 1920–August 1921*. Berkeley: University of California Press, 1984.

Hurley, Andrew. *Beyond Preservation: Using Public History to Revitalize Inner Cities*. Philadelphia: Temple University Press, 2010.

"Growing the Middle Class: Connecting All Miami-Dade County Residents to Economic Opportunity; Immigration, Florida, Cities, Jobs and the Economy, Demographics." Report, The Brookings Institution, June 2004, http://www.brookings.edu/reports/2004/06cities.aspx.

Investigation of Communist Activities in the State of Florida: Hearings Before the Committee on Un-American Activities, Eighty-Third Congress. Parts 1 and 2. Washington, D.C.: Government Printing Office, 1955.

Jacobs, Jane. *The Death and Life of Great American Cities*. New York: Random House, 1961.

Johnson, Whittington B. *Post-Emancipation Race Relations in the Bahamas*. Gainesville: University Press of Florida, 2006.

Jonas, Andrew E. G., and David Wilson, eds. *The Urban Growth Machine: Critical Perspectives Two Decades Later*. Albany: State University of New York Press, 1999.

Jones, Maxine D., and Kevin M. McCarthy. *African Americans in Florida*. Sarasota: Pineapple Press, 1993.

Kahrl, Andrew W. *The Land Was Ours: African American Beaches from Jim Crow to the Sunbelt South*. Cambridge, Mass.: Harvard University Press, 2012.

Kanter, Rosabeth Moss. *World Class: Thriving Locally in a Global Economy*. New York: Simon and Schuster, 1995.

Kaufman, Ned. *Place, Race, and Story: Essays on the Past and Future of Historic Preservation*. New York: Routledge, 2009.

Kayden, Jerold S. *Privately Owned Public Space: The New York City Experience*. New York: John Wiley & Sons, 2000.

Keier, Allan. *Marian Anderson: A Singer's Journey*. New York: Scribner's, 2000.

Kelley, Robin D. G. "'We Are Not What We Seem': Rethinking Black Working-Class Opposition in the Jim Crow South." *Journal of American History* 80, no. 1 (1993): 75–112.

Kelly, James. "South Florida: Trouble in Paradise." *Time*, November 23, 1981.

Kennedy, Stetson. *Jim Crow Guide: The Way It Was*. 1958; repr., Boca Raton: Florida Atlantic University Press, 1990.

———. "Miami: Anteroom to Fascism." *The Nation*, December 22, 1951, 546–47.

———. *Palmetto Country*. New York: Duell, Sloan & Pearce, 1942.

———. *Southern Exposure*. 1946; repr., Boca Raton: Florida Atlantic University Press, 1991.

———. "Way Down Upon . . . Gathering Tales of Folklife in Suwannee Country." *FHC Forum* 17 (Spring/Summer 1993): 22–27.

———. "The W.P.A. Florida Writers Project: A Personal View." *FEH Forum* 12 (Spring 1989): 1–4.

Kirsch, George B. "Municipal Golf and Civil Rights in the United States, 1910–1965." *Journal of African American History* 92, no. 3 (2007): 371–91.

Kohn, Margaret. *Brave New Neighborhoods: The Privatization of Public Space*. New York: Routledge, 2004.

Knebel, F., and B. Kociva. "One Man's Progress . . . and the Fight Ahead." *Look*, April 14, 1959.

Kotkin, Joel. *The City: A Global History*. New York: Modern Library, 2005.

Kruse, Kevin. *White Flight: Atlanta and the Making of Modern Conservatism*. Princeton, N.J.: Princeton University Press, 2005.

Lardiner, George, Jr. "Epidemic of 'Law and Order.'" *The Nation*, February 19, 1968, 231–34.

Lassiter, Mathew D. *The Silent Majority: Suburban Politics in the Sunbelt South*. Princeton, N.J.: Princeton University Press, 2006.

Lawson, Steven. *Running for Freedom: Civil Rights and Black Politics in America since 1941*. New York: McGraw Hill, 1997.

Lears, Jackson. "Reconsidering Abundance: A Plea for Ambiguity." In *Getting and Spending: European and American Consumer Societies in the Twentieth Century*, edited by Susan Strasser, Charles McGovern, and Matthias Judt, 449–66. Washington, D.C.: Smithsonian Institution and Cambridge University Press, 1998.

———. *Something for Nothing: Luck in America*. New York: Viking, 2003.

Lee, David, ed. *The World as Garden: The Life and Writings of David Fairchild*. West Charleston, S.C.: Createspace, 2013.

Lenck, Lena, and Gideon Bosker, *The Beach: The History of Paradise on Earth*. New York: Penguin Books, 1998.

Lenck, Lena, and Gideon Bosker, eds. *Beach: Stories by the Sand and Sea*. New York: Marlowe and Company, 2000.

Leopold, Aldo. *A Sand County Almanac with Essays on Conservation from Round River*. New York: Ballantine Books, 1966.

Lichtenstein, Alex. "'Putting Labor's House in Order': The Transportation Workers Union and Anti-Communism in Miami during the 1940s." *Labor History* 39 (February 1998): 7–23.

———. "'Scientific Unionism' and the "Negro Question': Communists and the Transport Workers Union in Miami, 1944–1949." In *Southern Labor in Transition, 1940–1995*, edited by Robert Zeiger, 58–85. Knoxville: University of Tennessee Press, 1997.

Lightfoot, Greg. "Judge Worley and FEC Waterfront Access in Miami." Unpublished paper in author's possession.

Lindbergh, Anne Morrow. *Gift from the Sea*. 1955; repr. New York: Pantheon, 1991.

Lingeman, Richard. *Don't You Know There's a War On? The American Homefront 1941–1945*. New York: Nation Books, 1970.

Lippard, Lucy *The Lure of the Local: Senses of Place in a Multicultural Society*. New York: The New Press, 1997.

Lloyd, Robert. "Resilience: An Investigation of Tropical Coastal Community." MA thesis, University of Miami School of Architecture, 2011.

Locke, Alain. "An Evaluation of the New Negro." *Opportunity* 1 (August 1923): 231.

———. *The New Negro: An Interpretation*. New York: A. and C. Boni, 1925.

Lombard, Joanna. "The Memorable Landscapes of William Lyman Phillips." *Journal of Decorative and Propaganda Arts* 23 (1998): 260–87.

Longa, Ernesto. "Lawson Edward Thomas and Miami's Negro Municipal Court." *St. Thomas Law Review* 18 (2005): 125–38.

Louv, Richard. *Last Child in the Woods: Saving Our Children from Nature-Deficit Disorder*. Chapel Hill, N.C.: Algonquin Books of Chapel Hill, 2008.

———. *The Nature Principle*. Chapel Hill, N.C.: Algonquin Books, 2011.

Low, Setha, and Neil Smith, eds. *The Politics of Public Space*. New York: Routledge, 2006.

Low, Setha, Dana Taplin, and Suzanne Scheld. *Rethinking Urban Parks: Public Space and Cultural Diversity*. Austin: University of Texas Press, 2005.

Lowenthal, David. *Possessed by the Past: The Heritage Crusade and the Spoils of History*. New York: Free Press, 1996.

Mabee, Carleton. "Evolution of Non-Violence." *The Nation*, August 12, 1961.

Macguilles, Alex. "The Ruse of the Creative Class." *American Prospect*, January 2010, http://prospect.org/cs/articles?article=the_rise_of_the_creative._class.

Mailer, Norman. *Miami and the Siege of Chicago*. New York: Signet, 1968.

Mason, Gilbert R. *Beaches, Blood, and Ballots: A Black Doctor's Civil Rights Struggle*. Jackson: University Press of Mississippi, 2000.

"Miami Klan Tries to Scare Negro Vote." *Life*, May 15, 1939.

Miami Pictorial Number. *The Crisis*, March 1942.

Miller, Lloyd. *Biscayne National Park: It Almost Wasn't*. Redland, Fla: Lemdot Publishing, 2008.

Mitchell, Don. *The Right to the City: Social Justice and the Fight for Public Space*. New York: Guilford Press, 2003.

Mitchell, Jerry. *Business Improvement Districts and the Shape of American Cities.* Albany: State University of New York Press, 2008.

Mitchell, Katharyne. "The Culture of Urban Space." *Urban Geography* 21 (2000): 443–49.

Mohl, Raymond. "Black Immigrants: Bahamians in Early Twentieth Century Miami." *Florida Historical Quarterly* 65 (January 1987): 271–97.

———. "Elizabeth Virrick and the 'Concrete Monsters': Housing Reform in Postwar Miami." *Tequesta* 61 (2001): 5–37.

———. "Making a Second Ghetto in Metropolitan Miami, 1940–1960." *Journal of Urban History* 21 (May 1995): 395–427.

———. "The Origins of Miami's Liberty Square." *Florida Environmental and Urban Issues* 12 (July 1985): 11.

———. "The Pattern of Race Relations in Miami since the 1920s." In *The African American Heritage of Florida*, edited by David R. Colburn and Jane L. Landers, 326–66. Gainesville: University Press of Florida, 1995.

———. "'South of the South?' Jews, Blacks and the Civil Rights Movement in Miami, 1945–1960." *Journal of American Ethnic History* 18 (Winter 1999): 3–36.

———. "Trouble in Paradise: Race and Housing in Miami during the New Deal Era." *Prologue: Journal of the National Archives* 19 (Spring 1987), 9–10.

Mohl, Raymond, Matilda "Bobbi" Graff, and Shirley M. Zoloth. *South of the South: Jewish Activists and the Civil Rights Movement in Miami, 1945–1960.* Gainesville: University Press of Florida, 2004.

Mohl, Raymond A., and George E. Pozzetta, "From Migration to Multiculturalism: A History of Florida Immigration." In *The New History of Florida*, edited by Michael Gannon, 391–417. Gainesville: University Press of Florida, 2012.

Morganthau, Tom, and Vincent Coppola. "Clouds on the Beach." *Newsweek*, February 11, 1980, 40–41.

Mormino, Gary. *Land of Sunshine, State of Dreams: A Social History of Modern Florida.* Gainesville: University Press of Florida, 2005.

———. "Midas Returns: Miami Goes to War." *Tequesta* 57 (1997): 5–51. http://digitalcollections.fiu.edu/tequesta/files/1997/97_1_01.pdf.

Munroe, Mary Barr. "Pioneer Women of Dade County." *Tequesta* 3 (1943): 49–56.

Munroe, Ralph Middleton. *The Commodore's Story: The Early Days on Biscayne Bay.* 1930; repr., Miami: Historical Museum of Southern Florida, 1990.

Murray, Willie Mae Rolphe. "Black Education in Miami." *The Crisis*, March 1942.

Myrdal, Gunnar. *An American Dilemma: The Negro Problem and Modern Democracy.* New York: Harper and Row, 1944.

Nash, Roderick Frazier. *The Rights of Nature.* Madison: University of Wisconsin Press, 1989.

National Conference on Citizenship. "A Tale of Two Cities: Civic Health in Miami and Minneapolis-St. Paul." January 24, 2011, http://ncoc.net/Civic_Engagement_in_Miami_and_MinneapolisSt_Paul.

National Oceanic and Atmospheric Administration (NOAA), *Biscayne Bay: Environmental History and Annotated Bibliography.* Silver Spring, Md.: NOAA, 2000.

Nieves, Angel David. "'We Are Too Busy Making History . . . to Write History': African American Women, Constructions of Nation, and the Built Environment in the New South, 1892–1968." in *We Shall Independent Be: African American Place Making and the Struggle to Claim Space in the United States*, edited by Angel David Nieves and Leslie M. Alexander. Boulder: University Press of Colorado, 2008.

Nijman, Jan. "Globalization to a Latin Beat: The Miami Growth Machine." *Annals of the American Academy of Political and Social Science* 551, (1997), 175.

———. *Miami: Mistress of the Americas*. Philadelphia: University of Pennsylvania Press, 2011.

Nixon, Richard. "Remarks to a Young Voters Rally in Miami, Florida." August 22, 1972, The American Presidency Project, http://www.presidency.ucsb.edu/ws/index.php?pid=353.

Nye, David. *Electrifying America: Social Meanings of a New Technology*. Cambridge, Mass.: MIT Press, 1990.

———. "Technology, Nature, and American Origin Stories." *Environmental History* 8 (January 2004): 8–24.

O'Connell, Kim A. "The Keepers of the Keys." *National Parks*, May–June 2003, 30–33.

Ortiz, Paul. *Emancipation Betrayed: The Hidden History of Black Organizing and White Violence in Florida from Reconstruction to the Bloody Election of 1920*. Berkeley: University of California Press, 2005.

Paddon, James, and Daniel Suman. "The Virginia Key Campground." In *Urban Growth and Sustainable Habitats: Case Studies of Policy Conflicts in South Florida's Coastal Environment*, edited by Daniel Sumna, Manoj Shivlani, and Maria Villabueva, 155–69. Miami: University of Miami, 1995.

Parks, Arva Moore. *Miami: The Magic City*. Miami: Community Media, 2008.

"Police: Patch of Blue." *Time*, March 15, 1968.

Patricios, Nicholas. *Building Marvelous Miami*. Gainesville: University Press of Florida, 1994.

Peters, Thelma. *Biscayne Bay Country*. Miami: Banyan Books, 1981.

———. *Lemon City: Pioneering on Biscayne Bay, 1850–1925*. Miami: Banyan Books, 1976.

———. *Miami 1909*. Miami: Banyan Books, 1984.

Phelts, Martha Dean. *An American Beach for African Americans*. Gainesville: University Press of Florida, 1997.

Pinkney, Enid. "Growing Up in Overtown." In *Miami: The American Crossroad*, edited by Arva Parks and Gregory Bush, 115–18. New York: Simon and Schuster, 1996.

"Planning and the Public Voice: Charrettes, Democracy and the Growth Management Process." Democracy in Miami: A Work in Progress, Spring 2004, http://scholar.library.miami.edu/community_forum/growthTranscript.html.

Pleasants, Julian M. ed. *Orange Journalism: Voices from Florida Journalism*. Gainesville: University of Florida Press, 2003.

"Police: Patch of Blue." *Time*, March 15, 1968.

Porter, Harry. "The Lanham Act." *History of Education Journal* 3, no. 1 (1951): 1–6.

Porter, Bruce, and Marvin Dunn. *The Miami Riot of 1980: Crossing the Bounds*. Lexington, Mass.: Lexington Books, 1984.

Portes, Alejandro, and Alex Steppick. *Miami: City on the Edge*. Berkeley: University of California Press, 1993.

Potter, David. *People of Plenty*. Chicago: University of Chicago Press, 1954.

Powell, Stewart. "The Struggle to Regain Paradise Lost." *U.S. News & World Report*, February 24, 1986, 21–22.

Powers, Richard Gid. *Secrecy and Power: The Life of J. Edgar Hoover*. New York: Free Press, 1987.

Proctor, Samuel. *Napoleon Bonaparte Broward: Florida's Fighting Democrat*. 1950; repr., Gainesville: University Press of Florida, 1993.

Rabinowitz, Howard. *Race Relations in the Urban South, 1865–1890*. Urbana: University of Illinois Press, 1980.

Rameau, Max. *Take Back the Land*. Miami: Nia Press, 2008.

Ramsey, Kate. *The Spirit and the Law: Vodou and Power in Haiti*. Chicago: University of Chicago Press, 2011.

"Ransom Christmas, 1902." *Update* 7, no. 4 (1980): 8–10.

Raub, Patricia. "True to Life: *Life* Magazine's Coverage of African Americans, 1936–40." *Prospects* 25 (October 2000): 607–40.

Read, Gary. "Many Miamis: The Theater of Public Space." In *Miami Modern Metropolis: Paradise and Paradox in Midcentury Architecture and Planning*, edited by Allan T. Shulman, 60–81. Miami Beach: Bass Museum of Art, 2009.

Redford, Polly. "Small Rebellion in Miami." *Harper's Magazine*, February 1964.

"The Reverend John Edwin Culmer, 1891–1963." The Church Awakens: African-Americans and the Struggle for Justice, http://www.episcopalarchives.org/Afro-Anglican_history/exhibit/leadership/culmer.php.

Richardson, Joe M. "Florida's Black Codes." *Florida Historical Quarterly* 47 (April 1969): 365–79.

"Rides Crest of Motorboat Boom." *Life*, June 13, 1955, 35–38.

Roberts, Kenneth. *Sun Hunting*. 1922; repr., Ithaca, N.Y.: Cornell University Press, 2009.

Rogers, Daniel. *Age of Fracture*. Cambridge, Mass.: Harvard University Press, 2011.

Rogers, Kim Lacy. *Righteous Lives: A Narrative of the New Orleans Civil Rights Movement*. New York: New York University Press, 1993.

Rose, Chanelle. "Neither Southern nor Northern: Miami, Florida and the Black Freedom Struggle in America's Tourist Paradise, 1896–1968." PhD diss., University of Miami, 2008.

———. *The Struggle for Black Freedom in Miami: Civil Rights and America's Tourist Paradise 1896–1968*. Baton Rouge: Louisiana State University Press, 2015.

———. "Tourism and the Hispanicization of Race in Jim Crow Miami, 1945–1965." *Journal of Social History* 45, no. 3 (2011): 1–22.

Rose, Mark. *Castles in the Sand: The Life and Times of Carl Graham Fisher*. Gainesville: University Press of Florida, 2000.

Rosentraub, Mark S. *Major League Losers: The Real Cost of Sports and Who's Paying for It.* New York: Basic Books, 1997.

Rosenzweig, Roy, and David Thelen. *The Presence of the Past: Popular Uses of History in American Life.* New York: Columbia University Press, 1998.

Rothman, Hal. *Neon Metropolis: How Las Vegas Started the Twenty-First Century.* New York: Routledge, 2003.

———. "Shedding Skin and Shifting Shape: Tourism in the Modern West." In *Seeing & Being Seen: Tourism in the American West*, edited by David M. Wrobel and Patrick T. Long, 100–20. Lawrence: University Press of Kansas, 2001.

Rymer, Russ. *American Beach: A Saga of Race, Wealth, and Memory.* New York: HarperCollins, 1998.

Sanders, Rickie. "The Public Space of Urban Communities." In *Public Space and the Ideology of Place in American Culture*, edited by Miles Orvell and Jeffrey Meikle, 263–89. Amsterdam: Ropopi, 2009.

Sassen, Saskia. *Territory, Authority, Rights: From Medieval to Global Assemblages.* Princeton, N.J.: Princeton University Press, 2006.

Schnably, Stephen "Safe Zones and Invisibility in *Pottinger v. City of Miami*." Paper presented at the Law and Society Association, Toronto, June 2, 1995.

Schuyler, David, and Patricia M O'Donnell. "The History and Preservation of Urban Parks and Cemeteries." In *Preserving Cultural Landscapes in America*, edited by Arnold R. Alamen and Robert Z. Melnick, 70–93. Baltimore, Md.: Johns Hopkins University Press, 2000.

Schweizer, Errol. "Environmental Justice: An Interview with Robert Bullard." *Earth First! Journal* (July 1999), http://www.ejnet.org/ej/bullard.html.

Sennett, Richard. *The Fall of Public Man.* New York: W. W. Norton, 1976.

———. *Flesh and Stone: The Body and the City in Western Civilization.* New York: W. W. Norton, 1994.

Sewell, John. *Memoirs and History of Miami.* 1933; repr., Miami: Arva Parks & Co., 1988.

Shearer, Boyd. "Narrative." The Daily Aesthetic, http://www.uky.edu/Projects/TDA/narrativ.htm.

Shell-Weiss, Melanie. *Coming to Miami: A Social History.* Gainesville: University Press of Florida, 2009.

Shofner, Jerrell H. "Custom, Law and History: The Enduring Influence of Florida's 'Black Codes.'" *Florida Historical Quarterly* 55 (January 1977): 277–98.

Singer, Isaac Bashevis. "Introduction." In Richard Nagler, *My Love Affair with Miami Beach.* New York: Simon & Schuster, 1991.

Sitkoff, Harvard. *A New Deal for Blacks: The Emergence of Civil Rights as a National Issue: The Depression Decade.* New York: Oxford University Press, 1978.

Small, John Kunkle. *From Eden to the Sahara: Florida's Tragedy.* 1929; repr., Sanford, Fla.: Seminole Soil and Water Conservation District, 2004.

Smith, Eileen M. "Black Churchgoers, Environmental Activism, and the Preservation of Nature in Miami, Florida." Dissertation abstract, January 1, 2003. Digital

Commons: Florida International University. http://digitalcommons.fiu.edu/dissertations/AAI3126427.

Smith, Lillian. *Strange Fruit*. 1944; repr.; New York: Harcourt, Brace, Jovanovich, 1992.

Sorkin, Michael, ed. *Variations on a Theme Park: The New American City and the End of Public Space*. New York: Hill and Wang, 1992.

Spain, S. Brent. "Florida Beach Access: Nothing but Wet Sand?" *Journal of Land Use & Environmental Law* 115 (1999), http://archive.law.fsu.edu/journals/landuse/vol151/spain1.htm.

Sprout, Michael D. "A Beach Too Far." *Sarasota Magazine*, June 2005, , https://sarasotamagazine.com/2005/06/01/a-beach-too-far/.

Stegner, Wallace. *One Nation*. Boston: Houghton Mifflin, 1945.

———. *Where the Bluebird Sings to the Lemonade Springs*. 1993; repr., New York: Penguin, 2002.

Stodolska, Monika, Kimberly Shinew, Myron Floyd, and Gordon J. Walker, *Race, Ethnicity and Leisure*. Champaign, Ill.: Human Kinetics, 2014.

Stofik, M. Barron. *Saving South Beach*. Gainesville: University Press of Florida, 2005.

Stuart, John A. "Constructing Identity: Building and Place in New Deal South Florida." In *The New Deal in South Florida: Design, Policy, and Community Building, 1933–1940*, edited by John A Stuart and John F. Stack Jr., 31–70. Gainesville: University Press of Florida, 2008.

———. "Liberty Square: Florida's First Public Housing Project." In *New Deal in South Florida: Design, Policy, and Community Building, 1933–1940*, edited by John A. Stuart and John F. Stack Jr., 186–222. Gainesville: University Press of Florida, 2008.

"The Task for the Future—A Program for 1919." In *Report of the National Association for the Advancement of Colored People for the Years 1917 and 1918* (New York, 1919). Reprinted in Thomas R. Frazier, ed., *Afro-American History: Primary Sources*. Chicago: Dorsey Press, 1988.

Terkel, Studs. "Stetson Kennedy, 77." In Terkel, *Coming of Age*, 391–400. New York: New Press, 1995.

Tichi, Cecilia. *Shifting Gears: Technology, Literature, Culture in Modernist America*. Chapel Hill: University of North Carolina Press, 1996.

Thomas, Donna. "'Camp Hell': Miami during the Spanish-American War." *Florida Historical Quarterly* 57, no. 2 (1978): 141–56.

Thomas, Lawson E. "The Professions in Miami." *The Crisis*, March 1942, 85.

Trouillot, Michel-Rolph. *Silencing the Past: Power and the Production of History*. Boston: Beacon Press, 1995.

Tscheschlok, Erick. "Long Time Coming: Miami's Liberty City Riot of 1968." *Florida Historical Quarterly* 74 (Spring 1996): 440–60.

Tuan, Yi-Fu. *Topophilia: A Study of Environmental Attitudes and Values*. New York: Columbia University Press, 1974.

Tweed, Thomas. "An Emerging Protestant Establishment: Religious Affiliation and Public Power on the Urban Frontier in Miami, 1896–1904." *Church History* 64, no. 3 (1996): 412–37.

Uguccioni, Ellen J. "Black Police Precinct and Courthouse, 1009 NW 5th Avenue." City of Miami Designation Report, 2002, http://www.historicpreservationmiami.com/pdfs/Black%20Police%20Precinct.pdf.

Valle, Victor M., and Rodolfo D. Torres. *Latino Metropolis*. Minneapolis: University of Minnesota Press, 2000.

Vanclay, Frank, Matthew Higgins, and Adam Blackshaw, eds. *Making Sense of Place: Exporting Concepts and Expressions of Place through Different Senses and Lenses*. Canberra: National Museum of Australia, 2008.

Vickery, George. "TV Newsman Makes News By Bringing Peace to City Torn by Racial Conflict." *The Quill*, September 1956, 15–16.

Virginia Key Public Planning Coalition with City of Miami Planning Department. "Virginia Key Master Plan: 2010." Accessed November 1, 2015. http://www.miamigov.com/planning/docs/plans/vk/VaKeyPresentationJuly222010.pdf.

Vonk, Carita Swanson. *Theodore R. Gibson: Priest, Prophet and Politician*. Miami: Little River Press, 1997.

Vought, Kip. "Racial Stirrings in Colored Town: The UNIA in Miami during the 1920s." *Tequesta* 45 (2000): 56–77.

Wachs, Martin. "The Evolution of Transportation Policy in Los Angeles: Images of Past Policies and Future Prospects." In *The City: Los Angeles and Urban Theory at the End of the Twentieth Century*, ed. Allen Scott and Edward W. Sofa, 106–59 (Berkeley: University of California Press, 1996).

Wagy, Tom. *Governor LeRoy Collins of Florida: Spokesman of the New South*. Birmingham: University of Alabama Press, 1985.

Walmsley, Jan. "Life History Interviews with People with Learning Disabilities." In *The Oral History Reader*, edited by Robert Perks and Alistair Thomson, 184–97. New York: Routledge, 1998.

"W. E. B. Du Bois and the NAACP." Virginia Historical Society, http://www.vahistorical.org/civilrights/naacp.htm.

Wachs, Martin. "The Evolution of Transportation Policy in Los Angeles: Images of Past Policies and Future Prospects." In *The City: Los Angeles and Urban Theory at the End of the Twentieth Century*, edited by Allen J. Scott and Edward Soja, 106–59. Berkeley: University of California Press, 1996.

Walmsley, Jan. "Life History Interviews with People with Learning Disabilities." In *The Oral History Reader*, edited by Robert Perks and Alistair Thomson, 184–97. New York: Routledge, 1998.

Waters, Maxine. "Foreword." In *The Quest for Environmental Justice: Human Rights and the Politics of Pollution*, edited by Robert D. Bullard, ix–xiv. San Francisco: Sierra Club Books, 2005.

Weaver, Timothy. *Blazing the Neoliberal Trail: Urban Political Development in the United States and United Kingdom*. Philadelphia: University of Pennsylvania Press, 2016.

Weigall, T. H. *Boom in Paradise*. New York: Alfred H. King, 1932.

Weisbrot, Robert. *Father Divine and the Struggle for Racial Equality*. Urbana: University of Illinois Press, 1983.

Wilkerson, Isabel. *The Warmth of Other Suns: The Epic Story of America's Great Migration*. New York: Random House, 2010.

Williams, Terry Tempest. *The Open Space of Democracy*. Great Barrington, Mass.: Orion Society, 2004.

Wiltse, Jeff. *Contested Waters: A Social History of Swimming Pools In America*. Chapel Hill: University of North Carolina Press, 2007.

Wingard, G. L. et al. "Ecosystem History of Southern and Central Biscayne Bay: Summary Report on Sedimentary Core Analyses." U.S. Geological Survey Open File Report 03-375, September 15, 2003, http://sofia.usgs.gov/publications/ofr/03-375/.

Winsboro, Irvin D. S., ed. *Old South, New South, or Down South? Florida and the Modern Civil Rights Movement*. Morgantown: University of West Virginia Press, 2009.

Wolch, Jennifer, John P. Wilson, and Jed Fernbach. "Parks and Parks Funding in Los Angeles: An Equity Mapping Analysis." *Urban Geography* 26 (2005): 4–35.

Wolfe, Tom. "Art and Real Estate: The Secret of Urban Renewal." Address delivered at Miami's Freedom Tower, October 7, 2007.

Wollcott, Victoria. *Race, Riots, and Roller Coasters: The Struggle over Segregated Recreation in America*. Philadelphia: University of Pennsylvania Press, 2014.

Whyte, William H. *The Social Life of Small Urban Spaces*. New York: Project for Public Spaces, 1980.

Works Progress Administration and Florida State Planning Board. *Planning Your Vacation in Florida: Miami and Dade County, including Miami Beach and Coral Gables*. Northport, N.Y.: Bacon, Percy, and Daggett, 1941.

Wright, Roberta Hughes, Wilbur B. Hughes, and Gina Renee Misiroglu. *Lay Down Body: Living History in African American Cemeteries*. Detroit, Mich.: Visible Ink Press, 1995.

Yehle, Jean. "The History of the Rosenstiel School of Marine & Atmospheric Science: 1940–1950's." Rosenstiel School of Marine & Atmospheric Science, http://www.rsmas.miami.edu/about-rsmas/history/.

Zukin, Sharon. *The Culture of Cities*. Boston: Blackwell, 1995.

———. *Landscapes of Power: From Detroit to Disney World*. Berkeley: University of California Press, 1991.

———. *The Naked City: The Death and Life of Authentic Urban Places*. New York: Oxford University Press, 2010.

Zelizer, Julian. "Reflections: Rethinking the History of American Conservatism." *Reviews in American History* 38 (June 2010): 367–92.

Index

GREGORY BUSH is director of the Institute for Public History at the University of Miami and associate professor of history. Born and raised in Essex Fells, New Jersey, Bush joined the faculty of the university in 1983 after completing his PhD in American History at Columbia University. Prior to that he received his MA degree from George Washington University and his BA from Colgate University.

Professor Bush is the author of *Lord of Attention: Gerald Stanley Lee and the Crowd Metaphor in Industrializing America* and coauthor, with Arva Moore Parks, of *Miami: The American Crossroads*, which won the Tebeau Prize in 1997 for best book in Florida history from the Florida Historical Society.

Bush is also one of the founders of the Florida Moving Image Archive and the former editor of *Film and History*. He has been involved in assisting with, reviewing, and completing numerous documentary projects, including *Patriotic Parades: Wartime Miami, 1898–1945* and a documentary about Virginia Key Beach.

Concerned about civic involvement and the loss of public space along Miami's waterfront, Bush helped create the Urban Environment League in 1996 and subsequently served as its president from 1998 to 2002. He is now vice-president. As president, he helped initiate creation of a civil rights park on Virginia Key Beach in 1999 and played a leading role in other major waterfront issues, including saving the Miami Circle and preserving open space in Bicentennial Park on the waterfront. He wrote the enabling legislation for the city's Parks Advisory Board and served as its first chair, from 2000 to 2002. He also wrote the enabling legislation and served as vice-chair of the Bicentennial Park/Waterfront Renewal Committee of the city of Miami.

Bush wrote the historical component of a feasibility study for Virginia Key Beach Park for the National Park Service in 2006. He was also involved in initiating the Florida Community Studies Consortium with local history/social science and science teachers. This project included setting up a civil rights archive with teachers at Turner Tech High School. He has completed numerous oral history interviews across Miami-Dade County and is preparing several volumes for publication.

Bush has also initiated a project called Nature Links for Lifelong Learning (www.naturelinks.net), which helps young adults with middle-range intellectual disabilities. It was located at Virginia Key Beach Park (in affiliation with the city of Miami) and at J. R. E. Lee Educational Center in south Miami (part of Miami-Dade County Public Schools). Its three programs are now housed at the Patricia and Philip Frost Science Museum, the Coral Gables Congregational Church, and the City of Miami's Simpson Park. Nature Links seeks to empower young adults through storytelling, travel training, and news production using iMovie instruction, and focuses on culinary skills, organic gardens, habitat restoration, cultural expression, other educational/cultural elements, job readiness, and independent life skills.